THE BEST, OF
BOYS' LIFE

Lyons Press is an imprint of Globe Pequot Press

Library of Congress Cataloging-in-Publication Data is available on file.

ISBN 978-1-59921-992-9

Printed in China

10 9 8 7 6 5 4 3 2 1

Staff Credits

Text supplied by   J. D. Owen
Consultant Editor   Jonathan Wells
Executive Editor   Jennifer Barr
Additional editorial work   Alice Payne
Design Manager   Darren Jordan
Design   Chris Francis
Additional design work   Stephen Cary and Emily Clarke
Production   Karin Kolbe

With special thanks to the staff of *Boys' Life*, including Karen Rash, Adryn Shackleford and Lenore Bonno.

THE BEST OF BOYS' LIFE

Lyons Press
Guilford, Connecticut
Lyons Press is an imprint of Globe Pequot Press

CONTENTS

INTRODUCTION

Boys' Life entered the American scene in March 1911. The first issue cost a nickel. The cover was a two-color illustration of a locomotive crashing through a barrier, illustrating the fiction piece "The Lost Express." The other 47 pages were black and white, packed with other fiction, features, Scouting articles, and games. To promote its "Learn to Read" campaign, the Boy Scouts of America bought the magazine from George S. Barton, the founder and publisher, in June 1912 for $6,000. The price was based on $1 for each subscriber. The circulation now is 1.1 million.

Today, the magazine is a full-color, glossy publication full of photography and artwork, and costs $1 an issue for Scouts. Each issue features Scouting outings, fiction, hobbies, games, profiles of young achievers, nature, science, entertainment, comics, jokes, and more. Originally subtitled the "Boys' and Boy Scouts' Magazine," the BSA changed the subhead to the "Boy Scout's Magazine," and today the subhead reads simply "For all boys."

This collection of a variety of content from the pages of **Boys' Life** is divided into six categories that highlight the chief attractions of the magazine: Survival, Scout Life, Sports, News, Stories, and Features. As stated in the first issue "We feel that the boys of this country are not namby-pamby youths, devoid of imagination, and who know nothing and care nothing about the great world awaiting them. They want to read and know something beyond the dull level of their own street and town."

For the first several decades, the magazine was edited for boys 12 and older (the age at which they could join Scouting). Over the years the program has expanded, and the magazine now reaches boys ages 6 to 18. As a result, demographic editions for younger and older readers were introduced in 1995.

Much of the content is the same for all readers, but 12 to 16 pages are exchanged for age-appropriate content each month. The magazine has carried advertising since its inception.

Noteworthy writers contributing to the magazine over the years include Isaac Asimov, Ray Bradbury, Van Wyck Brooks, Arthur C. Clarke, Thomas Fleming, Alex Haley, Robert A. Heinlein, John Knowles, Gary Paulsen, Ernest Thompson Seton, and Isaac Bashevis Singer. Works of noteworthy artists and photographers appearing in the magazine include Ansel Adams, Harrison Cady, Joseph Csatari, Salvador Dali, Phillipe Halsman, and Norman Rockwell. When he was 18, Rockwell was hired by **Boys Life'**, eventually becoming the art editor, a position he held until 1917. It was the beginning of a life-long affiliation with the Boy Scouts of America. Like Rockwell, Csatari also served as the art director of **Boys' Life** before launching his career as a freelance illustrator. The works of Rockwell and Csatari have helped to define the merit and usefulness of Scouting almost since its birth.

The quality displayed by the magazine over the years has consistently been cited for excellence, being recognized by such groups as the International Reading Association, EdPress, Western Publishing Association, and the Society for Children's Book Writers and Illustrators.

The original object of the magazine, as explained in the first issue, was "to furnish the Boy Scouts with a paper they may consider their own....and to place in the hands of all boys a paper of which they may be proud." That mission continues to this day. As a general-interest magazine for boys, undergirded by the values of Scouting, the always-evolving **Boys' Life** has become an American institution.

BOYS' LIFE
SURVIVAL

Boys' Life is a not only a reflection of the Boy Scouts of America in words, photos, and art, but also a reflection of the interests and aspirations of boys. Almost anything that is of interest to boys will be found between the covers of the magazine. Surviving—even thriving—in intense conditions is definitely of interest.

The first edition of the *Boy Scout Handbook* asked: "Would you like to be an expert camper who can always make himself comfortable in the out of doors, and a swimmer that fears no waters? Do you desire the knowledge to help the wounded quickly, and to make yourself cool and self-reliant in an emergency?"

Millions of boys have answered yes.

Outdoor adventures: that's the lure of Scouting. But the outdoors can be treacherous, with extreme heat and cold, snow, rain, and wind conspiring to wreck an outing. Scouting trains boys to handle foul weather and almost all conditions, from parched deserts to snow-covered mountains. Scouts even seek out these environments to test their skills. The lure of high adventure appeals to older Scouts, while younger Scouts begin learning and practicing the skills that will enable them to feel confident in all conditions, even some of the most adverse. Scouts today embark on outings early Scouts would never have dreamed of.

First-aid training is a one of the first skills a Scout learns. Hiking and camping can result in blisters, cuts, burns, scrapes, stings, and sprains— even broken bones. Scouts learn to treat injuries properly, call for help if needed, and plan a course of action. They travel with first-aid kits and other Scout basic essentials (sometimes kept in "ditty bags"). In addition to first aid, Scouts are taught rescue skills—cardiopulmonary resuscitation or retrieving someone floundering in the water. No one expects a Scout to have the skills of a doctor—they are expected to do the best they can—but quick-thinking Scouts have saved many lives.

"Be Prepared" is the motto of Scouting worldwide (with variations). Sir Robert Baden-Powell, the founder of the Scouting movement, was once asked what a Scout should be prepared for. He responded, "Why, for any old thing." That covers a lot of ground, and over the decades the pages of *Boys' Life* have shown Scouts how to be prepared for all types of situations and in all climates, how to be prepared not only with clothing and gear, but physically and mentally as well.

Boys' Life has brought stories of this rugged life to Scouts over the decades, showing how Scouts test their skills and knowledge against the elements. To become an expert camper and hiker requires practicing skills in the outdoors; *Boys' Life* features articles on how to do this as well as showcasing the skills in action. The appeal is in showing how it can be done, in stories of Scouts snowshoeing, kayaking, or living off the land. The magazine is a manual and a travelogue, page after page of possibilities.

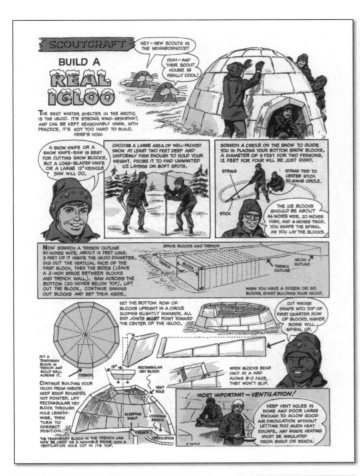

SCOUTCRAFT

BUILD A REAL IGLOO

HEY—NEW SCOUTS IN THE NEIGHBORHOOD!

YEAH—AND THEIR SCOUT HOUSE IS REALLY COOL!

THE BEST WINTER SHELTER IN THE ARCTIC IS THE IGLOO. IT'S STRONG, WIND-RESISTANT, AND CAN BE KEPT REASONABLY WARM. WITH PRACTICE, IT'S NOT TOO HARD TO BUILD. HERE'S HOW.

A SNOW KNIFE OR A SNOW KNIFE-SAW IS BEST FOR CUTTING SNOW BLOCKS, BUT A LONG-BLADED KNIFE OR A LARGE 12" KEYHOLE SAW WILL DO.

CHOOSE A LARGE AREA OF WELL-PACKED SNOW AT LEAST TWO FEET DEEP AND UNIFORMLY FIRM ENOUGH TO HOLD YOUR WEIGHT. PROBE IT TO FIND UNWANTED ICE LAYERS OR SOFT SPOTS.

SCRATCH A CIRCLE ON THE SNOW TO GUIDE YOU IN PLACING YOUR BOTTOM SNOW BLOCKS. A DIAMETER OF 9 FEET FOR TWO PERSONS, 12 FEET FOR FOUR WILL BE JUST RIGHT.

STRING TIED TO CENTER STICK TO MAKE CIRCLE.

THE ICE BLOCKS SHOULD BE ABOUT 46 INCHES WIDE, 20 INCHES HIGH, AND 6 INCHES THICK. YOU SHAPE THE SPIRAL AS YOU LAY THE BLOCKS.

NOW SCRATCH A TRENCH OUTLINE 30 INCHES WIDE, ABOUT 12 FEET LONG, 3 FEET OF IT INSIDE THE IGLOO DIAMETER. DIG OUT THE VERTICAL FACE OF THE FIRST BLOCK, THEN THE SIDES (LEAVE A 2-INCH SPACE BETWEEN BLOCKS AND TRENCH WALL). SAW ACROSS THE BOTTOM (20 INCHES BELOW TOP), LIFT OUT THE BLOCK. CONTINUE SAWING OUT BLOCKS AND SET THEM ASIDE.

WHEN YOU HAVE A DOZEN OR SO BLOCKS, START BUILDING YOUR IGLOO.

SET THE BOTTOM ROW OF BLOCKS UPRIGHT IN A CIRCLE SLOPING SLIGHTLY INWARDS, ALL END JOINTS MUST POINT TOWARD THE CENTER OF THE IGLOO.

CUT WEDGE SHAPE INTO TOP OF FIRST QUARTER, ROW OF BLOCKS, HIGHER ROWS WILL SPIRAL UP.

PUT A TEMPORARY BLOCK IN TRENCH AND BUILD WALL ACROSS IT.

CONTINUE BUILDING YOUR IGLOO FROM INSIDE. KEEP ROOF ROUNDED, NOT POINTED. LIFT RECTANGULAR KEY BLOCK THROUGH HOLE LENGTHWISE, THEN TURN TO CORRECT POSITION.

THE TEMPORARY BLOCK IN THE TRENCH CAN NOW BE USED AS A MOVABLE DOOR, WITH A VENTILATION HOLE CUT IN ITS TOP.

WHEN BLOCKS BEAR ONLY AT A END ALONG B-C FACE, THEY WON'T SLIP.

MOST IMPORTANT—VENTILATION!

KEEP VENT HOLES IN DOME AND DOOR LARGE ENOUGH TO ALLOW GOOD AIR CIRCULATION WITHOUT LETTING TOO MUCH HEAT ESCAPE. ANY INSIDE HEATING MUST BE INSULATED FROM SHELF OR BENCH.

"Okpik," the snowy owl, has spread its wings and flown to the rugged Rocky Mountains of Colorado. *Okpik* is the Inuit, or Eskimo, word the BSA chose for the popular winter outdoors program that began at the national

In the BSA's Okpik program, Scouts learn cross-country skiing, snowshoeing, tracking, and cold-weather cooking.

high adventure base in northern Minnesota. But now Western Scouts are also learning the secrets of Okpik.

Winter comes early to the high country of Colorado. The razor-edged winter wind can bring more than 300 inches of snow during the season. To survive—and even

---

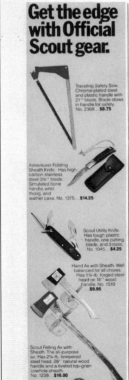
Trash-Can Cooking

BY WARREN AND JOE ASA

The lid is all you need to bake a pie or other treat in camp.

Pies, biscuits, casseroles, and cobblers—sound tasty, don't they? And you can bake them in camp with a metal trash-can lid.

Before starting, be sure you have a rake, shovel, hooked stick, gloves, all cooking supplies, and a clean trash-can lid with a handle. (Make sure it will cover your baking dish.)

On flat, dry mineral soil, keep a hot fire burning for 30 to 60 minutes. The best woods for baking coals are hard woods like oak, maple, or ash. (During this wait, use the fire for other cooking, and get your pie or biscuits ready.) Next, rake away the fire down to the soil, and place the food—in a pie pan or other shallow baking dish—on three, ½-inch pebbles over the hot spot.

Immediately, cover the food with the metal trash-can lid, and shovel some hot coals onto the lid. Check the baking progress by lifting the lid slightly with a hooked stick.

Don't pile too many hot coals on top, or you may scorch the food. In general, 15 to 30 minutes will do for biscuits, 45 to 50 minutes for pies, and an hour for casseroles.

TRASH-CAN APPLE PIE

At home: Mix most ingredients, and pack in two plastic bags.

• For the crust, use a prepared mix, or press together with a fork: 2¼ cups flour;

¾ teaspoon salt; and ⅔ cup shortening.

• For the filling, mix ½ cup sugar; ½ teaspoon cinnamon; ⅛ teaspoon nutmeg; ½ teaspoon grated lemon peel; and ¼ cup flour.

You will also need six apples and two tablespoons of margarine.

In camp: After starting your fire, add two to four tablespoons of cold water to the crust. Knead until it forms a solid ball. Roll it out with a bottle or a rolling pin, or just press the dough evenly into the pie pan. Reserve half of the dough for the top crust.

• Core, peel, and slice apples. Place half on the pie crust, and sprinkle with half the sugar-spice mixture. Repeat for another layer. Dot the top with margarine, and add strips of dough for a lattice top crust.

• After about 10 minutes of baking, tilt the lid just enough to check the pie.

If the top is slow to bake, replace the coals with new, hot ones. (You may have to keep a second fire going during the baking, for an adequate supply of coals.)

If the top of the pie is baking too fast, remove some coals from the lid. Your pie should bake in about 50 minutes, if the ground is hot enough.

Try these other lip-smackers:

Beef stew with biscuits on top. Cook the stew in a pot first, then add biscuit dough and bake until golden brown.

Cobbler made with fresh, frozen, or canned berries, or other fruit. Mix berries with sugar and a little cornstarch, then heat to boiling. Or use a canned pie filling. Add sugar and cinnamon to biscuit dough, spoon fruit mixture on top, and bake.

THE PEDRO PATROL — Pioneer Know-How!

SCOUTS HAVE USED PIONEER KNOWLEDGE FOR YEARS TO HELP WITH WILDERNESS ENGINEERING!

USE THIS SLOPING TRENCH TRICK TO SET A HEAVY POST!

WHEN POST IS UPRIGHT, REMOVE PLANK AND FILL HOLE WITH ROCKS AND EARTH! TAP IT DOWN FIRMLY!

STONE HOLDS THE PLANK IN PLACE.

EARLY SETTLERS FASHIONED AIDS OUT OF MATERIAL AT HAND! A BIPOD HELPS LIFT THE HEAVY POST!

THROW THE ROPE OVER THE BIPOD, THEN PULL! THE MORE THE MERRIER!

STAY AWAY FROM THE POLE UNTIL IT'S SET TIGHTLY IN THE HOLE!

LOADING LOGS OR HEAVY BARRELS ONTO TRUCKS? DOUBLE YOUR HOISTING POWER WITH THIS PARBUCKLE!

MULTIPLY YOUR STRENGTH WITH BACKWOODS ENGINEERING, WHEN MUSCLE POWER ISN'T ENOUGH!

STUDY THE WAY THE ROPE IS LOOPED AROUND THE ANCHOR PLANK! IT'S SO SIMPLE! EXERT AN EVEN PULL!

BREATHING FOR THE BREATHLESS

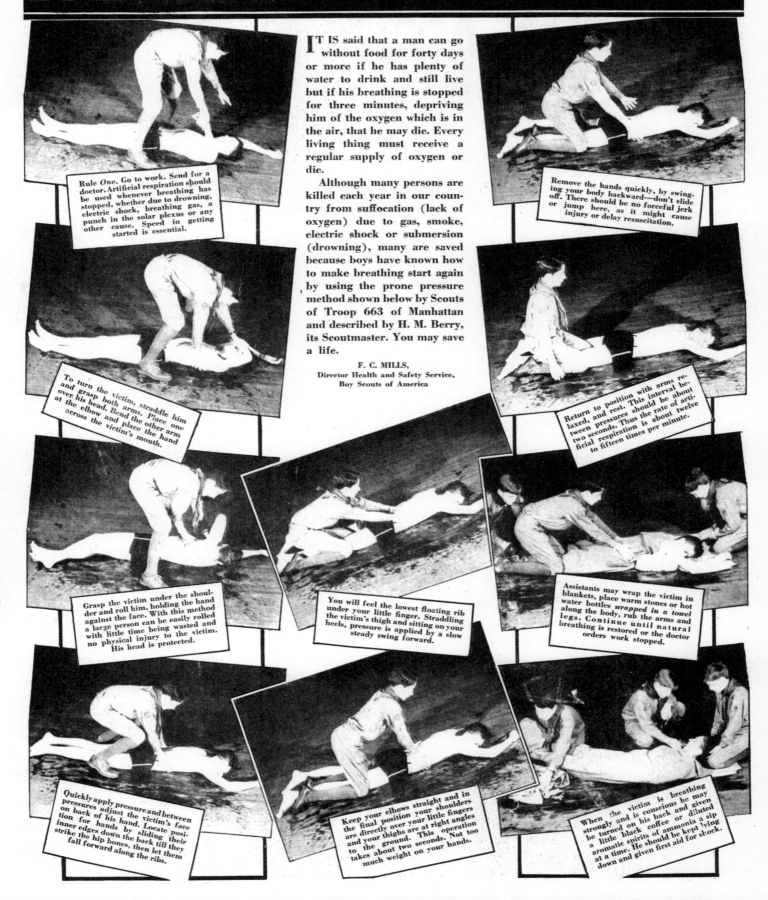

IT IS said that a man can go without food for forty days or more if he has plenty of water to drink and still live but if his breathing is stopped for three minutes, depriving him of the oxygen which is in the air, that he may die. Every living thing must receive a regular supply of oxygen or die.

Although many persons are killed each year in our country from suffocation (lack of oxygen) due to gas, smoke, electric shock or submersion (drowning), many are saved because boys have known how to make breathing start again by using the prone pressure method shown below by Scouts of Troop 663 of Manhattan and described by H. M. Berry, its Scoutmaster. You may save a life.

F. C. MILLS,
Director Health and Safety Service,
Boy Scouts of America

Rule One. Go to work. Send for a doctor. Artificial respiration should be used whenever breathing has stopped, whether due to drowning, electric shock, breathing gas, a punch in the solar plexus or any other cause. Speed in getting started is essential.

To turn the victim, straddle him and grasp both arms. Place one over his head. Bend the other arm at the elbow and place the hand across the victim's mouth.

Grasp the victim under the shoulder and roll him, holding the hand against the face. With this method a large person can be easily rolled with little time being wasted and no physical injury to the victim. His head is protected.

Quickly apply pressure and between pressures adjust the victim's face on back of his hand. Locate position for hands by sliding their inner edges down the back till they strike the hip bones, then let them fall forward along the ribs.

Remove the hands quickly, by swinging your body backward—don't slide off. There should be no forceful jerk or jump here, as it might cause injury or delay resuscitation.

Return to position with arms relaxed, and rest. This interval between pressures should be about two seconds. Thus the rate of artificial respiration is about twelve to fifteen times per minute.

You will feel the lowest floating rib under your little finger. Straddling the victim's thigh and sitting on your heels, pressure is applied by a slow steady swing forward.

Assistants may wrap the victim in blankets, place warm stones or hot water bottles *wrapped in a towel* along the body, rub the arms and legs. Continue until natural breathing is restored or the doctor orders work stopped.

Keep your elbows straight and in the final position your shoulders are directly over your little fingers and your thighs are at right angles to the ground. This operation takes about two seconds. Not too much weight on your hands.

When the victim is breathing strongly and is conscious he may be turned on his back and given a little black coffee or diluted aromatic spirits of ammonia a sip at a time. He should be kept lying down and given first aid for shock.

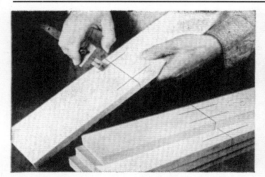

Make the six frames first. Square up stock according to rectangle sizes in plan. Cut tapers on ends. Lay out batten notches and bottom tapers. Cut.

Lay out the bow block. Saw and plane the angles at each end. Cut out the batten notches with a sharp chisel; note these notches are not same size.

Stern block. Scribe center line along top batten. Center. Brad together. Drill body and lead holes for 1½" No. 10 screws.

Water Scooter

By

GLENN A. WAGNER

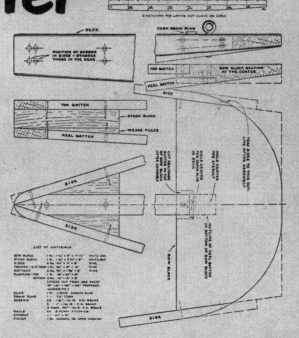

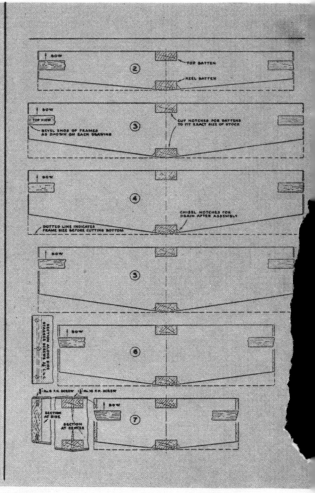

THERE'S nothing to equal this Water Scooter (modeled after the 14 foot Hawaiian surfboards) for all-around water sport. Construction is not difficult, but to make the job easy, BOYS' LIFE has reproduced these plans full-size and will mail them to you postpaid for 15 cents. Send your full name, correct address, and 15 cents to BOYS' LIFE, 2 Park Avenue, New York 16, N. Y.

List of Materials

Bow block, 1 pc. 1½" x 8" x 17½", white oak
Stern block, 1 pc. 1½" x 5¼" x 8", white oak
Sides, 2 pcs. ¾" x 4" x 8', pine
Battens, 2 pcs. ¾" x 1⅝" x 8', pine
Frames, cut from 1 pc. ¾" x 6" x 10', pine
Planking—top, 1 pc. ⅛" x 24" x 8'
        bottom, 2 pcs. ⅛" x 12" x 8'
    (pieces cut from one sheet of ⅛" x 48" x 96" tempered Masonite)
Glue, 1 pt. liquid marine glue
Drain plug, 1 ⅞" cork
Screws, 32 1½" No. 10 flat head brass
       2 1" No. 10 flat head brass
       3 gross, ¾" No. 6 flat head brass
Nails, 24 8-penny finishing
Eyebolt, 1¼" x 2"
Finish, 1 qt. enamel or spar varnish

Glue and fasten stern block in position. Cut top batten exactly 89" long. Assemble the six frames—be certain that the bevels on ends face the right direction fore and aft. Use one 1½" No. 10 screw at each joint. Glue. Check parts for squareness before glue sets.

Turn frame over. Clamp top batten to bench to keep it straight until the sides are fastened securely in place. Lay keel; start at bow block. Allow stern end of strip to extend beyond stern block until wedge shape filler strip is fitted between the two pieces.

Cut keel to length and trim taper with a plane. Use one 1½" No. 10 screw at each frame, and two screws at the stern block. Prepare the sides. Follow plan dimensions. You can rough-cut the curve on the bottoms before fastening the sides to the frames.

CUT TOP BATTEN 89" LONG

FIT WEDGE FILLER STRIP

Screw sides to stern block. Pull sides together with a tourniquet. Use glue and two eight-penny finishing nails at each frame joint.

Now carefully plane the taper on the keel and the sides. Fair out all of the curves; then check each one with a straightedge.

Also plane the bow block to a nice, even sweeping curve. Be careful not to gouge the surface or the edges. Trim off the sides.

PLANKING ⅛ × 12 × 96

BRADS

CHISEL DRAINAGE NOTCHES

Planking. Line up one sheet at center. Make gauge to scribe centerline. Plane bevel on keel edge: cut outside curve ¼" oversize.

Make another gauge to lay out lines for screws; set dividers at 2¼" and step off screw centers. Drill holes, and countersink.

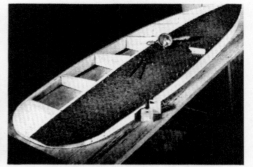

Next apply a generous coat of marine glue to all of the exposed surfaces. Securely fasten the planking with ¾" No. 6 screws.

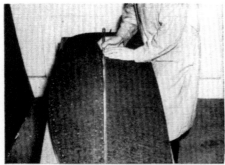

Fit rest of planking. Brad to anchor. Use dividers to scribe parallel keel line. Glue.

Trim outside edges. Paint inside. Fit the top, apply glue, and fasten in place. Fit eyebolt

and drainage cork. Fill all nail and screw holes with hard-setting crack filler. Paint.

Trash-Can Cooking

BY WARREN AND JOE ASA

The lid is all you need to bake a pie or other treat in camp.

Pies, biscuits, casseroles, and cobblers—sound tasty, don't they? And you can bake them in camp with a metal trash-can lid.

Before starting, be sure you have a rake, shovel, hooked stick, gloves, all cooking supplies, and a clean trash-can lid with a handle. (Make sure it will cover your baking dish.)

On flat, dry mineral soil, keep a hot fire burning for 30 to 60 minutes. The best woods for baking coals are hard woods like oak, maple, or ash. (During this wait, use the fire for other cooking, and get your pie or biscuits ready.) Next, rake away the fire down to the soil, and place the food—in a pie pan or other shallow baking dish—on three, ½-inch pebbles over the hot spot.

Immediately, cover the food with the metal trash-can lid, and shovel some hot coals onto the lid. Check the baking progress by lifting the lid slightly with a hooked stick.

Don't pile too many hot coals on top, or you may scorch the food. In general, 15 to 30 minutes will do for biscuits, 45 to 50 minutes for pies, and an hour for casseroles.

TRASH-CAN APPLE PIE

At home: Mix most ingredients, and pack in two plastic bags.

• For the crust, use a prepared mix, or press together with a fork: 2¼ cups flour; ¾ teaspoon salt; and ⅔ cup shortening.

• For the filling, mix ¾ cup sugar; ½ teaspoon cinnamon; ¼ teaspoon nutmeg; ½ teaspoon grated lemon peel; and ¼ cup flour.

You will also need six apples and two tablespoons of margarine.

In camp: After starting your fire, add two to four tablespoons of cold water to the crust. Knead until it forms a solid ball. Roll it out with a bottle or a rolling pin, or just press the dough evenly into the pie pan. Reserve half of the dough for the top crust.

• Core, peel, and slice apples. Place half on the pie crust, and spinkle with half the sugar-spice mixture. Repeat for another layer. Dot the top with margarine, and add strips of dough for a lattice top crust.

• After about 10 minutes of baking, tilt the lid just enough to check the pie.

If the top is slow to bake, replace the coals with new, hot ones. (You may have to keep a second fire going during the baking, for an adequate supply of coals.)

If the top of the pie is baking too fast, remove some coals from the lid. Your pie should bake in about 50 minutes, if the ground is hot enough.

Try these other lip-smackers:

Beef stew with biscuits on top. Cook the stew in a pot first, then add biscuit dough and bake until golden brown.

Cobbler made with fresh, frozen, or canned berries, or other fruit. Mix berries with sugar and a little cornstarch, then heat to boiling. Or use a canned pie filling. Add sugar and cinnamon to biscuit dough, spoon fruit mixture on top, and bake. ♣

While your hardwood fire is heating the ground, prepare the pie. This isn't hard, since you mixed many ingredients at home. A pie bakes in about 50 minutes.

Place the pie on three small pebbles over the heated soil; then, cover with the lid.

Next, cover the lid with hot coals, so the pie will bake from bottom and top.

Tilt the lid slightly with a stick after about 10 minutes to see if the pie is baking too fast or too slowly. You may have to adjust the coals on top.

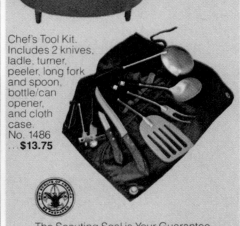

WHAT WOULD YOU DO?

By WILLIAM HILLCOURT

National Director of Scoutcraft

YOU are out hiking with your Patrol in strange territory. For some reason or other, you lag behind the gang. You decide to take a short cut. Suddenly you find yourself at the edge of a cliff. As you quickly draw back, you trip. The rocks crumble under your feet. You tumble down and land twenty feet below, badly scratched, head swimming and with a stabbing pain in your right arm.

What would you do in that situation?

Well, if you have learned First Aid, you should be able to figure out what to do. If you are trained in PERSONAL FIRST AID, you'll be even better off.

It's one thing, and not a very difficult thing at that, to put a sling on some other person. But it's something entirely different to make a sling for your own arm.

It's one thing to stop the blood spurting from a cut artery on someone else. But it's quite a different story when you have to stop your own blood, and keep yourself from passing out from the shock you are suffering at the same time.

On these two pages you will find the photographs of accidents that may happen to you and what to do about them. But don't just look at the picture and read the captions. Actually DO the things shown. Make a tourniquet around your arm while you are lying on your back; put your left arm in a sling, using only your right hand and your teeth; put a sprained ankle bandage on yourself, and so on.

Our Scout Motto is "BE PREPARED." You are completely prepared for emergencies only if you know how to care for yourself as well as help others if an accident should happen.

You have been working out in the open sun. You begin to feel faint, with cold sweat on your forehead. Watch out: HEAT EXHAUSTION.

Since heat exhaustion may be considered "shock from heat," do what you would for shock: lie down, head low, keep warm with anything handy.

You are on the last lap of a long hike. The weather has turned hot, humid. Your head is throbbing, your face red, without perspiration.

Get into the shade quickly to prevent SUN STROKE. Strip to waist, lie down, head high. Cool body and head by dousing yourself with water.

On a hike through rocky territory, you happen to step on a loose rock. It gives under you. The result: SPRAINED ANKLE. Do not remove your shoe. Use shoe as a support as you tie special ankle bandage around leg and shoe to keep your ankle steady.

What would you do if you were the fellow in the main picture? Coming to, he discovered his right ARM BROKEN. Using his good hand and his teeth, he made a neckerchief sling for the injured arm. Can you?

You have been working out in the open sun. You begin to feel faint, with cold sweat on your forehead. Watch out: HEAT EXHAUSTION.

Since heat exhaustion may be considered "shock from heat," do what you would for shock: Lie down, head low, keep warm with anything handy.

You are on the last lap of a long hike. The weather has turned hot, humid. Your head is throbbing, your face red, without perspiration.

Get into the shade quickly to prevent SUN STROKE. Strip to waist, lie down, head high. Cool body and head by dousing yourself with water.

WHAT WOULD YOU DO?

By WILLIAM HILLCOURT

National Director of Scoutcraft

YOU are out hiking with your Patrol in strange territory. For some reason or other, you lag behind the gang. You decide to take a short cut. Suddenly you find yourself at the edge of a cliff. As you quickly draw back, you trip. The rocks crumble under your feet. You tumble down and land twenty feet below, badly scratched, head swimming and with a stabbing pain in your right arm.

What would you do in that situation?

Well, if you have learned First Aid, you should be able to figure out what to do. If you are trained in PERSONAL FIRST AID, you'll be even better off.

It's one thing, and not a very difficult thing at that, to put a sling on some other person. But it's something entirely different to make a sling for your own arm.

It's one thing to stop the blood spurting from a cut artery on someone else. But it's quite a different story when you have to stop your own blood, and keep yourself from passing out from the shock you are suffering at the same time.

On these two pages you will find the photographs of accidents that may happen to you and what to do about them. But don't just look at the picture and read the captions. Actually DO the things shown. Make a tourniquet around your arm while you are lying on your back; put your left arm in a sling, using only your right hand and your teeth; put a sprained ankle bandage on yourself, and so on.

Our Scout Motto is "BE PREPARED." You are completely prepared for emergencies only if you know how to care for yourself as well as help others if an accident should happen.

On a hike through rocky territory, you happen to step on a loose rock. It gives under you. The result: SPRAINED ANKLE. Do not remove your shoe. Use shoe as a support as you tie special ankle bandage around leg and shoe to keep your ankle steady.

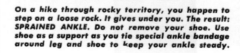

What would you do if you were the fellow in the main picture? Coming to, he discovered his right ARM BROKEN. Using his good hand and his teeth, he made a neckerchief sling for the injured arm. Can you?

While your hardwood fire is heating the ground, prepare the pie. This isn't hard, since you mixed many ingredients at home. A pie bakes in about 50 minutes.

Place the pie on three small pebbles over the heated soil; then, cover with the lid. Next, cover the lid with hot coals, so the pie will bake from bottom and top.

Tilt the lid slightly with a stick after about 10 minutes to see if the pie is baking too fast or too slowly. You may have to adjust the coals on top.

This, of course, wouldn't happen to you. You would know enough about the proper use of the knife to prevent getting ARTERIAL BLEEDING OF FOREARM.

Not a moment to spare! Place the bleeding hand in the crook of the other arm. Then, with the thumb of the good hand, press artery in injured arm against the bone.

You feel shock coming on. You can't keep on pressing. So you slip down on the ground, head low, hold injured hand high and get a neckerchief tourniquet around the arm.

Another bad slip you wouldn't make: Your foot was too close to the log when the axe came down. You cut into it boldly causing ARTERIAL BLEEDING OF FOOT.

The blood is spurting. You go into action immediately. Place a stick under your knee, draw up the leg, and tie your neckerchief firmly around the lower leg and thigh.

The blood is stopped temporarily. You lie down to get over the dizziness of onsetting shock. Then, as the faintness leaves you, you lay a tourniquet around thigh.

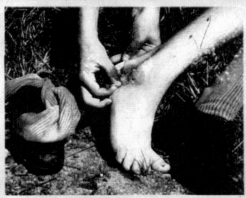

We are all clumsy at times. This time you've upset a pot of boiling water. You pull your stocking off quickly: Your foot and leg are red from SCALD. Care for it with boric acid ointment, burn ointment, or with vaseline applications, from first aid kit.

On the Fourteen-Mile Hike your heel is getting sore. You take off the shoe and stocking and find that a BLISTER is forming. You know enough about blisters not to open it. Instead, you protect it with a band aid against being broken by rubbing against the stocking as you continue your hike.

Clumsy again. You run too fast, stumble, your face hits the ground: NOSEBLEED. Sit up, with your head bent back. Pressing side of nostril from which blood oozes may stop the blood. Pressing your upper lip against your teeth is fairly certain to do it.

The Scouts of Troop 15, Charlotte, N.C., explore their surroundings. Later that evening, Evan Doyle lays low during a kayaking trip through the mangrove tree maze.

THE CALL THE WILD

BY AARON DERR

PHOTOGRAPHS BY JOHN R. FULTON JR.

Alex Ronan, Troop 869, Midlothian, Va., makes a nice catch while deep-sea fishing.

The mysterious crabmaster ceremony: You'll have to come to Big Munson to see what it's all about.

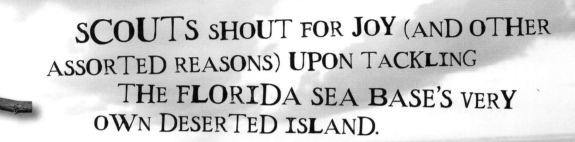

SCOUTS SHOUT FOR JOY (AND OTHER ASSORTED REASONS) UPON TACKLING THE FLORIDA SEA BASE'S VERY OWN DESERTED ISLAND.

Can't quite make out the air-conditioned hotel? That's because there isn't one. See that sandy beach? That's your home on Big Munson.

NCE EVERY FEW HOURS – sometimes more often, sometimes less – you hear the call.

"MUNSON!"

It might come from just around the next sand dune. It might sound as though the wind carried it from the other side of the island.

It's a greeting – a friendly "hello" from the Scouts and Venturers who are living on Big Munson Island as they participate in the Florida National High Adventure Sea Base's Out Island Adventure program.

It's also a sort of rallying cry, because living on Big Munson isn't easy. Five days and four nights with no running water, no electricity and lots and lots of sand that gets into everything – your hair, your ears, that space between your toes, your food....

It's also partly a taunt, a Scout's way of saying: "I have seen the challenges of Big Munson, and I am thriving. Is that all you got? Bring it on."

In many ways, camping on this island is like all those other summer camping trips. It's hot, and after a long day, you might feel like trading it all for a warm shower and a soft bed.

But after a few days, you realize that showers are overrated and your sleeping pad is actually quite comfortable, **especially after a day of snorkeling, fishing, kayaking or just horsing around in the cool waters off the Florida Keys.**

And it helps greatly if, every few hours, you gather your fellow Scouts around and yell at the top of your lungs: *"Munson!"*

continued »»

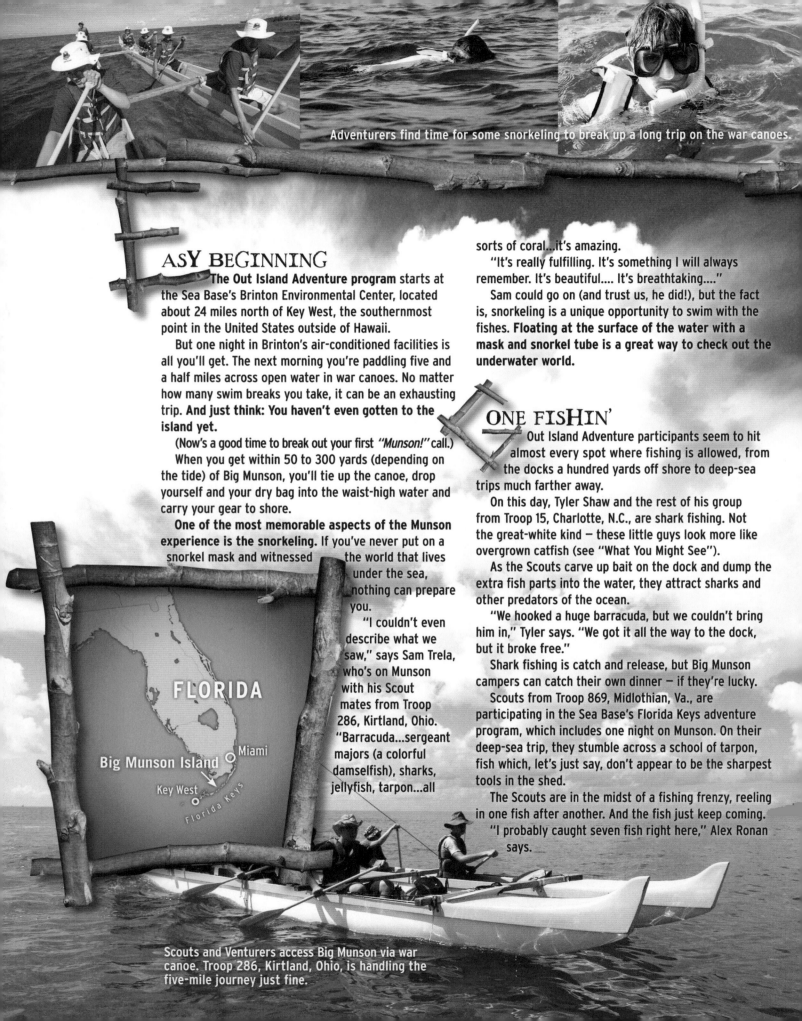

Adventurers find time for some snorkeling to break up a long trip on the war canoes.

EASY BEGINNING

The Out Island Adventure program starts at the Sea Base's Brinton Environmental Center, located about 24 miles north of Key West, the southernmost point in the United States outside of Hawaii.

But one night in Brinton's air-conditioned facilities is all you'll get. The next morning you're paddling five and a half miles across open water in war canoes. No matter how many swim breaks you take, it can be an exhausting trip. **And just think: You haven't even gotten to the island yet.**

(Now's a good time to break out your first *"Munson!"* call.)

When you get within 50 to 300 yards (depending on the tide) of Big Munson, you'll tie up the canoe, drop yourself and your dry bag into the waist-high water and carry your gear to shore.

One of the most memorable aspects of the Munson experience is the snorkeling. If you've never put on a snorkel mask and witnessed the world that lives under the sea, nothing can prepare you.

"I couldn't even describe what we saw," says Sam Trela, who's on Munson with his Scout mates from Troop 286, Kirtland, Ohio. "Barracuda...sergeant majors (a colorful damselfish), sharks, jellyfish, tarpon...all sorts of coral...it's amazing.

"It's really fulfilling. It's something I will always remember. It's beautiful.... It's breathtaking...."

Sam could go on (and trust us, he did!), but the fact is, snorkeling is a unique opportunity to swim with the fishes. **Floating at the surface of the water with a mask and snorkel tube is a great way to check out the underwater world.**

GONE FISHIN'

Out Island Adventure participants seem to hit almost every spot where fishing is allowed, from the docks a hundred yards off shore to deep-sea trips much farther away.

On this day, Tyler Shaw and the rest of his group from Troop 15, Charlotte, N.C., are shark fishing. Not the great-white kind — these little guys look more like overgrown catfish (see "What You Might See").

As the Scouts carve up bait on the dock and dump the extra fish parts into the water, they attract sharks and other predators of the ocean.

"We hooked a huge barracuda, but we couldn't bring him in," Tyler says. "We got it all the way to the dock, but it broke free."

Shark fishing is catch and release, but Big Munson campers can catch their own dinner — if they're lucky.

Scouts from Troop 869, Midlothian, Va., are participating in the Sea Base's Florida Keys adventure program, which includes one night on Munson. On their deep-sea trip, they stumble across a school of tarpon, fish which, let's just say, don't appear to be the sharpest tools in the shed.

The Scouts are in the midst of a fishing frenzy, reeling in one fish after another. And the fish just keep coming.

"I probably caught seven fish right here," Alex Ronan says.

FLORIDA

Big Munson Island — Miami

Key West

Florida Keys

Scouts and Venturers access Big Munson via war canoe. Troop 286, Kirtland, Ohio, is handling the five-mile journey just fine.

First comes the catching, then comes the cleaning. Leftover parts go back into the water and are gobbled up in no time by sharks, like the one caught (and released) by Munson staffer Craig Bonfield.

WHAT YOU MIGHT SEE

On your snorkeling or diving trip to the Florida Keys, keep your eyes peeled for the following fascinating sea creatures:

DOLPHINFISH: Also called Mahi Mahi. Different from the animal you know as Flipper.

BRIAN SKERRY/NATIONAL GEOGRAPHIC/GETTY IMAGES

GREAT BARRACUDA: This fearsome-looking predator will often attack a fish that you've already hooked.

SOUTHERN STINGRAY: Don't get too close – this guy has a dangerous, poisonous barb on its tail.

GETTY IMAGES

TARPON: Puts up a great fight when hooked. Can get up to six feet long and 150 pounds.

NURSE SHARK: Not exactly Jaws, this shark is just a few feet long and is considered harmless.

⁘ FIXING THE BEACH

The slew of hurricanes that ripped through the Gulf of Mexico in 2004 and 2005 did not spare Big Munson Island. Vegetation was pulled out of the soft sand, and normally fertile ground was rendered sterile because of excess salt that was dumped there from the ocean.

Without the plants to hold the sand in place, the island could suffer from excess erosion in the coming years. Scouts who stay on the island can participate in a service project to help correct the problem.

The solution lies in the island's Sargassum, a plant that you probably know better as seaweed. When spread out and buried under the sand, the Sargassum acts as natural fertilizer, rejuvenating the soil and encouraging the growth of new plants.

Troop 286, Kirtland, Ohio, spent one afternoon collecting Sargassum from the shore, spreading it across a barren area, and covering the area with sand.

"We're fixing the beach," says Senior Patrol Leader Sam Trela. "In some time, with a little luck, this area will come back to life."

Michael Brettrager, Troop 286, hauls a load of Sargassum to a barren spot near the beach, where it is buried by the rest of the Scouts.

To truly experience Munson, you have to experience the crabmaster ceremony. We won't spill the details, but there's a lot of...enthusiasm.

On their journey through the mangrove maze, Scouts navigate tight places in their kayaks. It's easy to get lost in there — sometimes even veteran staffers get turned around.

A NEW PERSPECTIVE

After five days on Munson Island, adventurers stuff their belongings back into their dry bags and hop into kayaks for the paddle back to the mainland.

After a closing ceremony back at Brinton, the Scouts head home for air conditioning and soft beds but also chores and schoolwork.

Maybe Munson isn't so bad after all?

"The heat gets annoying, but you just drink lots of water," says Jeff Woods, Troop 564, Bel Air, Md. "You're in the water a lot, so it's not too bad.

"We slept on our pads right out on the beach. It was actually pretty cool."

In the meantime, another group is just now arriving on Big Munson Island.

On a quiet evening, when the sound really carries, you can hear the call from miles around....

"MUNSON!"

Emerging unscathed from the mangrove maze, Richard Dobberstein and Forest Boylston watch the sun set before heading back to camp.

CHOOSE YOUR OWN ADVENTURE

The BSA's National Council owns and operates three high adventure bases. Talk to your Scoutmaster about them to find out which is best for your troop.

The Florida National High Adventure Sea Base: The Sea Base offers two Bahamas programs in which participants spend the week on a boat, sailing, snorkeling, fishing and swimming. There's also a coral-reef sailing program and a scuba program.

For more information, click on www.bsaseabase.org or write to The Florida Sea Base, P.O. Box 1906, Islamorada, FL 33036.

Northern Tier National High Adventure Bases: Northern Tier offers wilderness canoe trips from bases in Ely, Minn.; Bissett, Manitoba, Canada; and Atikokan, Ontario, Canada. From December through early March, campers participate in programs such as cross-country skiing, dog sledding, shelter building and ice fishing.

For more information, click on www.ntier.org or write to Northern Tier National High Adventure Bases, P.O. Box 509, Ely, MN 55731.

Philmont Scout Ranch: Philmont offers backpacking treks ranging from 50 to 100 miles and also offers fall and winter programs. The Double H High Adventure Base is part of the Philmont program and features seven-day backpacking treks with no trails.

For more information, click on www.scouting.org/philmont or write to Philmont Scout Ranch, 17 Deer Run Road, Cimarron, NM 87714.

Desert Survival

TEXT AND PHOTOGRAPHS
BY DAVID CUPP

They lived in the Stone Age land of the Anasazi where nobody ever heard of matches, machines, or three meals a day.

How long could you and your patrol survive in the arid desert of southern Utah? Could you last five days in the blazing wilderness with nothing more than the clothes on your backs, your pocketknives, bedrolls, and a sack of flour?

That's just about what four Scouts from Colorado and Montana did last summer. Mike Kozak, Paul Savio, Jay Trotter, and Paul Olsen brought along only two "extras" as part of their survival gear.

The "extras" were Larry Dean Olsen and Dick Jamison, who operate a survival school in Stevensville, Mont. Olsen and Jamison pattern their skills on what they have learned about the lives of the original survivalists in the area, the Indians known as the Anasazi or "Ancient Ones." Hundreds of years ago, the Anasazi built cliff dwellings in Comb Wash near Blandings, Utah.

Clues left by the long-vanished Ancient Ones were helpful to the modern Scouts. By searching the wash near the site of some Indian ruins, the group located two water holes that must have been used by the Indians. These were not springs but catch basins in the rock. The holes held run-off from one infrequent rainfall to the next.

Some of the Scouts had felt thirsty as they searched the rocky wash, but when they saw the water holes they were not so sure. The liquid was brownish, murky, and filled with insects.

"Don't worry." Larry Olsen grinned. He told them if they saw living things in water they found in a desert wilderness, the water was not poisonous.

The next job was to find a campsite.

Like the Indians, they headed for the high ground. They chose a spot on the highest rise within walking distance of the water.

"The sun will strike here all day," Larry said, "but it will be breezy. At night when the air cools, the ground will stay warm."

Now that they had water and a campsite, they began construction of brush shelters and started to think of food. They hadn't had time to gather anything from the land, so they used the bag of flour.

Jay Trotter and Paul Savio mixed flour with a little water and kneaded it into thick dough.

Mike Kozak labored with a bow and drill to create a glowing coal, while Paul Olsen stood by with tinder and kindling to build a cooking fire. When the fire burned down, the lumps of dough were dropped into the hot ashes. In a few minutes the Scouts had ash cakes—hard, blackened, and practically tasteless. But it was food.

Food was the subject next morning also as the Scouts learned to eat yucca blossoms, cactus flowers, and the peeled stalk of the common thistle. They also learned they could eat the tender shoots of the cattail and grind its roots into flour. A kind of yeast found on juniper berries could make bread rise.

Meat was another matter. It had to be caught or killed in the primitive deadfalls they learned to build. Olsen told them the tails and hind legs of lizards could be cooked in a tasty stew with wild clover.

To build the deadfalls they made cord from the fiber of the dogbane. Now all they needed was luck. ▶

Unfortunately, luck was against them. No small animals tripped the deadfalls. Even a ground squirrel they spotted entering his burrow managed to make an escape. It was ash cakes for dinner again. They could at least improve the taste of their water by making "lemonade" from berries of the squaw bush, and a warm beverage from the green stems of the Brigham tea bush.

In the days that followed, they studied other Indian skills such as making rabbit sticks to throw at small game. And they also practiced the patient art of chipping flakes from a kind of volcanic glass called obsidian to make razor-sharp knife blades and spear or arrow points. As they awkwardly removed flakes of stone with a deer antler point, they gained respect for the Anasazi who made such beautiful stone objects.

Stone, antlers, bone, pitch, and sinew were all part of the daily life of the Indians. Such were the articles Larry Olsen carried in a leather pouch he called his "possible" bag. "With this bag, I can survive indefinitely in the wilderness," Larry said.

One feature in everybody's possible bag was not visible, but the whole crew had plenty of it. It was alertness sharpened by hunger. On the fourth day, someone spotted a rattlesnake near the campsite and beat the snake to the strike.

The snake was skinned and coiled into a jar full of water for storage. That night the Scouts had the unusual experience of dreaming about broiled snake for breakfast.

In the morning, Mike Kozak wound the reptile around a stick and cooked it evenly over a low fire. To the delight of everyone, the snake was delicious.

"We're used to so much," Larry said. "We expect three meals a day. The old Indians didn't have them, and they lasted here for 1200 years."

As the Scouts packed their bedrolls for the trip out to a world of super markets and fast-food chains, they thought about the quiet place they were leaving. For a time, they had been very close to nature in Comb Wash. There was harmony there. Every plant and creature had a purpose. There was even a place for man. ♣

(Top.) When heated, squaw bush bends easily to make handle for stone ax chipped out by Scouts. Berries of same bush make tasty lemonade, or may be eaten. Bird's nest tinder catches fire from hot coal made with bow and drill. (Bottom.) Making sandals from yucca fiber. Obsidian arrow point made by Larry Olsen with antler flaking tool. Deadfall failed to catch a meal.

BUILD A REAL IGLOO

"HEY — NEW SCOUTS IN THE NEIGHBORHOOD!"

"YEAH — AND THEIR SCOUT HOUSE IS REALLY COOL!"

THE BEST WINTER SHELTER IN THE ARCTIC IS THE IGLOO. IT'S STRONG, WIND-RESISTANT, AND CAN BE KEPT REASONABLY WARM. WITH PRACTICE, IT'S NOT TOO HARD TO BUILD. HERE'S HOW:

"A SNOW KNIFE OR A SNOW KNIFE-SAW IS BEST FOR CUTTING SNOW BLOCKS. BUT A LONG-BLADED KNIFE OR A LARGE 12" KEYHOLE SAW WILL DO."

CHOOSE A LARGE AREA OF WELL-PACKED SNOW AT LEAST TWO FEET DEEP AND UNIFORMLY FIRM ENOUGH TO HOLD YOUR WEIGHT. PROBE IT TO FIND UNWANTED ICE LAYERS OR SOFT SPOTS.

SCRATCH A CIRCLE ON THE SNOW TO GUIDE YOU IN PLACING YOUR BOTTOM SNOW BLOCKS. A DIAMETER OF 9 FEET FOR TWO PERSONS, 12 FEET FOR FOUR WILL BE JUST RIGHT.

STRING

STRING TIED TO CENTER STICK TO MAKE CIRCLE.

STICK

"THE ICE BLOCKS SHOULD BE ABOUT 46 INCHES WIDE, 20 INCHES HIGH, AND 6 INCHES THICK. YOU SHAPE THE SPIRAL AS YOU LAY THE BLOCKS."

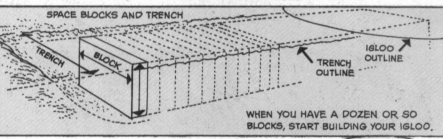

NOW SCRATCH A TRENCH OUTLINE 50 INCHES WIDE, ABOUT 12 FEET LONG, 3 FEET OF IT INSIDE THE IGLOO DIAMETER. DIG OUT THE VERTICAL FACE OF THE FIRST BLOCK, THEN THE SIDES (LEAVE A 2-INCH SPACE BETWEEN BLOCKS AND TRENCH WALL). SAW ACROSS THE BOTTOM (20 INCHES BELOW TOP). LIFT OUT THE BLOCK. CONTINUE SAWING OUT BLOCKS AND SET THEM ASIDE.

SPACE BLOCKS AND TRENCH

TRENCH

BLOCK

TRENCH OUTLINE

IGLOO OUTLINE

WHEN YOU HAVE A DOZEN OR SO BLOCKS, START BUILDING YOUR IGLOO.

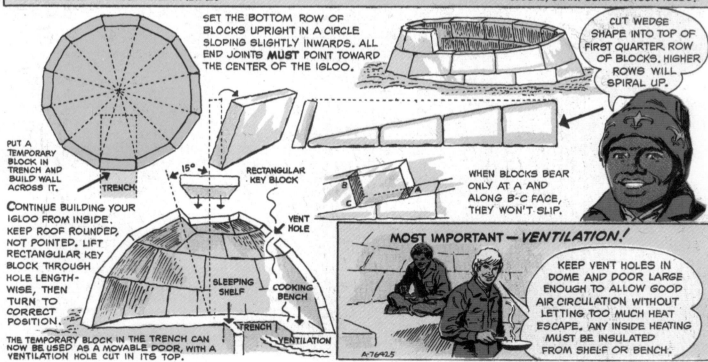

SET THE BOTTOM ROW OF BLOCKS UPRIGHT IN A CIRCLE SLOPING SLIGHTLY INWARDS. ALL END JOINTS **MUST** POINT TOWARD THE CENTER OF THE IGLOO.

CUT WEDGE SHAPE INTO TOP OF FIRST QUARTER ROW OF BLOCKS. HIGHER ROWS WILL SPIRAL UP.

PUT A TEMPORARY BLOCK IN TRENCH AND BUILD WALL ACROSS IT.

TRENCH

RECTANGULAR KEY BLOCK

VENT HOLE

15°

B A C

WHEN BLOCKS BEAR ONLY AT A AND ALONG B-C FACE, THEY WON'T SLIP.

CONTINUE BUILDING YOUR IGLOO FROM INSIDE. KEEP ROOF ROUNDED, NOT POINTED. LIFT RECTANGULAR KEY BLOCK THROUGH HOLE LENGTHWISE, THEN TURN TO CORRECT POSITION.

THE TEMPORARY BLOCK IN THE TRENCH CAN NOW BE USED AS A MOVABLE DOOR, WITH A VENTILATION HOLE CUT IN ITS TOP.

SLEEPING SHELF

COOKING BENCH

TRENCH

VENTILATION

MOST IMPORTANT — VENTILATION!

KEEP VENT HOLES IN DOME AND DOOR LARGE ENOUGH TO ALLOW GOOD AIR CIRCULATION WITHOUT LETTING TOO MUCH HEAT ESCAPE. ANY INSIDE HEATING MUST BE INSULATED FROM SHELF OR BENCH.

A-76425

What to Do With Your Staff

DO you know, I find that lots of Scouts are never taught to make any use of their staffs—except to carry them about on parade.

I think that's an awful shame. There's practically no end to the number of useful things you can do with staffs—if you know how, and every Scout should know row.

This month I'll tell you how to play

QUARTERSTAFF

because quarterstaff is a rattling good game and a useful one, and now is the time of the year to take it up—in your headquarters.

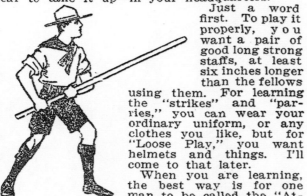

Just a word first. To play it properly, you want a pair of good long strong staffs, at least six inches longer than the fellows using them. For learning the "strikes" and "parries," you can wear your ordinary uniform, or any clothes you like, but for "Loose Play," you want helmets and things. I'll come to that later.

When you are learning, the best way is for one man to be called the "Attacker," and the other the "Defender." The umpire

FIG. 1.

calls each strike, "No. 1," "No. 2," and the attacker has to give the strike, and the defender parry it in the correct way.

THE "READY" POSITION

To start, the combatants fall in opposite each other at such a distance apart that they cannot touch each other with their staffs without leaning forward.

On the word to get "Ready" they fall in to the "Ready" position (Fig. 1). The left foot is about twelve inches to the left front of the right one. Both feet should be flat on the floor and the weight of the body distributed evenly upon them. Knees should be

FIG. 2

slightly bent, and the whole body should be held well back.

The right hand holds the staff about six inches from the "butt"—the thick end—and the left hand about a foot from it.

THE LUNGE

At the word "Lunge," the attacker takes a step forward with his left foot, throwing his whole body well forward, and bringing his staff up and forward at the same time, as in Fig. 2. He lets his left hand slide some little way down towards his right, so as to get as long a reach as possible with the staff.

FIG. 3.

From this position, as quickly as he can, he delivers his strike.

No. 1 Strike is made by bringing the tip of the staff round and down in a diagonal motion, striking at his opponent's right shoulder.

To parry it the defender draws slightly back and brings his staff up across his body, hands well apart, and strikes his opponent's staff outwards (Fig. 3).

No. 2 Strike is the same as No. 1, but is delivered at the left shoulder. The parry is the same, but on the opposite side of the body, of course.

No. 4 Strike is the same as No. 3, but is aimed at the left side.

FIG. 4.

LOOSE PLAY.

When you know the strikes and parries well you can indulge in "Loose Play"—just whacking away at each other as if you were having a real fight, like Robin Hood and his men used to do.

But whatever you do, don't on any account go in for loose play without properly protecting your bodies. However gentle you may try to be, you'll get nasty knocks—and quite possibly broken collar-bones and cracked heads.

You want wicker fencing-helmets, going right over your head—you can buy them at any sporting goods store. Your body should be protected with a padded fencing-jacket, or, if you can't get that, two or three coats, one over the other. You want the padding principally on your shoulders and sides.

Football pants and shin guards are the best things possible to protect your legs, and boxing-gloves will save you from broken knuckles.

Got up like this, you can go in for as much and as fast and hard loose play as you like.

The parry, of course, is the same, on the other side.

In proper quarterstaff there is no striking at the legs. But

FIG. 5.

some fellows do it—or sometimes a No. 3 or No. 4 strike may unintentionally be delivered rather low.

To parry a strike like this, swing the staff down as in Fig. 4, but let the tip rest firmly on the ground, well away from the body, and slip the right hand round on to the top of the butt.

No. 5 Strike is usually delivered after parrying a strike from the other fellow. Slide both hands quickly down to the tip of the staff and swing the butt right over in a semi-circle straight down at your opponent's head.

It is the best strike of all, but you have to be pretty smart to bring it off successfully.

To parry it, grip the staff firmly with both hands, each about a foot from the centre, and hold it horizontally above your head, catching the force of the blow with all the resistance of your stiffened arms.

These are the principal strikes and parries in quarterstaff. At another time I'll give you some tips for tricks and feints.

THE PEDRO PATROL LIGHTS FIRES WITHOUT MATCHES

REMEMBER—HANDLE FIRE CAREFULLY, *ALWAYS!*

LEARN TO LIGHT FIRES WITHOUT MATCHES!

THIS SKILL COULD SAVE YOUR LIFE IN AN *EMERGENCY.*

WE START WITH A BOW AND DRILL—MAKE THE BOW WITH A 24" STICK AND A 35" THONG.

HOLDER — SPINDLE
THONG — BOW
FIREBOARD
DRY, FLUFFY TINDER

THE HOLDER FITS YOUR PALM. CARVE THE SPINDLE WITH POINTS TOP AND BOTTOM. IN FIREBOARD AND HOLDER, CARVE CUPS FOR SPINDLE.
MAKE A SLIT IN THE FIREBOARD SO SPARKS FALL ON TINDER BELOW.

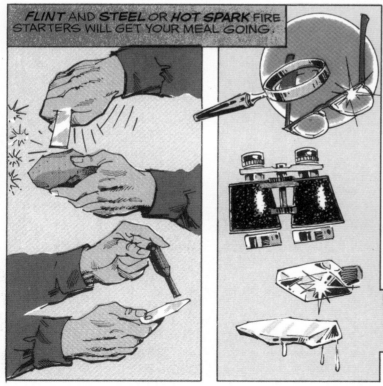

FLINT AND *STEEL* OR *HOT SPARK* FIRE STARTERS WILL GET YOUR MEAL GOING.

STEEL WOOL FROM YOUR KITCHEN KIT CAN BE A FIRE STARTER. PUT TWO FLASHLIGHT BATTERIES TOGETHER IN YOUR HAND. TUCK ONE END OF LOOSELY SHREDDED PAD UNDER THE BOTTOM CELL, THEN TOUCH TOP OF PAD TO CONTACT BUTTON. WHEN IT BURNS, TRANSFER HOT MATERIAL TO TINDER.

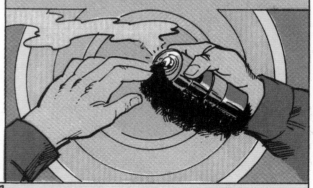

FOCUS SUN'S RAYS WITH MAGNIFYING GLASS! YOU CAN ALSO DO IT WITH BINOCULARS, CAMERAS, EYEGLASSES, WATER IN A BOTTLE— EVEN *CLEAR ICE!*

A-77153

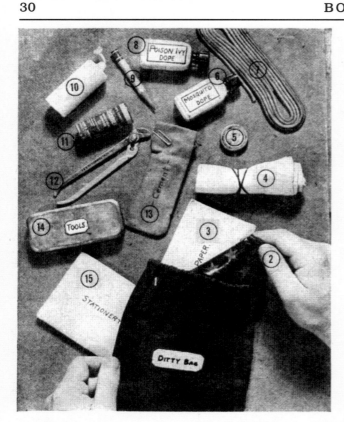

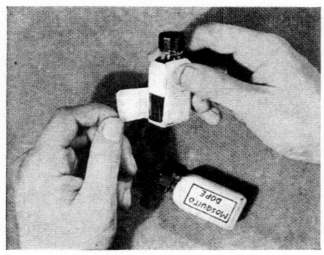

YOUR Ditty Bag is an important piece of equipment! To an outsider it might look like a weird accumulation of junk, but to a real camper the little collection of essentials in his Ditty Bag spells the difference between misery and comfort in the field.

The bag itself should be about 6 x 8 inches in size. This one is made of a tight, tough cloth and has a drawstring top. Most of its contents can be found around the house, but be careful not to include too much. Keep it "light but right." If each item can do several jobs so much the better. For instance, the waterproof cement and the handkerchief are also a canoe repair kit. But keep that cement in a tight canvas case!

"Non-melting" candles are best, but to light them do not use the waterproofed matches in the tool box. Those are strictly for emergencies. The foot powder will help your feet almost as much as that little can of salve or cold cream helps your sunburned lips.

Keep your flag in a plastic or cloth case—except, of course, when it flies over your canoe on the sparkling blue waters of some wilderness lake or from the summit of a faraway mountain.

Litepac Ditty Bag contents (upper left): 1. Cloth bag, 2. American Flag, 3. Toilet paper, 4. Handkerchief, 5. Cold cream or lip salve, 6. Mosquito dope, 7. Boot lace, 8. Poison ivy dope, 9. Pencil, 10. Candle, 11. Foot powder, 12. Pliers, 13. Cement (waterproof), 14. Tool box, 15. Stationery. Not shown: Dark glasses.

A Ditty Bag

AND A FIRST AID KIT

By ERNEST F. SCHMIDT

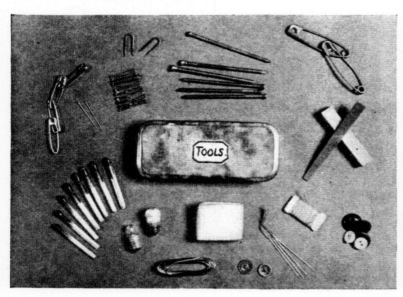

A LITEPAC FEATURE

YOU'D be surprised at the number of First Aid Kits that aren't really *first* aid kits at all. They're "second" aid—or "third" aid or maybe even *last* aid kits. It all depends on where you carry 'em. If you're on a hike, and your kit is at home, then it's a last aid kit. If you've left it in camp, then it's definitely third aid. In your packsack it becomes a second aid kit—but in your pocket—Ahh, Now it's a FIRST Aid Kit!

The trouble with most commercial kits is that they are so big and bulky that most fellows hate to lug them along. What you really need is a compact lightweight affair that can be slipped into a pocket. The best way to get such a First Aid Kit is of course to make it yourself.

The Litepac First Aid Kit illustrated here may give you some ideas. It's a one-man kit, small and light and inexpensive. You will find that it's just about the best two ounces of life insurance you've ever had.

A container is the first thing you need. Boullion cube boxes, typewriter ribbon boxes, plastic cigarette cases, tobacco tins and tin cough drop boxes are all good. You can get the filler materials from your family medicine chest and the corner drug store, or from some of the big First Aid equipment or mine safety companies that sell lightweight articles.

Wind your adhesive tape on a matchstick or a piece of cardboard. A small tight bottle is O.K. for antiseptics but ampules are better because they won't spill. However, an ampule can be used only once. Halazone (for purifying water) ages quickly. Be sure to renew it twice a year. And be sure too to keep your sterile dressings sealed. Wrap aspirin and halazone tablets in cellophane. Before starting on a trip seal the whole kit with a strip of adhesive tape to waterproof it. To prevent breakage, all bottles should also be wrapped with adhesive tape. (See middle photograph, left-hand page). The picture below that one shows the contents of your tool chest: nails, pins, needles and thread, extra matches (waterproofed), flashlight bulbs, tape, buttons, wire, a small file and whetstone.

Litepac First Aid Kit contents (shown at left): 1. A metal or plastic box, 2. Matches (waterproofed), 3. Halazone tablets, 4. Adhesive tape (½" x 2'), 5. Burn salve, 6. Sterile gauze pads (2" x 2"), 7. Ammonia ampule, 8. Antiseptic ampules, 9. Band-aids or Handi-tapes, 10. Needle and thread, 11. Pins, 12. Razor blade, 13. Aspirin.

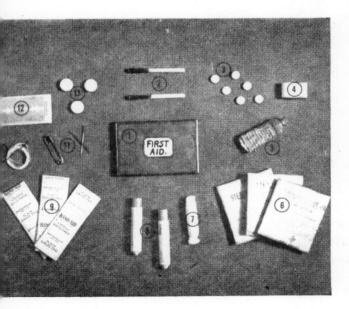

"Okpik," the snowy owl, has spread its wings and flown to the rugged Rocky Mountains of Colorado. *Okpik* is the Inuit, or Eskimo, word the BSA chose for the popular winter outdoors program that began at the national

In the BSA's Okpik program, Scouts learn cross-country skiing, snowshoeing, tracking, and cold-weather cooking.

high adventure base in northern Minnesota. But now Western Scouts are also learning the secrets of Okpik.

Winter comes early to the high country of Colorado. The razor-edged winter wind can bring more than 300 inches of snow during the season. To survive—and even

Winter Survival in the Rockies

TEXT AND PHOTOGRAPHS BY BRIAN PAYNE

enjoy—winter in such a place demands a keen knowledge of the outdoors.

December's harsh cold greeted a group of first-time Okpikers at the gates of Camp Tahosa, the Denver Area Council's 50-year-old Scout camp. The camp, though closed as a summer camp in 1981, was

Top: **A well-bundled Scout enjoys a beautiful—but frigid—ski trip across a frozen mountain meadow in the Colorado Rockies.** Inset: **Scout Sam Southam turns down his gas lantern, preparing to retreat to the warmth of his sleeping bag.**

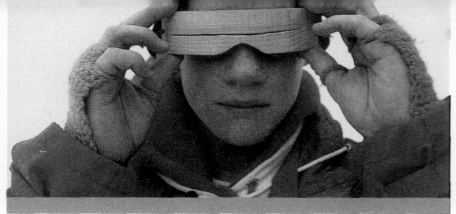

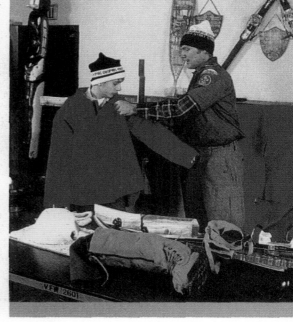

Clockwise from top left: **Carved wooden goggles with slit to block light reflected off snow; layered clothing; synthetic fleece garments; ski poles; bear-paw snowshoes; shoepacs that can be strapped onto skis.**

reopened last year for the winter Okpik program.

Under the guidance of camp director Lorren ("Smitty") Smith, a retired Denver fireman, Scouts can now learn cross-country skiing, snowshoeing, tracking, and cold-weather cooking.

Scouts here camp at elevations above 9,500 feet, where the thin, dry air can cause dizziness and dehydration. They are cautioned not to overexert themselves and to drink at least three quarts of water per day.

Scouts at Tahosa are also taught to protect the fragile mountain environment by practicing low-impact camping.

The Tahosa program runs Friday evening through Sunday noon. Camp director "Smitty" opened the program by displaying a "C.O.L.D." chart that states important points of winter survival: *keep clean* ("C"), *don't overheat* ("O"), *wear layers* ("L"), and *stay dry* ("D").

"Imagine your body is a house," Smitty said. "Your head is the roof and if left uncovered, over 80 percent of your body heat will escape. The feet and hands are the windows and doors and need to be covered too." Smitty also warned that wet, sweaty clothing will conduct away body heat much faster than dry clothes.

Clothing materials have improved greatly over

Scouts at Tahosa camp above 9,500 feet, where the thin, dry air can cause dizziness and dehydration.

the years, but wool is still considered the ideal outdoor fabric. It stays warm when wet and dries quickly. The new pile garments and other synthetic insulations are also good. But cotton, including that in denim jeans, is not recommended. Likewise, down garments, though very warm when dry, become useless when wet.

For footwear, use mountaineering boots, or try mukluks (winter overboots) or shoepacs with felt liners. (Shoepacs combine a leather upper with a waterproof rubber bottom.) At night the felt liners should be removed and put inside your sleeping bag to be dried by your body heat.

Eating plenty of calories is also important for staying warm. Camp staffer Rick Smith explained food requirements to the Scouts.

"You'll need to eat about 5,200 calories per day," Rick said. The average person at sea level needs about 1,800 calories per day. But vigorous exercise at high altitude burns up much more food. For every 1,000 feet in elevation gain, it takes 5 percent more energy just to breathe.

At Tahosa, the 5,200 calories are served up as 40 percent carbohydrates, 40 percent fats and 20 percent proteins. Staples in the camp are oatmeal; hot soup; hot, liquid Jell-O; hot stews; tortillas; and breads.

For shelters, Scouts build quinzhee snow houses, or igloos. Quinzhees, made of packed snow, "breathe," and allow moisture to escape. Snow is piled 10 feet high and is allowed to set for an hour. Then it's dug out, leaving walls 12 inches thick. A plastic garbage bag serves as a door.

Scouts at Tahosa learn to get around on cross-country skis. They pull lightweight sleds to carry food and extra gear.

Up early Saturday morning, the Scouts from the Denver Area Council faced blowing snow and dropping temperatures. They layered on clothes, gobbled down oatmeal and were ready for the trail.

"I wanted to take a formal training program like Okpik to convince my mom I could do it," said Brian Thomas of Troop 600, chartered to the St. Joan of Arc Church in Denver.

"It's so cold, I can't think," shouted William Deere, 17, of Troop 249 from Commerce City, Colo.

Just living in Colorado doesn't automatically make one a mountaineer.

"I really enjoy winter camping," said Scout John Adams, 15, of Troop 148, Aurora, Colo. "But I thought I should learn the correct way to prepare and better enjoy Colorado winter."

At mealtime the topic of conversation was ava-

Top: **A properly built snow shelter can last for months. Sticks pushed through the snow help the builder achieve uniform thickness in the wall.** Above: **A skier can load gear on a lightweight plastic sled and pull it behind him.**

lanches. Hundreds of avalanches occur each winter in Colorado. The Scouts learned:

● Most avalanches occur on slopes of 40 degrees or more.

● Snow is most unstable after snowfalls or prolonged heating by the sun.

● Slopes facing south are most dangerous.

● You should not follow old tracks across a slope.

● Snow crystals in the shape of needles or pellets signal unstable conditions.

● Rapid changes in wind and temperature affect snow stability.

● Big cracks in the snow should be avoided.

After digging out their snow houses, the Scouts had plenty of time left for skiing. But once the winter sun started setting, they had to cook dinner quickly. The light faded fast. Temperatures dropped even faster. But once inside their quinzhees, the Scouts were soon comfortable.

Morning brought gentle winds and warmer temperatures. A few Scouts scrambled atop their snow houses and were surprised to find the houses were strong enough to hold their weight.

Before the weekend ended, director Smitty added final words of wisdom. "Why snow camp?" he asked. "Because there are no bugs and no crowds," he explained.♣

Scouts are distinguished by the code of conduct that they pledge to follow. This code is embodied in the Scout Oath and Scout Law:

Scout Oath:

On my honor I will do my best to do my duty to God and my country and to obey the Scout Law; to help other people at all times; to keep myself physically strong, mentally awake and morally straight.

Scout Law:

A Scout is trustworthy, loyal, helpful, friendly, courteous, kind, obedient, cheerful, thrifty, brave, clean and reverent.

Other features of Scouting's code are the Scout Motto (Be prepared), the Scout Slogan (Do a good turn daily) and, since Scouting's classroom is the outdoors, the Outdoor Code (As an American, I will do my best to be clean in my outdoor manners, be careful with fire, be considerate in the outdoors and be conservation-minded).

These serious aspirations to lead a life of virtue, service and self-reliance set Scouting apart from most other youth organizations. The attempt to live up to these standards is described as "Scout spirit," and all Scouts are expected to demonstrate this spirit in their daily lives.

Scouts are taught the skills to grow into responsible adults through Scoutcraft, and the skills to be confident in the outdoors through campcraft. They gain a deep appreciation for nature through woodcraft. Through the decades, the pages of *Boys' Life* have brought the Scouting "code" and Scouting "crafts" to life.

Messages from Scouting leaders (even U.S. presidents) in the pages of the magazine have encouraged Scouts in acts of service and leadership.

Every aspect of a young man's life is fodder for the magazine, from how to get a job to how to date girls (with advice from Miss Teen America). Scouting is an international movement and world brotherhood, and Scouting practices in other countries have appeared in the magazine.

The great occasions for Scouts to gather together are large encampments known as "jamborees." World jamborees, which are now held every four years, promote international understanding among Scouts. National jamborees, also held every four years, promote fun and fellowship, and they too are visited by international contingents. Jamborees provide Scouts an opportunity to get involved in the wider world, and although most Scouts are not able to visit a jamboree in person, they can at least experience this special area of Scouting through articles in the pages of *Boys' Life*.

The most popular feature of *Boys' Life* is "A True Story of Scouts in Action." These illustrated tales of quick-thinking and heroic Scouts depict the incidents that earned Scouts recognition by the National Court of Honor in the form of lifesaving awards—the Honor Medal (issued in exceptional cases with crossed palms,) the Heroism Award, or the Medal of Merit.

While "Scouts in Action" is the most popular feature in the magazine, the most popular content remains the humor—jokes and cartoons that have prompted many readers to start at the back of the magazine (where the humor section is located) and work their way forward to the front. Scouting has a serious purpose, but it's administered with fun!

Jamboree '89 Moments to Remember

BY JON C. HALTER
Photographs by Brian Payne

Chief Scout Executive Ben Love introduced the nation's chief executive to 33,000 jamboree Scouts and leaders.

Jamboree Scouts took home a duffel bag of unforgettable experiences, from the mud of "Challenge Valley" to a visit from President Bush.

Eagle Scout Spielberg talked cinematography.

"WE feel like we are a part of history."

That's how Mike Ernette, of Scottdale, Pa., felt about attending the 12th national jamboree last August at Fort A.P. Hill, Va.

Mike and the other 33,000 Scouts and leaders at the jamboree had good reason for excitement. Few will forget experiences like

• romping through a muddy, mile-long obstacle course called "Challenge Valley."

• riding a hot air balloon, sailboard, BMX bicycle, kayak, canoe, and Olympic rowing shell.

• scuba diving, snorkeling, trapshooting, shooting an air rifle or black-powder rifle, archery, and fishing for prizewinning catfish.

• meeting famous visitors.

Fireworks and laser lights greeted Scouts and throngs of visitors for the opening arena show. Two Eagle Scouts were the evening's biggest stars: movie director Steven Spielberg and freestyle bicycle champion Ron Wilkerson.

"Scouting got me started on my career when I earned the Photography merit badge," Spielberg told Scout hometown news reporters assembled for a press conference. Only moments before, the director of blockbuster films like "Indiana Jones and the Last Crusade" had made jamboree history by introducing a brand-new merit badge, Cinematography. Scouts immediately streamed to the Cinematography pavilion to begin working on the new badge.

Spectators at Saturday's mid-jamboree show heard another famous Eagle Scout—Bill Bradley, Senator from New Jersey and former professional basketball star.

Each day brought more headline visitors, including space shuttle astronaut Bruce McCandless. Retired basketball superstar Julius "Dr. J" Erving and skateboard whiz Tim Morris shared tips on doing well in their sports.

NBC weatherman Willard Scott met Pedro the Mailburro at the *Boys' Life* exhibit and made live reports for the "Today" show.

ALMOST 450 Scouts came to the jamboree from other countries. Making friends was easy, said Mark Soler, from the Mediterranean nation of Malta. "Being a Scout means you are never a stranger when you're with other Scouts," he said, "no matter what country you're in."

On Monday morning, Aug. 7, all jamboree activity paused. For the first time in 25 years, the President of the United States was visiting a jamboree.

President Bush offered greetings—and challenges—for Scouts everywhere. "[You] Scouts...will face challenges unimagined by your parents," he said to a hushed crowd in the jamboree arena.

Become more personally involved in the fight against drug abuse, the President urged. "Ask yourself if you know someone [who is abusing drugs]," he suggested. "And if so, have you done everything you can to help him or her?"

The conquest of space is another challenge, the President declared. "Your generation will have a broader, greater

---

Among these colored sands pioneers lost their way and died of thirst. The survivors named the place Death Valley.

Death Valley Adventure

Where Scouts explore the mysteries of this weird desert land

By JOHN WOODBURY

The famous castle of fabulous Death Valley Scotty.

THE Indians called it Tomesha—"ground afire"—this long, low bowl of burning desert in southeastern California, a region of desolation nearly twice as large as the state of Delaware and lower in places than the level of the sea. But white men, blundering into it in their march to the California gold fields and almost perishing there before they escaped, gave it the name that it bears today, more than a century later. They called it Death Valley, and this is how it happened.

It was the winter of 1849, the year of the great gold rush. All America was bewitched by the news of prodigious wealth that lay waiting to be taken for Sutter's Fort, on the banks of the Sacramento. Thousands of emigrants struggled westward through the wilderness. Haste was the watchword of the day, for the gold would not last forever.

And so it was that one particular band of '49ers—perhaps a hundred of them—broke away from the established trail in quest of a short cut. They squirmed their way through a mountain pass and dropped into the great barren valley where no white man had ever ventured before. There they found themselves confronted with a high wall of mountains on the west. Their food and water were running low. Despair and panic overtook them, and the little band began to splinter.

One group, known as the Jayhawkers, burned its wagons, killed its oxen for meat and finally made its way out of the valley to the north. Another group, called the Bennett-Arcane party, camped along the vast salt flats of the valley floor and sent two of its men to hunt an exit to civilization.

More than three weeks passed before the two men returned. Enduring profound hardships, they had found a pass through the mountains. They assembled the gaunt travelers and led them out of the salt flats and up the mountain slopes toward safety. Reaching the crest, the '49ers paused. They looked back upon the huge sinkhole which had almost become their graveyard and spoke the words which gave the region its name:

"Good-bye, Death Valley!"

It was just 100 years plus a few months later that we followed the trail of the '49ers into this region of doom and despondency. There were about 700 of us—Scouts, Explorers and their leaders from all over the Hoover Dam Area Council, from Troops in Nevada, Arizona and California. This was the Council's second annual Death Valley Trek, and by far the biggest.

We'd picked a good time for it—March of this year. For we knew that within a month or so Nature would turn the heat on in Death Valley and transform it into something that was once described as "a reasonable facsimile of a first-class

---

A FRIEND TO ALL

By Arthur A. Schuck
Chief Scout Executive

ALONG, long time ago a fierce dragon threatened an ancient city. The people mustered to destroy it, but the monster's breath was so foul they fled in panic. To appease the beast, the people fed it sheep, and when there were no more sheep — human beings. One day the lot fell to the King's own daughter. She stood facing death when a brave young knight rode up, impaled the dragon on his lance, rescuing the maiden and saving the city.

The knight was St. George, who has come to stand for the spirit of chivalry, for lending a hand to the weak and the persecuted. Scouts throughout the world celebrate St. George's Day, April 23, rededicating themselves to the Scout Oath and Law. They are the counterparts of St. George — modern dragon slayers. The dragons they slay are not the legendary, fire-spouting breed. They are even more deadly and poisonous — dishonesty, treachery, malice, prejudice, hatred, cruelty, and cowardice.

How many of these dragons have you fought lately? How many cruel or cowardly acts have you seen in your neighborhood or town? Did you react in a helpful or brave manner? The smallest gesture of kindness or courtesy has real meaning. And you do not stand alone. There are millions of Scouts throughout the world, and if each does a single Good Turn daily . . . Well, it is difficult to total all these contributions. But they add up to kinder, more friendly relations among people.

Scouting carries friendship across all sorts of boundaries, across mountains, continents and oceans, across boundaries of race and religion. The Scout uniform is a universal sign of friendliness, his handshake its seal. "He is a friend to all and a brother to every other Scout."

The Scouts on the color page opposite are your brothers in friendship and service. They may look and dress differently, even speak a language foreign to your ears, or eat strange, exotic foods. But hiking and camping, they walk under the same sky and sleep under the same stars you do. They are your brothers, friends through Scouting.

If you are going to the national jamboree in July, you will meet foreign Scouts and can express your friendship face to face. Even if you are unable to be at Colorado Springs, you can show your friendship with pen pal letters or donations to the World Friendship Fund. Perhaps you have already helped by preparing, with members of your troop, a Scrapbook of Friendship to send to a foreign land.

This year we are celebrating the Golden Jubilee of Scouting. As a Cub Scout, Boy Scout, or Explorer you will be taking part in a pack project, a camporee, or a field day. You will be acting out with your buddies the true spirit of friendship.

Scouts on the facing page are framed in simulated stamps so that you can identify the uniform of each country. These are not real stamps.

A TRUE STORY of SCOUTS IN ACTION
by ALSTEN

ON APRIL 18, 1965, TWO-YEAR-OLD TRACY BOYD CLARK RAN DOWN THE BANK OF LEONARD DAUGHERTY LAKE NEAR VAN ALSTYNE, TEX. HE STRUCK A SLIPPERY SPOT, HIS FEET SLID FROM UNDER HIM AND HE PLUNGED INTO THE DEEP LAKE!

SCOUT LARRY LEE COLLIER, 12, SAW A SMALL HAND RISE UP OUT OF THE WATER...

LARRY RUSHED DOWN THE BANK AND HOOKED HIS FEET AROUND A TREE ROOT...

REACHED OUT INTO THE WATER AND, WHEN TRACY'S HAND APPEARED A SECOND TIME, GRABBED IT FIRMLY.

THEN HE HAULED LITTLE TRACY OUT AND CARRIED HIM UP THE BANK JUST AS THE CHILD'S MOTHER CAME RUNNING...

TRACY! OH, THANK GOD YOU SAW HIM, LARRY. I LOOKED ALL OVER FOR HIM! I WAS FRANTIC!

ALL I SAW WAS A LITTLE HAND POP OUT OF THE WATER. ARE YOU OK NOW, TRACY?

FOR HIS PROMPT AND EFFICIENT HANDLING OF THIS EMERGENCY, SCOUT LARRY LEE COLLIER WAS AWARDED THE CERTIFICATE FOR HEROISM BY THE NATIONAL COURT OF HONOR, BOY SCOUTS OF AMERICA.

LARRY IS A MEMBER OF TROOP 4, VAN ALSTYNE, TEX., SPONSORED BY A GROUP OF CITIZENS.

REACH OUT... AND SAVE A LIFE!

MANY SWIMMING ACCIDENTS HAPPEN WITHIN EASY RESCUE DISTANCE OF SOMEONE ON SHORE, ON A DOCK OR IN A BOAT... USE YOUR HEAD AND REACH FOR THE DISTRESSED SWIMMER. DON'T ENDANGER BOTH YOUR LIVES BY LEAPING FRANTICALLY INTO THE WATER.

EXTEND A STOUT BRANCH, A POLE OR A LONG STICK — OR FLIP A LENGTH OF STRONG MATERIAL ...

GET A FIRM HOLD ON SOMETHING, THEN EXTEND YOUR LEG OR YOUR ARM FOR THE VICTIM TO GRAB.

OR, FORM A HUMAN CHAIN — THE HEAVIEST, HUSKIEST FELLOW AS ANCHOR MAN WITH A SECURE HOLD.

HOLD TOGETHER WRIST TO WRIST.

Sir Robert Baden-Powell's
Message to the Boy Scouts.

Given to O. D. Griswold, Special Representative BOYS' LIFE, The Boy Scouts' Magazine

"I AM glad to be among you in response to the very flattering invitation to me to visit America. Your Chief Scout tells me there are 400,000 Scouts in this country.

I only wish I could come and see all of you, and I mean to see as many as I can while I am in America, but I am not able to stay as long as I could wish, as I have to go around the world visiting other centres of our great Brotherhood.

You Boy Scouts of America live in a great country, full of the good things of life and whose history is replete with the adventures of courageous and red-blooded men. On the world's roll of honor and high at the top are the names of such great Americans as Washington, Lincoln, Lee, Grant, Dewey and Evans, mighty men of war and statecraft. The nations of the world honor as well your Edison, Westinghouse, Fulton, Wright, mighty men in science and industrial progress.

The histories of such great men teach us that they were great boys before they became great men. They were poor boys, mainly, who depended upon their own courage, industry and thought to win their laurel wreaths. They were fresh air boys with red blood in their veins. They studied hard, played hard, worked hard and took their honors modestly. They knew that discipline was good for character building, and they were good soldiers, whether in the ordinary walks of life or on the battlefield.

You are least of all soldiers, most of all good citizens. Remember the main duty of Scouts, the doing of good turns to others, and it will very soon develop that you will be doing big things that others will recognize and appreciate.

The nine troops of Boy Scouts in Panama asked me to bring a greeting to you. And the Boy Scouts of England also send a hearty greeting to the Boy Scouts of America.

"Be prepared," is the motto of all Scouts. I want you to develop that spirit of manliness, fair play and chivalry for which you are already noted. Keep up the Scout spirit and good work of helping others, and you are sure to be good sons, good men and good citizens. I congratulate the Boy Scouts of America on the rapid growth of their organization.

My last message to you is, "Study hard, recognize discipline, live honestly and simply, breathe deep the good fresh air God gives to us all so bountifully, love your flag and fight for right in times of peace as well as in times of war."

This is the message of Lieut.-Gen. Sir Robert Baden-Powell, founder of the Boy Scout Movement and the defender of Mafeking during the Boer War, to the 400,000 Boy Scouts in this country through the columns of BOYS' LIFE, The Boy Scouts' Magazine.

It was in the tiny anteroom back of the platform of Tremont Temple that Baden-Powell stood, surrounded by dignitaries of the State and of the city, the staff of the Governor in full regimental uniform, and members of the British Naval and Military Veterans of Massachusetts, officers of the Boy Scout Movement and Boy Scouts themselves. Over his

LIEUTENANT-GENERAL BADEN-POWELL
Founder of the Boy Scout Movement

heart was the badge of the British Naval and Military Veterans, which had been presented to him through the hands of the British Vice-Consul, Gordon T. Maclean, while hundreds of Boy Scouts cheered their leader until the auditorium rang in echo. It was there that he sent this message of the Boy Scouts in America through this magazine.

You have all heard by this time of the wonderful greeting Baden-Powell received in New York and Boston; how Walter W. Waller of Brooklyn, N. Y., one of the seventeen Scouts winning the honor medals for saving human lives, greeted the soldier-leader at New York;

ENGLISH BOY SCOUTS

how the Boy Scouts of old New England gathered in the drill hall of the Boston Latin School, cheering until it was impossible for him to speak, and how troop after troop saluted him as he entered Tremont Temple for his lecture.

That is history, but how many realize the man himself? Tall, erect and soldierly, with eyes now flashing with conviction as he told of the heroic deeds of members of the Boy Scout fraternity, now aglow with humor as he related a tale of amusing occurrences during his long and varied life. The founder of the Boy Scout Movement is every inch a man. Nevertheless, he has the heart of the boy.

In this country they have astonished Baden-Powell with their determination and success. The snap and precision with which the boys in the armory performed their evolutions under the leadership of their Scoutmasters brought expressions of pleased wonder from beneath the grizzled mustache of the "Hero of Mafeking," and he warmly complimented them upon their work.

The veteran of many a bloody campaign in war, he is a greater leader of a campaign against war. For witness, his ringing words to the thousands that heard him in Tremont Temple, after he had related his stories of his service in the army of England and his dangerous jaunts into the jungles of South Africa, are sufficient:

"The basis of a successful career is not the A, B, C nor the three R's. It is the character of the man in 99 cases out of 100 that carries him to the top. Character should be one of the first aims of education instead of being, as in the old world, about the last."

"Now there has been such a thing as scouting in history, and it teaches character. In fact, there is a form of scouting in peace that is of infinitely greater value than of war. War is a very easy thing to recommend, but a very bad thing to enter upon and put through."

"That is why we ask you boys to join our Boy Scout Movement. We are essentially a peace organization trying to help on the education of the people in these matters, and there is an enormous number of boys everywhere who are eager to join our movement. We mean to join them all together as brothers, whatever their nationality may be.

This is the message that the founder of our splendid, aggressive, helpful, manly organization sends to the Boy Scouts of America, and those are the ideals toward which every Scout, from the leaders to the littlest kiddie, should strive with heart and soul.

Let us all work to the end that as the "Hero of Mafeking" watches the progress of the Boy Scouts of America, he will be proud of his comrades across the sea and will use our organization as a model for the many that will follow as the movement girdles the world.

A FRIEND TO ALL

By Arthur A. Schuck
Chief Scout Executive

A LONG, long time ago a fierce dragon threatened an ancient city. The people mustered to destroy it, but the monster's breath was so foul they fled in panic. To appease the beast, the people fed it sheep, and when there were no more sheep — human beings. One day the lot fell to the King's own daughter. She stood facing death when a brave young knight rode up, impaled the dragon on his lance, rescuing the maiden and saving the city.

The knight was St. George, who has come to stand for the spirit of chivalry, for lending a hand to the weak and the persecuted. Scouts throughout the world celebrate St. George's Day, April 23, rededicating themselves to the Scout Oath and Law. They are the counterparts of St. George — modern dragon slayers. The dragons they slay are not the legendary, fire-spouting breed. They are even more deadly and poisonous — dishonesty, treachery, malice, prejudice, hatred, cruelty, and cowardice.

How many of these dragons have you fought lately? How many cruel or cowardly acts have you seen in your neighborhood or town? Did you react in a helpful or brave manner? The smallest gesture of kindness or courtesy has real meaning. And you do not stand alone. There are millions of Scouts throughout the world, and if each does a single Good Turn daily . . . Well, it is difficult to total all these contributions. But they add up to kinder, more friendly relations among people.

Scouting carries friendship across all sorts of boundaries, across mountains, continents and oceans, across boundaries of race and religion. The Scout uniform is a universal sign of friendliness, his handshake its seal. "He is a friend to all and a brother to every other Scout."

The Scouts on the color page opposite are your brothers in friendship and service. They may look and dress differently, even speak a language foreign to your ears, or eat strange, exotic foods. But hiking and camping, they walk under the same sky and sleep under the same stars you do. They are your brothers, friends through Scouting.

If you are going to the national jamboree in July, you will meet foreign Scouts and can express your friendship face to face. Even if you are unable to be at Colorado Springs, you can show your friendship with pen pal letters or donations to the World Friendship Fund. Perhaps you have already helped by preparing, with members of your troop, a Scrapbook of Friendship to send to a foreign land.

This year we are celebrating the Golden Jubilee of Scouting. As a Cub Scout, Boy Scout, or Explorer you will be taking part in a pack project, a camporee, or a field day. You will be acting out with your buddies the true spirit of friendship.

Scouts on the facing page are framed in simulated stamps so that you can identify the uniform of each country. These are not real stamps.

THE SCOUT WORLD

Edited by — James E. West, Chief Scout Executive

Tr. 71, Welch, W. Va., gets books for U.S.O. Tr. 7, Buffalo adds its trophies to scrap. Chico, Calif. Scouts picking apricots were among thousands who helped the farmers.

Vegetables from Minneapolis Camp Victory Garden. Medford, Oregon Scouts load scrap metal and rubber.

THE summer just ending has seen Scouts, Cubs and Scouters busier than ever before. Throughout the vacation months, despite good attendance at Council-conducted camps thousands of Scouts devoted much of their leisure time to man-sized projects.

The collection of scrap rubber goes on. In a month Scouts brought in over thirty million pounds of it. In addition Scouts have been requested by the Conservation Division of the War Production Board to comb literally the nation's attics, cellars and barns for every available scrap of iron, steel, brass, copper, lead and other metals.

The Conservation Division's director, Lessing J. Rosenwald, in a telegram to the Chief Scout Executive, said:

"The Conservation Division of the War Production Board is deeply appreciative of your past efforts which have already brought in large amounts of scrap metal and rubber from the farms. The shortage of scrap is so critical that we must renew and redouble these efforts in the national scrap harvest to make up the deficiencies. Our nationwide goal of seventeen million tons of scrap metal, before the snow flies, is certainly possible of achievement and we are counting on your continued vigorous support not only to reach your share of this goal, but to surpass it in building a reserve scrap pile that will insure capacity operation of our war production industries."

Manpower on the farms has been diminished by calls to the Armed Forces and in war production plants. Again, as during the first World War, thousands of Scouts maintained their own Victory Gardens or cooperated in growing Troop gardens, community gardens and school gardens. At Council camps they planted, tended and harvested hundreds of gardens, and in many areas helped to bring in fruit and vegetable crops.

Collect ton of iron at Meriden, Conn. Scout Camp. Credit 6 Cubs of Pack 20, Omaha for 10 tons scrap.

Ft. Benning, Ga. Scouts, Cubs get 4 tons metal, 2½ tons rubber.

5,500 Brooklyn, N. Y. Scouts each bring 2 lbs. scrap or used records as admission fee to Dodgers game.

U.S.O. funds from 7 tons scrap of Little Neck, N. Y. Scouts, Cubs.

Troop 29, Mankato, Minn., signed up 900 Bond pledges in one day.

First aid trailer made of old lumber by Troop 396, Cincinnati.

Troop 5's scrap rubber is part of the 5,000 lbs. collected by Huntington, W. Va. Scouts in one day.

AT THE request of the Office of Civilian Defense, Boy Scouts successfully met a test of their thoroughness by distributing to 25,000,000 homes throughout the nation pamphlets prepared by the Office of Price Administration, entitled "What You Should Know About Price Control."

Their work won the admiration of two national leaders, Price Administrator Leon Henderson and Civilian Defense Director James M. Landis, a recognition that puts every Scout, Cub and Leader on Uncle Sam's team.

"By putting this leaflet into millions of American homes," said Mr. Henderson in a Scout tribute he gave to the press, "the Boy Scouts of America are helping OPA do an important part of its job of telling the public what price control is all about."

"The nation's civilian defense effort already owes an immeasurable debt to the Boy Scouts of America for the help they have given in the past," Mr. Landis said. "The service the Scouts are now performing places them in the front ranks of those who are fighting the battle against the rising cost of living."

One of the oldest Troops of the Boy Scouts of America in point of continuous existence is Troop 5, Honolulu in the Territory of Hawaii. It is a 32-year old Troop and one of its former Scoutmasters, Wade Warren Thayer, is Scout Commissioner of the Honolulu Council. Known as the "Queen's Own" as it dates back to the time when Queen Liliuokalani was alive, Troop 5 has taken active part in national defense projects. As evidence of its faith in America and confident of its own continued progress the Troop was proud to buy a $500 War Bond. With several of the Scouts in the photo are Mr. Thayer (left) and Scout Executive Fred B. Forbes (right).

Independence, Kans. Scouts turn in rubber.

Troop 111, Altanta, Ga., amassed 3,874 lbs. scrap rubber.

Fairhaven, Mass. Scouts on duty at Civilian Defense Report Center.

Troop 5, Honolulu, proud of its $500 Bond.

Tr. 90, University City, Mo., sees incendiary bombs put out.

Messenger Corps of Tr. 40, Duluth, also takes first aid training.

Boy Scouts place price data in 25,000,000 homes.

Minneapolis Scouts learn to put out fire bombs.

Boy Scouts of United Nations enjoy camping at Youlbury, England.

King George visits London Scout headquarters.

The King greets ex-Scoutmaster Griffiths of Norfolk, Va.

Salvage photograph of late Lord Baden Powell from bombed Scout headquarters at Malta.

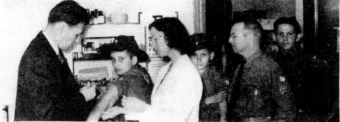

Troop 14, Beaumont, Tex., pays for its typhoid inoculations from its Troop Budget.

KING GEORGE VI recently visited the Imperial Scout Headquarters in London where he met and chatted with Scouts of the United Nations. One photo shows him passing through a Scout Guard of Honor, with Lord Somers, the Chief Scout. He enjoyed a long talk about Scouting with Sergeant R. S. Griffiths of the U. S. Army who was Scoutmaster of Troop 7 at Norfolk, Va.

The Ad Alta Dei Cross is awarded by the Catholic Church to First Class Scouts of that faith who achieve distinction in both knowledge of their religion and service to their Church. It was a proud moment for Mrs. Rose McCarthy when her son Daniel, of Troop 22, Davenport, Iowa, received his Ad Alta Dei Cross from Bishop H. P. Rohlman.

Harry Sloan was a Philadelphia Scout over thirty years ago. His son Robert is a Scout of Troop 18, Pitman, N. J. The composite photo showing both in their Scout Uniforms spans nearly the full history of Scouting in the United States.

When Rear Admiral Frederick C. Sherman, commander of the ill-fated U.S.S. *Lexington* visited his native city of Port Huron, Mich., Scouts of Eagle Rank and Sea Scouts of the Blue Water Council acted as his Guard of Honor.

First Air Scout Patrol at Chelsea, Mass., grows into a Squadron.

Bishop Rohlman presents an Ad Alta Dei Cross.

Absorbed by General Motors' arms exposition at Dayton.

Aviation enthusiasts thrilled by model plane at Houston meet.

Composite photo of Scout and father as a Scout.

Honor Guard at Port Huron, Mich., for Admiral Sherman.

Ja'89mboree
Moments to Remember

BY JON C. HALTER

Photographs by Brian Payne

"WE feel like we are a part of history."
That's how Mike Ernette, of Scottdale, Pa., felt about attending the 12th national jamboree last August at Fort A.P. Hill, Va.

Mike and the other 33,000 Scouts and leaders at the jamboree had good reason for excitement. Few will forget experiences like

• romping through a muddy, mile-long obstacle course called "Challenge Valley."

• riding a hot air balloon, sailboard, BMX bicycle, kayak, canoe, and Olympic rowing shell.

• scuba diving, snorkeling, trapshooting, shooting an air rifle or black-powder rifle, archery, and fishing for prizewinning catfish.

• meeting famous visitors.

Fireworks and laser lights greeted Scouts and throngs of visitors for the opening arena show. Two Eagle Scouts were the evening's biggest stars: movie director Steven Spielberg and freestyle bicycle champion Ron Wilkerson.

"Scouting got me started on my career when I earned the Photography merit badge," Spielberg told Scout hometown news reporters assembled for a press conference. Only moments before, the director of blockbuster films like "Indiana Jones and the Last Crusade" had made jamboree history by introducing a brand-new merit badge, Cinematography. Scouts immediately streamed to the Cinematography pavilion to begin working on the new badge.

Spectators at Saturday's mid-jamboree show heard another famous Eagle Scout—Bill Bradley, Senator from New Jersey and former professional basketball star.

HAROLD TATE

Chief Scout Executive Ben Love introduced the nation's chief executive to 33,000 jamboree Scouts and leaders.

Jamboree Scouts took home a duffel bag of unforgettable experiences, from the mud of "Challenge Valley" to a visit from President Bush.

Eagle Scout Spielberg talked cinematography.

Each day brought more headline visitors, including space shuttle astronaut Bruce McCandless. Retired basketball superstar Julius "Dr. J" Erving and skateboard whiz Tim Morris shared tips on doing well in their sports.

NBC weatherman Willard Scott met Pedro the Mailburro at the *Boys' Life* exhibit and made live reports for the "Today" show.

ALMOST 450 Scouts came to the jamboree from other countries. Making friends was easy, said Mark Soler, from the Mediterranean nation of Malta. "Being a Scout means you are never a stranger when you're with other Scouts," he said, "no matter what country you're in."

On Monday morning, Aug. 7, all jamboree activity paused. For the first time in 25 years, the President of the United States was visiting a jamboree.

President Bush offered greetings—and challenges—for Scouts everywhere. "[You] Scouts...will face challenges unimagined by your parents," he said to a hushed crowd in the jamboree arena.

Become more personally involved in the fight against drug abuse, the President urged. "Ask yourself if you know someone [who is abusing drugs]," he suggested. "And if so, have you done everything you can to help him or her?"

The conquest of space is another challenge, the President declared. "Your generation will have a broader, greater

Above: **About 450 Scouts from other countries shared the jamboree fun.** Right and Below: **Sailboarding and kayaking were new experiences for many.** Clockwise from bottom left: **An Army fife and drum corps provided entertainment. Scouts cooled off with scuba diving. While thousands pondered the *Boys' Life* code game, others pedaled the BMX course.**

Top: **A Scout band provided a musical interlude.** Above: **Challenge Valley "survivors" agreed that the muddy obstacle course was well worth a long wait in line.**

opportunity to live in space, to travel to establish an outpost on the moon and explore the mysteries of Mars," he predicted.

FOR the moment, however, jamboree Scouts were concerned with another kind of challenge—Challenge Valley.

Before sunrise each day, Scouts lined up for a crack at 10 obstacles over a gooey, grimy one-mile course.

Afterward, most Challenge Valley "survivors" agreed with Kansas Scout Sean Brewer: "It was really cool—the best thing at the jamboree."

Action never stopped at Jambo '89.

Patrols staged spirited competitions in pioneering and camping skills, volleyball, flagpole raising, tug-of-war, and in the *Boys' Life* patrol flag contest.

Each day the Merit Badge Midway overflowed with visitors. Guided by expert counselors for 58 different badges, Scouts earned nearly 10,000 badges and completed requirements on 35,000 others.

Every day was show time. Scouts saw helicopter rescue demonstrations, hot air balloon rides, precision parachute jumpers, military drill teams, and band concerts of all kinds. Meanwhile, under every tree, Scouts traded patches, hat pins, and names and addresses.

And then—too soon for most—it was over. On Tuesday night at regional closing shows, the Scouts bid farewell.

In four years, a new group will gather for yet another great festival of Scouting.

And they'll make their own bit of history.✤

"I Appeal to the American Boy to Remember That—

Unless He Thinks of Others He Cannot Fit Himself to Do the Best Work in Any Emergency"

By

THEODORE ROOSEVELT

Ex-President of the United States; Chief Scout
Citizen of the Boy Scouts of America

Copyright, Underwood & Underwood

THEODORE ROOSEVELT ON HIS RETURN FROM A BEAR HUNT IN
COLORADO

COL. ROOSEVELT, because of his great interest in American boys, wrote this message while on his way to South America, and sent it to Mr. James E. West, Chief Scout Executive of the Boy Scouts of America, as his contribution to the Christmas number of BOYS' LIFE.

ON BOARD THE "VAN DYCK,"
October 7, 1913.

THROUGH BOYS' LIFE I wish to send this message, not only to the Boy Scouts, but to all the boys of America. The prime lesson that the Boy Scout move- ment is teaching is the lesson that manliness in its most vigorous form can be and ought to be accompanied by unselfish consideration for the rights and interests of others.

Indeed I can go a little further. I wish that I could make the especial appeal to the American boy to remem- ber that unless he thinks of others he cannot fit himself to do the best work in any great emergency.

The names in our history to which we now look back with pride are the names of men who have rendered great service. This service may have been rendered at the same time that they themselves gained glory or reputation. But neither the glory nor the reputation would have been gained save as an incident to the service.

In our history there is now practically no mention of any great financier, of any great business man, who merely made money for himself. If at some crisis in the nation's history that financier rendered a great national service, or if he identified himself in useful fashion with some great movement for good, whether in art or philanthropy or otherwise, then his name remains. But even under these conditions it remains as of secondary value. America's contribution to permanent world history has been made by the statesmen and soldiers whose devotion to the country equaled their efficiency, by men of science, men of art, men of letters, by sane and honest reformers and social workers, who did great work and treated that work as in itself a great reward.

The two greatest men in our history are Washington and Lincoln. They possessed great ability, great intellect, and especially great sanity of mind; but it was the fact that they each possessed the highest character, a character both very strong and very unselfish, which gave them their pre-eminence over their fellows.

There have been very able and very unscrupulous statesmen in our history. But not one of them has ever come within even measurable distance of the achievements of Washington and Lincoln, or of the reputation of Washington and Lincoln; and this precisely because they were unscrupulous, because they lacked character.

Let me illustrate what I mean by a small example taken from my own experience:

When fifteen years ago I was helping to raise the regiment of Rough Riders, I did my best to get both as officers and enlisted men those men, and those men only, who I believed would make formidable fighters in a battle, rugged men in a campaign, and men of indomitable purpose to see the war through. I would not take any man who was not strong, hardy, brave, able to live in the open, able to handle both horse and rifle.

But even if the man had all these qualities, if he were quarrelsome or egotistical, or bent only on his own selfish advancement, and if I knew that this was the case, I would not take him. If he cared only for himself I was sure that he would be apt to be a bad instead of a good element in the regiment. There were some men from the plains whom I refused, although I knew that they were formidable fighting men, because I also knew that they were quarrelsome bullies and would wish to exalt themselves at the expense of their comrades; and I did not wish any man with me unless he was prepared to put the honor of the regiment and the army and the flag first of all.

If a man of the wrong type got into the regiment and I found that though brave he was thinking only of his own advancement and shirked doing work that might help others, or intrigued against them, or failed to support them, I got rid of him or discriminated against him or else took the first chance to punish him as roughly as I could. The best work could be done only by the men who, in addition to possessing formidable fighting qualities, had the desire to help others and the willingness to sink his own advantage in the common advantage.

What was true on a very small scale in my regiment is true on a very big scale of American citizenship as a whole. The boy is not worth anything if he is not efficient. I have no use for mollycoddles, I have no use for timid boys, for the " sissy " type of boy. I want to see a boy able to hold his own and ashamed to flinch. But as one element of this ability to hold his own, I wish to see him contemptuously indifferent to the mean or brutal boy who calls him " sissy " or a mollycoddle because he is *clean* and *decent* and *considerate* to others. If a boy is not fearless and energetic, he is a poor creature; but he is an even poorer creature if he is a bully of smaller boys or girls, if he is guilty of cruel mischief, and if *in his own home, and especially in his relations with his own mother and sisters,* he is selfish and unfeeling.

I believe in play with all my heart; but I believe in work even more. While boy or man plays, I want to see him play hard; and when he works I don't want to see him play at all.

Theodore Roosevelt

A TRUE STORY OF
SCOUTS IN ACTION
BY ALSTEN

The Blazing Wreck Was About To Explode!

ABOUT 11 P.M., ON SEPT. 7, 1975, A GROUP OF SCOUTS RETURNING FROM A BACKPACKING TRIP IN THE HIGH SIERRAS CAME UPON AN ACCIDENT. A SMALL CAR HAD CRASHED THROUGH THE GUARDRAIL, PLUNGED DOWN A 50-FOOT EMBANKMENT, AND WAS ENGULFED IN FLAMES!

WHEN A DAZED SURVIVOR WAS SEEN WANDERING CLOSE TO THE FIRE, SCOUT KALANI JENSEN, 16, RAN DOWN THE EMBANKMENT, SCOOPED UP YOUNG SHERRI RUSSELL, AND CARRIED HER TO SAFETY—JUST AS THE CAR EXPLODED!

BACK ON THE ROAD, SCOUT JENSEN ORGANIZED THE THREE OTHER SCOUTS, NOW WIDE-AWAKE, TO HELP KEEP SIGHTSEERS AWAY FROM THE BURNING HILLSIDE, HELP GUIDE TRAFFIC, AND TREAT THE GIRL FOR SHOCK UNTIL AN AMBULANCE ARRIVED.

MEANWHILE, HE CHECKED ON A MAN SEEN AT THE WRECK AND REPORTED THAT IT WAS THE DRIVER, DEAD. IN ALL, TWO PEOPLE DIED AND FOUR WERE HURT IN THIS ACCIDENT.

THE SCOUTS, WITH SCOUTMASTER HAROLD RING, THEN SET OUT TRAFFIC FLARES AND DIRECTED TRAFFIC TO KEEP OPEN LANES FOR RESCUE, FIRE, AND POLICE EQUIPMENT.

KALANI, ALONG WITH LIFE SCOUT ROBIN MARCHE, 15; STAR SCOUT MIKE WAY, 14; AND TENDERFOOT SCOUT BRIAN RING, 11, ARE ALL MEMBERS OF TROOP 131, NEIGHBORHOOD TROOP COMMITTEE, VENICE, CALIF.

EAGLE SCOUT KALANI JENSEN WAS AWARDED THE HONOR MEDAL FOR HIS UNUSUALLY HEROIC ACTIONS BY THE NATIONAL COURT OF HONOR, BOY SCOUTS OF AMERICA.

BOY SCOUTS of AMERICA

A-78L90

Bombers away on new Hart Hornet junior racing skis!

When we give young hotshots an edge on the competition —gangway! It's a fantastic spring steel "L" edge. On the most advanced junior ski—ever. With the fastest race base going—Har-Co Poly P-T-X.

Hornets have 14 laminate construction of spring steel and aircraft aluminum, dampened to a whisper with fiberglas and woodcore. And one-piece thru-the-ski edges.

Guaranteed for Life against delaminating or ripping an edge . . . and for 2 years against breakage.

Carve a place for yourself on Hornets. Maybe first place! $89.50

hart hornet NEW JUNIOR COMPETITION SKI

Take a tip from Jim Whittaker.

James Warren Whittaker, first American to scale Mt. Everest and leader of the Mt. Kennedy expedition, shown with his Vibram-soled boots.

"I take a firm stand when it comes to Vibram soles," says Big Jim. "They're the ideal sole for any tough job . . . work or sport. They give sure-footed, safe traction and long, rugged wear. Why not have Vibram soles put on your boots and go for that hiking merit badge?"

QUABAUG RUBBER COMPANY
NORTH BROOKFIELD, MASSACHUSETTS

Trails start and end with this TRAILBLAZER Official Boy Scout Compass. It has all the features needed for passing all compass tests and cross-country hiking. Show Dad the special features of the TRAIL-BLAZER: The liquid-damped needle settles instantly for quick, sure sighting. Has see-through rotating capsule for easy map viewing and orientation. The azimuth ring is marked for every 5° to make plotting more accurate. Dad will see what a valuable compass you can have for only $1.75. He (or you) can get one from your Boy Scout distributor.

Taylor INSTRUMENT COMPANIES, ASHEVILLE, N. C.

Miss Teenage America 1967

GETTING ALONG WITH US

By SANDY ROBERTS

When it comes to dating, I have some very firm opinions, pet peeves and suggestions for you! Most of my ideas, I think you'll find, are shared by many, many teen-age girls. So here goes.

Personally, I don't like to go steady. When you come right down to it, going steady is a family matter. Many parents—probably the majority—do not like their children to go steady until they are out of high school.

However, one of the big problems a girl has to face is that boys *think* she is going steady. Sometimes, if you date a boy once or twice, other fellows get the idea you're going steady. And they won't even bother to ask you for a date. This really cuts down on a girl's social life.

So if you're not sure about a girl's status, don't hesitate to call her anyway. Remember, if she's going steady, she'll certainly tell you, and if she isn't—you'll probably get the date!

Another thing, when it comes to asking out a girl: Don't hold back just because she's pretty! You can't imagine how many pretty girls I know who sit home on weekends because of this! Here again, find out for yourself—no matter how pretty or popular the girl may be. She may be waiting for you to call!

If a girl says "no," that usually just means she can't go because she has other plans. Too many boys feel they're being put down when refused a date, but they're not necessarily. This depends on the sincerity of the girl, and you can really tell the difference if you try! It never hurts to ask her again.

I don't think a boy should worry about money, having a car or making expensive date plans; he should concentrate on his personality, on being himself and showing a girl a good time.

When you call a girl for a date, suggest something to do. Don't ask her what she wants to do; I'm never sure what to say because I don't know how much the boy wants to spend or what he'd like. Sometimes,

I'd like to see a show, but it might be too expensive; you don't know!

I love it when a guy asks me out and has something planned—like, "I have tickets to go see so-and-so and would like you to go with me." It flatters a girl, that the boy has really put some thought into the date of time and planned the evening for her.

Otherwise, you can make two or three suggestions to the girl, and decide together what you'd prefer to do. Many times, I've had a date when we decided to go to the movies, then waited until he arrived before we pulled out the movie section, sat down and decided on our choice. That's fun.

Another reminder: It's always a good idea to let a girl have some idea ahead of time what to wear. And on a date a boy should always look well-groomed and neat, even if they're only going to a ball game. He should be dressed so that the girl can be proud to be with him. Of course, she should look the same!

There's no favorite place to go on a date with me. The main thing I like is variety. You get sick of seeing 300 movies a year! I just want to have a good time; it really depends on the boy!

Here's a pet peeve. I think it's kind of disgusting for a boy to grab a girl on the first date, as if it's something to be expected. A boy should have enough respect for a girl so that he doesn't expect a good-night kiss as a "thank-you." It should mean a little more than that. Otherwise a girl would be kissing every boy who took her out.

To conclude, I like to date many different boys, I like to go many different places on dates, I like good grooming, courtesy and respect. Most teen-age girls agree, I'm pretty sure!

Incidentally, I'll be crowning my successor in Dallas this month and maybe you'd like to see all the girls on television. The Miss Teenage America Pageant will be telecast on CBS, live and in color, from 10 to 11:30 P.M. EST, November 11. Be sure to watch. ∎

HOW TO GET A JOB

By Albert Fancher

ILLUSTRATED BY STUART HAY

Keep your chin up

III. Getting an Interview

HE WAS lounging on the side-lines, watching the first and second teams in a scrimmage. He was in his football uniform and, from the way he criticized the plays, seemed to know the game quite well. But he wasn't playing, nor making any effort to join the others.

Two boys, behind him, were watching, also.

"Gee," exclaimed one, "that Bill Smith makes me sick. Look at him—all dressed up and no place to go. He could make the first team easy, if he wanted. But he's waiting for someone to ask him to play. The big sap!"

"Yeah," the other agreed, "and by the time he gets ready to play the season will be over. Why doesn't he get wise to himself? If I knew as much about football as he does I'd be out there right now."

What has this to do with jobs? Plenty.

You may know what you have to sell; you may learn the methods of finding an opening and getting an interview. But unless you use your knowledge, unless you get actively into the game, you will be like Bill Smith on the side-lines—waiting to be asked to play. And in business, to-day, mighty few employers are begging people to apply for positions. You are out to make the team, and it will take all your skill and grit to do it—most of all, it will take initiative.

Now let's see where you stand. You know that you must first of all have some plan. You must determine what you have to offer and where to offer it. These things you have discovered in our other articles, which appeared in the November and January issues. You have found out how to uncover an opening, by answering advertisements, publishing ads of your own, talking with employment agencies, writing letters, calling on friends and acquaintances, and selling yourself through ideas. You know, also, how to write an outline of yourself and your ability—and how to use that outline in following up leads.

Your present interest is in getting an interview, for the interview is the last barrier between yourself and

"Say, you oughta have me playing end for you!"

your first job. That sounds like a pretty high hurdle, but it isn't; not if you have followed the suggestions given in our other talks. This whole business of finding a job is, as you know, based on a plan. You chart yourself; next you see where your experience and talent will best fit, then you go after openings.

Perhaps, however, you are wondering how to answer a help wanted advertisement, or write a letter of application, or an ad of your own. To you these things may sound difficult and bewildering. They needn't be, at all; they are really quite simple, when you know how.

Suppose you are away from home and need money. You don't have any trouble in writing your parents for it, do you? It's easy enough to paint your needs in the most vivid colors. You put your whole heart into your plea for cash—and usually you get it. You do the same thing when you are writing a friend about some interesting thing you are going to do—something he would enjoy if he could be there. You have no difficulty selling him on the good time that is coming.

It's the same thing in writing a business letter, or in answering a help wanted advertisement. You put your whole heart into the job. But you do more than that. First you study that advertisement and find out just what that employer wants. You picture to yourself, from his description, the kind of a boy that man is interested in, and what sort of a job is being offered.

Then you take your outline and check it against the advertisement, point by point. Does your age tally with that of the boy described in the ad? Is your education sufficient? Does the employer insist upon some experience? If so, what kind? Are you fitted for this work?

SUPPOSE we take an advertisement and see how it might be answered. Here is one: "YOUNG MAN — responsible, steady, for clerical work. Write, stating experience. Box 230 ——."

This employer wants a young man, and on that point you can immediately qualify. He wants one who is responsible and steady. From this emphasis on these two things we may assume that he has perhaps had trouble with other boys in that job; they have *not* been reliable. This job is a clerical one, so we must bear that in mind. It will help, too, if you have some experience to offer, since that is mentioned.

Now, what does your outline tell you? We will assume that you are both dependable and reliable, and that you have proven this, either through regular attendance at school or by holding some position of trust and responsibility. But what about this clerical work? Well, that need not be so difficult. You know how to write—neatly, we hope. You are at least fairly good at figures. You have an orderly mind and can easily handle such routine clerical duties as filing papers, etc. That leaves only your experience.

Thus far, your outline checks with the ad in every respect. Let's see how we will go about writing that letter. You know what this employer is looking for; you know what you have to offer him. It is simply a matter of presenting your case so as to make the strongest appeal, in the light of his own interests.

We suspect, you remember, that this man has been disappointed by some of the boys he has previously employed. This seems quite clear from the fact that it is the first thing he mentions and also that he has emphasized it. It would appear wise, then, to make this the basis of your approach. Our letter, therefore, might read something like this:

DEAR SIR:

Believing that you would be more interested in proof of my ability than in claims or promises, I submit my qualifications for the position you advertised in the. . . . . . .

I am seventeen, American, and a High School graduate. For the past two years I served as Treasurer of our Athletic Association. I was responsible for all money collected from games and prepared all reports on funds, expenditures, etc. I enclose a copy of a letter of appreciation for the work I did while in this position.

This was excellent clerical training, but in addition I clerked in a drug store during part of one summer, and last year spent several weeks in my uncle's law office, filing papers, looking up references and doing some typing.

I am ambitious and will work hard to make good. I believe you would find me reliable and steady and that you could depend upon me to do my work promptly and as you wanted it done.

If my experience and ability interest you as much as your position interests me, I would very much appreciate the opportunity of telling you more about myself. Should you wish to reach me by telephone, the number is . . . . . .
                    Respectfully,

This is not the best letter than can be written; probably you can write a much better one. But it does illustrate one thing; it shows the value of thinking of the job in terms of the other man's interest, and of fitting your experience to his needs.

Remember this, for in answering an ad, in writing letters of application, or in any detail of getting a job, you must put yourself in the other fellow's place. That is rule number one in business; the other man's viewpoint comes first. So get into your letter your special qualifications, those extra values that count so tremendously. And when you set them down, do so with the interests of your prospective employer foremost in your mind.

In some cases you may wish to suggest how your experience might prove helpful, but be sure you are justified in making such a ➤

How to Get a Job

suggestion and are not doing it merely because you think it will help you get the job.

Above everything, avoid boasting, for that will ruin your chances at the outset. After all, you are only a beginner in business, and to tell a man that you can run his company for him and make him a lot of money, or something equally absurd, is simply to invite his ridicule and eliminate you from consideration.

And that's exactly what you do *not* want to do.

Make your letter natural. Remembering that the man you are addressing is older than you, and furthermore is your prospective employer, you should be respectful. Some boys feel it necessary to be brisk or individual or different, and in their efforts to do this they are fresh, or smart or flippant. They try trick openings for their letters, or promise the moon, or in some manner get off on the wrong foot. Be natural and you won't run into this snag; but in being natural try to be interesting as well.

Certainly what you have to tell this man is of great importance to you; it concerns what to you is the most interesting and vital thing in the world—yourself. Knowing of his needs, you should be able to make this subject of interest to the employer, because your training and ability and extra values are what he is advertising to find. Once you realize this, you will find it easy to write a reply to his advertisement—a reply that should bring a favorable response.

WRITING a letter of application is somewhat different. In this case you have no list of qualifications against which to measure your experience; but since such a list is necessary you must provide it yourself. First you must find out what kind of a job you are after, and the duties you will be required to perform. You can do this by talking with people in companies similar to those you intend to canvass, or with boys who are filling jobs similar to the one you seek. They can tell you a good deal of what you want to know; the rest is up to you. After checking your outline with these requirements, you will want to add, again, those extra values we have mentioned so many times before. And you will want to stress them, for they are the things that will win you preferment over other applicants; they will make your letter individual and interesting.

Some people feel it is necessary to insist upon an interview when they write a letter. Because they want so much to talk with the man about that job they forget that others have the same thought. But no employer wants to interview people unless he is convinced they can qualify for the position. It takes time to talk with them and, as he is busy, he must protect himself. That is why the most urgent plea for an appointment is wasted unless that plea is backed up with definite, compelling evidence that that person is well worth considering for the job.

Your letter must do its own pleading for an interview, and it must do it by convincing the man that you have something that he wants; by showing him that your experience is better than that offered by others. In other words, you must sell him on the idea that you are the one best equipped for the post he is offering. Having done this you can feel justified in asking for an appointment.

Suppose you are captain of your football team and you need a new end. A boy comes to you and says,

"Say, you oughta have me playing end for you. I'll put your old team on the map. I'll win that game for you Saturday—and run up a big score, too."

And he goes on to tell you how good he is and how much you need him. Possibly you are impressed, because you do want a new player in that important position, but somehow you don't like his approach. He's too boastful, too fond of his own ability—which, so far, has not been demonstrated at all, but is just talk.

Next day another chap comes along. He doesn't say anything about playing end at first; just gets out on the field and joins the practise. He spears four or five high passes out of the air—then goes dodging and twisting down the field. He's fast as a flash and a splendid runner. Knowing the weakness of your team, he looks mighty good to you. So, when *he* suggests that you let him play end, you are glad to put him on the team. He showed you before he told you.

Make your letter show, before it tells.

Prove that you are qualified for that position by showing what you have done; then your request for an interview will be all the more effective. But prove instead of promising—and show instead of telling. Do you get the idea?

Your extra values are your proof—the experience you had selling goods that summer; the work you did on the school paper or magazine; the letters you won in athletics—the special things you have done, that many other boys have not done. These are your extra values; they are the proof in which an employer will be interested.

WHEN you call at an employment agency you will want to do the same thing. Present your outline and let that tell your story. You will find it more businesslike and more effective than trying to tell about yourself, verbally. You are appealing to the man with visible evidence; something he can see. You will be making a very definite and a favorable impression on him.

Undoubtedly, you have been wondering how to get the names of companies to write to, or the names of the men in these companies. There are several sources you can use: the telephone and city directories, the public library, advertisements in the magazines and newspapers, and news items (concerning new organizations, combines, mergers and so on). From these you can secure the names of the concerns you feel you would like to work for; you can obtain the names of the individuals by calling at their offices, or by phoning and asking for the name of the man who does the hiring.

If you are aiming at some particular department, get the name of the advertising manager, sales manager, or whatever his title may be. If you cannot get his name, use his title and address him as "Dear Sir." It is always better, of course, to have the man's name, since this gives you a more personal approach. But take care not to misspell his name and be sure you have his initials right; any mistake of this sort is certain to irritate him and is therefore poor strategy on your part.

In answering an ad, in writing your own, in preparing a letter of application, always consider the man who will read what you have to say. Try to put yourself in his place, and determine what his reactions to it will be. It may help you to take your ad or letter to some older person, whose judgment you respect, and get their opinion. Be positive that your letter checks, in all details, with your outline of yourself. You must prove your claims with facts, otherwise you are not being honest with yourself or with your prospective employer.

Here is a chap who has picked up typewriting on the side. He also has worked a short time in an office and knows something of office routine. He wants a job and decides to advertise his services. He can not say very much in his ad, because it costs money, so every word must count. He has two things to sell: his previous experience and his ability to use a typewriter. But he knows the importance of dressing up his wares so as to make them as attractive as possible. Note how he does it in his ad:

"BOY—ambitious, willing, reliable, with some business experience, wishes position where knowledge of office work and typewriting will be helpful. Box R821."

SELLING yourself through ideas may sound difficult, but it isn't. It does, however, require imagination, energy and determination. When you use this method you are not looking for a job; you are making one for yourself. You are not applying to fill a vacancy; you are creating an opportunity which others have overlooked. And if you can do this now, when you are just starting out in business, you need not worry about jobs later on; you have demonstrated your ability to sell yourself into a position.

Pick out one firm at a time and study it. Talk with the people in the organization; find out what methods are being used, how the business is being run. Then see if you can discover something that is lacking; some little job that needs doing; some new idea that would be of value to that company.

For instance, one young fellow had canvassed nearly all the business houses in town without finding any opening. Conditions were bad and there just didn't seem to be any vacancies. After weeks of discouraged tramping, he went into a one-man grocery store, on an errand. He waited fifteen minutes or more until the man got around to take his order. In that time he noticed that several others were also being detained. Two or three of them left, and went to the store across the street.

This set the boy thinking. He came in again the next day and had the same experience. He repeated his visits for a week and each time saw the grocer losing sales because he couldn't take care of the orders in time. And the store across the way was getting more and more of this business.

Here, apparently, was an opportunity, so the young chap went to the grocer and pointed out the sales he was missing because he was shorthanded. He suggested that the man could not only afford to hire him as a clerk, but that he was losing money by not doing so. He got that job.

NOW we come at last to the interview. You are finally going to see a man about a job. Naturally, you will want to look your best. Your clothes should be clean and neatly pressed, your shoes polished, and so on; for your prospective employer will judge you to a large degree by your initial appearance—just as you judge other people.

When you go in to his office, forget yourself and how badly you want that job. Think of him and how you can fit yourself in with his plans.

Once again, remember not to tell him but to show him. Hand him your outline and let it present your story. Answer any questions he may ask, but let him do most of the talking. Too many boys spoil their chances by trying to dominate the interview, by bragging of how good they are, or promising things they can not perform and which the employer knows they can not. Others, of course, are like clams, and everything has to be pried out of them. This is almost as irritating as the boastful type; but if you must run to an extreme, it is better by far to say too little than too much. Furthermore, your outline, if you have prepared it properly, will do a great deal of your selling for you.

Let the man know you want the job, and that you are sure you can handle it to his satisfaction. But prove this to him, as well as you can, by referring to the facts in your outline. They are your best recommendation; use them as such.

What you actually say will depend, obviously, upon the job you are after and the man who is interviewing you. You will want to adapt yourself to him and present your case so that it will interest and convince him. If he wants you to do most of the talking, he will let you know. If he prefers to ask questions, you will be wise in confining yourself to suitable answers. This will be a real test of your aptitude for business, because one of the most important requirements is the ability to get along with other people, and to see things from their viewpoint.

Be courteous, respectful and keep to the point. Try to leave the man with the conviction that you are the boy he wants for the job—but do this by proving your ability, and not by promises or boasts. Show him, by your manner and the things you say, that you are interested in the work—and that, in hiring you, he will be getting a boy who will work with him and whom he can trust to handle the job satisfactorily and well.

It may take all your persistence and grit to land a position in these days. You will have to keep everlastingly at it, and learn to overcome discouragement. But the experience of looking for a job is wonderful training in itself, whether you connect now or not. You learn how to determine your own worth; you discover where you are weak and what your assets are. And you get a valuable, first-hand knowledge of the business world, of business men and methods.

You can, however, depend on this: If you keep at it; if you follow every lead you have, and those you get through your letters, ads and other sources; if you do a really thorough, sound job on that outline of yours, you will eventually land a position.

It may take weeks or even months; it may be merely a matter of days, but you should find a job, if you make up your mind to it. Business is no place for quitters; game, gritty fighters are the ones who win out. So keep your courage high, your chin up, and go after that job hard, with all that's in you. Here's luck!

IT'S ALL YOURS

THESE THREE EDITORIALS, *written by boy readers of* BOYS' LIFE, *were chosen as the best of many received by the editors. They tell how much fun there is in Scouting, and at the same time they give evidence of how much value they have received from it.*

"Every hike, in hail or heat, was kept alive by hearty singing and joking," says Eagle Scout David Leigh, who goes on to say also, "In my personal estimation, the most effective preparation for my manhood has come through Scouting."

"A Fellow Scout," writer of the anonymous editorial, says, "I came from a broken home." At one time he "stole money and ransacked cars," and was sent to a house of correction. He was fortunate that later he was invited to become a Sea Explorer. He says, "The Scout Law has given me new goals to reach and a different outlook on life."

To Edward Romano the Scout Oath was at first just something to memorize. As time passed, he understood its real meaning. "It is good to know," he said, "that we can be helpful in making a better world to live in."

These three boys, writing from their hearts, make us feel that Scouting is indeed doing what all of us want it to do—giving you adventure and good times with your friends and leaders, and at the same time a training that will make you better citizens, and will equip you for success and happiness when you are grown.

May we all, with Edward Romano, "respect those with whom we have contact and respect the God in whom we believe."

The editorial by a "Fellow Scout" is left anonymous for obvious reasons. It would be unfortunate to have his past interfere with his obviously promising future.

Arthur Schuck

CHIEF SCOUT EXECUTIVE

THE WORLD WE LIVE IN

The youngest of our winners, 11-year-old Edward Romano comes from Springfield, Pa., where he's a sixth grade student and a Scout working on his First Class badge. He likes swimming, reading, stamp collecting, and chemistry. He serves as an altar boy.

FROM DAY TO DAY we read, and hear, or see in some form or another that things about us are either right or wrong. Sometimes I become confused. What can I do to help make this a better world? Must there be speed, must there be fast thinking to get ahead of someone else, must there be selfishness? I go to my room where it is quiet and think. Then it comes to me in the quiet. "Faith!"

How can we boys of this generation go out into a world, which at present seems so large, without faith? First we must be at peace with ourselves, then

WHAT SCOUTING HAS MEANT TO ME

I WAS WHAT YOU might call a boy from the other side of the tracks. I came from a broken home, the eldest of five children. Being older, I perhaps understood more and felt more cheated than the others.

At home I didn't get the things I felt a boy my age should have; and with that feeling, I went out to get them for myself.

This I did to satisfy myself for not having the happy home and security I needed. To get what I wanted and to heck with everyone else was my attitude towards life. I stole money, ransacked cars, and did everything a good boy should not do.

Then came the day I got caught. My mother and I were called to appear at the Probate Court, and that is a day I shall never forget. My mother carried my little brother, then about nine months old, to court. With all the responsibility of trying to hold the family

THE SCOUTING WAY

A former Explorer who earned Eagle rank, Bronze Palm, and Ad Altare Dei Award, David Leigh is a 17-year-old from Seattle, Wash. He combines "sports, dates, and summer camping" with work on his school paper—and honor grades at school.

I AM APPROACHING manhood. Senior prom, final exams, then graduation from high school—these coming events will mark for me the final steps on to the treadmill of life. Balloons, tricycles, and squirtguns have long been only memories. Gradually all the restless freedoms of boyhood are sinking deeper into the past. As my evolution into the world of maturity progresses, a lone question rises: Am I prepared?

To prepare is to make ready, to do *now* that which will be of benefit in the future. Prompted by ⟶

The World We Live In

respect those with whom we have daily contact, and respect the God in whom we believe. Every day you can see or hear that there is a definite link between us and the hereafter—prayer is that link.

We have faith in knowing that too that grass can grow and trees bear fruit. Scientists have faith in whatever they put in test tubes to heal or produce for mankind. Cannot our faith be stronger? It must be, for the world's population is growing and needs faith. Faith is a rare gift and those who have it must share it with all.

Some months ago I became a Boy Scout. My father and I went to the troop meeting. In order for me to become a member of the Scouts, I had to know the Scout Law and what it means. At first it was something I had to memorize to get by. As the weeks passed, I became aware of the meaning of the words. Two things stood out. One was Scout spirit and the other, Scout participation. These two requirements form the good things that can make us better people for the future.

"Scout participation" made me stop and think. You have to know about your patrol and troop, your community, and the country of which you are a part. Can we go wrong when we start like this? Are we able to make it a better world to live in? The men who give up so much of their time in our Scouting units have that faith in us, knowing that as the boys of today, we will be the responsible men of tomorrow.

Thinking in this way, I find the cloud of confusion is lifting. I can look forward to a brighter future. Faith, hope, and charity—the three things that are taught to us at home, at school, at church, and of course in our Scouting program—are what will lead me to this happier future. It is good to know that we can be helpful in making this a better world to live in. In my small way I will help. If all the youth of America have faith, we can and will grow into a bigger and better nation.   THE END

What Scouting Has Meant To Me

together, my trouble only added to her worries. The judge said it would be necessary for me to be sent to a house of correction. I stayed there for two years. When I left, I had just about the same attitude I had had when I first arrived. I failed to see the fault was within myself and not others.

Within two months after I returned to my home town, I was right back in the old rut with the same gang. This time the court sent me to a juvenile home, and later I was placed in a foster

home. Not until then had I ever found the security and understanding love I needed. I met the right kind of companions who helped me to realize and appreciate the laws of society and to accept the right way to live and enjoy life.

One of my friends had been in Scouting for years and belonged to a Sea Explorer ship. He asked me to join. I did, and I have learned to appreciate the Scout Law and live by it. The Law has given me new goals to reach and a different outlook on life. I had never known that there could be such enjoyment in a group of good Scouts.

The companions I had had were so unlike my new friends. Thinking back to those days, I can truthfully say, "There is greater satisfaction in being a good Scout than the boy I used to be."

I am glad the court gave me a chance to get on the right side of the tracks. Now that I have joined the Scouts, they have helped make me feel secure by being my companions. This has given me happiness, and now I understand what Scouting means. I have advanced quite rapidly since I became a Sea Explorer; I've achieved the rating of Star and Ordinary. I have a goal to reach, and I am working for that rating now.

It must be pleasing to the vol-unteer workers in Scouting to know that the time they give is not wasted. They are helping to curb juvenile delinquency and are giving boys all over the world a chance to enjoy the better things in life, making better citizens like myself.

It is hard work for these skippers and leaders to know each boy's problems; but in working with them, their influence and guidance is doing much to keep boys like myself interested in Scouting and out of trouble.

Only hard work and proper guidance can change one's thinking completely to good deeds when you have had to grow up as I have.

In my foster home and new home town and with my new friends, I feel like a new boy. With these rules I shall try to be a better boy and find my place in life and be a more useful citizen in my community.

When I say, "A Scout is trustworthy, loyal, helpful, friendly, courteous, kind, obedient, cheerful, thrifty, brave, clean, and reverent," it is a prayer and a promise that has helped me to be a better boy and Scout. To me, Scouting has been one of the most helpful things to make my adjustment in my new way of life. It is my wish that other unfortunate boys could find the right way through Scouting as I have.

THE END

The Scouting Way

the wisdom of years, the American Indians presented severe gauntlets of trial for the prospective brave, their young man. A full-fledged member of their tribes was expected to have undergone rigorous ordeals and have demonstrated physical and mental prowess. The accepted warrior had to be thoroughly prepared.

In my personal estimation, the most effective preparation for my manhood has come through Scouting. Grade school days leave delightful memories, with my own favorite recollection centering around my first Cub Scout meeting, the laughter of the older

Cubs, the warm smile of the Den Mother. From that initial acquaintance onward, the entire ladder of the Scouting program has provided rungs of encouragement. It is with a sense of worthwhile accomplishment that I am trying to pour forth a few of the indelible meanings which I have received from Scouting.

First delighting my imagination are the frequent activities that combine to demonstrate the portion of the Scout Law that reads "A Scout is Cheerful." Every meeting was sparked by one patrol's leading the way with some novel skit or lively contest. Every hike, in hail or heat, was kept

alive by hearty singing and joking. Every summer session at camp was highlighted by water carnivals, sectional field days, and yarns around glowing campfires.

Whenever our troop traveled with other Scouts, we always noticed that the spirited groups also proved to be top-flight competitors in every phase of the Scout game. We did our best to surge forward in the same light-hearted manner of these well-knit units. Looking back, I am proud to state that my troop never failed to give me, as well as every Scout on its registration list, the happiest time of our lives.

Yet laughter was only one attraction that kept my interest focused on the wide screen of the Scouting program. It provided the necessary charm which eventually drew me to the more serious goals cited in the other eleven points forming the Scout Law.

To me as an individual, the four central ideas—helpfulness, friendliness, courtesy, and kindness—have been my greatest aids in preparing for life as a man. Too typical was I of modern youth: a driving, struggling lad whose favorite hero was himself. But as these staunch requirements were enforced in my troop and were obeyed by the advancing Scouts, a change for the better was wrought upon me. Influenced by the helpful interest among the leaders, by the friendly attitude of the patrol members, and by the courteous and kind brotherhood shown by all ranks of Scouts, I was drawn into the world-encompassing circle of friendship.

Certainly Scouting has an enthusiastic supporter in myself. Every moment during my more than three years of work in the movement has imprinted itself in my handbook of guiding principles. A firm handshake of gratitude is all I can give to each leader who has used his time and experience to lighten my pack and direct my footsteps along the path of advancement. Thanks to these men and to the assistance of the Great Scoutmaster, I am able to wear the medallion of the highest rank in Scouting. I have the honor of being an Eagle Scout.

With this medal of hardiness on my chest, I make ready for the grave decision of a lifetime vocation. The Scouting way has produced men since its foundation in England nearly fifty years ago. And because the movement has proved itself through modern American history, I consider it my insurance for a hopeful future. So, without a trace of self-importance but with self-confidence, I honestly believe Scouting has developed my character, has molded my personality, and has given me the power to "Be Prepared."

THE END

ARE YOU MOVING?

If you expect to move, and IF you know your new address now, and IF you don't want to miss any issue of BOYS' LIFE, here are three things you can do *right now!*

1 Tear your name and address sticker off the cover of this issue and paste it in this box, right over these words.

2 Print your name and NEW post office address in the lines below:

55

(NAME)

(Number and Street—or Route)

(City)   (Zone)   (State)

3 Cut out this whole box and mail it to: BOYS' LIFE, New Brunswick, New Jersey.

IF you don't like to cut your magazine, make a complete and accurate copy of your old address sticker on a sheet of paper. Print your name and new post office address right under it.

IF you have already moved and did not notify BOYS' LIFE, you're going to miss some exciting issues unless you send in the change of address pronto.

Note: It is not enough to notify your local post office of a change of address. You must notify us so that your mailing stencil may be corrected.

THEY CALL THEM "PATHFINDERS"—AND THEY ARE

Scouting in the Land of the Kaiser

By LUDVIG S. DALE

NATIONAL FIELD SCOUT COMMISSIONER

YOU might address a letter to "Boy Scout Headquarters" in any of the capital cities of Europe and it would, without doubt, reach its destination—the only exception being Berlin. You will understand the reason for this when you read the following paragraphs from a "Flying Leaflet," published by Dr. Carl Hellwig, Berlin, who, by the way, bids fair to become the real leader of scouting in the German empire.

"If one compares the second edition of the 'Pathfinder' book with the first, he finds one important difference. Whereas the former, published in 1909, was founded on those principles which form the foundation for scouting in every land, with 'Scouting for Boys,' by Baden-Powell, at least in part as a model, the latter edition tries to do away with everything which might remind you of the English idea. And the excuse given is that 'a movement patterned after an English ideal can never enjoy the favor of the German people.' If this supposition is correct, it will not prove 'the national consciousness of Germany' but simply cultural backwardness. To refuse to accept any new movement, the worth of which has been proved by another nation, simply because that nation is not our own, is a theory which no real student of culture can accept.

"Local prejudices and politics have made weak more than one movement. But scouting should not be in any way connected with politics. It is not a movement of any party, or of any people; it is the movement of youth, the youth of this land or any other land. And if we want to help this movement in our land we must unite our efforts with those of other lands; we must recognize that the movement is a worthy one because its roots reach down into the feeling and willing of every hale and hearty youth.

"One of the chief aims of scouting is to develop patriotism. But patriotism founded upon knowledge, not upon prejudice, a patriotism which is none the less ardent because it understands and appreciates the worth of other nations."

You will understand from the above extract, first that the German "pathfinder" is not exactly a "scout," and second, that there is a movement on foot to get into line with the scouts of every other land.

"Deutsche Spaherkorps" was founded September 16, 1911, in Berlin, and already many troops have been formed throughout the empire. This organization is built upon the English idea. The members carry the scout dress, and are united with the scouts of other lands through common laws and common badges and medals. Their motto is "Sei bereit," and they carry the "lily" as the national emblem.

Now that you know that a beginning has been made along the right line, it might be of interest to make the acquaintance of some of the "pathfinders." I can think of no better way than to let you come along on a two-day excursion from München to Tölz. Nor can I describe it better than the one who had charge of it, so I will let him repeat the report which he handed the boys a few days after we got home.

"We left München central station at 9 o'clock A. M., one hour late. At Holzkirchen we changed for Tölz. Here we march through town by patrols. We notice especially a monument to a war hero, as well as the picturesque houses on the main street. Then we pass the Isar bridge, health resort Krankenheil (heal the sick) and arrive at Blomberg. Rest fifteen minutes. We supply ourselves with water and begin the ascent of the Blomberg mountains. At the top we get a beautiful view of a number of villages and the fine forests round about. We rest here nearly two hours. Return to Tölz by another route, arriving there a quarter past seven.

"Had supper, consisting of noodle soup and calf steak, at the Cloister Inn, and slept on straw, etc., in the hallways and in a few chambers placed at our disposal at a health resort.

"The next day we arose at a quarter to five. At five-thirty coffee, at 6 o'clock all Catholics attended mass. Visit military storehouse at a quarter to eight, after having eaten bread and potatoes. March until we reach Urfeld, where we camp for three hours and a half. Dinner, consisting of pea soup, preserved meat and potatoes. From here we march via Kochel and Tuzing to München. Arrive home at a quarter to nine. Both days we had fine weather.

"The ascent.—Very slowly we march, but steadily we move upward. This method is the least fatiguing. A lady left quite a while before us, and she walked quite rapidly. In a little while we overtook her, because she had been obliged to rest. While we ascend we carry our jackets and vests over our shoulders, and we have our shirt fronts open. We take no short cuts; they take too much energy.

"At rest.—Always button your shirts and put on vests and jackets, even if it is warm, for you can easily catch cold. Select a dry place, protected from wind and rain. And when you leave, no one must be able to tell that you have been camping there. Therefore, do not forget to remove such things as paper bags, bottles, orange peelings, etc. Rubbish often destroys our enjoyment of nature.

"Drinking.—Well water, or water from mountain brooks, always good. But never drink lake water, or water taken from a river on the plains. The water of ponds and bogs is always poor. Drink as little as possible. The more you drink the more thirsty you become. A good many of you had bottles with you, and every five minutes you gulped down a little. That won't do. Pop, especially that which is colored, only makes you more thirsty. And besides it costs more than water. And when you have such an abundance of such good water, why do you carry along fancy drinks?

"Bathing.—Four days ago there was snow on the banks of the Walchensee. And yet you repeatedly begged to go in swimming. That is pure madness. Even if the water feels warm at the top, you must remember it is always colder underneath. And we take our outings to remain well, not to get sick.

"Marching in file.—You marched well, people told me, and covered one another well. Remember to hold your head up; never study the tracks of the one ahead of you. Also lift your feet properly, so the one behind you won't have to swallow so much dust. Never leave ranks without permission.

"Sleeping.—You had plenty of straw and heavy, warm blankets. If ever you have only a coat or a mantle, be sure to use it as a cover; do not put it on. Always take off your shoes and loosen up your clothing.

"Guards.—The guard must feel that he has an important mission. For instance, in case a fire should break out, and the guard should be asleep, he would have been to blame if any of his comrades had lost their lives.

"One of the guards at Walchensee had been told to stand on the banks of the lake and hinder any one from wading out too far when they took a foot bath. When I looked for him I found him a good distance from the lake, by a cooking fire. Did he do his duty?

"On the train.—When you are warm, do not stand on the platform. Never look toward the locomotive when you look out through the window; you might get a cinder in the eye.

"Punctual.—You must be more punctual. When I say eleven o'clock I do not want three or four boys reporting at eleven-ten.

"Comradeship.—I will be frank with you; you did not exhibit much comradeship. Just think of that everlasting chattering at night. You had no regard for the boys that wanted to sleep. You just kept at it, talking, laughing, cutting up. Then the soldiers are much

The Scouts Discover the Sea Serpent

True Stories of the Boone Scouts of the Sixties

By DANIEL CARTER BEARD

NATIONAL FIELD SCOUT COMMISSIONER

BOONE came running along the street, the street in front of Hi's house, and gave the old Indian call of whoo—whoo-ah! whoo-ah! Whooah Hi! Hi poked his head over the back fence; he was busy feeding the pigs. Boone held up two fingers. Hi nodded. Boone next whoo-ahed in front of Tom's house and went through the same mystic performance with Tom, and so on until he had rallied all the scouts. They met up in Grosbeck's woods. Here Boone explained to his followers that he had heard there was a sea-serpent in the river, and he had seen bubbles come up himself, whereupon he immediately began to strip off his clothes and conceal them in the bushes. This was necessary because if Clint Butts found them swimming without bathing suits he would arrest them, as none of the urchins owned a bathing suit, or, in fact, had ever seen one. They knew that Clint could not arrest them while they were out in the water, and they could stay in the water as long as the constable could stay on the bank. Follow the leader cried Boone, who's afraid of sea-serpents, so running lightly down the muddy bank and hopping from one leg to the other on the floating raft, he dove into the sluggish water of the river, followed by all his troop of scouts. Then in a procession they swam down the stream, laughing and disporting themselves in the water as only boys and porpoises can. Suddenly Boone felt a cold, clammy thing strike him on the chest and wiggle all the way down his body to his toes; he gave a wild whoop and splashed overhand for the shore. Hi was following him and Hi, of course, thought that Boone was only trying to frighten him. So Hi reached the same spot where Boone had met the awful thing. Hi gave a blood-curdling yell and he too splashed for the shore. After him came Tom. Tom also struck the uncanny, slimy thing, and he gave a shriek like a girl and followed Hi to the shore. By this time the other boys were all laughing so that they could hardly swim, all of them firmly believing that it was a put-up game to frighten them. But each in his turn had the same adventure, and each in his turn made for the shore in the same frantic manner; then they all sat down in the mud and compared notes. Hi said it must be a giant eel; Tom said it was an alligator; Dick said it was a big water snake, but Boone began to have suspicions that it was not alive, and after a while he ventured out to investigate. After scouting around the spot cautiously for some time, he at last made a desperate plunge and again felt the slimy, wiggling object; but this time he caught ahold of it with his hand and found it was the frayed end of a piece of cable attached to a water-logged log. It had been in the water so long that the fibres of the rope had become overgrown with green vegetable substance, and the sluggish current was only sufficiently strong to keep it waving under the surface of the water. The boys did not disturb it, but left the sea-serpent where it was for other swimmers to find.

About this time a one-armed figure was silhouetted against the sky on the river bank. "Whiz," cried Boone in alarm; "there's Clint Butts, but he don't see us." All of the boys hastened to swim back upstream with their little heads as low as possible in the water so as not to attract the attention of the policeman. Of course I know now that the good-natured Clint Butts did not want to see the boys and always gave them a chance to make their escape. However, at that time, we thought that the poor officer's principal delight was persecuting the boys.

When they reached Grosbeck's disaster awaited them. The river rats had found their clothes and tied their little shirts up in hard knots, which they had wetted in the river so as to make them more difficult to undo. Then, as the scouts sat in a row biting on the knots in their efforts to untie them with their teeth, the wicked river rats sat on the bank and sang in a chorus:
" Boone scouts, Boone scouts, Boone scouts dapples,
Chaw, chaw, chaw green apples."

This was lots of fun for the river rats, but the scouts had been there before and had learned to take their medicine philosophically, so they worked away at the hard knots in their shirts without complaint and when they were dressed Boone shouted: " It's all right for you fellows to tie green apples in our shirts, but I dare you to swim down and find the sea-serpent below the bridge."

The river rats were mean, but they were not cowards, and they seldom, if ever, refused to take a dare; in a jiffy their clothes were off and they were swimming in procession down the river.

"Wow—wow," said Red, as he struck the slimy rope's end.

"Whoop—ee," yelled Sofy.

" Murder, police, fire," shouted Sweaty Quinn, and one after another splashed ashore. This was a good time for disappearing, and the scouts took advantage of it. They were not mean enough to tie green apples in the river rats' shirts, but they were boys enough to enjoy the discomfiture of their enemies when they met the supposititious sea-serpent.

Scouting in the Land of the Kaiser

better comrades. If there are ten men in a tent and only one is asleep, you may be sure that the other nine won't disturb him. And when you were after water I noticed that the big boys always were first. You will never see an officer in the army drink before all of his men have been supplied. So comradeship you did not seem to possess; this you will have to acquire. But wait. One instance of comradeship I did see. When we were marching up the Blomberg one of the boys had an attack of the cramps in the leg. After treating it, one of the others took the sick boy's heavy knapsack off and carried it for him the rest of the way. That was nice of him.

"Obedience.—This a good many of you do not seem to understand. How many times were you not told to be quiet during the night, and all without any result? Scarcely had your master left the room before you were cutting up again. The next day I told you not to take water from a certain well. A little later I caught some of you doing that very thing. Do you call that obedience?

"Energy.—This I must reservedly praise. To march thirty miles in two days and make such an ascent as you did at Blomberg, without previous training, is a splendid showing, especially considering that a good part of the time you carried heavy knapsacks. To arrive home in such splendid condition as you did after such a trip is certainly going some."

This gives you an idea of an outing in Germany. It proves a good many things, but I will leave it to you to draw conclusions.

With words and pictures a California senior presents his view of

HIGH SCHOOL DAYS

By EVAN PESKIN

Gabbing with other boys—and girls—before school starts is popular and relaxing. Students dash for class when the bell rings.

UPPER LEFT: Rehearsal before one of Monterey Peninsula's song festivals eases tension. (That's me, fifth from left, top row.)

ABOVE: Everyone at Carmel High gets some background in chemistry. Some spend free periods in the lab doing special assignments.

LEFT: Elected members of our student body meet with administrators to run the school affairs and iron out problems. It's real democracy.

These guys are smiling, but you should see them when they're through. Huffing and puffing are part of Carmel's well-rounded phys ed program.

You need cheerleaders for any athletic event. No matter what the score is, they are sure to be flying high in the air and leading the students.

Whenever problems crop up, counselors are a great help. We ask them everything from what college to attend to how to improve study habits.

A look at Carmel, California, High School is a peek at high schools around the country. Classes, labs, buddies, phys ed and teachers are universal.

Among these colored sands pioneers lost their way and died of thirst. The survivors named the place Death Valley

Death Valley Adventure

Where Scouts explore the mysteries of this weird desert land

By JOHN WOODBURY

The famous castle of fabulous Death Valley Scotty

THE Indians called it Tomesha—"ground afire"—this long, low bowl of burning desert in southeastern California, a region of desolation nearly twice as large as the state of Delaware and lower in places than the level of the sea. But white men, blundering into it in their march to the California gold fields and almost perishing there before they escaped, gave it the name that it bears today, more than a century later. They called it Death Valley, and this is how it happened:

It was the winter of 1849, the year of the great gold rush. All America was bewitched by the news of prodigious wealth that lay waiting to be taken from Sutter's Fort, on the banks of the Sacramento. Thousands of emigrants struggled westward through the wilderness. Haste was the watchword of the day, for the gold would not last forever.

And so it was that one particular band of '49-ers—perhaps a hundred of them—broke away from the established trail in quest of a short cut. They squirmed their way through a mountain pass and dropped into the great barren valley where no white man had ever ventured before. There they found themselves confronted with a high wall of mountains on the west. Their food and water were running low. Despair and panic overtook them, and the little band began to splinter.

One group, known as the Jayhawkers,

burned its wagons, killed its oxen for meat and finally made its way out of the valley to the north. Another group, called the Bennett-Arcane party, camped along the vast salt flats of the valley floor and sent two of its men to hunt an exit to civilization.

More than three weeks passed before the two men returned. Enduring profound hardships, they had found a pass through the mountains. They assembled the gaunt travelers and led them out of the salt flats and up the mountain slopes toward safety. Reaching the crest, the '49-ers paused. They looked back upon the huge sinkhole which had almost become their graveyard and spoke the words which gave the region its name:

"Good-bye, Death Valley!"

It was just 100 years plus a few months later that we followed the trail of the '49-ers into this region of doom and despondency. There were about 700 of us—Scouts, Explorers and their leaders from all over the Hoover Dam Area Council, from Troops in Nevada, Arizona and California. This was the Council's second annual Death Valley Trek, and by far the biggest.

We'd picked a good time for it—March of this year. For we knew that within a month or so Nature would turn the heat on in Death Valley and transform it into something that was once described as "a reasonable facsimile of a first-class ➡

Death Valley Adventure

Inferno, in a state of suspended animation."

But now the nights were still cool and the days mild and warm. The Scouts made camp at Death Valley Monument headquarters, in a cluster of old wooden buildings that stood scoured and scarred by the sun and the blasts of sand which sweep every once in a while across the valley floor.

Our Camp in the Desert

Jim Moss, Scout executive of the Boulder Council, was there with his famous "chuck wagon"—the big trailer kitchen which I had last seen a year before when the Council staged its first Aquarado at Lake Mead. Ted Werner, camping and activities chairman for the Las Vegas, Nevada, district, had left his automobile business to fend for itself while he worked himself into a lather to keep the grub moving out of the "chuck wagon" and across the serving counters.

Camp was a busy place mornings and evenings. But between times it looked almost abandoned as the Scouts fanned out in a sort of mass evacuation to take in the sights which have made Death Valley one of the prime tourist meccas of the West and to probe its endless lore. For there is a story behind almost everything the Scouts saw in the valley: Bad Water, the lowest spot in the Western Hemisphere. The ghost towns of Rhyolite, Ryan, Skidoo and Panamint City. The tumbled borax mills, and the paths once pounded by the famous twenty-mule teams. Stovepipe Wells and the Sand Dunes. And Scotty's Castle, the fantastic $2,000,000 desert edifice of Death Valley Scotty, who is the region's most famous living legend.

Bad Water is Good for You

The Scouts swarmed southward along the valley to Bad Water, 280 feet below sea level. Some of them clambered up the nearby cliff to the "Sea Level" marker mounted high on its precipitous face. (It's something to be able to say that you went *up* to sea level!) The others gathered to hear the park naturalist, L. Floyd Keller, tell the story of how Bad Water got its name from a man who made a mistake.

He was a map-maker, and he found the place many years ago—a small pool of water standing in a depression of the salt flats. The salt there is 1,800 feet deep, but the water, fed by an underground river, runs to a depth of only a few inches. The map-maker tasted it, made a wry face and reported to his bureau in Washington that it was bad water.

But it wasn't bad at all. Actual tests revealed that it's really very good water. It contains epsom salts in just the right proportion, and Keller recommended, with an impish grin, that every Scout should drink a half-glass of it. Recommendation rejected.

There's a story, too, behind the ghost town of Rhyolite—several stories, really, and as with almost everything else in Death Valley, it's hard to tell where fact leaves off and fiction begins.

But it seems to be pretty well established fact that Rhyolite was born because an Indian called Johnnie Shoshone discovered gold there and then sold his rights to a man named Bob Montgomery for two dollars and a pair of new overalls. The mine yielded up about $5,000,000 worth of treasure and Rhyolite burst into life and became one of the wildest and richest mining towns in the region. It had a railroad and 10,000 people. It flour-

ished for five years, but when it died, it died quickly.

The Scouts found it a typical Western ghost town. They prowled gingerly through its dusty, ramshackle ruins, its famous Bottle House, with walls made of bottles laid horizontally in adobe clay, its old railroad depot. They met Rhyolite's one permanent resident. His name is Norman Westmoreland, and he describes himself as Rhyolite's "barkeep, cook and chambermaid" and adds that 'when there isn't any wind, I blow to keep the flag flying."

Then some of the Death Valley trekkers swung over in the direction of Skidoo and Panamint City, on the western slope of the valley's mammoth bowl. They were once as rich and woolly as Rhyolite, and they died just as abruptly. And the ghosts that took them over were the first and second cousins of the ghosts that took over Rhyolite.

Ghostly Cousins Took Over

Skidoo, as the Scouts learned, got its name from a bit of slang that was fashionable in that early period. The town didn't even have a name, in fact, until quite awhile after it was established. That bothered the townsfolk a little. Then a leading citizen announced that he was going to install a pipeline to bring water in from springs on Telescope Peak, which was all of twenty-three miles away. "Twenty-three skidoo!" came the inevitable wisecrack from someone in the immediate vicinity, and Skidoo it was forever after.

Wading deeper into the ghost town legendry of Death Valley, the Scouts discovered that Panamint City also earned its name from a popular expression of the time and locale. Prospectors heading up into the mountains were wont to receive a cheery sendoff from their friends. "Pan a lot of it!" someone would sing out. Or— "Pan a mint o' gold!"

Thus Panamint City, a town so wild and lawless that even Wells Fargo, that hardy operator of stagecoaches through the badlands, refused to haul silver bullion out of it. As the tale was told to the Scouts, someone finally contrived a solution to the problem. He had the silver cast up in 500-pound cannonballs, big enough and heavy enough so that they could be shipped out in unguarded wagons without fear that anyone would try to hijack them.

Ryan is a ghost town, too, but not as ghostly as the others, the Scouts perceived. Crouching on a mountain shelf up above Death Valley to the east, Ryan was once a center of borax operations. And a very important place it was, since borax had become the white gold of Death Valley. It was dug from the mines in huge quantities and moved out of the valley in high-wheeled wagons pulled by strings of twenty mules.

Ryan died when the borax play shifted elsewhere. But the Pacific Coast Borax Company keeps the town in a good state of repair for the benefit of tourists. Many of the Scouts saw it on their way up the road to Dante's View. This is the most accessible of Death Valley's high places and afforded the trekkers much the same spectacular view that they would have had if someone obligingly had moved in the Empire State Building, complete with elevator service.

Stovepipe Wells, located over on the west side of the valley, near the Sand Dunes, isn't one of the ghost towns, but it also has a story, as the Scouts

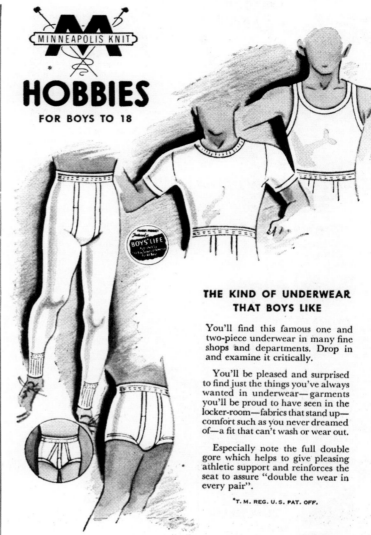

found out. Prospectors trudging between Rhyolite and Skidoo would pause at a half-way point along the trail to drink from an underground spring. But they had to dig eighteen inches below the surface to get the water, and between visits the hole would be covered up with shifting sand. Some unnamed genius finally hit upon an answer. He planted a piece of stovepipe to mark the location of the water hole. Presto! Stovepipe Wells.

But the Scouts found the people of Death Valley even more interesting than its places. For the history of that fabled area is so recent that there still reside there some of those who helped to make its history, or saw it being made.

Johnny is 106 Years Old

There's Johnnie Shoshone, the Indian who sold a $5,000,000 mine for two dollars and a pair of overalls. The Scouts learned that he's still alive and watches time go by at the tiny Indian village south of Furnace Creek Ranch, in the heart of the valley. Johnnie is a very, very old man. He thinks he's about 106 or 107 years old, and if that is true, he was there in the valley when the '49-ers stumbled in and struggled out again.

And there's Louie Blum, an old bearded prospector of seventy-two with a face that is browned and seamed by many summers of fiery heat and many winters of sharp desert cold. I visited Louie with two Scouts, Kenny Searles and Jimmy Cameron-Stuart of Troop 69 in Las Vegas, and he told us how he quit the sea nearly forty-five years ago and drifted in to Death Valley to hunt for gold and silver.

He's been there ever since, and we doubted if he's found very much gold and silver. But he watched the mining towns spring up, flourish briefly and then sputter out like a spent Roman candle.

What with his three burros and a little prospecting on the side, Louie manages to live. In the winters he poses with his burros for camera-toting tourists at two bits a picture. Then, come summer, he blows his earnings on gunpowder and supplies and shuffles into the Panamint Mountains to mine for silver and lead.

Louis told Kenny, Jimmy and me that he doesn't go to town very often. Last time he was in Las Vegas was five years ago, and he didn't stay long, because he couldn't find a place to park his burros.

He loves those burros—Shorty, Mike and Johnny. Shorty is the oldest—a ripe nineteen—and Louie says "he's liable to outlast me." The venerable prospector snorted when the Scouts asked him about the popular notion that burros are stubborn.

"They're not," he said firmly. "They're just smart."

When Louie makes camp, he turns his burros loose in the desert. They wander as far as a mile and a half away, but when they see the smoke of the campfire, back they come for their dinner. Try doing that with a horse, says Louie scornfully.

How Smart Can a Burro be?

The Scouts learned that burros run wild in and around Death Valley and they multiply fast. Since it is their irritating habit to pollute springs and ravage the grazing grounds of mountain sheep, the Park Service occasionally sanctions a burro hunt to thin out the population. This has resulted in a favorite Death Valley fable—or maybe it isn't a fable at all, but a true story—about the burro with a bell.

This particular burro, a fugitive from some prospector, had a bell wired around his neck, and, of course, the bell would jangle as he moved. That would have made him a sitting-duck target for a burro hunter, except that, whenever a hunt was on, the burro would stand stockstill. His companions would bring him fodder and he'd move his head only enough to reach down for a mouthful of grass, without the slightest betraying tinkle.

Well, anyway, that's the story the Scouts heard around Death Valley, and Death Valley folk say it only goes to show how a smart burro is.

But of far greater renown than the burros and Louie Blum and Johnnie Shoshone all put together is the man they call Death Valley Scotty. His real name is Walter Scott, and he's somewhere in the neighborhood of eighty, with a wild shock of snowy hair and a face that's white and soft because he sleeps in the daytime, out from under the fierce Death Valley sun.

Thirty-odd years ago, in strange and lordly isolation up on the northern slope of Death Valley, the incredible place known as Scotty's Castle was built. And that's precisely what it is— a Spanish-style castle replete with drawbridge, donjon, turret and rugs and furnishings so costly that the Scouts had to wear felt slippers over their shoes as they went through.

Death Valley Scotty

To the hundreds of Scouts descending en masse upon the castle it seemed to lack only a king. And then, for a moment, it seemed to have one. There suddenly, on the ornate balcony overlooking the courtyard, appeared Scotty himself, peering down up on the horde of Scouts for all the world like a monarch greeting his subjects. But his first remark didn't sound regal. "Where d'y'all come from?" asked Scotty.

Then he came down into the courtyard, to be engulfed in a tide of khaki. He blinked into the clicking cameras of half a hundred Scout shutter bugs while he chatted about the early days in Death Valley, when he was a swamper, or No. 2 man, on a twenty-mule team and a prospector for gold.

One day Scotty found a fantastically rich gold mine and that this is how he came to do the things which made him a legend in the West. Once he chartered a Santa Fe train for a run from Los Angeles to Chicago that broke the world's record. And the Scouts were told how he scattered gold coins on the streets of San Francisco and Sam Bernardino and flipped out fifty dollar bills for one of his famous red neckties, telling startled clerks to "keep the change."

What We Found

But the skeptics say Scotty didn't have a gold mine at all, unless you could call Albert Johnson his gold mine. Johnson was a wealthy Chicago financier who took a fancy to Scotty and to Death Valley. The skeptics claim it was Johnson's money that erected the Castle and financed Scotty's fabulous exploits. They say Johnson did it just for the fun of watching Scotty build himself into a legend.

Johnson, his wife, and Scotty resided in the castle until the financier's death two years ago. Scotty lives now at a ranch a few miles away, and his prospecting days are far behind him. But he likes to talk about the gold of Death Valley. And something he said about it came back to me one night as we had our big campfire.

The fire was built up against a short bluff. The dancing flames threw grotesque and monstrous shadows upon the bluff as though it were a screen for some huge stereopticon machine gone berserk. The sky was a carpet of stars, and in the starlight we could see the shadowy bulge of the mountains close by us to the east. Up from the campfire and out across the silent reaches of Death Valley floated the muted words of the Scout vesper song. "Softly falls the light of day, as our campfire fades away . . ."

And it was then that I remembered what Scotty had said about the gold of Death Valley. He'd said there's still gold a-plenty in the valley, but it's all beneath the surface and "it would take a million to get a million out." But Scotty was wrong. We found the golden treasure that night around the campfire, hard alongside the starlit mountains, and along the trails which the '49-ers trod. We found it in the wondrous places and the endless lore of Death Valley, and in the pleasures of comradeship in the out-of-doors.

THE END

A TRUE STORY OF SCOUTS IN ACTION
by ALSTEN

ON APRIL 18, 1965, TWO-YEAR-OLD TRACY BOYD CLARK RAN DOWN THE BANK OF LEONARD DAUGHERTY LAKE NEAR VAN ALSTYNE, TEX. HE STRUCK A SLIPPERY SPOT, HIS FEET SLID FROM UNDER HIM AND HE PLUNGED INTO THE DEEP LAKE!

SCOUT LARRY LEE COLLIER, 12, SAW A SMALL HAND RISE UP OUT OF THE WATER...

LARRY RUSHED DOWN THE BANK AND HOOKED HIS FEET AROUND A TREE ROOT...

REACHED OUT INTO THE WATER AND, WHEN TRACY'S HAND APPEARED A SECOND TIME, GRABBED IT FIRMLY.

THEN HE HAULED LITTLE TRACY OUT AND CARRIED HIM UP THE BANK JUST AS THE CHILD'S MOTHER CAME RUNNING...

TRACY! OH, THANK GOD YOU SAW HIM, LARRY. I LOOKED ALL OVER FOR HIM! I WAS FRANTIC!

ALL I SAW WAS A LITTLE HAND POP OUT OF THE WATER. ARE YOU OK NOW, TRACY?

FOR HIS PROMPT AND EFFICIENT HANDLING OF THIS EMERGENCY, SCOUT LARRY LEE COLLIER WAS AWARDED THE CERTIFICATE FOR HEROISM BY THE NATIONAL COURT OF HONOR, BOY SCOUTS OF AMERICA.

LARRY IS A MEMBER OF TROOP 4, VAN ALSTYNE, TEX., SPONSORED BY A GROUP OF CITIZENS.

REACH OUT... AND SAVE A LIFE!

MANY SWIMMING ACCIDENTS HAPPEN WITHIN EASY RESCUE DISTANCE OF SOMEONE ON SHORE, ON A DOCK OR IN A BOAT... USE YOUR HEAD AND **REACH** FOR THE DISTRESSED SWIMMER. DON'T ENDANGER BOTH YOUR LIVES BY LEAPING FRANTICALLY INTO THE WATER.

GET A FIRM HOLD ON SOMETHING, THEN EXTEND YOUR LEG OR YOUR ARM FOR THE VICTIM TO GRAB.

EXTEND A STOUT BRANCH, A POLE OR A LONG STICK —OR FLIP A LENGTH OF STRONG MATERIAL...

OR, FORM A HUMAN CHAIN—THE HEAVIEST, HUSKIEST FELLOW AS ANCHOR MAN WITH A SECURE HOLD.

HOLD TOGETHER WRIST TO WRIST.

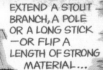

BULLETIN

Official News
What every Scout wants to know
Department conducted by JAMES E. WEST, Chief Scout Executive

BULLETIN

Scout Wartime Activities

Intensive Campaign for Third Liberty Loan The Boy Scouts' intensive campaign in the Third Liberty Loan will be from April 27th to May 4th, both inclusive. These are the dates agreed upon by the Treasury Department officials with the officers of the National Council of the Boy Scouts of America. There can be no exception. Awards for service will be confined to work done during these dates. Scouts may be trusted on their honor not to claim credit for work done at any other time.

Likewise all awards will be based upon subscriptions, secured upon the boy scout official application blanks, provided by the Treasury Department. The coupon received will be as a basis of making reports by all scoutmasters and scout officials alike.

The boy scout posters will be displayed April 6th and will continue on public display until after the close of the campaign.

Scouts will not make use of these for room decorations or for private purposes until after the close of the Liberty Loan Campaign.

Resolved:— No Slackers Among Us The National Council, at the eighth annual meeting of the Boy Scouts of America, passed a resolution pledging 100 per cent patriotism and energetic support of the Government in every way. These resolutions, which are reproduced in this Boys' LIFE, commit every scout and scout official to apply himself in carrying out the plans as agreed upon for national service by the representatives of the Boy Scouts of America and the representatives of the United States Government. There must be no slackers among scouts and scout officials, and there can be no exception to the plan agreed upon for the nation-wide campaign.

Every scout should make it his business to have his troop qualify for the honor roll. This roll is to be made up of troops in which every available scout participates in the Third Liberty Loan.

War Savings Stamp Campaign Booming The War Savings Stamp Campaign is going along very merrily. Indeed the local war savings stamp committees throughout the country are enthusiastic in reporting on the splendid spirit and effective co-operative work of Boy Scouts.

Many scouts have already earned the achievement button which is reproduced on this page.

Ace Medal for Sale of War Savings Stamps

A Decoration Worth Wearing

Already 12,000,000 red post cards have been printed and distributed; 8,000,000 more are now being printed, and if the demand keeps up as at present, it will require at least 20,000,000 additional cards to take care of the needs of the scouts between now and July 1st.

Just think what this means—35,000,000 red post cards. It depends upon the earnestness of each scout and scout official as to how many of these red post cards actually count for practical results. If each card averages $3.00, it will mean well over $100,000,000 secured through the War Savings Stamp Campaign of the Boy Scouts of America. Let's aim to make our cards count for just as much as possible.

Each scout is urged to warn the letter carriers and post office officials as to the importance of forwarding the red post cards to the National Council Office, Fifth Avenue Building, New York City. All awards will be based upon the cards as delivered at the National Office. The cards are now coming in at the rate of 10,000 a day. Achievement buttons and ace medals will be awarded without the necessity of further correspondence or further reports of any kind. The buttons and medals we hope will be delivered before May 1st.

Get Assistance for Your War Gardens The food production and garden campaign of the Boy Scouts of America is well under way. Every scout and indeed every troop and every local council, according to reports, is definitely interested in some way.

This year every scout is asked to be responsible for securing one adult to agree to work with him on the scout's individual garden or on the troop garden or on the local council garden. The adult might be a scout's father, his brother or his sister's best fellow, his uncle or indeed any man who will faithfully stick to the job until the crops are harvested.

Our Wartime Economy As a wartime economy, a change has been made in the membership certificates for scouts and scout officials. For the duration of the war and perhaps indefinitely, it has been necessary to arrange for a substitute for our celluloid certificate.

Happily the new certificate is proving very satisfactory. It is made on the finest quality of linen lined coated paper. A special envelope has been provided to protect the certificate. Additional enrollments must be paid for.

Understand Registration Rules

It is important that all scouts understand the registration rules. The best evidence of registration is the membership certificate. If, for any reason, your certificate has not been given to you by your scoutmaster, ask about it. There was a slight delay in mailing certificates during March, but this has all been taken care of, and from now on certificates will be mailed very promptly upon the receipt of registration fees.

All additional enrollments to the troop must be paid for at the rate of 25 cents from nine to twelve months, 20 cents more than six and less than ten months; 15 cents for six months or less.

Where to Wear the Badge when Sleeves Are Rolled Up

During the summer, and in some parts of the country all the year round, the weather is such as to make it advisable for boys to have the sleeves of the shirt rolled up. This would very naturally cover the badge.

With the National Headquarters office scouts an experiment has been tried of having them wear the embroidered badge on the left-hand breast pocket.

What Is a Senior Patrol Leader

From time to time inquiries have been received asking as to the status of the rank of senior patrol leader. While this title has occurred in the Official Handbook the duties have never been defined. Indeed, official action has never been taken. We are inclined to agree that here are functions which might properly be performed by a scout too young to be an assistant scoutmaster who, while not attached to any patrol, could be

To All Whom It May Concern, Be It Known:

THAT THE NATIONAL COUNCIL OF THE BOY SCOUTS OF AMERICA (ORIGINALLY INCORPORATED FEBRUARY 8TH, 1910 AND CHARTERED BY CONGRESS JUNE 15TH, 1916) AT ITS EIGHTH ANNUAL MEETING, HELD IN THE CITY OF NEW YORK, MARCH 25TH, 1918, PASSED THE FOLLOWING RESOLUTION:

Whereas—The National Council of the Boy Scouts of America, representing a definitely organized, uniformed and disciplined group of 397,208 boy scouts and scout officials, all pledged on their honor to do their duty to God and to their country, recognizes their responsibility in the present world crisis, and

Whereas—Each of these scouts and scout officials is anxious to do his utmost in helping to win the war.

Be It Resolved—That the actions of the Executive Board since the declaration of war in giving definite leadership to a National program of war activities be approved and continued, and that the President of the United States and other Governmental officials at Washington be assured that the Boy Scouts of America may be depended upon for any and all service of the character for which the boy scouts have been trained and which they are qualified to render, and

Be It Further Resolved—That the Boy Scouts of America stands for 100% patriotism and unqualified and energetic support of the Government in every way, and that it is expected that every scout and scout official will earnestly apply himself as a scout in carrying out such program for National service, as may be agreed upon by the authorized representatives of the National Council, and the representatives of the U. S. Government.

Be It Further Resolved—That a certified copy of this resolution be transmitted to the President of the United States, the President of the United States Senate, and the Speaker of the House of Representatives at Washington, D. C.

In Testimony as to the Passage of the Foregoing Resolution, the Officers of the Boy Scouts of America Hereto Affix their Signatures and the Seal of the Boy Scouts of America.

President, Boy Scouts of America.

James E. West
Secretary, National Council, and Chief Scout Executive, Boy Scouts of America.

of general service to all of them. Possibly some better designation than senior patrol leader can be suggested by the field.

Pioneer Scouts to Aid in War Work

All pioneer scouts will be glad to know that they are to have another opportunity to serve their Government through participation in the War Savings Stamp Campaign and the Third Liberty Loan. Special printed matter will be sent them as rapidly as can be managed. These boys reach a class of people that are very often not reached in any other way.

Veteran Scout Registration Fee Need Only Be Paid Once

In answer to various inquiries it may be stated officially that the fee of $1.00 paid by veteran scouts covers their registration in that rank perpetually.

Live in Your Country's Memory

The memory of the boys of the Revolutionary and Civil War days who answered the call of their country is beloved by all of us who live and read about them today. In the same way will future generations revere the memory of the boys of today who have answered their country's call.

How many of you scouts who are reading this page will live in future memory because of the vital work you are doing in this war? Every boy who has sold bonds, War Saving Stamps, worked on gardens or done other patriotic service, is ANSWERING HIS COUNTRY'S CALL.

The spirit with which you work and the results secured are the big things to keep in mind. The fighters on the battle line are doing their share for you and me and for all at home. Let us who are at home do our share to help them achieve victory for our righteous cause.

THE WHITE HOUSE
Washington

March 28, 1918.

My dear Mr. West:

I have your letter of March twenty-sixth, enclosing the very admirable and gratifying resolutions of the National Council of the Boy Scouts of America, adopted March twenty-fifth, and I want to beg that you will take some occasion to express to the members of that convention not only my deep appreciation of the resolutions but also my entire confidence that those resolutions will be acted upon to the limit.

Cordially and sincerely yours,

(Signed) WOODROW WILSON.

SPEAKER'S ROOM,
House of Representatives
Washington, D. C.

March 27, 1918.

Dear Mr. West:

I wish to acknowledge your letter of the 26th, transmitting resolution passed by the National Council of the Boy Scouts of America, at its 8th Annual Meeting.

The Resolution will be presented to the House today.

The sentiments expressed in the resolution are very highly commendable. I hope that the Boy Scout movement will grow until it contains millions of young Americans. I am very strongly in favor of it and can see many good results to be expected from it.

Cordially yours,

(Signed) CHAMP CLARK.

THE BROWN RECLUSE ... VIOLIN ...
LOXOSCELES RECLUSA ...
THEY'RE ALL ONE SPIDER ...

ACTUAL SIZE

MAGNIFIED TO SHOW ITS PRINCIPAL MARKS: VIOLIN SHAPE ON ITS HEAD; ITS SIX EYES.

MORE POISONOUS THAN THE INFAMOUS BLACK WIDOW.

THE BROWN RECLUSE HAS ONLY RECENTLY BEEN GIVEN MUCH ATTENTION IN THE U.S. BECAUSE ITS RANGE HAS INCREASED AS IT WAS BROUGHT ALONG WITH TENS OF THOUSANDS OF PEOPLE RELOCATING TO NEW AREAS. UNLESS ITS SPREAD IS CHECKED, THE SPIDER COULD BECOME A HEALTH HAZARD.

■ ORIGINAL RANGE
■ INCREASING RANGE

ORIGINALLY THE BROWN RECLUSE WAS FOUND OUTDOORS IN WARM, HUMID CLIMATES. THE PREVALENCE OF CENTRAL HEATING IN HOMES HAS ALLOWED THE SPIDER TO SURVIVE IN COLDER CLIMATES WHERE IT WAS NEVER BEFORE FOUND.

AS THE NAME "RECLUSE" IMPLIES, THIS SPIDER PREFERS TO LIVE QUIETLY BY ITSELF. IT BUILDS ITS LOOSE, IRREGULAR WEB IN, BEHIND AND UNDER FURNITURE, IN CLOTHING AND BLANKETS, IN CLOSETS, STORAGE BOXES, ETC. IT STAYS IN THESE RETREATS UNTIL NIGHT, WHEN IT COMES OUT TO FORAGE FOR FOOD.

PESTICIDES (LIKE LINDANE) HELP CONTROL THE SPIDER BUT CANNOT ALWAYS REACH ITS HIDING PLACES. THOROUGH HOUSECLEANING AND A VIGOROUS SHAKING OF BLANKETS AND CLOTHING OUTDOORS WILL GET RID OF MOST BROWN RECLUSE SPIDERS.

70013

THERE IS LITTLE CHANCE OF BEING BITTEN BY A BROWN RECLUSE. BUT THE BITE IS DANGEROUS, BECAUSE THERE IS NO QUICK ANTIDOTE FOR ITS VENOM.

THE EFFECTS OF THE BITE MAY BE FELT IMMEDIATELY OR FROM TWO TO EIGHT HOURS LATER. IF YOU THINK YOU HAVE BEEN BITTEN, CHECK THE SUSPECTED SKIN AREA. IF POSSIBLE, KILL AND KEEP THE SPIDER SO THAT IT CAN BE IDENTIFIED AS A BROWN RECLUSE AND PROPER MEDICAL TREATMENT GIVEN. SIGNS OF THE BITE: GENERAL DISCOMFORT; BLISTERS, PAIN, SWELLING AT THE BITE SITE.
FIRST AID: ICE PACKS ON THE BITE. GET THE VICTIM TO A DOCTOR IMMEDIATELY— THE BITE CAN BE FATAL!

WHEN · WHERE · AND HOW TO PROPERLY HONOR THE COLORS AND THE NATIONAL ANTHEM

OUR FLAG AND OUR NATIONAL ANTHEM ARE SYMBOLS OF OUR HERITAGE OF FREEDOM. AS SUCH THEY COMMAND OUR RESPECT AND ARE ENTITLED TO CERTAIN HONORS.

IN UNIFORM	NOT IN UNIFORM
WHEN THE NATIONAL ANTHEM IS PLAYED, STAND AT ATTENTION AND SALUTE WITH OR WITHOUT HAT ON. IF FLAG IS VISIBLE, FACE IT. IF IT ISN'T, FACE BAND; IF BAND IS NOT VISIBLE OR MUSIC IS RECORDED, FACE STRAIGHT AHEAD — HOLD SALUTE FROM FIRST TO LAST NOTE.	AT THE PLAYING OF THE NATIONAL ANTHEM, STAND AT ATTENTION, FACE FLAG, BAND OR STRAIGHT AHEAD (AS EXPLAINED BEFORE), REMOVE HAT, HOLD HAT WITH RIGHT HAND OVER HEART. WITHOUT HAT HOLD RIGHT HAND, PALM OPEN, OVER HEART. WOMEN ALWAYS HOLD RIGHT HAND, PALM OPEN, OVER HEART.
THIS IS THE CORRECT PROCEDURE BOTH INDOORS AND OUTDOORS.	THIS SAME PROCEDURE IS CORRECT FOR HONORING THE FLAG WHEN IT PASSES BY IN A PARADE OR REVIEW.
INDOORS AND OUTDOORS, WITH HAT OR WITHOUT, SALUTE WHEN...	DURING THE CEREMONY OF RAISING OR LOWERING THE FLAG OR POSTING THE COLORS,
THE PASSING FLAG IN A PARADE OR REVIEW IS SIX STEPS AWAY. HOLD SALUTE UNTIL FLAG HAS PASSED SIX STEPS BEYOND YOU...	DURING RECITATION OF THE PLEDGE OF ALLEGIANCE,
DURING RAISING AND LOWERING OR POSTING OF THE COLORS, AND...	THESE RULES APPLY BOTH INDOORS AND OUTDOORS.
DURING RECITATION OF PLEDGE OF ALLEGIANCE.	WHEN IN ATHLETIC UNIFORM, STAND AT ATTENTION, HOLD CAP OR HELMET IN RIGHT HAND AT SIDE.
(NOTE: EXPLORER BLAZER OR SIMILAR OUTFIT IS CONSIDERED A UNIFORM.)	

70136

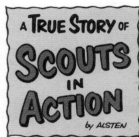

A TRUE STORY of SCOUTS IN ACTION

by ALSTEN

ON OCTOBER 24, 1964, A NEIGHBOR RUSHED TO THE HOME OF SCOUT JOHN MARK WHITE IN PHENIX CITY, ALA., CRYING...

DOES JOHN KNOW HOW TO GIVE ARTIFICIAL RESPIRATION?

BEFORE ANYONE HAD TIME TO ANSWER THE 17-YEAR-OLD SCOUT WAS OUT THE DOOR AND ON HIS WAY.

CALL AN AMBULANCE WHILE I GIVE HER FIRST AID!

REACHING THE NEIGHBOR'S HOME, JOHN FOUND 14-YEAR-OLD MARGY NELL JONES LYING UNCONSCIOUS ON THE FLOOR, GRASPING HER THROAT AND UNABLE TO BREATHE.

MARGY HAD BEEN KNOCKED OUT BY AN ELECTRIC SHOCK WHILE WORKING WITH HER TV SET. JOHN BEGAN MOUTH-TO-MOUTH RESUSCITATION. IN A SHORT WHILE MARGY BEGAN TO BREATHE FREELY.

YOU'RE GOING TO BE OK, MARGY. JUST LIE QUIETLY AND TAKE IT EASY!

JOHN STAYED WITH HER UNTIL THE AMBULANCE ARRIVED AND TOOK MARGY TO THE HOSPITAL. THERE SHE QUICKLY RECOVERED. FOR HIS ACTION SCOUT JOHN MARK WHITE WAS AWARDED THE CERTIFICATE OF MERIT BY THE NATIONAL COURT OF HONOR, BOY SCOUTS OF AMERICA.

I WANT TO ADD MY THANKS, JOHN... AND PROMISE NOT TO FOOL WITH A TV SET AGAIN—EVER!

JOHN IS A MEMBER OF TROOP 149, SPONSORED BY THE FIRST BAPTIST CHURCH OF PHENIX CITY, ALA.

Don't fool with Electric wires!

This could cost him his Life!

IN THE DECEMBER, 1965, ISSUE OF **BOYS' LIFE** A PICTURE OF A BOY RETRIEVING HIS MODEL AIRPLANE WITH A LONG STICK FROM SOME OVERHEAD WIRES WAS SHOWN IN THE ARTICLE, "WORLD SERIES IN THE AIR."

DON'T EVER FOLLOW THIS DANGEROUS EXAMPLE!

IF YOUR KITE OR MODEL AIRPLANE BECOMES ENTANGLED IN WIRES OF ANY KIND—CALL THE POWER OR TELEPHONE COMPANY FOR HELP. THEY'RE EQUIPPED TO HANDLE SUCH SITUATIONS SAFELY.

THIS SAME ADVICE APPLIES IF A PERSON IS ENTANGLED IN A FALLEN POWER LINE. CALL THE POWER CO. IMMEDIATELY—THEN, WHEN THE VICTIM IS FREED YOU MAY APPLY FIRST AID IF NECESSARY.

66031

Think & Grin

A man was driving around in his car, trying to find a parking place. He couldn't find one, so he parked in a "no parking" zone, and left a note on his windshield that said, "Don't give me ticket—just going to take a minute." When he came back, he found another note on his windshield that said, "I gave you a ticket—just going to take five dollars."—*Hy Ginsberg, Smithtown, N.Y.*

Then there was the guy who was so dumb, he thought the Red Sea was parted with a sea-saw.—*Mike Mathews, Harlingen, Tex.*

Dimm: Why are crawdads so greedy?
Whit: Because they're shellfish!—*Whitney White, Arlington, Tex.*

Said a Florida man, picking up a watermelon in a California field, "Is this the largest grapefruit you can grow in these parts?"
"Stop!" cried the Californian, "you're crushing that raisin!"—*Jack Dull, Wilmington, Del.*

Henny: Why did the chicken cross the road?
Penny: To see his friend Gregory Peck!—*John Bourque, Fort Lawton, Wash.*

Tom: Even a policeman can't arrest the flight of time.
Jerry: Can't he? Why, only this morning I saw a policeman go into a store and stop a few minutes.—*Scott Caltrider, Belleville, W. Va.*

Spike: What is a ghost's favorite pie?
Spook: "Boo"-meringue!—*Keith Neal, Hanover, Ind.*

Father, talking to his son who marched in the band during halftime at the football game: "I'm proud of you, son—everyone was marching out of step but you!"—*Kimsey Fowler, Dublin, Ga.*

A teacher was telling his barber about the excitement at school when classes were dismissed for vacation. "There was foot-stomping, table-banging, and all-around rejoicing," said the teacher.
"Real wild, huh?" asked the barber.
"Yeah," replied the teacher, "and that was just in the teachers' lounge!"—*Thomas Frosina, Seaford, N.Y.*

Hortense: Did you hear about the invention that lets you look through walls?
Aloysius: No—what's it called?
Hortense: The window!—*Tony Burgess, Weott, Calif.*

Driver: I think my turn signal is burned out. Stick your head out the window and see if it's working.
Passenger: Yes! No! Yes! No!—*Greg Dulin, Denton, Tex.*

Patient: Doc, I hate to bother you at 3 A.M., but I have a bad case of insomnia.
Doctor: Well, what are you trying to do, start an epidemic?—*Sam Morris, Braintree, Mass.*

Tenzing: Why do mountain climbers rope themselves together?
Hillary: To keep the smart ones from going home!—*Greg Schafer, Malvern, Pa.*

"One time I get 1,201,347,265, and the next time 1,201,347,266!"

Mutt: My shirts must laugh a lot at the laundry.
Jeff: Why do you say that?
Mutt: Well, the last batch came back with their sides split!—*J. Eldred, Orinda, Calif.*

Two hunters were tracking a bear along a trail; when they came to a fork in the trail, they lost him. Then they came across a sign that said, "Bear left," so they went home.—*Greg Wisyanski, Monongahela, Pa.*

Sam: What do you get when you cross a goat with a lamb?
Pam: I know—an animal that eats tin cans and gives steel wool!—*Rusty Houde, North Smithfield, R.I.*

Son: Dad, will you help me find the least common denominator in this math problem?
Dad: Don't tell me it hasn't been found yet—they were looking for it when *I* was a kid!—*Tom Brack, Kansas City, Mo.*

The inventor, he chortled with glee
As they fished his airship from the
   sea,
"I shall build" (and he laughed),
"A submarine craft,
And perhaps it will fly," remarked
   he.
—*Jesse Aronson, Brooklyn, N.Y.*

Byrd: Why does Ferd have high
shoulders and a flat forehead?
   Nerd: Because he's so dumb that
when you ask him a simple question,
he shrugs his shoulders, and when
you tell him the answer, he slaps his
forehead and says, "Oh, yeah!"—
Jeff Burnette, New Whiteland, Ind.

Movie director, to actor: Do you
have any experience in acting?
   Actor: Sure—my leg was in a cast
once!—*Scott Richards, Rochester,
Mich.*

Small boy, on telephone: The next
problem is on page four, number six.
What did your dad get for that one?
—*Wendy Scott, Wilmington, Del.*

Mother: Timmy! What was that
crash?
   Timmy: Mom, you know that an-
tique glass bowl that you were always worried about me breaking?
   Mother: Yes?
   Timmy: Well, your worries are
over!—*Louis Buonpane, New Haven,
Conn.*

Sally: What kind of dog would a
chemistry professor have?
   Silly: A laboratory retriever!—
Randy Hoekstra, Grand Rapids, Mich.

Susie: Where do flying fish swim?
   Woozie: In airstreams, of course!
—*Perry Meronyk, Carpentersville,
Ill.*

Silly: What did the lollipop say to
the wrapper?
   Sally: I don't know, what?
   Silly: Stick to me or I'm licked!
—*Jeffrey Botvinick, Los Angeles,
Calif.*

"Give him more line, Slim!"

Spacey: Knock knock!
   Tracy: Who's there?
   Spacey: Hugh.
   Tracy: Hugh who?
   Spacey: Hugh must be sick and
tired of knock-knock jokes!—*Greg
Hveston, Oxnard, Calif.*

Tall Tales Department: A man was
driving across the desert when he
had to stop because of a flat tire.
When he opened the door to get out
and fix it, he saw that he was parked
beside a rattler den, so he shut the
door and waited. Finally, one of the
rattlers bit the flat tire; the tire
swelled up to regular size, and the
man drove away.—*John Baker, Se-
quin, Tex.*

Daffynishion: Double stitch—Another name for a sew-and-sew.—*Arthur Peevy, Jr., Utica, N.Y.*

Billy: What kind of phone call is
it when one preacher calls another
preacher?
   Graham: I know—a parson-to-par-
son call!—*Patti Sienko, Arlington,
Tex.*

Milkman: How can you get a set
of teeth inserted free?
   Mailman: Easy—tease a watch-
dog!—*Leon Smith, Charleston, S.C.*

Guinevere: Why do dragons sleep
in the daytime?
   Lancelot: So they can hunt
knights!—*Brian Meyers, Alexandria,
Ohio.*

Nervous usher at a wedding: I'm
sorry, but this pie is occupewed. May
I sew you to another sheet?—*Peter
Gibbs, Kettering, Ohio.*

GUS

"Gus! What have you done now?"

"To keep myself physically fit" is part of the Scout Oath, and playing sports is an ideal way to accomplish this goal. Most sports are part of the Scouting program in some shape or form, with Boy Scouts able to earn merit badges in Archery, Athletics (track and field), Canoeing, Climbing, Cycling, Fishing, Fly Fishing, Golf, Horsemanship, Motorboating, Orienteering, Rifle Shooting, Scuba Diving, Shotgun Shooting, Skating (ice and roller), Small-Boat Sailing, Snow Sports, Sports (team play), Swimming, Water Sports, and Whitewater. Cub Scouts may earn more than two dozen belt loops in a variety of sports, from badminton to soccer to volleyball. Varsity Scouting, a program for older boys, also puts emphasis on sports. Varsity Scouts earn letters and activity pins for participating in seasonal sports (there are 12 to choose from). Aside from the physical benefits, the aim of these programs is to develop skills and the concept of sportsmanship.

Legendary athletes are featured in *Boys' Life*. These articles are not just about the individual sports stars, rather they explain how to play particular positions or give tips on aspects of the game. In other words, they allow the stars to serve as mentors to young readers. However, the athletes' personalities still manage to shine through in the stories, as the stars dispense advice not only about their sport but about larger issues that underpin the values of Scouting—doing your best, persevering, taking care of your body, being unselfish.

Such personalized profiles, full of anecdotes, "secrets," and how to's, have been an integral part of the magazine. Sports fiction has figured prominently, as well as studies of young athletes who have excelled in a sport. These young men, many of them Scouts or former Scouts, are seen as realistic role models for the readers of *Boys' Life*, although the popularity of the superstars of professional sports remains undiminished.

Sports features have also helped to keep sports in perspective. Athletes are shown to be talented, but also to be hard working, focused, and capable of dealing with adversity—attributes that have propelled them to the top of their game. These are the same qualities that also help boys grow into men. In the pages of the magazine, almost every feature reinforces the values embodied in the Scout Oath and Law. But the lesson is delivered with a light touch.

Humor, one of the hallmarks of *Boys' Life*, even finds its way into sports. Pedro, the magazine's mascot and "mailburro" (he carries the mailbag around the office and answers reader's letters), predicted the Major League Baseball results of the 1968 season—the top statistical players and the World Series champions. Whereas he picked the Pittsburgh Pirates over the New York Mets in six games, the Detroit Tigers beat the St. Louis Cardinals in seven games. In fact, every one of Pedro's predictions was wrong. Pedro put away his crystal ball.

BOYS' LIFE 71

80 BOYS' LIFE

Superstar Bill prefers being a team player.

Bill Walton Perfect in the Pivot

By BILL LIBBY

Meet the shy giant who's keeping UCLA No. 1.

Suddenly Bill Walton appeared in the play. He came from the corner of the court in three great strides. He went up high, seemingly all legs and arms and elbows, to smother the ball in two massive hands as it bounced off the backboard. Still in the air, he fired a football pass to fast-breaking UCLA (University of California at Los Angeles) teammates who converted it into a lay-up at the other end.

A grin creased Bill Walton's face as he joyfully jiggled up and down on the toes of his sneakers. Then he clapped his hands together in soft applause for his teammates and a play well executed.

This was one of many scenes of success in last season's NCAA championship game at the Sports Arena in Los Angeles. Before the competition was over, Walton passed through many moods. An animated athlete, he shook a fist in triumph each time he hit on a hook-shot, a turn-around jump-shot or a follow-up shot. He slapped hands with teammates who scored off his passes. During time-outs, he kept time to the band music by snapping his fingers. And when he was roughed up by foes or had fouls called on him, his face was set in a grimace of anguish and he complained outrageously. He got into foul trouble and his Bruin teammates had to struggle to stave off Florida State by five points. Afterwards, while everyone else on his side was celebrating, the Player of the Year as a sophomore in college basketball seemed strangely disappointed. He complained, "We didn't dominate the way we should have. I don't even feel as though we won."

The 6-11, 19-year-old youngster is accustomed to success. When he graduated from Helix High School in San Diego he had led his team to 49 straight victories. His freshman team at UCLA won 20 in a row. And after last season's 30-0 by the Bruins—Bill's first varsity campaign—Walton's teams now have won 99 consecutive contests. The Bruins beat their foes by an average margin of 32 points per game, an NCAA record. No team came closer than Florida State's five points in the final game. The schedule was not tough and most opponents were destroyed. Texas A&M fell by 64 points, Texas by 50, and Denver by 47.

As this new season began, UCLA was within 15 victories of the NCAA basketball record of 60 in a row, set by Bill Russell's University of San Francisco teams in the late 1950's. This is the only major record that has eluded Coach John Wooden's Bruins, who are bidding for their seventh straight national title and ninth in 10 seasons. Since they figure to have their strongest team yet, they are strong favorites to extend their dynasty of domination.

The UCLA campus is located in Westwood, a swank section of Los Angeles. The athletic department building is adjacent to the Pauley Pavillion, a modern concrete pillbox, which the Bruins fill with more than 12,000 fans for every home game. It is harder to get a seat to a Bruin game than to a game of the pro champion Lakers at their Forum in the suburbs. A team led by Gail Goodrich and Walt Hazzard launched UCLA on the incredible decade that concludes this season. Lew (Kareem Abdul-Jabbar) Alcindor's teams picked up the pace, and clubs led by Sidney Wicks carried on. Now, the Walton era.

Sitting surrounded by trophies in the university's basketball office, Bill shrugs and says, "I don't think much about records. I don't even think about basketball during the off-season. I enjoy basketball. It's a game, isn't it? That's what it's called. And everyone likes to play games. Games are to have fun. But it's not always fun."

He looks like an elongated Tom Sawyer, with a thatch of uncombed rust-red hair and a lot of freckles on his long, lantern-jawed, boyish face. He slouches some as though to hide from his height and he shies from interviews as though this will turn off the spotlights that follow him everywhere. And when he speaks to an outsider he stammers some, as though reluctant to give much of himself away. But it is impossible for Bill Walton to slip through shadows unseen. He is too good and too prominent.

Before last season he was not as publicized a sophomore as Tom McMillen, the Pennsylvanian at the University of Maryland and U.S. Olympic team member. However, Tom and his team had their troubles. They failed to win the Atlantic Coast Conference and so did not even qualify for the NCAA tournament, although they did go on to win New York's NIT classic. Meanwhile, UCLA swept the major honors and by season's end Walton was the most celebrated collegian since Alcindor.

Walton suffers from tendonitis, a condition sometimes caused by rapid growth. The tendons in his knees are inflamed and they flare up painfully with exertions. His knees are packed in heat pads before every game and soaked in ice afterward. Despite this, Walton was wonderful last season. He averaged 21 points and 15 rebounds a game, but statistics do not measure his value. He per-

??
OUT ON A LIMB...
AFTER YEARS OF BEING CHICKEN, BOYS' LIFE HAS DECIDED TO PUT ITS REPUTATION ON THE LINE WITH PREDICTIONS OF THINGS TO COME IN THE 1968 MAJOR LEAGUE BASEBALL SEASON.
SAVE OUR PREDICTIONS TIL THE END OF THE SEASON, AND CHECK US OUT. IF WE'RE RIGHT, LET'S HEAR THOSE CHEERS. IF WE'RE WRONG, WAIT TIL NEXT YEAR!
AMERICAN LEAGUE
MVP AND HOME-RUN LEADER... HARMON KILLEBREW. THE "KILLER" SHOULD HIT ABOUT 47, FINISHING AHEAD OF HIS BIGGEST RIVALS, FRANK ROBINSON AND CARL YASTRZEMSKI. A STRONG YEAR AT BAT, WITH THE TWINS WINNING THE PENNANT, SHOULD MARK HIM AS MOST VALUABLE PLAYER.
RBI LEADER...FRANK ROBINSON. FRANK SHOULD COME BACK STRONG AFTER A SEASON IN WHICH AN EYE INJURY KEPT HIM OUT OF ACTION FOR A-WHILE, AND HIS ORIOLES WEREN'T AS CONVINCING AS THEY WERE THE YEAR BEFORE. HE SHOULD DRIVE IN 125 RUNS. PRESSING FRANK WILL BE KILLEBREW, YASTRZEMSKI AND AL KALINE.
BA LEADER... TONY OLIVA. WE EXPECT TONY TO BOUNCE BACK FROM WHAT, FOR HIM, WAS AN OFF YEAR. FIGURE HIM TO HIT ABOUT .332, WITH YASTRZEMSKI AND FRANK ROBINSON CLOSE ON HIS HEELS.
TOP PITCHER... JOEL HORLEN. JOEL SHOULD COME THROUGH WITH THE BEST WON-LOST PERCENTAGE—23-8—ALTHOUGH HE'LL HAVE TOUGH COMPETITION FROM TWO TWINS: DEAN CHANCE AND JIM KAAT. JIM LONBORG'S INJURY MAKES HIM A QUESTION MARK.
TOP TEAM... MINNESOTA TWINS.
ANOTHER TIGHT RACE. BOSTON, DETROIT, CHICAGO AND THE ANGELS (ALMOST, BUT NOT QUITE).
NATIONAL LEAGUE
HOME-RUN LEADER... HENRY AARON. HANK WIELDS THE BOOMING BAT IN THE SENIOR CIRCUIT. HIS 39 HRs SHOULD SHADE ORLANDO CEPEDA AND WILLIE McCOVEY. WILLIE MAYS COULD BE AN UNEXPECTED CANDIDATE, BUT WE DOUBT IT.
BA LEADER, RBI LEADER AND MVP... ROBERTO CLEMENTE. IT'S HARD TO PICK ANYONE OVER THE PIRATES' BIG MAN, EVEN ORLANDO CEPEDA (LAST YEAR'S RBI BOSS). CLEMENTE SHOULD SEND 135 RUNNERS ACROSS THE PLATE.
WHO ELSE HITS WITH THE SEASON-LONG CONSISTENCY OF THIS PITTSBURGH POWERHOUSE? HIS .340 SHOULD TOP THE LIKES OF HENRY AARON AND RON SANTO.
HE'S A SHOO-IN FOR MVP, ESPECIALLY IF THE PIRATES TAKE THE PENNANT.
TOP PITCHER... JIM BUNNING. BEING WITH THE PIRATES SHOULD BRING NEW LIFE TO THE FORMER PHILLIES' MEAL TICKET. JIM SHOULD POST A 23-11 RECORD.
TOP TEAM...PITTSBURGH. DESPITE CARDS AND CUBS, THE PIRATES IN THE CATBIRD SEAT.
TWINS
WORLD SERIES... PIRATES SINK TWINS IN SIX GAMES.

USA
USA-USSR-POL
107
AAU

72 BOYS' LIFE

A great Olympic star—"Trackman of the Age"—reveals three SECRETS OF A CHAMPION ATHLETE

By Jesse Owens

Last year, sports writers and broadcasters named Jesse Owens "Trackman of the Age." In a career which began in 1928 in junior high, Jesse tied or set world records in the high jump, broad jump, 100-yard dash, the 220-yard, 60-meter, and 60-yard-dashes. As a sophomore at Ohio State, he became the only track and field athlete in history to set three world records and to tie a fourth in a single track meet! The events: 100-yard-dash (9.4 seconds, tied record); the 220 (20.2 seconds); 220 low hurdles (22.6 seconds); and broad jump (26 feet, 8¼ inches—still the world's record).

At 1936 Olympics, Owens was tops in three events. Above he breaks tape in 100 meters race.

THE PRESSURE WAS really on. I'd fouled on my first two tries in the 1936 Olympic broad jump preliminaries, and I had only one chance left to make the qualifying distance of 23½ feet.

What should I do? I asked myself. You travel all these miles to Berlin, you're the guy who's supposed to win (because you broke the world record the year before at Ohio State University), and now you've put yourself in a position where one mistake—any old kind of a mistake—will spell *o-u-t* for good.

I knew I had two choices. First, go ahead as usual. Take my jump and be as careful as possible about not fouling. The second (suggested to me after my fouls by a German broad jumper who'd become my friend) was: draw a line a safe distance in back of the take-off board and jump from there. It would mean throwing away valuable distance, but I'd be sure of not fouling. So the question was: could I afford to sacrifice those inches?

What would you have done? I figured it was a tossup. No matter which course I chose, the risk was great. It had to be; I'd already tossed away my first two jumps. Finally, one thing made me decide to draw a line of my own a foot in back of the take-off board. It was a thing that was always a personal secret with me, even though I've known a lot of athletes who felt the same way. *I wanted to do my best.* I minded losing, sure—but one thing I hated worse was not getting a chance to show what I had, losing by fouling out. Win or lose, I wanted to make some kind of a showing in the Olympics, and not just have the word 'disqualified' by my name. So I drew my own line a full foot in back of the board, and felt secure knowing that now I could be free to do my best, to give it all I had without any fear of fouling. If my best wasn't good enough for an extra foot above the 23-6, then okay.

I laid my sweat shirt by the line as a marker, and jogged back down the runway. Just before I started my run, I glanced at the shirt and suddenly all the terrific tension seemed to ease. I could feel my skin and muscles start to tingle with that peculiar sense of confidence you get when you know you're going to perform up to your capability.

Now I could see that Olympic gold medal I'd dreamed of ever since I first laced on the spikes. Even more important, sitting 50 yards away in the stands glaring at me were Adolph Hitler and his crew. They'd made a lot of noise about the "master race" and all that, and even though I was good friends with many of the German athletes, I wanted to show them that old Uncle Sam's boys weren't push overs, and Negroes in particular.

I took a deep breath and started my run. The assurance that I wasn't going to foul had really relaxed me, because the second my foot left the ground I knew the jump was good. I didn't know how good until they measured it. Twenty-five feet, 9 inches.

As it was, that jump turned the tide for me in the '36 games. The same day I won the 100 and 200 meters. And the next day took first in the broad jump finals, breaking the Olympics record with a jump of 26′ $5\frac{5}{16}$″. It also helped the American relay team win.

Needless to say, I was glad I had gone with my best effort rather than depending on holding back a little and leaving it up to the take-off board or the judge's eyesight. Not that I'm agreeing with the bigots who say that the German refs were unfair to me in the Olympics. They were as honest as you and I. But even an honest ref can make a mistake once in awhile, and I couldn't afford to chance another mistake.

It may sound a little corny, but it's doing your best, not just coming in first, that will make you champion. It's like what they say about making money: you'll never get rich just by trying to make a dollar—you've got to enjoy doing the thing that's making you the money.

Pierre de Coubertin, founder of the first modern Olympics, said it like this: "The important thing in life isn't winning, but fighting well."

Take a look at all your top athletes and you'll see that that's their first secret. What

Today Jesse Owens conducts sports clinics and makes speeches for Illinois Youth Commission.

A great Olympic star—"Trackman of the Age"—reveals three SECRETS OF A CHAMPION ATHLETE   By Jesse Owens

Last year, sports writers and broadcasters named Jesse Owens "Trackman of the Age." In a career which began in 1928 in junior high, Jesse tied or set world records in the high jump, broad jump, 100-yard dash, the 220-yard, 60-meter, and 60-yard-dashes. As a sophomore at Ohio State, he became the only track and field athlete in history to set three world records and to tie a fourth in a single track meet! The events: 100-yard-dash (9.4 seconds, tied record); the 220 (20.2 seconds); 220 low hurdles (22.6 seconds); and broad jump (26 feet, 8¼ inches—still the world's record).

At 1936 Olympics, Owens was tops in three events. Above he breaks tape in 100 meters race.

THE PRESSURE WAS really on. I'd fouled on my first two tries in the 1936 Olympic broad jump preliminaries, and I had only one chance left to make the qualifying distance of 23½ feet.

What should I do? I asked myself. You travel all these miles to Berlin, you're the guy who's supposed to win (because you broke the world record the year before at Ohio State University), and now you've put yourself in a position where one mistake—any old kind of a mistake—will spell o-u-t for good.

I knew I had two choices. First, go ahead as usual. Take my jump and be as careful as possible about not fouling. The second (suggested to me after my fouls by a German broad jumper who'd become my friend) was: draw a line a safe distance in back of the take-off board and jump from there. It would mean throwing away valuable distance, but I'd be sure of not fouling. So the question was: could I afford to sacrifice those inches?

What would you have done? I figured it was a tossup. No matter which course I chose, the risk was great. It had to be; I'd already

tossed away my first two jumps. Finally, one thing made me decide to draw a line of my own a foot in back of the take-off board. It was a thing that was always a personal secret with me, even though I've known a lot of athletes who felt the same way. *I wanted to do my best.* I minded losing, sure—but one thing I hated worse was not getting a chance to show what I had, losing by fouling out. Win or lose, I wanted to make some kind of a showing in the Olympics, and not just have the word 'disqualified' by my name. So I drew my own line a full foot in back of the board, and felt secure knowing that now I could be free to do my best, to give it all I had without any fear of fouling. If my best wasn't good enough for an extra foot above the 23-6, then okay.

I laid my sweat shirt by the line as a marker, and jogged back down the runway. Just before I started my run, I glanced at the shirt and suddenly all the terrific tension seemed to ease. I could feel my skin and muscles start to tingle with that peculiar sense of confidence you get when you know you're going to perform up to your capability.

Now I could see that Olympic gold medal

I'd dreamed of ever since I first laced on the spikes. Even more important, sitting 50 yards away in the stands glaring at me were Adolph Hitler and his crew. They'd made a lot of noise about the "master race" and all that, and even though I was good friends with many of the German athletes, I wanted to show them that old Uncle Sam's boys weren't push overs, and Negroes in particular.

I took a deep breath and started my run. The assurance that I wasn't going to foul had really relaxed me, because the second my foot left the ground I knew the jump was good. I didn't know how good until they measured it. Twenty-five feet, 9 inches.

As it was, that jump turned the tide for me in the '36 games. The same day I won the 100 and 200 meters. And the next day took first in the broad jump finals, breaking the Olympics record with a jump of 26' 5⁵⁄₁₆". It also helped the American relay team win.

Needless to say, I was glad I had gone with my best effort rather than depending on holding back a little and leaving it up to the take-off board or the judge's eyesight. Not that I'm agreeing with the bigots who say that the German refs were unfair to me in the Olympics. They were as honest as you and I. But even an honest ref can make a mistake once in awhile, and I couldn't afford to chance another mistake.

It may sound a little corny, but it's doing your best, not just coming in first, that will make you champion. It's like what they say about making money: you'll never get rich just by trying to make a dollar—you've got to enjoy doing the thing that's making you the money.

Pierre de Coubertin, founder of the first modern Olympics, said it like this: "The important thing in life isn't winning, but fighting well."

Take a look at all your top athletes and you'll see that that's their first secret. What

Today Jesse Owens conducts sports clinics and makes speeches for Illinois Youth Commission.

keeps Stan Musial, Sam Snead, and Sugar Ray Robinson on top of the list of champions year after year? I think the answer is that these men are perfectionists at what they do. Snead gets a lot madder when he blows a three-foot putt than when his opponent beats him by dropping a thirty footer!

Does this mean that Sam and Stan and Ray don't care if they lose, or that they just forget the competition and act like they're out for the fresh air? You bet your cleats it doesn't. They hate to lose. But they figure the worst thing of all is to ease up just because they're real far behind or way out in front. They always try their hardest, no matter what the situation. I know this personally about Sugar Ray; to him, not doing his best is dishonorable.

Choose the Sport for You

Of course, even Sugar Ray and Musial and Slammin' Sammy had to pick the right sport to become champs. If the three of them traded professions, they might be good, but not great. I think that the *second secret* of becoming a champion athlete is to *choose the right sport for you*. In my experience, there's always one game at which each man can excel. Sure, there are natural athletes who reach the top in any sport they tackle, but they're few and far between. I don't think any of the guys we named above are completely "natural athletes," and I know I never was.

When I was in grammar school, I found myself playing a lot of football and baseball. I did pretty well at them, but not great. The more I played these games, the more I began to see that the parts I excelled in and liked best were the running and jumping. Stealing home meant more to me than knocking in four runs. By the time I got to high school, I realized that track was the sport for me. I'm glad I did. I'm sure I never would have broken any Olympic records in swimming or skiing, no matter how hard I'd practiced.

Practice—that's the third "secret" of becoming a champ. *Don't lose off the field what you gained on it.* I put the word "secret" in quotes because good training habits are really no secret to anybody. It's just mathematical common sense that the twenty-two hours a day a guy spends outside the gym can be exactly eleven times as important as the two he spends inside it. It's no secret, but you'd be surprised how many promising athletes don't live up to their potentials just because they take the bus when they could walk, or sit in a movie on weekends instead of hiking in the woods once in a while. That's what I mean by *practice*. Not the obvious things that you do in the gym or on the field, but some of the subtler activities a guy takes part in that on the surface don't seem related to running or baseball or swimming.

I remember walking into my quarters in the Olympic Village in 1936 and being surprised because one of our runners was standing over in the corner juggling three rubber balls.

"Man, what are you doing?" I asked him. "You come three thousand miles to run and instead you take up juggling."

"Juggling's part of running, Jess," he answered me. "Remember that time I dropped the baton a few days ago in a warmup? Tomorrow's the relay finals. I'm not going to drop it this time."

I had to respect him for that. ➡

Secrets of a Champion

He was all through running for the day, but one way or another he still was able to improve some part of himself for the race.

Another way to keep in shape off the field is by making out a *goal chart*. I always used to keep track of how many miles I walked each day, how much sleep I got, and so on. Of course, when I was a boy it was hard *not* to walk enough. We didn't have any cars to drive around in, and the streetcars didn't come around very often. A *goal chart* on the field is a good thing, too, because just winning a race isn't an accurate indicator of whether a runner has improved or not. Only by beating your past records can you improve. I made a lot of mistakes as a runner and broad jumper (fouling twice in the Olympic preliminaries, for example!), but I always tried to do my best and keep in shape, once I'd found the right sport for me. That's why I think I won so many events by just a hair's width. I was running against the clock, and I would have rather lost the race by 50 yards and broken my record than win by dogging it. I went all out in 1936, and so it figures that my Olympic broad jumping record is still standing.

To me, though, there are a lot of men who are champions—even though they never set a record or won a gold medal or blue ribbon. I think Webster hit the nail on the head in his definition: "Champion: *combatant* or *fighter*." In my book, you measure an athlete not only by what he accomplishes, but by how hard he tries and how he plays the game. Even if Snead and Ray and Musial weren't winning, you'd be sure of one thing: they'd always do their very best.

(Jesse Owens today still shows the drive and versatility of a multiple champion. He is special representative of the President of the United States to the international Olympic Games, and for the state of Illinois, Jesse is administrative assistant to the chairman of the Illinois Youth Commission, and head of the Department of Juvenile Delinquency Prevention.—*Ed.*)

How We Got the Mind-Reading Pills

thought of poor Kai hoping we'd rescue him, and I couldn't turn back. I stepped in boldly, with Brains at my elbow.

The door clicked shut behind us. I tried it. It wouldn't open again. Sweat broke out all over me.

The room had glowing walls like mother-of-pearl, and seats as soft as marshmallows. It was like a doctor's reception room. Another door slid open and a man came in, blinking as if he'd been asleep.

He was bald and toothless like everyone we'd seen on our first trip, and skinny as a skeleton. When he

From WEAKNESS to STRENGTH

An Intensely Interesting and Helpful Series of Articles for All Boys

Conducted by JOSEPH J. LANE

It is, or should be, the ambition of every boy to become a well-developed, healthy specimen of physical manhood. Many lads have the desire, but they lack the necessary knowledge or instruction to achieve this very laudable object. It will be my object to give you in future issues of BOYS' LIFE a page of easily understood instructions, without the aid of expensive apparatus—as a matter of fact, simply with a piece of ordinary clothes-line and a broom-handle, two things that any boy can find in his own home—any lad who will follow the

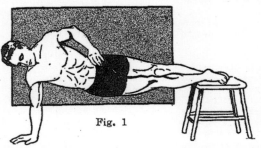

Fig. 1

instructions can, in the space of a few short months, develop his frame until he shall become the envy and admiration of every other lad he knows.

Not only this, but he will be building up in his body such a tower of strength which will fit him to undergo the most arduous labor without in the least feeling any ill effects.

To prove that I am not claiming more for these articles than they justify, I will tell my readers of the case of a young friend of mine. A year ago he was a helpless rheumatic cripple, unable even

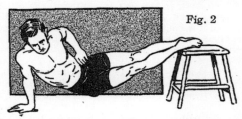

Fig. 2

to attend upon himself. By paying strict attention to a diet I suggested and by following these exercises I am now to tell you about, he not only obliterated all traces of the devastating illness which enfeebled him, but became one of the finest specimens of manhood in this country.

Any boy can do the same for himself. Start in today following the directions here set forth.

The Exercises

The exercises illustrated on this page are not too difficult or severe for the beginner.

A good way to test the strength of the body and arm muscles is to rest with the feet on a seat of a chair and one arm on the floor (Fig. 1). Gradually lower yourself until hip barely touches the floor (Fig. 2) and then raise yourself with one arm until the body is again in a horizontal position with the head level with the feet.

Fig. 3

By throwing practically the whole weight of the body on the arm and shoulder, and raising and lowering yourself, you will soon find that not only the muscles of the arm and shoulder, but also of the back and sides are beginning to bulge out beautifully.

Vary the exercise by using first one arm and then the other, so as to keep the muscles on both sides balanced. Apart from the great value of this exercise as a muscle-producer, it will help to reduce the waist measure and give to the whole body a delightful feeling of freedom and suppleness.

With an ordinary piece of clothes-line about five feet long you can add another very good exercise to your list for arm and leg developers.

Double the rope, put one foot through the loop, and, holding the ends of the rope in one hand, hoist up your foot. (Fig. 3). Then bear down with your foot and force

Fig. 4

the arm down again until your foot touches the floor. (Fig. 4). Vary the exercise by changing the rope from the right leg and right arm to the others from time to time.

by Willie Mays

with Charles Einstein

"I don't rate 'em—I just catch 'em."

I'm supposed to have said those words years ago, when somebody asked me to list the best plays I'd ever made in the outfield.

Maybe I did say it, but I doubt it. I just don't remember, and over the years a lot of stories have grown up, built around things I might have said but really didn't. But it isn't the kind of thing I'd say, unless I was kidding.

I do remember saying something else. I said, "It's nothing unless you catch it." I not only said this—I meant it.

I said it just after being asked, for something like the 300th time, about the catch I made off Vic Wertz in the first game of the 1954 World Series. Because of television, millions of people saw that catch. Because it came at a big moment in the first game and because, from that moment on, everything seemed to go the Giants' way in that World Series, they remembered it. Because that series only went the minimum stretch (the underdog Giants, you'll remember, beat the Cleveland Indians four straight to take that '54 series), there was just plain less of a chance—fewer innings—for some other big defensive moment to develop. And so my catch off Wertz in that first game was a turning point—it was a "money play"—and it was all by itself, so to speak, because those four games just didn't produce another similar big moment. Let's face it: When you look back on a World Series that went only four games, there are no turning points after the first game. There can't be.

And in a way, it's too bad. Especially if you're playing the outfield. Because the catch I made off Wertz wasn't that great a catch to begin with.

He did hit the ball a long way, but the Polo Grounds in New York, where that game was played, had the deepest center field in the majors. I just kept running back and the ball stayed up, so the two of us—the ball and I—arrived at the same spot at the same time.

There had been men on first and second, with the score tied in the top of the eighth and nobody out. We got out of the inning without being scored on.

But in the top of the 10th, with the score still tied, here came Mr. Wertz again, and there went a wicked, low, skipping shot, headed for the bullpen in deepest left center. That's inside-the-park-homer territory at the Polo Grounds. I was able to cut the ball off with a one-handed pickup of one of those mean bounces, and Wertz was held to a double. In my book this was a far more difficult play—and just as important—as the one two innings before. But nobody noticed it then, and nobody's remembered it since.

That's why I said, "It's nothing unless you catch it."

If you're going to play the outfield, you have to resign yourself to this in advance. The best move you make out there will seldom if ever be noticed by the fans, because they're not looking when you make it. The basic thing that made both those plays on Wertz possible was the "break" or "jump" I was able to make the instant the ball was hit. The fans don't see this, because they're not looking at you at that moment. They're watching the hitter as he connects.

At times, I even find myself starting in motion *before* the bat connects! Or at least it seems that way to me—there'll never be any way to prove it. But Joe DiMaggio, who had one of the greatest instinctive jumps on the batted ball of all the outfielders in history, told me the same thing happened to him. "I guess it must be instinct," he said. "I don't know how it can be taught."

But many things can be taught, and the good outfielder is the one who learns. On the San Francisco Giants, for example, we take throwing practice not only before but *during* our games at home! Every time we take the field for a new inning, while the pitcher's taking his warm-up throws and the first baseman is tossing grounders to the other infielders, the three outfielders throw a ball among themselves. This is because of the strong—and variable—wind factor

Another fabulous catch by the Giant of baseball. Fans may argue over which major leaguer can offer the best advice about playing the infield, but few will disagree with BOYS' LIFE that Willie the Wonder ranks as baseball's peerless outfielder.

at Candlestick Park. We're just running a little "weather bureau" of our own out there. You'd be surprised what wind can do to a long throw from the outfield—especially if the outfielder isn't prepared for it in advance.

Not only the weather, but the time of day, the time of year—even the ball park you happen to be playing in—can turn a good outfielder into a bum. In the majors and the fast minors, almost all parks are laid out with home plate to the west, to keep the sun out of the hitters' eyes. That's why left-handed pitchers, then left-handers generally, came to be known as southpaws; as the lefty takes his place on the mound, his pitching arm is to the south. This may help the hitters, but the outfielders take it on the chin.

In September of 1954 I set a new all-time Giant mark for the number of extra-base hits in one season, with a double to center field. What a double that was! It was a routine pop fly that Gus Bell, playing center for the Reds, camped under with ease and grace. And then—he simply "lost" the ball. It dropped 10 feet behind him.

What had happened was that our day game had started very late because of rain, and by now we were into the twilight zone. The white baseball had gone up above the background of the grandstand and simply became a part of the remaining daylight to the west.

If the center fielder has his problems in the daytime, the right fielder picks up problems of his own at night. From this standpoint, the Coliseum at Los Angeles, where the Dodgers played for the first four years after they moved from Brooklyn to the Coast, was the worst I ever saw—particularly during June and July. That's when the days are longest, and the 8 P.M. starting time for games left some daylight. Also, rather than furnishing any high, dark backdrop, the Coliseum stands were light colored and sloped away toward the sunset. Since the park was "correctly" laid out, with home plate due west, the right fielder in the first couple of innings would ➤➤➤

Willie making the memorable "Wertz catch" in the 1954 World Series. With his back to the infield, he outraced the ball, caught it, whirled and threw a strike.

be staring smack into the brightest part of the sky.

The most famous "bad field," though, is neither center nor right. It's left field—left field, that is, at Yankee Stadium at World Series time. The time of year and the way the haze from so many cigarettes in the packed stands seems to collect and hang result in one helpless moment after another for the man in the "dark pocket"—which at the stadium is the left fielder. And, of course, when you make a bad play in the World Series, half the world knows it. I have seen fine defensive men like Gene Woodling and Monte Irvin misjudge the easiest fly balls under those circumstances. And not all outfielders are as good as Woodling and Irvin were.

In the majors, in fact, many managers station their outfielders in terms of who's pitching that day for their side. Once, in 1961, we had so many injuries that Ed Bailey, a catcher, had to play the outfield. But Juan Marichal was pitching for us that night, and he's got quite a fast ball. So our manager, Alvin Dark, put Bailey in left field. He reasoned that not much of the Reds' right-handed power was going to get around soon enough on the Marichal fast ball to pull it to left. And he was right. They hit one ball—a routine fly—to Bailey all night.

You notice this even more at the lower levels and with younger players. I'll never forget watching a kid's pickup game—a bunch of boys about Little League age—in a San Francisco sandlot near my house one day last year. This team in the field had a little guy playing third base whose glove was bigger than he was. The left fielder was twice as small as the third baseman. The shortstop was playing back of second base. The center fielder was playing halfway into right field. I asked one of the kids what was going on. "Oh," he said. "Hoolihan's pitching." And—you guessed it—Hoolihan had a wicked fast ball. So there was nothing hit to the left side at all.

Not only who's pitching, but *what he's* pitching, is important information for the outfielder. In professional ball, whoever can pick up the catcher's sign the easiest—the second baseman if it's a right-handed hitter, the shortstop if the hitter's left-handed—will pick up the sign for the next pitch and relay it with a hand signal to the outfield. (By the way, a lot of times you see a runner on second being bluffed back to the base by the pitcher. It's not because he was taking too big a lead—it's to keep him busy and prevent him from standing there and picking off the catcher's signs.)

Different pitches will react differently when they're hit. A breaking pitch will tend to veer in the air, after it's hit, in the direction of the break. A line drive hit off a fast ball will tend to take off or sail; off a change-up, it may become a "dying quail" and suddenly drop.

For this reason, fungo practice is good only for certain things. Fly balls hit to you by a coach who tosses the ball in the air and then hits it will teach you several things, but only game conditions themselves—or batting practice—will gain you the experience as to how a ball behaves when hit off a pitch.

Fungo practice does teach you to time fly balls and to experiment with your stance. Find out whether you're more comfortable going back or coming in. You'll change your fielding depth in terms of who's at bat, of course, but even then you may play a little closer or a little deeper in terms of your own abilities. Larry Doby played a deep center field. I play a shallow center field.

As to your stance itself, test breaking in different directions and see which seems hardest for you. Then change your stance to favor that direction to begin with. Some outfielders play with feet well spread, others close together. Some don't actually face the hitter. Dominic DiMaggio, playing center field for the Red Sox, used to take a stance that was

practically sideways to the hitter.

In timing a fly ball, remember there are two kinds: the ones where you get there first, and the ones where you and the ball kind of arrive together. If you get there first, don't freeze while waiting for the ball to come down. The smallest misjudgment or puff of wind will leave you unable to untrack. Be on your toes—you can even do a little dance step or two; most professionals do. Your heels should never make contact with the ground while you're about to catch a fly. Most pros, you'll notice, tap their gloves a time or two while waiting for the catch. This again is motion—an instinctive guard against freezing.

If you are going to have to make a throw after the catch, practice circling a yard or so back of the line of the ball's descent. Then you will be coming forward as you make the catch, and your body will add its weight to the propulsion of your throw.

Speaking of throwing—nobody throws with his arm alone. This is particularly true of outfielders, who have to make the long throws. Also, outfielders frequently have the opportunity, as I just said, to be coming forward and adding momentum to the throw. It's a big factor.

One of the best throws I ever made—and just about the strangest play I can remember—came when I was playing center field for the Birmingham Black Barons of the old Negro National League, before the Giants signed me. There was one out and men on second and third against us, and the batter hit a fairly deep fly to me in center. I took it coming in, and with that momentum I threw a strike on one bounce to the plate—but too late to catch the man coming from third. The only reason I missed him was that he'd left third base before the catch. The funny thing was, the man on second had tagged up too, to go to third, and *he* left early too. So now we threw the ball to second and appealed to the umpire, and he upheld us. That was the

third out, and we all trotted to the dugout.

Too late we found out that the run, scored by the man who'd left third early, counted against us. The ruling was that he had crossed home plate before the third out was ruled, and since no appeal play had been made on him for leaving third too early, the umpire could not rule one way or the other. On appeal plays, of course, the umpire rules only when the appeal is made.

We found out that if, after winning the appeal at second base, we had then thrown the ball to third and appealed there, before leaving the field, then the run would not have counted. So this was a case where the defensive side should have made *four* put-outs in order to get out of the inning unscored upon!

I mentioned that my throw to the plate on this play was on one bounce. Most outfield throws should be. If your arm isn't strong enough to cover those big distances on the fly—and most young arms aren't—then you have to use the bounce. Or if you can reach your target on the fly, but need an arching throw to do it, forget it. The low throw on the bounce will get there faster anyway.

Furthermore, the low throw is handled more easily by infielders, especially in cutoff situations. So the only time the throw on the fly is permissible is when (1) it's the fastest way to get the ball there and (2) no other base runner is going to move up on the sequence.

I confess I've violated this rule from time to time. But I've never done it without a reason—though sometimes later I've agreed the reason wasn't a good one. Joe DiMaggio violated it under very special circumstances in the 1949 World Series. He was playing center for the Yankees against the Dodgers in that series, and his arm was dead—but the Dodgers didn't know it. So in fielding practice before each of those series games, he cut loose one fantastic throw, on the fly to home plate. It killed him to

Getting a fast jump on the ball and making the right moves is part instinct, part practice. As Mays puts it, "The good outfielder is the one who learns."

do it and ruined his arm for the rest of the day. But the Dodgers saw it and figured it would be suicide to run on him. And so they never tested him during the games!

In the 1954 World Series, Don Mueller, the Giants' right fielder, made an *error* that had a similar effect on the opposition. The batter had singled to right, and as he made his routine turn around first base, Mueller shot the ball back toward first—the throw *behind the runner*. It was a good notion, but the ball misfired and wound up in the dugout, so the hitter took off and made an extra base. Interestingly enough, though, the Indians didn't do any more running in that entire series. They figured if Mueller had enough confidence to try a stunt like that, what would Mays or Irvin be like? They wound up leaving 38 men on base in four games, and not one of those 38 was thrown out trying to advance.

I made a throw to the plate in 1951 that has become known as The Throw. Billy Cox of the Dodgers, a fast man, was on third, and Carl Furillo hit a medium-depth fly to my left. In catching it, I was going away from my throwing momentum. So I did a full spin and let fly and caught Cox coming into home plate. Charley Dressen, then managing the Dodgers, said afterward, "I'd like to see him do it again." If it's any comfort to Dressen, so would I.

Many tributes have been paid to my throwing arm, yet I don't think I've ever led the league in assists. Maybe one year or two. It doesn't matter, because that's a meaningless statistic. The outfielder with a lot of assists is a guy whose arm they're running on. I'd just as soon have no assists—except in starting an occasional double play by catching a ball the base runner didn't think I'd catch. The best tribute I can get is that they don't run on me. Like DiMag in that '49 World Series.

Getting back to those two categories of fly balls, let's talk here for a moment about the second kind—the ones where you and the ball are having a race. Here, fungo practice will enable you to do two things. First, it will teach you how to gauge a ball's flight so that you can take your eye off it for a time. This will enable you to run faster—also to measure your distance if you're getting close to the fence or another fielder. On balls that two men are chasing, always set it up in advance that you can "call." The Alphonse and Gaston act, where two fielders suddenly stop and let the ball drop between them, or—far worse—the collision of two men, are things that don't have to happen as frequently as they do. Particularly on balls where an outfielder and an infielder seem to have an equal chance, the infielder should *always* give way to the outfielder. This is just straight common sense. The outfielder is coming in; he has the ball, the play and any necessary throw all in front of him.

But nobody catches a ball "blind." It's fine to take your eye off it, but you've got to pick it up again before you can make the catch. I don't care what the fancy write-ups say, *nobody* ever caught a ball without looking. That includes me on the Wertz catch in '54. I may have been running full-out with my back to the plate, but in case anybody's interested, I looked back twice while I was running.

As you practice ranging to your left or right in fungo drills, one thing will fascinate you. Your body will automatically

"shift gears" so that you always come down on your leading foot—your right foot, if you're going to your right, your left foot, if you're going to your left—as you reach the ball. It's the same as in the running broad jump. Regardless of how far you run to the take-off board, you'll find the foot you favor for the take-off will always be the foot that hits the board.

The worst outfield sins are committed on ground balls. Why this isn't emphasized more, I'll never know. Every season I get as many grounders as I get fly balls —probably more. If you field a single and throw it back to the infield, it doesn't show in your fielding statistics. But you'd better know how to do it. In my case, I'm famous for taking *infield*, as well as outfield practice, before every game. An outfielder can't work too much on grounders. It's as simple as that.

Unless the ball is going to come to you on a predictable high bounce, the general rule is to field outfield grounders down on one knee. This is to block the ball and keep it from rolling on through. An infielder has someone to back him up. You don't.

If you can charge a grounder, field it like a shortstop and whip it back in, so much the better. But bear in mind your position, your talent and your situation. If you're ahead 1-0 with two out and nobody on in the ninth, and the batter singles to you in the outfield, why take a chance the ball can get past you?

In fact, *always* gauge your situation *before* the play. Know your score, your inning, your hitter, who's coming up next, who's left on the bench, how many are out, the speed and habits of any of the base runners.

When Bucky Harris was managing the Yankees in the late 1940s, he's supposed to have told the then-rookie Yogi Berra, "*Think* when you hit." And Berra is supposed to have replied, "How can you think and hit at the same time?"

There's something in what Berra said. If you can map your choice in advance, then you don't have to deliberate and act at the same time.

And three final tips:

1) *Never* throw the ball before you have it. Does this sound like unlikely advice? It's one of the commonest and worst of outfielding mistakes.

2) Once you have the ball, get rid of it. *Never* stand there and hold it or run in with it. The team that's trying to beat you is doing business in the infield. That's where the ball belongs.

3) Do I recommend the famous Willie Mays "basket catch"? *No!* It works for me. But it's part of the glove I like to use, the shoulder-angle of the throw I make the best, and about four other things that combine uniquely so they seem to work for me without being a pattern anyone else ought to follow.

If I've been at all helpful here, I'm glad. But nothing I've said is any good, if you don't have good physical shape to go with it. You outfielders especially— for you'll do more actual running than anybody else.

I've never smoked. I don't drink—except for two glasses of champagne, one when we won the pennant in 1951, the other when we won the pennant in 1954. The champagne was there too when, having moved from New York to San Francisco, we won the pennant in 1962. But I didn't drink any.

Champagne makes me sick. Twice was enough. ∎

Remember to gauge a ball's flight and know what to do with it when you catch it.

Superstar Bill prefers being a team player.

Bill Walton Perfect in the Pivot

By BILL LIBBY

Meet the shy giant who's keeping UCLA No. 1.

Suddenly Bill Walton appeared in the play. He came from the corner of the court in three great strides. He went up high, seemingly all legs and arms and elbows, to smother the ball in two massive hands as it bounced off the backboard. Still in the air, he fired a football pass to fast-breaking UCLA (University of California at Los Angeles) teammates who converted it into a lay-up at the other end.

A grin creased Bill Walton's face as he joyfully jiggled up and down on the toes of his sneakers. Then he clapped his hands together in soft applause for his teammates and a play well executed.

This was one of many scenes of success in last season's NCAA championship game at the Sports Arena in Los Angeles. Before the competition was over, Walton passed through many moods. An animated athlete, he shook a fist in triumph each time he hit on a hook-shot, a turn-around jump-shot or a follow-up shot. He slapped hands with teammates who scored off his passes. During time-outs, he kept time to the band music by snapping his fingers. And when he was roughed up by foes or had fouls called on him, his face was set in a grimace of anguish and he complained outrageously. He got into foul trouble and his Bruin teammates had to struggle to stave off Florida State by five points. Afterwards, while everyone else on his side was celebrating, the Player of the Year as a sophomore in college basketball seemed strangely disappointed. He complained, "We didn't dominate the way we should have. I don't even feel as though we won."

The 6-11, 19-year-old youngster is accustomed to success. When he graduated from Helix High School in San Diego he had led his team to 49 straight victories. His freshman team at UCLA won 20 in a row. And after last season's 30-0 by the Bruins—Bill's first varsity campaign—Walton's teams now have won 99 consecutive contests. The Bruins beat their foes by an average margin of 32 points per game, an NCAA record. No team came closer than Florida State's five points in the final game. The schedule was not tough and most opponents were destroyed. Texas A&M fell by 64 points, Texas by 50, and Denver by 47.

As this new season began, UCLA was within 15 victories of the NCAA basketball record of 60 in a row, set by Bill Russell's University of San Francisco teams in the late 1950's. This is the only major record that has eluded Coach John Wooden's Bruins, who are bidding for their seventh straight national title and ninth in 10 seasons. Since they figure to have their strongest team yet, they are strong favorites to extend their dynasty of domination.

The UCLA campus is located in Westwood, a swank section of Los Angeles. The athletic department building is adjacent to the Pauley Pavillion, a modern concrete pillbox, which the Bruins fill with more than 12,000 fans for every home game. It is harder to get a seat to a Bruin game than to a game of the pro champion Lakers at their Forum in the suburbs. A team led by Gail Goodrich and Walt Hazzard launched UCLA on the incredible decade that concludes this season. Lew (Kareem Abdul-Jabbar) Alcindor's teams picked up the pace, and clubs led by Sidney Wicks carried on. Now, the Walton era.

Sitting surrounded by trophies in the university's basketball office, Bill shrugs and says, "I don't think much about records. I don't even think about basketball during the off-season. I enjoy basketball. It's a game, isn't it? That's what it's called. And everyone likes to play games. Games are to have fun. But it's not always fun."

He looks like an elongated Tom Sawyer, with a thatch of uncombed rust-red hair and a lot of freckles on his long, lantern-jawed, boyish face. He slouches some as though to hide from his height and he shies from interviews as though this will turn off the spotlights that follow him everywhere. And when he speaks to an outsider he stammers some, as though reluctant to give much of himself away. But it is impossible for Bill Walton to slip through shadows unseen. He is too good and too prominent.

Before last season he was not as publicized a sophomore as Tom McMillen, the Pennsylvanian at the University of Maryland and U.S. Olympic team member. However, Tom and his team had their troubles. They failed to win the Atlantic Coast Conference and so did not even qualify for the NCAA tournament, although they did go on to win New York's NIT classic. Meanwhile, UCLA swept the major honors and by season's end Walton was the most celebrated collegian since Alcindor.

Walton suffers from tendonitis, a condition sometimes caused by rapid growth. The tendons in his knees are inflamed and they flare up painfully with exertions. His knees are packed in heat pads before every game and soaked in ice afterward. Despite this, Walton was wonderful last season. He averaged 21 points and 15 rebounds a game, but statistics do not measure his value. He per-

The powerful 6-11, 225-pound pivot man says,

"I look forward to playing pro basketball—

with the best—but I doubt it will be fun."

forms with the wisdom of a veteran. He unselfishly orchestrates games to see that each player on his well-balanced team plays his part.

This lanky, but quick, graceful, and agile giant does many things well. He defends, blocks shots, rebounds, and makes the quick pass out to start fast breaks about as well as any young center ever. While he is accurate with a variety of shots, he looks first to pass to teammates. When they miss, he manages to get there to follow up for scores. He is not as spectacular a shooter as Abdul-Jabbar, but may be more versatile.

His coach, Wooden, says, "I don't like to compare players, but I must say that while Lewis Alcindor, as he was known when he played here, was taller, Bill Walton is every bit as dominating." Others go further. One opposing coach, Marv Harshman, said, "I almost wish Alcindor was back with them instead of Walton. Walton is an awesome force, who intimidates foes." One foe, Shelby Metcalfe, said, "I thought the Lord divided things up evenly, but He gave it all to Walton."

One after another heaped similar praise on the sophomore.

However, Walton says, "Don't compare me to Abdul-Jabbar. He is the greatest. I'm just beginning. I'm not the first player to win with the teams John Wooden puts together at UCLA. Without any one of my teammates last season, we would not have won as we did. I don't like it when I'm singled out for attention. I wish we would only be interviewed as a team, in a group. The other guys have all been great players all their lives and here they got into a situation where they had to sacrifice themselves. The way they

handled it is a lot more admirable than anything I accomplished."

We walked across campus, the heads of students turning as the towering youngster went by. We drove to a dark restaurant, where more heads turned as he walked in and folded himself into a booth. Not only several customers, but the owner as well, came to tell him they thought he was the greatest and to ask him for autographs.

Wistful with wonder, he shook his head and said, "I haven't done anything yet. I think autographs are the most useless things around, but I sign them because it's easier than not signing them. When people I don't know praise me or make jokes about my height, I smile and reply politely, but I'm not paying much attention because they're not an important part of my life and my mind usually is on other things.

"I avoid places where I'll be hassled too much, but generally I go where I want to go because you can't let strangers dictate your life. They only want to talk basketball to me. They think basketball is my whole life. But there are other things in my life."

A growing boy who now weighs 225 pounds, Bill has an enormous appetite. The waitress asked him if he wanted soup or salad with his steak for lunch and he said, "Both, please, and not one of those little-bitty cups of soup, but a big bowl, please." And the food simply disappeared into his skinny frame as he spoke of his life.

He was born in November of 1952. His father is a district chief of the San Diego Department of Public Welfare, which may have stirred in his son sentiments for the underprivileged. His mother is a librarian, which may have stirred in him some book-

ishness. He got good grades in high school, graduating 29th in a class of 575, and has an average of 2.9 (out of 4.0) in college. He says he is majoring in history simply because he likes it and not because he knows how he will use it later. He especially likes courses in African culture. He says he is inclined to go on to law school and would like to set up a free practice to serve needy minority groups.

His father is 6-4 and his mother is 5-10. He has an older brother, Bruce, who is 6-6 and a 250-pound starting tackle at UCLA, and a younger brother, Andy, who is a 6-5 basketball forward at Helix, Bill's old high school, as well as a 5-11 sister, Cathy, who plays girls' basketball at the University of California at Berkeley. Bill grew fast and naturally turned to basketball. He became a schoolboy star and received more than 100 college bids before settling on UCLA, "because of its combination of athletics and scholastics."

He says he is fairly happy at UCLA, especially since he moved from a crowded dormitory to one small room, where he lives alone without even a telephone. He explains, "I prefer privacy. I don't need a lot of people. I'm suspicious of strangers because I feel they're interested in me only as a basketball player, not as a person. I almost didn't come to UCLA because my brother was here and I felt it was time we went our own ways some. I have only a few close friends. I select my friends carefully, because they're important to me. The main thing I ask of them is that they let me be myself, not some all-American boy image of an athlete."

He spends a lot of time in his ➡

"I don't like it when I'm singled out for attention. I wish we'd only be interviewed as a team. The other guys are great players."

room. He says, "I study, but not to excess. I read a lot. I listen to a lot of different kinds of music. Because I shy from the public, I've been called a hermit, but I go out. I have a small car. I go to movies. I go to parties. But I don't like big parties. I'm happy sitting around rapping with a few friends. I date. I have a girl, but I'm a long way from marriage. I don't go overboard. I go my own way. Even Coach Wooden doesn't know where I go."

In a *Boys' Life* article last year, Tom McMillen said he set himself a strict schedule daily, hour by hour, so he could cram the most into his time. Bill Walton, cut from different cloth, shudders at the thought. He says, "Aside from the commitments I have in season and with some classes, I don't even want to plan what I'll do tonight. And if tomorrow comes, I'll let it take care of itself. I don't know what I'll do with the rest of my life."

One summer afternoon we sat in a parked car on a tree-lined side-street, listening to contemporary pop music. Even in a big car Bill was uncomfortable, almost doubled up with his knees drawn up against the dashboard. He looked at me, almost twice his age, and said, "I'm sympathetic to the causes of young people. I don't trust politicians. I think war is senseless. Bigotry really bothers me. I think I get extra attention because most good basketball players today are black and I'm white. I resent being in that position."

We sat in the sunshine listening to the music and he said, "I have strong feelings, but I don't speak out much because I don't want people to listen to me just because I'm a basketball star."

Some of us wish we were celebrities and some do not. If you are a sports star and feel singed by the spotlight, life can be difficult, which is one reason Bill so far has turned down pro offers of up to $200,000 a season. He says, "Money doesn't mean much to me. I know people with money who are unhappy and all I want right now is to enjoy life, to have some fun."

He sighs and points out, "I doubt that the pro grind will be fun. I'll have to learn to live with a lot of publicity and attention. And I'm not sure I can take the schedule. It's been said I'll grow out of my knee problems, but the doctors don't promise that. I decided to pass up the Olympics to save my knees. They ached so much late last season I couldn't wait for the season to end.

"I think I'll improve enough in the next year or two to hold my own with the pros. I look forward to playing with the best. And to not being double-teamed and triple-teamed, which was another reason basketball wasn't much fun last season.

"It bothers people that UCLA always wins and it bothers me when teams go into stalls in an effort to beat us. That's not basketball. It bothered me when the referees acted as though, because I'm big, it was all right for opposing players to beat on me. I was called a 'crybaby' for complaining, but I thought I had a right to complain, and I tend to get emotional on court."

Coach Wooden says, "His main weakness on court is that he tends to let his emotions get away from him, but he is a spirited young man and a big reason we had the best team spirit of any team I've coached. He is a fine young man of many changing moods who is trying to find himself."

Bill says, "The coach is a fine man who coaches not only the player, but also the person and wants only that we make the most of ourselves. But he is of an older generation and does not always understand the feelings of the young. For example, I wish he'd let us wear our hair longer.

"I don't feel comfortable with older people. I love the young guys on our club and I wanted to stay with them instead of going into pro ball. We have a coach who knows how to win and a great bunch of guys who are winners. I look forward to the season because I think we'll be better than ever."

He continues, "I wish I were taller because it would make me a better basketball player, but I wish I were shorter because it would make my life easier. I sense people staring at me. I try not to pay any attention, but I could live without it."

He looks down at his large hands and says, "I don't understand why people go crazy over basketball. The money it took to build all the fancy arenas could have fed a lot of hungry people. Basketball is beautiful in its place, but it's made too much of. I play it because it's something I do well, but I want to do other things, too."

He sits quietly for a moment, then concludes, "I don't mind the pressure of having to produce up to potential, but it wouldn't worry me if we weren't able to win all the time. It's more important for people to just live one day at a time, trying to be nice to one another, in peace, trying to get some fun out of life. Life is too short to worry all the time about being the best."

And then he was gone, long and lean, loping across the street to find some friends to rap with. ●

"I wish I were taller because it would make me a better player. but I also wish I were shorter because that would make my life easier."

I'm playing basketball again for the New York Knickerbockers.

What a simple statement. But few people in this world know how much those nine words mean to me; how much it means to be an active member of another National Basketball Association champion.

For most of the 1971-72 season, I was a captain without a uniform. A painful knee condition took a year out of my basketball life. There were times when I wasn't sure I'd ever be able to play again. An operation that was supposed to have cured this condition had failed. I was depressed, discouraged.

As I began the course of exercise and therapy that doctors promised would enable me to

Willis Reed talks about Coach...

ies and are still playing. This isn't the way you want to go out."

Minor injuries not connected with my knee slowed my comeback against Baltimore and Boston in the first two rounds of the playoffs, but it wasn't until we got to the finals against Los Angeles that I finally felt I had put it all

When the series ended, I was named the most valuable player in the finals but, to me, even more important were these words from Coach Hobdy when he phoned to congratulate me: "Big-un, you ran out there like you were 19 years old."

When my old coach told me that, I knew for sure I'd made it back.

I first started having trouble with my knee during the 1969-70 season when we won our first NBA championship. It really began to bother me the next year and after the season I agreed to undergo surgery. We all thought the operation would provide an escape from pain, but it did not. After I tried to play a few games the next year, the pain became too intense and I was forced to quit. The doctors finally decided that I needed a full year of therapy.

During these depressing months, I thought often about another time Fred Hobdy had been there when I was discouraged and in pain. That was just before my greatest moment in basketball, the night the Knickerbockers won that first title.

Four nights earlier, during the fifth game of the play-off finals against Los Angeles, I had torn a muscle in my right hip. My

You Have to Be a Man

resume my career, I went back to Grambling College and to the man who started me on my way —my old coach, Fred Hobdy.

Fred and I don't have a player-coach relationship any more. He's an old friend and he was there when I needed him. During those trying days, we went fishing together, and he invited me to watch his team practice. He told me about the problems he was having with his boys, and then we'd reminisce about the years when I was playing for him and the good games and the good guys I'd played with.

These talks took my mind off my problems and also reminded me of the good times I'd had with the Knickerbockers. They made me more determined than ever to get back to the game.

Fred Hobdy is a very positive man. He never acknowledged the possibility of my not coming back. "I know you're very depressed now," he'd reassure me, "but don't let it get you down so you give up all those things you worked so hard to achieve. A lot of guys have had injur-

back, but I was satisfied because I knew I was making a contribution to the team's success. I had some good games

...Fred Hobdy—not just a coach.

together. We lost our first game to the Lakers, then beat them four in a row for our second championship in four years.

teammates had gone on to win that game without me but, two nights later, as I watched unhappily from the bench, the Lakers won easily in Los Angeles to square the best-of-seven series at three games apiece.

Then came the night before the seventh game, back in New York. It would be the most important game the Knickerbockers had ever played. They had been charter members of the NBA when it was formed in 1946, yet they had never won a championship. It was the biggest game of my professional career, too. I knew I would have to try to play despite my injury. My teammates had told me they felt they didn't have a chance without their center and captain. Could I play the next night? At this point even the doctors weren't sure.

As I rested my aching body, the phone rang in my apartment. Fred Hobdy was on the line. He was keeping a promise he once had made to me—and to all the other boys he had ever recruited at Grambling: "I'm not promising you a car or a nice new wardrobe or $200 a month spending money," Hobdy had told me as I was finishing high school, "but whenever you need me, even after you've finished playing at Grambling, I'll be there."

That night, my old coach gave me a pep talk from more than 1,400 miles away. "Reed," he said, "you've got to be out there when they throw that ball up tomorrow night. If you've got an ounce of breath in you, you've got to be out there."

If I needed any extra inspiration, that was it. The next evening, the team doctor assured me that I would risk no permanent damage to my leg by trying to play. Even though I'd been given pain-killing injections, I was still hurting as I limped out on the floor. But my teammates said my appearance gave them the lift they needed to beat the Lakers for New York's first pro basketball championship.

I received a lot of honors after the Knicks won the championship, more than any basketball player who ever came out of Grambling, and I know Coach Hobdy is proud of me. But he's just as proud of all his boys. He once told a newspaper reporter, "Willis Reed is my most famous player, but he would have made good without Fred Hobdy. But those boys who come to Grambling from bro-

Hobdy says of a little-used substitute on the same team, who averaged under two points a game, "I'm just as proud of Leon Moore, because he's getting his diploma."

Fred Hobdy knows there's a lot more security in a college degree than in dreams of professional basketball.

Being from Bernice, only 26 miles from Grambling, I had known all about the school and Coach Hobdy. I wanted to play pro basketball, and I knew I could get the coaching, as well as a good education, at Grambling. My mother also was happy, because she had been impressed by Coach Hobdy's sincerity when he came to visit our little house.

One reason I chose Grambling was because freshmen could play with the varsity. Only that opportunity didn't seem to be doing me any good as I sat on the bench through the opening games of the season. Folks around Grambling were wondering out loud if Coach Hobdy hadn't wasted one of his scholarships on me. I was wondering if I had made a mistake, too, in thinking I could play basketball.

One day after practice dur-

Coach didn't argue. "OK, get your things and I'll take you," he said.

My mother was surprised to see us, but Coach Hobdy started chatting with her as if we were simply paying a little visit. I just listened. Finally, Coach said, "Well, Reed, you ready to go back?" He knew I would be too ashamed to admit to my mother in front of him that I was quitting, and he was right. I just got up and marched out to his car.

A couple of weeks later, I had improved enough to make the starting lineup, and we went on to win the National Association of Intercollegiate Athletics championship for small colleges. If Coach Hobdy hadn't handled me just right when I was so discouraged, who knows if I'd ever have returned to basketball?

One of my teammates on that championship squad, 5-9 Bobby Ricks, was too small ever to make it as a pro, and Coach Hobdy knew it. He also knew that this boy from tiny Raysville, La., had few prospects in life without a college degree. So he battled to keep Bobby in school and got him jobs to help him pay his way. Today Bobby is a successful high school coach in Chicago.

Another teammate, who eventually made All-American, came from a broken home. Nobody had ever taught him the importance of fulfilling obligations. His first year or so in college, he'd think nothing of skipping practice, or his lessons, to visit his girl friend in the next town. But Coach Hobdy straightened him out, and now my teammate is a coach in a high school in Arkansas.

At a school like Grambling, where today 80 percent of the student body requires some kind of financial aid, a few dollars at the right time can mean a lot to students who are struggling to complete their education. Coach Hobdy has made countless trips up dirt roads to little unpainted shacks to plead with parents to try to sacrifice just a little bit more to keep their children in school. He knows that a college degree can open the way to a new life and, often, he'll dig into his own pocket to help, too.

Coach Hobdy knows what it's like for his players to overcome obstacles to get through college because he had to travel the same path himself. He was born in Winnfield, La., in 1922, and his father died when he was seven, leaving his mother to raise a family of seven boys and three girls.

The family owned a farm, so there was always plenty to eat, but little left over for extras. ➡

By WILLIS REED with LARRY FOX

ken, unstable homes or from the most deprived economic conditions and who end up as productive citizens—they are my greatest successes."

Ask Fred Hobdy about his greatest players, and he will tell you about his nine All-Americans and the half-dozen Grambling stars who have played in professional basketball, both amazing figures for an all-black college of less than 4,000 students that is known primarily for its football team. But Coach also will list, just as proudly, his former players who are now coaches, teachers, and principals.

Two seasons ago, one of Grambling's star players, Fred Hilton, was a high draft choice by both professional basketball leagues. Hilton came to Grambling from an orphanage in Baton Rouge, La. His prospects were poor, but Coach Hobdy kept him in school and saw to it that he was able to support his wife and two small children while continuing his education. Hilton won a lot of honors for Grambling, and will win more, and Coach says, "This is a boy I'd be proud to have as my son." But, in the same breath,

ing the Christmas holidays, I went up to Coach Hobdy and mumbled, "I'm going home. I'll never be able to play here."

Willis Reed—a dynamo on court.

Those who wanted to go to school were encouraged, but higher education definitely was not taken for granted. Two of Coach's brothers have masters' degrees and two of them are still working in the sawmill, which is where he would have ended up if it hadn't been for Joseph Simpson, principal of Winn Parish Training School, five miles, by foot, from the Hobdy farm.

Simpson was 30 years ahead of his time. He and his wife both had masters' degrees, which was unheard-of in a small black high school in the Thirties, and, even then, he was preaching that self-pride and education would be the means for our people to improve their lives. Mr. Simpson stressed sports because he knew this would keep the boys interested in school. He even bought them some basic equipment out of his own meager $30-a-month salary.

More important, he proposed goals beyond anything the students had ever imagined before. "You've got to take the right courses so you can graduate and go on to college," he told Hobdy back then, "because you're going to be a great player and a great coach." He kept repeating it and soon the young Hobdy began to believe him.

Coach wasn't a great athlete at the beginning in high school. He was kind of awkward, the way I used to be, but he worked hard and he was a star by his senior year. After he graduated, and other colleges passed him by, Mr. Simpson drove him down to enroll at Grambling.

There's a lot of Mr. Simpson in Coach Hobdy, according to people who know them both. In fact, it could be the old principal speaking when Coach says, "My greatest reward is not if they become professional athletes, but if they become better citizens. I require a boy to get his degree, not just to teach, but because it aids his dignity. If these boys play and I have not been able to improve their economic situation or improve their thinking, then I have used them as tools to better myself."

When Coach Hobdy first arrived at Grambling, it was a junior college of some 300 students. The meals were served family style in the dining hall. The president then, and now, was Dr. Ralph Waldo Emerson Jones. We still call him "Prez," he still coaches the baseball team, and the school still uses the motto he lives by: "Everybody is Somebody."

Coach enrolled as a freshman in 1942 and played guard on Grambling's first undefeated football team. They called it the "Un" team—unbeaten, untied, and unscored-upon. He also played center on the basketball team at only 6-3½, and was a weak-hitting first baseman in baseball before entering the Navy that spring.

After 38 months of service, most of it in combat in the Pacific during World War II, Coach Hobdy returned to join the beginning of the famous Grambling sports dynasty. The school was now a full four-year college and hundreds of strong, hungry young men were streaming back to the campus. They had matured in service. They had seen the outside world and they wanted to be part of it. Sports would get them the education to make something of themselves.

Hobdy captained the football, basketball, and baseball teams as a senior. When he graduated in 1948 he simply moved across the street to become the coach at Grambling High school. Three years and two state basketball championships later, he returned to his alma mater as an assistant to the head coach of all sports, Eddie Robinson. In 1956, Hobdy succeeded Robinson as head basketball coach.

Coach now finds that some of his competitors tell high school prospects not to go to Grambling "because you won't be able to make their team." But he'll never bad-mouth the other schools. What he does is try to recruit boys who have pride in themselves and who believe they can be winners.

When I was wondering whether I'd be able to play in that big game for the Knicks, I could almost hear Coach Hobdy trying to inspire us during a game in which we weren't playing well.

"You should be proud to represent Grambling," he'd tell us scornfully, "but the way you're playing, you don't deserve to wear the Black and Gold. You have to be a man to represent Grambling."

Those words sank in and that's why I'll always be a Grambling man.

As for Coach Hobdy, he's resisted many offers from other colleges and even from pro teams. It's more than the promise of a good pension holding him there, it's dedication and loyalty—and the fraternity of the Grambling way of life. ●

"There's more security in a college degree than in dreams of professional basketball."

Reed drives ahead, despite an injured knee.

Fitness Tips for an Action Lifetime

BY BRUCE JENNER AS TOLD TO LOUIS SABIN
PHOTOGRAPHS BY FOCUS ON SPORTS

**Need help? Books
can be great coaches.
Bruce Jenner knows.**

EVERY TIME I'M ASKED which sport is best for a boy to get into, my answer is, any one he enjoys and gets some success from. But if you press me to name my number one choice, I'd have to say *running*. That's because running is the basis of all physical activities. It builds a young athlete's wind, stamina, muscles—every part of his body.

And, along with running, play sports all year 'round. There's no reason to specialize when you're young. That can come later, when your skill at certain sports shows you are ready to concentrate on them.

Take me as an example. I didn't start decathlon training until I was well into my teens. Before then, I played football, basketball, baseball—you name it—and ran all the time. Although I didn't know it, all of those sports were actually preparing me for the running, throwing, and jumping events of the decathlon.

And one more thing: Don't think about becoming a superstar. The hard truth is that most people don't ever reach that peak. If you set your goals too high, you'll only end up disappointing yourself. Just try to be as good as you can be in every sport you like—and in everything else you do. Nobody can ask more of you than that.

I really believe youngsters should get into at least one sport that lasts a lifetime. I remember my Scoutmaster talking about that when I was a Boy Scout in Tarrytown, N.Y. He said that we'd be smart to get into any sports we'd be able to play at 30 years or older. He was right. Even though I'm not training for decathlon competition any more, I play plenty of tennis and run whenever I can. It's not for medals —it's just that I feel good being active.

Fun and health are the two key words. To have the fun (and success you're after), you have to stay healthy. I don't want to sound preachy, but I really agree with the saying, "Get high on sports, not drugs." That goes for smoking and drinking liquor, too. You may hear that some athletes take pills and other drugs to get the most out of themselves. Don't believe it. The only thing *real* athletes need is for their adrenalin to start pumping. Their talent does the rest. Take my word for it, the greatest "high" is the one that comes from doing well in competition— without the aid of drugs.

No matter which sports you like, the best way to get into them is to begin slowly and build steadily. Let's say you're a beginning track man. Try running one mile. If you find yourself too tired before it's over, drop down to a half mile the next time out. Then, when you've done that for several days, try the mile again. Once that distance feels comfortable, and you feel you're not running far enough, move up to two miles, then three, and so on. A good way to tell how your body is taking it is the "next-day test." If you wake up sore all over, or too tired to get out of bed, you're overdoing it. Lower the distance and see how you feel the next morning. And here's a tip for running any distance. Pump your arms. They work directly with the legs. The faster you pump your arms, the faster your legs will go. That's why I encourage young boys to build up arm and upper body muscles. And, as I said, running is the foundation for *all* sports.

Would you believe I never had much coaching? It's true. From about the age of 12, when I first really became interested in football, basketball, and running, I taught myself. With books. You'd be surprised how much you can learn from how-to sport books. They tell you the rules of the games, how to play from Step 1 to Step 100, what to do, and what *not* to do. And I would read the book over and over if I had to, until I got everything clear in my mind. Only when the books couldn't answer a question did I ask someone for help, and then I'd usually talk to an athlete who was a little older than I was.

Experience—playing your sport—is the best teacher. Here are some examples of things I learned that I'd like to pass on to you.

When you get a cramp, rub the place that's cramped and try to play through it. It almost always goes away. Only if it seems to be getting worse should ▶

The world's greatest all-around athlete names the one activity that gets you ready for every other sport.

you stop. Then there's the "stitch" in the side, which sometimes comes when you're running. I just massage the place that hurts, relax for a short time, then get back into action. As for Charley horses and pulled muscles, the wise thing is to lay off until the injured area heals. That doesn't mean you should become inactive. Do something else that won't put a strain on the injured part of your body, but that will keep you in shape. Just use common sense. If it hurts no matter what sport you play, stop. You don't want to do permanent damage.

There are no strict rules for eating. Even while training for the Montreal Olympics, I always ate when I was hungry, and always the kind of food I liked. Meat, spaghetti, salads, and so on. I simply made sure I ate a balanced diet, and took vitamins in addition. Just avoid one thing: junk food. It does you no good and fills your stomach so there's no room for healthful food.

The only rule for sleep is, get as much as you feel you need. Some guys do well on six hours a night, others need 10. However, when you have a big game or race coming up, my advice is to get in solid sleep sessions on the *third* and *second* nights before the big day. That's because athletes can get so keyed up that they spend the night before the game tossing and turning, thinking about tomorrow. When you can't sleep well the night before, don't worry. If you slept well the two nights before, you'll be fine—and you'll sleep like a baby the night after you play.

Do you like to work out alone? Good. Do you like to work out with others? That's good, too. I found that running alone, or practicing field events by myself gave me time to solve personal problems as well as those connected to my sport. Then, anytime I wanted company, there'd always be some guys around, and I'd join them.

Finally, there's the best tip I can give to anyone seeking an active, rewarding, athletic life: Do it! Get into sports you like and play them as much as you can. And don't stop until you're 100 years old. Or more. ♣

Jenner wins the gold. As a teenager he began training for the decathlon. But his strength, skill, and fitness are rooted in even earlier habits and athletic interests.

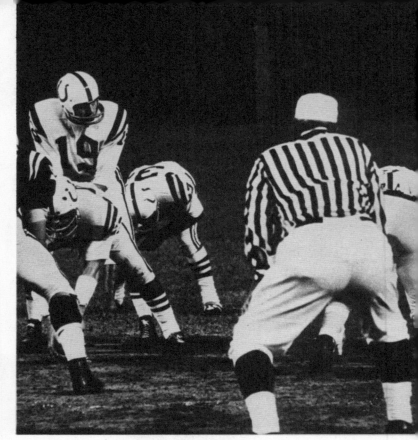

"Blue!"

By JOHNNY UNITAS

QUARTERBACK— A TOUGH POSITION TO TACKLE

The great Baltimore Colt QB passes on his know-how of running a pro team.

The quickest and best way to illustrate my philosophy of playing quarterback is to take you back ten years —to the most important football game I've ever played: the 1958 National Football League championship game against the New York Giants. More precisely, I'd like to go back to the winning series of downs in that game, the first overtime contest in pro-football history.

The score was tied, 17-17, when my team, the Baltimore Colts, got its first chance to move the ball on offense in that first sudden-death period. We worked the ball downfield till we had it on the Giant eight-yard line, first down and goal to go. My head coach, Weeb Ewbank, wanted me to call three running plays; then, if we hadn't scored a touchdown, we could settle for a comparatively easy field goal. That's sound, by-the-book football.

On first down, I gave the ball to our fullback, Alan Ameche. He hit the line but could gain only a yard. It was obvious why. I noticed that the experienced Giant defense was clogging up the middle, sensing that we would not risk a pass that might be intercepted. On the right side, the New York corner linebacker, Cliff Livingston, was forced to guard our fine end, Jim Mutscheller, one-on-one. Livingston was fast for his size, but not fast enough, I knew, to cover Mutscheller. I figured we could take advantage of this matchup.

I called for a pass on second down. Again Ameche pounded by me, but this time I did not give him the ball. Instead I looped a pass to Mutscheller as he ran a "flag pattern," slanting toward the goal-line pennant in the right coffin corner. He caught it on the one-yard line, then fell out of bounds.

On the next play, Ameche plowed over for the winning touchdown.

After the game, a lot of reporters second-guessed me. They wanted to know why I had passed when an almost certain field goal would have given us the title. What if the Giants had intercepted that pass? they asked. What if Livingston had grabbed it and run 99 yards to win the championship for the Giants? What if . . .?

I told them the only thing I could tell them. "When you know what you're doing," I said, "they're not intercepted."

That call may have seemed foolhardy from the press box, but not to me down on the field. I thought it was a good call —a daring call, maybe, an unorthodox call, maybe, but a good call. I saw a weakness in the defense and I took advantage of it. That's playing quarterback.

To me, the worst thing a quarterback can do is to type himself, to become predictable. If the defense can predict what you're going to do, if you fall into a signal-calling rut, they're going to stop you. But if you do something unexpected —like pass when a run seems likely— then you have the edge. That's why I passed to Mutscheller. I knew that play would go—and it did.

I remember another game—during my

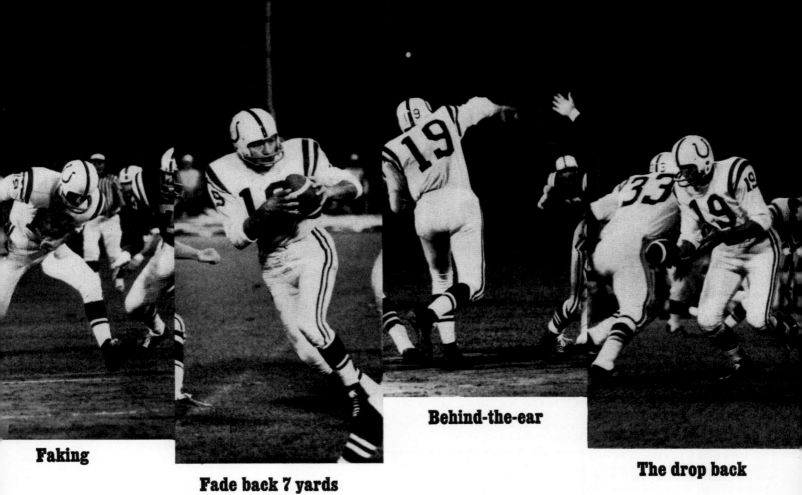

Faking

Fade back 7 yards

Behind-the-ear

The drop back

freshman season at Louisville University. We were playing Houston, and we had the ball on our 40, fourth and two. I wanted to go for the first down. I ducked into the huddle and called a pass play. Our fullback glared at me. "I can make two yards," he said. "Give me the ball."

I glared right back. "I'm calling the plays," I said. "You run when I tell you to run."

Actually, I figured Houston would look for a line plunge. Sure enough, their secondary packed in tight. Our end broke clear easily and we completed a 60-yard touchdown pass. Later in the game, facing the same fourth-and-two call, I passed again—for another TD. Finally, we had the ball on our three-yard line. I threw another pass. It went 97 yards for a third touchdown.

In modern T-formation football, the quarterback is the most important player on the field. He usually calls all the plays, he handles the ball on every play, and he is responsible for that football game-breaker, the forward pass. No quarterback, no matter how good he is, can do it alone, of course. He needs good ends, reliable blockers and running backs who can keep the defense honest. Still, what's the sense of kidding you, quarterback is the glamour position.

I think that good quarterbacks are made, not born. I wasn't always a quarterback. When I attended St. Justin's High School in Pittsburgh, I played end. I stood 5'11" and weighed about 145 pounds. I had never played quarterback

in my life, but a week before we opened the season, our regular quarterback broke his ankle. The coach had seen me throw the ball pretty well in practice, so he said, "Unitas, you're our new quarterback." I've played the position ever since.

Which brings me to the subject of desire. I believe that, given certain physical qualifications, the quarterback who really wants to be good, who will sacrifice to be good, has a better chance than the man who takes his skill for granted. Look at me. I wanted to go to Notre Dame, but they thought I was too small. I wound up at Louisville, and while I set some passing records I wasn't mentioned on any of the All-American teams. It was the same in the pros. The Pittsburgh Steelers drafted me in 1955, but dropped me. I was playing sandlot ball for six dollars a game when the Colts signed me in 1956. In my first pro game, I went in with the Colts leading, 20-14. J.C. Caroline of the Chicago Bears intercepted my first pass and ran 59 yards for a touchdown. I also fumbled three times and we lost, 58-27.

But, corny as it sounds, I always thought I could play pro ball. I had confidence in my ability. You have to. If *you* don't, who will? A quarterback must take charge; he must be a leader. That doesn't mean bawling out your team like a drill sergeant, but you have to be decisive. You must know what you want to do—and do it. Look, I was an unknown kid when I joined the Colts. But when I came into the huddle, I felt I was the boss. If the

coach had enough confidence in me to let me call signals, I was going to call them. And I've always called my own game—except that on the Colts, the coach calls the first three plays of the game. Of course, I don't object to getting advice from the bench or from our spotters; they help a lot. But basically, I like to think I'm in charge out there on the field.

To be in charge, a quarterback must be a student of defense as well as offense. He has to know the personnel on opposing teams as well as his own. He has to know each defensive back's strength and weakness. Does he play pass receivers loose, leaving himself open to the short pass? Or does he play the receivers nose to nose, so you can beat him deep? The quarterback had better know.

I realize that high-school players don't see the complex, shifting defensive alignments we face in the NFL. Most of the time they'll have to cope with a regular zone defense, in which each defender covers a predetermined portion of the field. The best way to attack a zone is to pick at the seams—the "dead spots" where one defensive player's responsibility ends and another's begins.

But whatever you do, remember this: You have to have a reason for every single play you call. And that means knowing defenses—"reading" defenses, as we say.

In schoolboy and college football, you find two different kinds of quarterback. One is the roll-out quarterback. The

other is the drop-back quarterback. The roll-out quarterback must be a strong runner, since he's called on to swing out wide with the football. He can either pass or run with it. But few roll-out quarterbacks are accurate passers; it's hard to throw the ball on the run, without setting your feet properly. Most roll-out quarterbacks who become pros must learn how to drop back into the protective pocket and set their feet before passing. Some players can do both. Joe Namath, of the New York Jets, was a good roll-out quarterback before he hurt his knee. He's also a good drop-back passer.

The drop-back passer falls back behind his wall of blockers and throws from the pocket their bodies form. I'm a drop-back passer, and so are all pro quarterbacks. About the closest thing to a roll-out quarterback that you'll find in pro ball is the scrambler. The most famous scrambler, of course, is Fran Tarkenton, traded by the Minnesota Vikings to the Giants during the winter. Franny drives people crazy by running out of the pocket—scrambling and dodging tacklers till he either finds a receiver open or sees running room. Lots of fans think Tarkenton does this on purpose. He doesn't. Franny scrambles only when he has to. If his protection holds up, he stays in the pocket. He knows that the quarterback who scrambles too often winds up third and 38—and what do you do then?

Me, I only run with the football if I have no other choice.

⟫⟫⟫→

A Tough Position to Tackle

And if I do carry the ball, I always try to head up the middle. Every offensive system is organized to open up the middle, so that's generally where you'll find some daylight.

Of course, drop-back quarterbacks have varying styles. Some backpedal into passing position—like Namath. Others, like me, turn around completely and run back into the pocket. Both styles have their advantages. By backpedaling, you keep the whole field in view; you never have to take your eyes off the defense. But personally, I don't believe that backpedaling gets you into position fast enough. After all, you can run faster forward than you can backward. In football, the act of establishing your passing position is called "setting up" —and I just don't think backpedaling sets you up very efficiently. You have a harder time stopping, you have to plant your feet, then step forward again to throw. It's a lot smoother if you run back the way most quarterbacks do.

Ordinarily, pro quarterbacks drop back seven yards. Sometimes they'll fade back eight or ten yards—when the play calls for a longer pass. But every additional yard you drop back costs you time. On the Colts, we figure that I have 2.5 to three seconds in which to set up in the pocket, look for my receivers and throw. It usually takes me from 1.2 to 1.5 seconds simply to get back there.

Once you're in passing position, you start playing games with those defensive halfbacks. They're taught to "play a quarterback's eyes." The principle is simple: Watch the passer's eyes and he'll give away the direction he's going to throw. To counter this, I use what's called a pump fake. I look to the right and pretend I'm going to throw that way; I give it a good, full arm feint. I have no intention of throwing to the right, but I want to fool the defensive back over on the left. If he thinks the pass is not coming in his direction, chances are he'll let up for a second.

My job at this point is to throw the football quickly and accurately. There are three passing techniques: overhand (or behind-the-ear), three-quarter overhand, and sidearm. I pass overhand; I think you can throw more accurately that way. But young quarterbacks should learn all three methods. You never know when you'll need one. As for gripping the ball, I hold it across the laces, with my little finger and fourth finger on the laces. I try to release the ball with its nose pointing up slightly. When you throw nose up, the receiver sees the majority of the football; nose down, he sees only the middle of the ball. The more of the ball he sees, the easier it is to catch.

When you throw the football, distance doesn't matter that much. A powerful arm helps, but don't overestimate its importance. You don't have to throw the length of the field. Matter of fact, you seldom get to throw a pass 50 yards in the air. It's very hard for your blockers to give you the time even Bob Hayes needs to run that far downfield. Forty yards is about the farthest you have to pass. Delivering the ball quickly, getting it to the receiver on time—that's the key. I call it "drilling the ball." Here it's important to follow

through on your passing motion, just like a baseball pitcher. It gives you more snap on your passes.

What should your passes look like? Well, it's nice to throw pretty spirals, to put plenty of spin on the ball. A rapidly spinning ball penetrates the air better and gets to the target a little faster. A wobbly ball is slowed by wind resistance. But there are exceptions. Like Bobby Layne's passes. Bobby did not always throw what you would call a pretty ball. Some of his passes looked as if they'd die before they got out there. But they didn't. Layne was a great pro quarterback. All right, his passes didn't look elegant, but he got results.

Naturally, you have to adjust your passing style to different game situations. Sometimes you lob the ball softly, leading your receiver, making him run under the pass. Otto Graham threw this way—great, big rainbow passes. I throw a harder ball, I think, although I can throw the rainbow just as I'm sure Otto could fire the bullet.

Sometimes a quarterback deliberately throws what seems to be a bad pass. In my workouts I often concentrate on throwing slightly behind the receiver, so he has to come back for the ball. I do this because frequently a receiver is tightly covered, and by forcing him to come back a little I complete a pass we have no business completing.

Interceptions! I hate them. They drive me crazy. They drive every quarterback crazy. They stop your momentum, they give the other team a lift—and the football. Who's responsible for an interception? It depends. A receiver can run a poor pattern, not cutting sharply but rather bending his pass route and drifting toward the defender. Or a quarterback can throw a rotten pass. Or the defensive rush can pressure you into getting rid of the ball without being certain where it's going.

Some quarterbacks are wonderful at "accidentally" throwing the ball away if they see they're going to be dumped for a big loss. I do it myself, but I don't like to. I'd rather settle for a seven-yard loss than put up the ball out of desperation; too often the wrong team catches it. That's a tough lesson for kid quarterbacks to learn—how to eat that football when you're awfully tempted to fire it away wildly.

To football fans, one of the most mysterious sides of the quarterback's profession is calling "automatics" (they're also known as "audibles" or "checkoffs"). Really, there's no mystery. When a quarterback calls an automatic, it means he's changing the play right at the line of scrimmage.

There are different ways of calling an automatic. Some teams use colors. Some use states of the union. Some use numbers (a double-digit number like 22 means look for an automatic; a number like 13 is meaningless).

On the Colts, we use colors. Let's assume that in the huddle I call a play known as 64-Pass. But when we come out over the ball, I see that the defense has changed so that 64-Pass can't possibly work. So I call an automatic. On this particular Sunday, for instance, all colors beginning with the letter B are "live"—meaning they signal an automatic is coming.

All right. I come over the center.

"Blue!" I shout. Now my team has to be alert. The next thing I say tells them what the new play will be.

"Thirty-eight!" Now everybody shifts his assignment mentally.

"Hut one . . ." And the play starts. All automatics go on the first count—"on one," we say. Occasionally, you'll see a quarterback check off twice before the ball is snapped, but that's rare. Your team can get confused if you keep switching, and there's just not enough time to get into a bind like this.

Actually, automatics aren't nearly as popular as they once were, I used to call them 65 percent of the time. Now I'm down to ten percent. There are three reasons for this decline. First, crowd noise makes it hard for everybody to hear the new signal (remember you've got to yell loud enough so your flanker can hear). Second, automatics increase the possibility of blown assignments and other mistakes. And third, most teams now prefer to solve opposing defenses by studying films the week before the game; they resort to automatics only when they must.

Playing quarterback isn't all passing and barking signals. Every good quarterback must master the mechanics of faking handoffs—and making handoffs—to his running backs. You have to execute each fake as if it were real; for instance, even if you've handed off, you should drop back and set up as if you're going to pass. It may look silly from the stands, but bear in mind that the defense is often screened off by bodies, and your deceit may make the play.

Basically, there are two kinds of fakes: the ball fake, in which you actually tuck it into the runner's belly, then pull it back; and the hand fake, which looks like a ball fake except that you yank the ball back at the last moment and carry out the fake with your empty hand. I like to hand fake because it causes fewer fumbles; there's no contact between ball and runner. It's also

important to make a little head fake after you hand off. In other words, hook the ball into the runner's belly, pull it away, then sneak a quick look back over your shoulder as if you've really given it to him. That little head fake can make a defensive back commit himself one step too far.

The list of quarterbacking techniques is almost endless. I've been a pro quarterback for 11 years, and I'm still learning. One of the most underrated techniques, one that's frequently overlooked, is the exchange between the center and the T-quarterback. It happens on every play, so you might as well get it right.

I'm right-handed, so I place my hands under center with my right hand on top, fingers extended and spread comfortably. The only right-handed quarterback I know who kept his left hand on top was Otto Graham. I either adopt a balanced stance with my feet, or a toe-to-heel stance (one foot a little behind the other). With my right hand, I nudge the center in the crotch so he knows I'm ready. He doesn't hand the ball to you point up; he feeds it to you on an angle, in a good passing position. Your left, or bottom, hand serves as a stopper, so you won't drop the ball.

By now I'm sure you realize how difficult and challenging it is to be a quarterback. Sometimes, however, I think fans make us out to be more than we are. We're not flesh-and-blood computers who can sort out hundreds of plays in 25 seconds, and generally choose the right one. It's true that there are about 300 plays in the Colt playbook, and I have to know them all thoroughly. But I never take all 300 into any one game. The coaches pick what we call a "short list" — usually 25 running plays, 15 passes, a few short-yardage plays and our two-minute series (when we're racing the clock late in a game).

I've tried to explain the various quarterbacking problems, but I want to warn young players against trying to copy me, or Bart Starr, or Joe Namath — or any pro. We have a lot more strength and experience. Sure, watch us. Study us. Try to pick up our good points and avoid our weaknesses (we all have them). But don't try to be "just like Johnny Unitas." Everybody is different. Develop your own style, a comfortable style. Don't get too tricky too fast. And whatever you do, LISTEN TO YOUR COACH.

It will help to do a lot of passing. I did, when I was a kid. I still play a little game in practice. I try to hit different parts of a receiver's body—right hand, left shoulder, right eye, helmet—putting more and more distance into my throws. I never aim below the waist, because they you fall into a bad habit, an interception habit. And don't worry about being a child prodigy. I don't believe in midget football, as a father or a quarterback. I think the boys are too young to learn much. High school is time enough to learn organized football. My son, John Unitas, Jr., is ten, and he has yet to play organized ball. He's got plenty of time.

Wouldn't it be funny if a young fellow reading this story came on to became a great quarterback — with the Baltimore Colts? Stranger things have happened. In that case, I hope you'll let an old geezer named Unitas earn a living. Heck, I taught you almost all I know!   ∎

OUT ON A LIMB...

After years of being chicken, Boys' Life has decided to put its reputation on the line with **predictions** of things to come in the 1968 major league **baseball season**.

Save our predictions til the end of the season, and check us out. If we're right, let's hear those cheers. If we're wrong, *wait til next year!*

AMERICAN LEAGUE

MVP AND HOME-RUN LEADER... *HARMON KILLEBREW.*
The "Killer" should hit about **47**, finishing ahead of his biggest rivals, Frank Robinson and Carl Yastrzemski. A strong year at bat, with the Twins winning the pennant, should mark him as *most valuable player.*

RBI LEADER... *FRANK ROBINSON.*
Frank should come back strong after a season in which an eye injury kept him out of action for a-while, and his Orioles weren't as convincing as they were the year before. *He should drive in 125 runs.* Pressing Frank will be Killebrew, Yastrzemski and Al Kaline.

BA LEADER... *TONY OLIVA.*
We expect Tony to bounce back from what, for him, was an off year. Figure him to hit about **.332**, with Yastrzemski and Frank Robinson close on his heels.

TOP PITCHER... *JOEL HORLEN.*
Joel should come through with the **best won-lost percentage—23-8**—although he'll have tough competition from two Twins: Dean Chance and Jim Kaat. Jim Lonborg's injury makes him a question mark.

TOP TEAM... *MINNESOTA TWINS.*
Another tight race. Boston, Detroit, Chicago and the Angels (almost, but not quite).

NATIONAL LEAGUE

HOME-RUN LEADER... *HENRY AARON.*
Hank wields the booming bat in the senior circuit. His **39 HRs** should shade Orlando Cepeda and Willie McCovey. Willie Mays could be an unexpected candidate, but we doubt it.

BA LEADER, RBI LEADER AND MVP... *ROBERTO CLEMENTE.*
It's hard to pick anyone over the Pirates' big man, even Orlando Cepeda (last year's RBI boss). Clemente should send **135** runners across the plate. Who else hits with the season-long consistency of this Pittsburgh powerhouse? His **.340** should top the likes of Henry Aaron and Ron Santo.

He's a shoo-in for **MVP**, especially if the Pirates take the pennant.

TOP PITCHER... *JIM BUNNING.*
Being with the Pirates should bring new life to the former Phillies' meal ticket. Jim should post a **23-11** record.

TOP TEAM... *PITTSBURGH.*
Despite Cards and Cubs, the Pirates in the catbird seat.

WORLD SERIES...
Pirates sink Twins in six games.

KAREEM ABDUL-JABBAR:

No list of great basketball centers is complete unless it includes the Lakers' "Big Guy."

Kareem Abdul-Jabbar soars skyward to grab the basketball banging off the backboard. He whirls and snaps it to his Los Angeles teammate, Lucius Allen. As Allen dribbles upcourt, Kareem lopes past him to a spot 10 feet away from the Laker basket, and begins the bump-and-shove battle for scoring position. The Lakers pass the ball around swiftly, looking for a chance to get it to their 7'2", 235-pound center. Three Knickerbockers form a human wall around Kareem, but he outmuscles the New York defenders and snares a looping pass from forward Cazzie Russell. Then, taking a giant step to his left, he fires a hook-shot that swishes like a rocket through the net. Laker fans roar gleefully as Kareem jabs a fist in the air. Grinning, he lopes to the other end of the court, to his job on defense. ▶

POWER IN THE PIVOT

BY LOUIS SABIN
PHOTOGRAPHS BY FOCUS ON SPORTS

The action goes back and forth until the game ends, and Kareem Abdul-Jabbar has piled up 35 points and 24 rebounds, leading the Lakers to their fifteenth straight home victory of 1977. It's a happy group of Los Angeles players who stream into the locker room, talking about another big night for the big guy and the team's dream of winning the National Basketball Association championship.

That kind of talk hasn't been heard in Los Angeles for a long time. It started in 1975 with The Trade that shook basketball, the one that brought Kareem to the Lakers in a swap that sent four top players to the Milwaukee Bucks. And sure enough, that year the huge pivot man scored, rebounded, blocked shots—did all the super things that have made him an all-league All-Star every year of his pro career. But the team wasn't strong enough to help him mount a challenge for the NBA title.

"Wait till next season," one of the Lakers promised. "The big guy's going to make winners of us in '77." And as L.A. flew higher and higher in 1977, Kareem's spirits rose, too. "I'm happy again," he said. "Winning makes me happy." (The Lakers won their division title last year, but fell to the Portland Trailblazers in the semifinals of the NBA playoffs, despite Kareem's 30 points per game average.)

Winning and the superstar nicknamed "The Big A," have always gone together. Just how much he hates to lose was clear back in his days as a schoolboy All-American playing for Power Memorial High School. When his basketball team's winning streak was broken after 71 games, he actually broke down in tears. He blamed himself, even though his coach and teammates pointed out that he had made the winning streak possible, and that the other team had almost buried him with defenders throughout the game. But the teenager just slumped on his bench, crying and repeating, "I should have done better."

Doing better, playing to the peak of his ability—that was the goal of Lewis Alcindor (he changed his name to Kareem Abdul-Jabbar, for religious reasons, in 1972) as he grew up in New York City. He was outstanding at track,

KAREEM ABDUL-JABBAR

baseball, football, and swimming, but his height and physical gifts made him the greatest schoolboy basketball player in the country. What's more, his intelligence made him a standout in the classroom. That was important, because his parents wanted him to give at least as much time to books as to basketball.

"The first choice was education," his father said years later. "We were determined to bring Lewis up properly and to give him proper goals. We are proud of his basketball talents, but we are just as proud of his college degree."

At Power Memorial High, Lew proved that bookwork paid off in As, and that after-class basketball paid off in high marks on the court. At first the seven-foot teenager had a hard time handling his height problems. For a while he was gawky and clumsy but then, he remembers, "By the time I was a sophomore, I was beginning to learn how to use my size. And when other teams ganged up on me, I learned how to pass off."

He learned a lot more than that, and by the time he graduated from Power, he had boosted his team to three straight city championships. More than 250 colleges wanted him. He chose the University of California at Los Angeles (UCLA) because, "I felt it would be good for me to travel, to see how people lived in another part of the country."

Also, Coach John Wooden's basketball teams were the finest. While Lew was a high-school senior, UCLA was winning the national championship. The next year, although they did not repeat as national champions, the Bruins had a top team again. However, the varsity lost one game not on their regular schedule, to UCLA's own junior varsity, led by a freshman named Lew Alcindor.

With that kind of center about to move into the UCLA pivot, the National Collegiate Athletic Association tried to even things up for the rest of the nation's college teams. They introduced what was soon called "The Anti-Alcindor Rule." It made dunking the ball illegal—but it didn't stop the young superstar from pouring in his points. In three years of varsity play, Lew was the king of collegiate basketball. UCLA took three straight NCAA

titles, racking up a fantastic won-lost record of 88-2. Naturally, each year Lew was named the NCAA tournament's Most Valuable Player and was chosen Player of the Year. He played on three All-American College teams.

Completing UCLA as a history major with excellent grades, he also boasted a 26.4 three-year scoring average, an awesome reputation for rebounding and shot-blocking, and secured a big-money contract to play for the Milwaukee Bucks of the NBA.

Going head-to-head with supercenters like Wilt Chamberlain, Lew quickly showed he belonged. He averaged 28.8 points and 14.5 rebounds a game, and was voted Rookie of the Year.

"I was worried at first," he said, "that I wouldn't be strong enough to last through that long season. But I used weights to build up my strength. Bill Russell was skinny, yet he led the Boston Celtics to 9 titles in 11 years. I decided if he could do it, so could I."

The Big A's 1969-70 rookie season was just a warm-up for the year to come. Spearheading the Bucks to a record 66 wins against only 16 losses, he powered Milwaukee all the way to the NBA championship in 1971. The league's MVP that year, he won that honor again in 1972, in 1974, and in 1976.

Yet despite his heroic efforts, Milwaukee wasn't able to repeat as champions. Then, in 1975, the club suffered its greatest loss—it agreed to his request to be traded either to New York (his hometown) or Los Angeles (his college town). The L.A. Lakers offered the best deal, and their success last year tells just how smart a deal they made.

Is it super scoring that makes Abdul-Jabbar so valuable? Yes, especially since his 30-point career average ranks him second only to Wilt Chamberlain on the all-time list. Is it super rebounding? Yes, again. Kareem's eight-season mark of 15.3 caroms a contest put him with the all-time best in that department. But it's also his unselfish dedication to defense and team play that have made him, along with Chamberlain and Russell, one of the greatest centers in the game. As far as Bill Russell is concerned, "Kareem Abdul-Jabbar will be remembered as the greatest center of all." ♣

From his parents' "coaching," Kareem learned to place education first and became a standout in the classroom.

Boys are interested in the world around them and in the future. With this in mind, *Boys' Life* publishes stories to help them understand both the events of the day and whatever tomorrow may hold. Although it has never been a magazine full of breaking news, *Boys' Life* publishes articles that distill the meaning of events in a way that appeals to boys.

The merit badge program of the Boy Scouts of America, with more than 120 subjects on offer, is a great tool for boys to explore their interests in a wide variety of fields. In fact, it leads many boys to their future careers and steers them toward lifelong ambitions. The magazine helps point the way with articles showing where opportunities may lie. From the telephone line connecting coast to coast, to space exploration, the pages of *Boys' Life* have filled the imaginations of generations of American boys.

Melville Bell Grosvenor, later president of the National Geographic Society, was only 13 years old when he became the first boy to speak on the telephone in a call from New York to San Francisco in 1915. His story was featured in the magazine, along with the statistics of stringing tons of wire across the continent to make communication possible. The topic of space exploration is a readers' favorite in articles as well as fiction. In 1972, Isaac Asimov, who wrote material for both genres in the magazine, was mostly accurate in his assessment of the future of the space program (space station,

space shuttle, satellites exploring planets, and comets). But a base on the moon is still somewhere in the future.

Covering current events, the magazine explained how Scouts proved their worth at the inauguration of President Woodrow Wilson in 1913, helping the police to keep order during the inaugural parade and giving first aid to onlookers who were injured in the crush of people. Scouts have served at every presidential inauguration since. When the United States entered the First World War in 1917, a call went forth in *Boys' Life* for Scouts to help with the war effort. Scouts responded by planting gardens and selling more than $200 million worth of Liberty Bonds and war savings stamps. After the devastation of the atomic bombs dropped on Hiroshima and Nagasaki in 1945, the magazine published an article on how and why the bombs worked—and ended with an appeal for the abolition of war.

In 1972, Pulitzer Prize–winning journalist Harrison Salisbury wrote an article about Russian youth for the magazine. He compared Russian schools to American schools, and the Communist youth programs to the Scouting program, citing the similarities and the enormous difference—indoctrination in Communist goals, ideals, and objectives. The article, in keeping with American ideals of freedom, concluded with the hope that signs of dissent among Russian youth would bring about a change to the totalitarian regime.

THE COMING DECADES IN SPACE

By ISAAC ASIMOV

Illustrated by ROBERT McCALL

In 1957, mankind launched its first satellite into space. That satellite, unmanned and small, circled Earth, barely skimming the main body of the atmosphere. In 1969, a large, three-man vessel traveled safely to the moon, 237,000 miles from Earth. There, it deposited the first human beings on the soil of an alien world, then brought them safely back.

So much for what can be done in a dozen years. What will we do in the next two and a half dozen?

Reaching the moon by three-man vessels in one long bound from Earth is like casting a thin thread across space. The main effort, in the coming decades, will be to strengthen this thread; to make it a cord, a cable, and, finally, a broad highway.

Can we stand the expense of doing this?

The manned space program has cost the United States $24 billion, but it was $24 billion spent right here in the United States (not on the moon). Part of it went into the development of many materials, devices, and techniques that will have—and already do have—applications here on Earth. Part of it went into laying the groundwork for future advances that will be less expensive and that promise greater returns.

To make the moon landing more than a sort of glorious feat and to bring it into the realm of the commonplace, we are going to need some sort of base between Earth and moon. We will need a large manned satellite, orbiting Earth permanently at a distance from us far less than the moon. The Soviet Union has been gearing its space program toward the establishment of such a "space station," and the United States plans to have its first space station in orbit in 1973. The American space station will be powered, in part, by solar batteries. It has been planned to include a large reflecting telescope.

The telescope indicates the most immediate use of the space station. It will be an observation post. Though the station may be just a few hundred miles up from Earth's surface, in a certain way it will be millions of miles closer to the rest of the universe than we are down here.

Why? Because it will be outside the atmosphere.

Our atmosphere is a crowded mass of molecules that lets hardly anything through. Most of the visible light gets through and most of a band of short-wave radio radiation called microwaves. Everything else is absorbed. What's more, the water vapor in the atmosphere forms mist, fog, and clouds that frequently cut off the visible light, too.

There are some areas in deserts and on plateaus where the air is clearer. But even there, temperature differences from one part of the atmosphere to another bend light beams, make stars apparently shift position, blur planet-surfaces. And even in the most isolated spots, the dust in the air is increasing, and distant light from man-made cities grows brighter. It becomes harder to see.

Every year the atmosphere becomes harder to look through, and a space station will take us beyond all that. Since the vacuum of space is absolutely clear, a telescope with no air between itself and the stars is an astronomer's dream come true.

One thing we would see most clearly from a space station (and something we cannot see at all from Earth's surface) is a large swath of Earth taken as a whole.

Earth can be mapped from space with an instant accuracy available by no other means, and the map always could be kept up to date. It would be an extraordinary map—one that would show details no other map could. It would show the character of the ground, and from small changes we could deduce the location of mineral and oil deposits. We could study geologic faults more precisely and perhaps learn to predict landslides and earthquakes. We could follow the changing patterns of vegetation, study the progress of plant diseases, make farming more efficient.

It may be only by studies from space stations that we will learn enough about the earth as a whole to make real progress in studying ecology; in studying the worldwide relationship of life-forms to each other and to the environment.

Nor is it only Earth that can tell us about Earth. From a space station, we can study the sun as it has never been studied. We can study *all* its radiation in detail and in full, and not just the radiation that gets through our thick and dusty atmosphere.

We will understand better the amount and kind of energy that Earth receives, and the amount and kind it radiates from different portions of its surface. We will understand its weather systems better and learn, perhaps, how to introduce controls that will make the environment better for man and for life generally.

We will understand better the cosmic-ray particles and the neutrinos that fill all of space, and learn what they can tell us of the inner workings of stars and the evolution of galaxies. We may discover new particles that will reveal mysteries now undreamed of. But—will new facts about these particles be useful?

Certainly! Knowledge is *always* useful; if not at once, then some day. Knowledge is all one piece. No matter where we increase the knowledge; no matter what we learn about the universe; no matter how far-off and unimportant it all seems, it could have ways of helping us right here on Earth.

For instance, what could seem more unimportant to the average human being than the fact that quadrillions of miles away from us there are dust clouds in space?

Well, by studying the kind of light emitted from the dust clouds and the kind of light they absorb, astronomers have been able to deduce what kind of atoms exist there. Mostly, they are hydrogen and helium atoms, but with some oxygen, carbon, and nitrogen atoms thrown in. These atoms are spread out so thinly that it didn't seem likely that very many would just happen to collide and stick together.

But then, in the 1960's, microwaves were studied instead of just light waves. That made more delicate decisions possible about any atom-combinations that could exist there. In 1963, oxygen-hydrogen combinations were detected. Then, beginning in late 1968, more and more atom-combinations were found: two, three, four, even six atoms in combination have been located in those clouds. To detect them requires the most delicate work with radio-telescopes.

In space, though, away from interference by Earth's man-made radio waves, →

Man continues the greatest adventure of all—exploring the universe.

LET'S fly one-third of the distance around the world, non-stop! Sounds fantastic, doesn't it? Before the B-19, built by Douglas Aircraft Company, had its successful maiden flight, such a proposal would have been scoffed at as impossible. But this 82 ton flying battleship, with its 11,000 gallon supply of gasoline, has a range of 7750 miles. It actually can fly non-stop from Santa Monica, Calif., to Oslo, Norway, and return to New York City for a landing.

The B-19 can carry an 18 ton bomb load, bigger than any three other planes, or transport a fully equipped troop of 125 soldiers. Even the famous *Flying Fortress* bombers are Lilliputian in comparison with this massive giant, whose wing spread (212') would cover two-thirds the length of a football field.

Although the U. S. Army Air Corps has officially accepted the B-19, tests will continue, for this plane is essentially an experiment which will serve as a guide in the design of huge cargo and troop transport planes yet to come; planes that will insure our hemisphere defense.

The B-19's three bladed propellers measure 17'1" in diameter; weigh 686 lbs.

The tail assembly stands 42'9" high and contains the rear gunner's compartment which is heavily fortified.

The radio system has four transmitters and as much equipment as a large broadcasting station.

The main wheels of the B-19 measure 11' in diameter; weigh 4000 lbs. each. The giant tires, of 28 ply, require 112 lbs. of air to inflate.

The pilot, his assistant, the commander, flight engineer, navigator, and radio operator ride on the "bridge deck"; the chief mechanic and three helpers complete the "crew."

The giant size of the B-19 is evident when it is compared with twin motored DC-3 transports (built by Douglas Aircraft Co.) and used by most commercial airlines.

Every part of the B-19, from nose to tail (132'), and from one landing light to another, can be reached by a series of companionways and hatches, allowing for repairs even when in flight.

For six years, from first blue print to first flight, the B-19 was known as Project D at the Douglas plant, and into its construction went 2,000,000 man hours of labor and $3,000,000.

RUSSIAN YOUTH

By HARRISON E. SALISBURY

A DISTINGUISHED newspaperman, Harrison E. Salisbury won the Pulitzer prize for international reporting in 1955 for articles on the Soviet Union. He has toured Siberia and Central Asia, visiting areas usually sealed off from the outside world. The author of five books on the Soviet Union, his most recent is A New Russia? *Mr. Salisbury was born in Minnesota, where he was an Eagle Scout who liked to hike and camp.*

JUST AHEAD AS I walked down Gorky Street, Moscow's Fifth Avenue, one mild winter day were two teen-agers. Both wore identical gray Karakul hats and almost identical heavy wool coats with fur collars.

The boys were arguing. "There's no doubt about it," one of them said firmly. "The Chevrolet is clearly superior to the Ford. For one thing it has more horsepower."

His friend gave him a superior glance. "That's your opinion. Everyone knows the Ford is technically better. And it's faster as well."

"That may be," the first boy said. "But in my view the most advanced technology is found in the Kree-sler." He went on to describe a Chrysler limousine that he had seen outside the Metropole Hotel.

The boys walked down the street, happily chatting, spattering their conversation with the names of American cars (often mispronounced) and obviously trying to impress each other with their knowledge.

The boys were bright, healthy, well-fed and well looked-after. But for the difference in clothing and language they would have fitted into any American high-school class. Russian children start school at the age of seven, instead of six, as we do. I guessed that this pair was in eighth or ninth grade.

On another day not long after, I was walking through a narrow side street about a block off Gorky Street. In the gathering winter twilight I saw a dozen teen-agers straggling down a small hill. Suddenly a fight broke out. For a moment fists flew, and then I caugh the flash of a knife in an upraised hand—and a boy fell to the ground. In a twinkling the others fled.

The fallen youngster was the victim of a gang of what the Russians call *"gooligani."* The word comes from our term, "hooligan." In Russia's Cyrillic alphabet there is no letter "h"—so hooligan in transliteration becomes googligan. But it means much the same thing—a young roughneck or, as we might say, a teenage gangster.

Quite often in the long years I have spent as a correspondent in Russia, I have visited Soviet schools. Usually the principal acts as my guide. Each time we enter a classroom, the pupils spring to attention. They remain standing, with arms rigid at their sides and eyes straight forward, until given the order to be seated. When we leave the room, they rise again and remain standing until the door closes behind us. There are not many American schools where you will see the kind of rigid discipline enforced by the Soviet schools.

Each Russian schoolgirl wears a brown school dress with a white pinafore apron. She does her hair in pigtails, just like each of her neighbors. The boys wear gray school uniforms with brass-buckled belts and round-visored caps. Both boys and girls wear red Pioneer kerchiefs, almost identical with neckerchiefs that Boy Scouts wear. *But the Pioneers are not Scouts. They were founded by Lenin as a kind of grade-school auxiliary of the Communist Party.*

Which of these pictures is typical of Ivan? Is he a bright, industrious youngster with an inquiring mind? Is he a Soviet-style juvenile delinquent? Or is he nothing more than a robot, the product of Communist indoctrination and military discipline? The truth is that there are all kinds of Ivans. And this may be the most important thing of all, because for the past 45 years the Communist regime has been trying to "change the nature of man," to produce a new kind of Soviet individual.

The fact that, after all these years, after all the efforts at indoctrinization, discipline, propaganda and specialized training, Russian youngsters are still growing up pretty much the way they do in the United States—some good, some bad, some in-between—is testimony to the vitality of the human character. It is a testament to the ability of human beings to resist.

Russian young people are like young people everywhere. If something is forbidden, it is likely to acquire a special attraction. For years the Communist Party has tried to shield them from Western influences. They banned American music. What happened? Russian youngsters listened in to rock 'n' roll on the short-wave radio. They got X-ray plates from hospital laboratories and secretly cut their own records. These were bootlegged in the black market at $10 apiece. In the last two or three years the Soviet authorities have thrown up their hands. The ban on jazz has been lifted.

This may seem like a small matter. But in a totalitarian state—one which seeks to direct every aspect of human life—such things are important. In the worst days of Stalin, musicians actually were exiled to Siberian labor camps just because they played a hot trumpet.

Today in Moscow, youngsters ask a foreigner: "Excuse me, but do you know how to do the twist?" When asked how they heard about the twist, they reply that they read an article in the Party newspaper, attacking the dance as a "decadent Western invention."

"It sounded very interesting," the young Russians say.

For years the Party crusaded among young people against foreign fads, styles, clothes, even foreign words. What was called "bowing down to Western culture" was one of the worst of crimes. They even tried to make res-

A Boy Talks Across the Continent

Melville Bell Grosvenor, Age 13, Telephones from New York to San Francisco.

(1) Famous Men Who First Talked from New York to San Francisco.

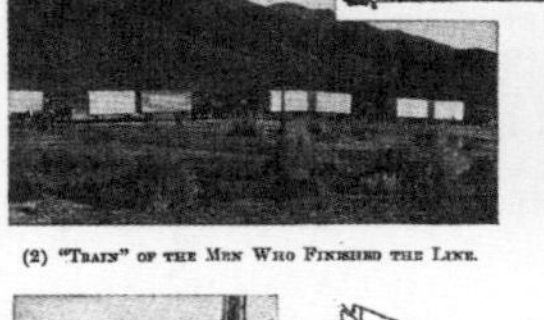

(2) "Train" of the Men Who Finished the Line.

(3) Hauling Poles in the Sage-Brush Country.

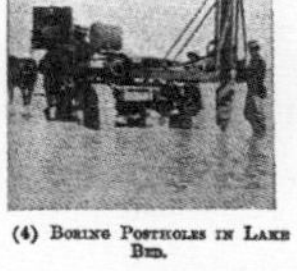

(4) Boring Postholes in Lake Bed.

(5) Map Showing Route of the Atlantic-to-Pacific Telephone Line.

(6) Setting a Pole in a Salt Sink.

THE first boy to telephone across the continent is Melville Bell Grosvenor, a thirteen-year-old lad of Washington, D. C. Melville is a grandson of Alexander Graham Bell, the inventor of telephony, and he was one of the guests of honor at the formal opening of the transcontinental telephone line on January 25.

Along with Mayor Mitchel of New York, "Grandfather" Bell and other distinguished guests at this opening ceremony, Melville conversed with distinguished men at the other end of the line in San Francisco, 3,400 miles away.

Of course every boy in the country has heard of this wonderful new telephone line connecting San Francisco with New York, Philadelphia, Boston and other eastern cities, and has felt a thrill of pride knowing that this remarkable achievement has been made possible through the genius and persistence of American inventors and electrical engineers. But there are some very interesting things connected with this new telephone achievement of the American Telephone and Telegraph Company which most boys probably have not heard about.

The Pictures

(1) *Beginning at the left end, those in the historic group at the top are: Mr. T. T. McCarty, Chief Engineer, American Telephone and Telegraph Company; Mr. George McAneny, President, Board of Aldermen, New York City; Mr. U. N. Bethell, Senior Vice-President, American Telephone and Telegraph Company; Dr. Bell, the inventor; Mayor Mitchel, of New York City; Mr. C. E. Yost, of Nebraska, and Mr. W. A. Prendergast, Comptroller, City of New York.*

(2) *In Nevada the construction crews, far from railroads, moved by these trains in finishing their great work.*

(3) *Carting poles in the roadless deserts was no easy job, as this picture shows.*

(4) *In Humboldt Lake, Nev., two miles of poles (80 in number) were set in water from 18 inches to 3 feet deep; the picture shows the machine used to bore the holes.*

(5) *Note the enormous distances between the largest cities on this transcontinental telephone line.*

(6) *This shows some of the difficulties of polesetting in the "wild" parts of the West.*

How the Voice Flies

Suppose a boy in New York were able to speak loud enough for his voice to carry to San Francisco. How long do you think it would take the sound to travel across the continent? Sound travels at the rate of 1,160 feet per second. The distance from New York to San Francisco is 3,400 miles. So it would take a boy's voice about four hours to travel from New York to the Golden Gate.

How, then, is it possible for your voice to be transmitted almost instantaneously over the telephone? As a matter of fact, transmission of sound by telephone is not instantaneous, although for short distances the length of time consumed is too brief to be measured. When Melville Grosvenor

PACKAGED Devastation

By CAPTAIN BURR LEYSON

If you ever wondered how and why bombs work, here is the answer

An explosion heard round the world! A single cataclysmic blow utterly devastated over four square miles of Hiroshima

NEVER in history has a nation reaped such a harvest as did the Japanese from the treacherous seeds they sowed at Pearl Harbor. Their wanton and unprovoked attack was returned with righteous wrath. Day and night American warplanes roamed the skies over Japan, blasted apart the enemy's factories, oil plants, shipping, airports, stores of munitions—all the myriad materials essential to the support of his war effort. The tempo of the air attack was constantly increased yet the full might of the world's greatest air power, the United States, was never brought to bear against the Japanese. It was not necessary. Into the scene came a weapon of such devastating power that it was at once apparent even to the fanatical Japanese that their dreams of conquest were ended and they faced either destruction or surrender. This weapon was the atomic bomb.

Wrapped in deepest secrecy, the details of the atomic bomb are withheld. Yet much can be revealed about it. It follows closely the same destructive pattern of the demolition bomb. By examining the manner in which the demolition bomb creates its effect the tremendous destructive power of the atomic bomb can be realized.

The demolition bomb, ranging in weight from a few hundreds of pounds to as much as 22,000 pounds, is a long heavy steel cylinder, rounded at the nose and brought to a point at the rear so that it presents a roughly streamlined shape. This facilitates its passage through the air, making it speedier in its fall and materially adding to its destructive effect, for its higher speed gives it a greater penetration into the target. Attached to the rear of the bomb are four flat steel vanes which act much in the same manner as the keel of a boat. They hold it to a straight course.

The mechanism of the demolition bomb is very simple. Set in the nose is a fuse which is actuated by impact with the target. To insure that the bomb is exploded a second fuse is set in the rear section. Both fuses can be adjusted to detonate the bomb either upon impact or a considerable time afterwards.

These fuses set in motion a train of explosions. First they detonate a small quantity of very sensitive high explosive. This fires a charge of several pounds of high explosive which is called a "booster" charge. Because the main charge of explosive in the bomb requires a very high degree of heat or a severe blow to set it off, the booster must be employed.

Were the main charge of explosive such that it would be detonated by the impact of the bomb with the target it would not be possible to control the time of the explosion. Where factories and other enemy installations are protected by armor or heavy concrete it is necessary for the bomb to penetrate these protective coverings and explode within for the best effects.

THE action of the bomb occurs with incredible speed but scientists have been able to calculate each cycle of its action to a nicety. Leaving the average bomber, the bomb will have a forward speed of 250 to 350 miles an hour. This speed, given the bomb by the speed of the plane dropping it, causes the bomb to continue forward for a considerable distance. For instance, if a bomber flying at 20,000 feet with a speed of 300 miles an hour releases a 2,000 pound bomb, the bomb will travel forward some 15,000 feet or nearly three miles before it strikes the earth. Its downward path is a long curve which grows sharper as it approaches the target. Here the bomb falls almost vertically.

There is nothing slow about this descent. Beginning at 300 miles an hour, the speed is augmented by gravity until the bomb attains a maximum velocity of about 1,000 feet a second or 720 miles an hour. As this speed builds up, so does the force of its impact with the target. The blow struck by a 2,000 pounder traveling at 1,000 feet a second staggers the imagination. It can be calculated with accuracy through the use of a simple formula.

If we multiply the weight of the bomb in pounds (2000) by the square of its velocity in feet per second (1000) and divide the product by twice the acceleration of gravity (32) it will give us the force of the blow struck by the bomb. Thus

$$\frac{(2000 \times 1000 \text{ squared})}{(2 \times 32)} = 31,250,000 \text{ ft. lbs.}$$

(This is a handy formula. You can use it to determine the striking force of any moving object—your body in a dive into the water, the blow the bullet strikes when fired from a .22, even an automobile bumping into an obstacle. If you want to be very accurate the exact figure for the acceleration of gravity is 32.1739 feet per second.)

To understand better the tremendous force of this blow—if we could harness its power it would lift an average automobile weighing 3,000 pounds over 10,417 feet into the air in one second! Or a ton of coal to a height of 15,625 feet!

ILLUSTRATED BY SEYMOUR THOMPSON

Packaged Devastation

But this is the least of the huge forces generated by the bomb. Watch what happens as the fuses set off the chain of events that results in the explosion of the bomb!

PACKED in the steel walls of the bomb are many cubic feet of high explosive, more powerful than the well known TNT. As the chain of explosions reaches the booster charge and it detonates this main charge events occur with unbelievable speed. In about 1/20,000 of a second every cubic foot of solid high explosive in the main charge changes into about 1,000 cubic feet of gases.

This huge volume of gases, a thousand times greater than the original volume of the solid contents of the bomb, exerts a stupendous pressure on the steel walls. The heat of the explosion further increases this pressure, for it causes the gases to expand into even greater volume. The steel walls swell out like a toy balloon being inflated. Finally, when the bomb is expanded to about one and one-half times its original diameter the steel can no longer withstand the pressure. The walls burst and disintegrate into thousands of jagged pieces. The pent-up gases rush out with a speed of over 7,000 feet a second—nearly 80 miles a minute!

At this speed and at the pressure they have been under inside the bomb —estimated at some 700,000 pounds to the square inch—the gases strike the surroundings. Everything in the immediate area is destroyed. But the gases rapidly cool, expand, and lose their speed. Not so the effects of their initial rush from the bomb.

The first rush of the gases from the disrupted casing of the bomb at a speed of 7,000 feet a second—4,800 miles an hour—forces back vast quantities of air around the point of the explosion. So rapid and so strong is this compression of the surrounding air that a powerful compression wave is set up in the air, a "shock" wave that travels outwards in all directions and covers a wide area like the effect of a stone dropped into water. While data on the strength of the shock wave set up by the larger and newer bombs are not yet released by the military authorities, figures for one of the smaller bombs, the 500 pounder, are available.

Suppose that we are standing 100 feet from the point where one of these bombs strikes and explodes. The shock wave set up by the explosion will travel outward at about 5,000 feet a second.

It will strike us with a force of approximately 300 pounds to the square foot. Presuming that we present seven square feet of surface as we stand erect this means that in 1/5000 of a second our body will be struck with a total force of 2,100 pounds. There is no necessity of elaborating on what would happen to us under those circumstances!

It is this shock wave that creates so much damage to buildings and other installations. With it is another wave, the product of the first. This second wave is the one that caused so much speculation when the German air forces were making their "blitz" on England.

People sufficiently far away from the explosion of the bomb to escape serious injury reported that they were knocked flat by the shock wave and then, even as they fell, their breath was "sucked from their lungs." Likewise walls of buildings and windows were observed to fall towards the point of the explosion rather than away from it as was to be expected.

The explanation proved simple. It lies in Newton's third law governing bodies: For every action there is an equal and opposite reaction. In other words, this shock wave, a wave of compression, had to be followed by a wave of opposite force, a wave of rarefaction or "suction". This is termed usually a wave of negative pressure to differentiate from the compression or positive pressure wave.

At a distance of 100 feet from the explosion of a 500 pounder our body would be subjected to a "suction" from this wave of 115 pounds to the square foot or a total of 805 pounds, with seven square feet frontal area. In other words, if we escaped the shock wave by some miracle and it didn't knock us flat the following suction wave would pull us forward flat on our face.

But the forces so far generated by the bomb are not all it sets in motion. Its impact with the earth and the shock of the subsequent explosion causes a second shock wave to be formed. This is in the earth itself and its action is that of a local but very severe earthquake. This wave travels through the earth and shatters foundations of buildings, breaks water and gas mains, disrupts sewers, shakes and weakens buildings, playing general havoc with the surroundings. So great is the force of this wave when the larger bombs are employed—4,000, 8,000, 22,000 pounders—that persons who have thrown themselves flat on the earth to avoid injury have had their lungs collapsed and sometimes even bones broken.

"This is what I get for keeping my nest so near a glider school!"

The remaining destructive force of the bomb is in its fragments, the thousands of jagged pieces of metal sent hurtling through the air at a speed of some 5,000 feet a second with the explosion and bursting of the bomb casing. Traveling about 3,000 miles an hour, their effect is deadly. A fragment weighing but one-half an ounce, less than the weight of the average letter, has been found driven over three inches into solid oak. In the 2,000 pound bomb these fragments, weighing from a fraction of an ounce to several pounds, are deadly as far away as 1,200 feet from the point where the bomb explodes.

TREMENDOUS as are the effects of the demolition bomb, its devastation is dwarfed into insignificance by the atomic bomb. Used only twice, this bomb utterly wrecked two great Japanese war centers. With but an estimated eleven to fourteen pounds of the material producing the atomic explosion these missiles developed the destructive effect of over 20,000 tons of TNT. They exceeded the havoc that would be wrought in such war centers if 2,000 of the huge 22,000 pound "earthquake" bombs were dropped at one time.

The exact details of how these atomic bombs function are a strict military secret, for in the hands of unscrupulous powers such as the Axis nations their use well might threaten an end to our present civilization. However, only the "modus operandi" is secret. The material from which they are made and the theory of their operation are known facts.

All matter—everything about us, even our bodies—is composed of ultra-microscopic particles known as atoms. These in turn are composed of still more minute particles. Their core is formed by a proton, a particle charged with positive electricity, or a neutron, a particle having no electrical charge. Around this central core, traveling at incredible speeds, are other particles termed electrons. These hold to an orbit somewhat in the same manner as the moon swings around the earth and they are charged with negative electricity.

While much is known about these ultra-minute particles a great deal still remains to be discovered or revealed if it has been found during the research on the atomic bomb. We know that tremendous power is packed in the atom, power that is far beyond anything we can comprehend as a source at the present. So far we have utilized but a fraction of one percent of this power and it is sufficient to make the atomic bomb the most powerful destructive

agent ever known to man. Illustrative of the terrific possibilities for power is the fact that for every fifty electron volts of energy we use to split the uranium atom we release over 200,000,000 electron volts when the division is made. For every electron volt we gain 4,000,000 electron volts of power.

To split the atom, that is, break up the formation of the central core with its clustered electrons whirling around it we use a device called a cyclotron. Atoms of hydrogen are placed in a vacuum and then the container set in the cyclotron, which is a complicated electrical device having coils that set up a very strong and whirling electro-magnetic field. This field causes the atoms of hydrogen to increase their speed until they are traveling at thousands of miles a second. The vastly augmented speed adds to their electrical energy until at the speed attained in the cyclotron the hydrogen atoms have an energy of some 5,000,000 volts. When they arrive at this stage they are directed against a particle of uranium.

The atom of uranium is the largest in the entire series and is the easiest to break up. As we have noted previously, for every volt of energy we use in breaking the atom the atom itself will release 5,000,000 electron volts of energy. It follows that if we can start a chain of events which will result in the disintegration of atoms an unheard of amount of energy will be released in an exceedingly short period. We have seen what happens under similar but far lesser circumstances when the solid explosive of a bomb is disintegrated. Obviously our scientists have discovered a way in which to start a chain of atomic disintegration with its concomitant release of vast amounts of energy. Further, the apparatus has been concentrated and simplified so that it can be packed within the limited confines of a bomb.

ATTEMPTS to effect this same chain of atomic disintegration or explosion were made by the Germans using as a prime mover in the chain "heavy water," that is, water containing atoms of heavy hydrogen. These atoms have a core made up of a neutron and the neutron possesses sufficient force from the rays it emanates to split the uranium atom and release its lethal energy in the form of an atomic explosion.

Until such time as the details of the bomb are released only its effects can be used to judge its force. In the experimental explosion of the first completed bomb observers who were ten miles from the explosion were thrown

flat and windows were rattled over 250 miles distant. The first used in warfare, that at Hiroshima, utterly destroyed over four square miles of that war production center. The second destroyed the munitions and naval center of Nagasaki.

THE explosion of the atomic bomb sets in motion the counterpart of the action of a demolition bomb but the effects are immeasurably greater. In addition it appears that in the atomic explosion there is a vast area covered by flame of very high heat intensity. It is not necessary to use an incendiary type of bomb to fire the wreckage caused by the atomic. Until the advent of the atomic bomb the incendiary held an important place in the reduction of war industries and other important military targets.

Our incendiary is another secret process. By adding a chemical in the form of a powder to high-test aviation gasoline we cause it to assume a jelly form. This jelly is packed into the bomb and when the bomb strikes the target the jelly is scattered far and wide by a small charge of explosive which fires and bursts the bomb. Wherever the jelly strikes it adheres and burns fiercely. It is practically impossible to quench the flame. Dropped in large containers holding up to as many as thirty or forty of these small bombs, a single raid can cover a large area for the containers are designed to fall free for a set distance and then open, hurling the small incendiaries in all directions and adding to their effect through dispersal.

The older type incendiaries generated a lot of heat, but too often the only damage was a hole in the floor. The spattering new gel-gas affects a wider area.

It is a far cry from the crude bombs first dropped by hand in World War One to those of the present. Those first bombs were empty cans filled with a collection of scrap iron and explosive, fired by a fuse which the bomber lit before hurling the missile overboard. So-called "visionaries" of that time who predicted that aerial bombing would become a vital factor in the winning or losing of a war were laughed at. Now their dreams have come true and with it one of their greatest hopes. This was that aerial bombing might become so devastating and frightful that the world would at long last realize the futility of war and cooperate to abolish it. With the development of the atomic bomb it seems that this era is at hand.

CAREERS IN THE STEEL IN-
DUSTRY by Captain Burr W. Leyson, who wrote the preceding article, describes opportunities for employment as skilled workers without technical training, and for specialized careers requiring formal technical training. The importance of steel, its processing, and its uses are presented. An appendix lists representative earnings of workers and executives in the industry. If you are interested in metals and chemistry or feel you have an aptitude for skilled or technical work in industry you'll find this book informative and helpful. Ask your librarian. The book is published by E. P. Dutton & Co., N. Y., at $2.50.

"Remember it'll cost you five cents for every minute you're up there"

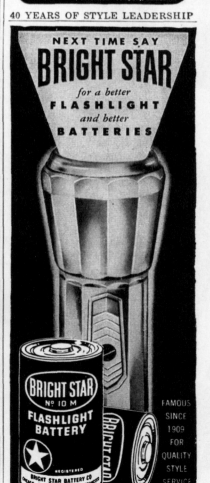

The World's Biggest Bomber!

LET'S fly one-third of the distance around the world, non-stop! Sounds fantastic, doesn't it? Before the B-19, built by Douglas Aircraft Company, had its successful maiden flight, such a proposal would have been scoffed at as impossible. But this 82 ton flying battleship, with its 11,000 gallon supply of gasoline, has a range of 7750 miles. It actually can fly non-stop from Santa Monica, Calif., to Oslo, Norway, and return to New York City for a landing.

The B-19 can carry an 18 ton bomb load, bigger than any three other planes, or transport a fully equipped troop of 125 soldiers. Even the famous Flying Fortress bombers are Lilliputian in comparison with this massive giant, whose wing spread (212') would cover two-thirds the length of a football field.

Although the U. S. Army Air Corps has officially accepted the B-19, tests will continue, for this plane is essentially an experiment which will serve as a guide in the design of huge cargo and troop transport planes yet to come; planes that will insure our hemisphere defense.

The radio system has four transmitters and as much equipment as a large broadcasting station.

The B-19's three bladed propellers measure 17'1" in diameter; weigh 696 lbs.

The tail assembly stands 42'9" high and contains the rear gunner's compartment which is heavily fortified.

The main wheels of the B-19 measure 11' in diameter; weigh 4000 lbs. each. The giant tires, of 28 ply, require 112 lbs. of air to inflate.

The pilot, his assistant, the commander, flight engineer, navigator, and radio operator ride on the "bridge deck"; the chief mechanic and three helpers complete the "crew."

The giant size of the B-19 is evident when it is compared with twin motored DC-3 transports (built by Douglas Aircraft Co.) and used by most commercial airlines.

Every part of the B-19, from nose to tail (132'), and from one landing light to another, can be reached by a series of companionways and hatches, allowing for repairs even when in flight.

For six years, from first blue print to first flight, the B-19 was known as Project D at the Douglas plant, and into its construction went 2,000,000 man hours of labor and $3,000,000.

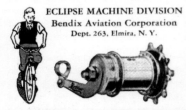
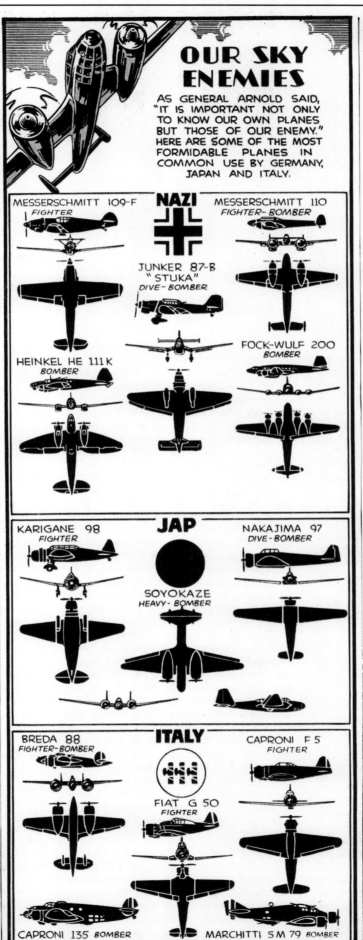

OUR SKY ENEMIES

AS GENERAL ARNOLD SAID, "IT IS IMPORTANT NOT ONLY TO KNOW OUR OWN PLANES, BUT THOSE OF OUR ENEMY." HERE ARE SOME OF THE MOST FORMIDABLE PLANES IN COMMON USE BY GERMANY, JAPAN AND ITALY.

NAZI

MESSERSCHMITT 109-F — FIGHTER
MESSERSCHMITT 110 — FIGHTER-BOMBER
JUNKER 87-B "STUKA" — DIVE-BOMBER
HEINKEL HE 111 K — BOMBER
FOCK-WULF 200 — BOMBER

JAP

KARIGANE 98 — FIGHTER
NAKAJIMA 97 — DIVE-BOMBER
SOYOKAZE — HEAVY-BOMBER

ITALY

BREDA 88 — FIGHTER-BOMBER
CAPRONI F 5 — FIGHTER
FIAT G 50 — FIGHTER
CAPRONI 135 — BOMBER
MARCHITTI 5 M 79 — BOMBER

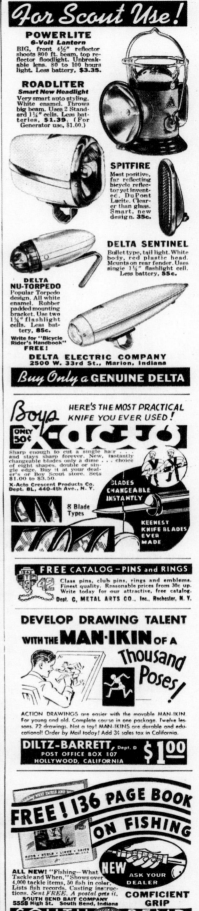

RUSSIAN YOUTH

By HARRISON E. SALISBURY

A DISTINGUISHED newspaperman, Harrison E. Salisbury won the Pulitzer prize for international reporting in 1955 for articles on the Soviet Union. He has toured Siberia and Central Asia, visiting areas usually sealed off from the outside world. The author of five books on the Soviet Union, his most recent is A New Russia? *Mr. Salisbury was born in Minnesota, where he was an Eagle Scout who liked to hike and camp.*

JUST AHEAD AS I walked down Gorky Street, Moscow's Fifth Avenue, one mild winter day were two teen-agers. Both wore identical gray Karakul hats and almost identical heavy wool coats with fur collars.

The boys were arguing. "There's no doubt about it," one of them said firmly. "The Chevrolet is clearly superior to the Ford. For one thing it has more horsepower."

His friend gave him a superior glance. "That's your opinion. Everyone knows the Ford is technically better. And it's faster as well."

"That may be," the first boy said. "But in my view the most advanced technology is found in the Kree-sler." He went on to describe a Chrysler limousine that he had seen outside the Metropole Hotel.

The boys walked down the street, happily chatting, spattering their conversation with the names of American cars (often mispronounced) and obviously trying to impress each other with their knowledge.

The boys were bright, healthy, well-fed and well looked-after. But for the difference in clothing and language they would have fitted into any American high-school class. Russian children start school at the age of seven, instead of six, as we do. I guessed that this pair was in eighth or ninth grade.

On another day not long after, I was walking through a narrow side street about a block off Gorky Street. In the gathering winter twilight I saw a dozen teen-agers straggling down a small hill. Suddenly a fight broke out. For a moment fists flew, and then I caugh the flash of a knife in an upraised hand—and a boy fell to the ground. In a twinkling the others fled.

The fallen youngster was the victim of a gang of what the Russians call *"gooligani."* The word comes from our term, "hooligan." In Russia's Cyrillic alphabet there is no letter "h" —so hooligan in transliteration becomes gooligan. But it means much the same thing—a young roughneck or, as we might say, a teenage gangster.

Quite often in the long years I have spent as a correspondent in Russia, I have visited Soviet schools. Usually the principal acts as my guide. Each time we enter a classroom, the pupils spring to attention. They remain standing, with arms rigid at their sides and eyes straight forward, until given the order to be seated. When we leave the room, they rise again and remain standing until the door closes behind us. There are not many American schools where you will see the kind of rigid discipline enforced by the Soviet schools.

Each Russian schoolgirl wears a brown school dress with a white pinafore apron. She does her hair in pigtails, just like each of her neighbors. The boys wear gray school uniforms with brass-buckled belts and round-visored caps. Both boys and girls wear red Pioneer kerchiefs, almost identical with neckerchiefs that Boy Scouts wear. *But the Pioneers are not Scouts. They were founded by Lenin as a kind of grade-school auxiliary of the Communist Party.*

Which of these pictures is typical of Ivan? Is he a bright, industrious youngster with an inquiring mind? Is he a Soviet-style juvenile delinquent? Or is he nothing more than a robot, the product of Communist indoctrination and military discipline? The truth is that there are all kinds of Ivans. And this may be the most important thing of all, because for the past 45 years the Communist regime has been trying to "change the nature of man," to produce a new kind of Soviet individual.

The fact that, after all these years, after all the efforts at indoctrinization, discipline, propaganda and specialized training, Russian youngsters are still growing up pretty much the way they do in the United States—some good, some bad, some in-between—is testimony to the vitality of the human character. It is a testament to the ability of human beings to resist.

Russian young people are like young people everywhere. If something is forbidden, it is likely to acquire a special attraction. For years the Communist Party has tried to shield them from Western influences. They banned American music. What happened? Russian youngsters listened in to rock 'n' roll on the shortwave radio. They got X-ray plates from hospital laboratories and secretly cut their own records. These were bootlegged in the black market at $10 apiece. In the last two or three years the Soviet authorities have thrown up their hands. The ban on jazz has been lifted.

This may seem like a small matter. But in a totalitarian state—one which seeks to direct every aspect of human life—such things are important. In the worst days of Stalin, musicians actually were exiled to Siberian labor camps just because they played a hot trumpet.

Today in Moscow, youngsters ask a foreigner: "Excuse me, but do you know how to do the twist?" When asked how they heard about the twist, they reply that they read an article in the Party newspaper, attacking the dance as a "decadent Western invention."

"It sounded very interesting," the young Russians say.

For years the Party crusaded among young people against foreign fads, styles, clothes, even foreign words. What was called "bowing down to Western culture" was one of the worst of crimes. They even tried to make res-

COLOR PHOTOS BY JERRY COOKE

RUSSIAN YOUTH

taurants stop serving "beefsteak" because the word was foreign!

What is the result?

Today young people in Moscow dance rock 'n' roll. The girls wear ponytails or beehive hairdos. The young men dress in conservative Madison Avenue styles or bright American-style sport shirts. They have picked up American slang. They call Gorky Street *"Brodvai"* and nickname their girl friends "Brigette," after Miss Bardot, or "Zhane," after the Jane of the Tarzan pictures.

But, of course, the life of the Russian youngster is not all Tarzan movies, rock 'n' roll and foreign slang. Ever since Sputnik flashed over the horizon in 1957, we have been hearing more and more about the Soviet schools. What are they like? Are Ivan's classes anything like yours?

The school buildings are not as fancy as some of yours. No modern decor. No pastel blackboards or "posture" desks and chairs. No single-floor buildings of gleaming glass and tile. Many Russian schools have no gyms and no auditoriums. None of them have swimming pools. Often there is no playground for youngsters to run on at recess time.

And there is no quarrel between Ivan and his parents over whether he should be allowed to have a car in high school or college. Only a handful of Russian parents own a car, and there probably isn't a single high-school boy in all of Russia who drives his own car to school. Indeed, even in remote country areas, there are very few school buses. In the city Ivan walks to school or rides a streetcar or subway. In the country he walks.

In other words, going to school in Russia is pretty much like it was in the United States about 50 years ago. The school buildings, the classrooms, the old-fashioned wooden desks and benches, the schoolmistress with her high-necked shirtwaist and pointer—all of this in Russia has a turn-of-the-century appearance to us.

But don't be deceived by the often shabby appearance of the schools. They are serious institutions, and the Russians—students, parents, teachers, the whole community, in fact—take education as a very serious matter. School starts September first and runs until about the middle of June. You go to school six days a week—no Saturday holiday. The winter and spring vacations are a little shorter than ours, and there aren't many holidays scattered through the year. No Thanksgiving, Christmas, Columbus Day or George Washington's Birthday holidays. Only November seventh—the anniversary of the Bolshevik Revolution.

In many ways the curriculum is likely to be toughter than that of many American schools. Russians get more math and physics by the time they are through high school than many of our college students who specialize in these fields have after four years in a university. They bear down heavily on languages. Every boy and girl begins to study a foreign language in fourth grade. Some special schools have been set up recently in which most of the instruction, beginning in the lower grades, is given in a particular foreign language. These schools are designed to turn out letter-perfect linguists. English is far and away the favorite language. There are more than 12,000,000 Russian youngsters studying English. Only a handful study Chinese.

Even though the schools are apt to be short on recreation facilities, they are strong on labs. It is not unusual for a high school to have physics facilities which would put some of our small colleges to shame. The same is true of chemistry and other natural sciences.

High-school youngsters have what they call "circles" or, as we would call them, hobby clubs. They may be for stamp collectors or chess players (chess is far and away the favorite Russian game). Or they may be for wireless hams, sharpshooting, dramatics, Russian poetry (poetry is very, very popular in Russia), botany or electrical engineering.

Just a few years ago 10 years of schooling was made compulsory for Russian youngsters in cities and seven in country districts. Before then it was seven years in the city and four in the country. Boys and girls go to school together, although for a few years separate schools for boys and girls were tried out.

One of Russia's big problems is persuading youngsters *not* to go to college. There isn't room for them all in the universities and higher educational centers. Besides, they are needed in the factories and on the farms. College entrance exams are made extremely stiff. So stiff, in fact, that parents use every kind of pull to get Ivan admitted. Bribery, threats, influence—anything goes. Last year a whole group of university officials and Communist Party bureaucrats were sent to jail in one provincial town because of scandals over college admissions.

To try to persuade youngsters to take up manual jobs, Russia has an extensive network of technical and trade schools. Many youngsters transfer to these schools after eighth grade. Two years of practical work in a factory or on a farm has also been introduced as a prerequisite for college admission. But this has not worked out well. Premier Khrushchev has insisted that high-school classes be geared more closely to actual life—that youngsters spend part of their time on apprentice jobs, that study be practical and not just theoretical.

The Party carries on a big propaganda campaign against boys and girls with "lily-white hands"—those who don't want to go out and help with the plowing or work on factory assembly lines.

Two organizations play a big role in propagandizing youngsters. One is the Pioneers, which is concerned with boys and girls from the age of seven to fourteen. The other is the Komsomols, or Communist Youth organization, which deals with youth from the mid-teens to the mid-twenties, or even later years. Both of these organizations are part of the Communist apparatus, designed to carry out the policy of the Party.

The program of the Pioneers is a curious blend. Some of its activities resemble those of Scouting. The fact is that there was a Scout organization in Russia before the revolution, founded on the principles of Lord Baden-Powell. It was suppressed by the Bolsheviks, and the Pioneer program was set up in its place. The red kerchief of the Pioneers, for example, was simply taken over from the Scout neckerchief.

The Pioneers have a program of camping, hiking, physical activities, hobbies and civic duties. Their motto is *"Sigda gatov,"* which

A girl takes notes as a 15-year-old boy works in lab of a Moscow secondary school.

Young Pioneers parade in the rain in Leningrad's "Park of Centuries." Millions of boys and girls— ages seven to fourteen—belong to this organization.

means "Always Ready." Or as Scouts would say, "Be Prepared." They say "On my Pioneer's honor," just as Scouts say, "On my honor."

But the purpose of the Pioneers differs greatly from that of American Scouting. The policy of the Boy Scouts of America is not dictated by a political party or by the government. The policy of Russian youth groups is dictated by the Communist Party. The major purpose of the Pioneers—and to an even greater degree, the Komsomols—is to indoctrinate youngsters in Communist goals, in Communist ideology and objectives.

The leaders of the Pioneers are usually active members of the Komsomols or teachers. The Pioneers are tied in closely with the schools. Almost every youngster belongs. If they misbehave in school, fail in their exams or get into trouble outside of school, they will be expelled or suspended from the Pioneers. Their kerchief will be taken from them, and they will be excluded from the whole program of extra curricular activities carried on by the Pioneers. It is a serious punishment.

The Komsomol movement is not as universal in membership as the Pioneers. Still there are nearly 20,000,000 Soviet young people in its ranks. The Komsomols are much more political. They are used to bring pressure on youngsters to "volunteer" for many kinds of more-or-less unpleasant public service, such as going out to Siberia to work on the new

farms of the so-called virgin lands, where living and working conditions are primitive; going to eastern Siberia to work on the big new hydroelectric-dam projects, where the temperature in winter drops to 60 below zero; or going to the northern taiga to help with prospecting and construction projects.

If 99 percent of the schoolchildren belong to the Pioneers, the percentage in the Komsomols probably is about 75. It is from the ranks of the Komsomols that the Communist Party recruits many of its adult members. Here they were trained in leadership and indoctrination. However, for the vast majority of Soviet youngsters, membership in the Komsomols is more a matter of routine than of strong political conviction. They belong because it is easier to sign up than to be subject to the pressures and ostracization which non-membership may produce.

The Komsomols are expected to be in the vanguard of whatever campaign the Communist Party carries·out. They, for example, launched a drive against ruffianism and drunkenness among young people in Moscow cafés and on the Moscow streets. They formed patrols which they sent to dance halls, restaurants and bars. They tried to persuade young people not to drink, not to dance in Western style and not to engage in brawls. Heavy drinking is common among young Russians, particularly because of a lack of facilities for recreation. The Komsomol campaign touched

off some serious incidents, including several in which young people were killed. The Communist Party then set up what are called "*druzhina*"—voluntary auxiliary police. Originally they were mostly Komsomols.

In Soviet Russia almost every kind·of activity is organized. In the past few years demonstrations have been organized outside the American Embassy and other embassies whenever the Soviet government wants to make a particularly dramatic protest against some incident—such as the U-2 flight, or the Lumumba murder in the Congo or the Cuban situation.

The Komsomols usually organize these "spontaneous" affairs, assigning detachments of youngsters from various schools, providing them with banners, telling them what slogans to shout and how long the demonstration is to last. Once when a couple of thousand young Muscovites were shouting outside the American Embassy, a visitor complained to a policeman who was standing by quietly, asking how he could get into the embassy. "Oh," said the policeman, looking at his watch. "You have only a few minutes to wait. The demonstration will be over at 5:30." It was too. Right on the dot.

Sometimes the activities of the Communist Youth are more sinister. Several times in the last two or three years Komsomol members have lured visiting foreign young people into serious trouble by deliberately involving them

RUSSIAN YOUTH

in scandalous incidents which the Communist *propaganda* apparatus then used to blacken the reputation of young visitors from the West.

The Komsomols also are the principal arm of the Soviet government that tries to persuade or compel Soviet youngsters to accept jobs or enter professions which they may not really want to.

The Soviet boy or girl is theoretically free to choose his own career. But if the government needs engineers, the Komsomols will do all they can to persuade boys and girls to go to an engineering school.

The government does not order students to study engineering. But if it needs more engineers, youngsters find that the quota for students in the literature or arts faculties is filled up. If they want an university education, they had better go into engineering, where there are plenty of openings.

Schools, including university levels, are free in Russia. But when you graduate you are compelled to repay the government by accepting the job which it allots to you for a period of three years. There is no way of evading this. So the law goes. In fact young people very effectively pull strings to get jobs in the big cities. They avoid faraway places like Kamchatka and Kazakhstan because living conditions are so bad. In the United States there's not too much difference between life in Montana and life in North Carolina—except for the weather. But in Russia, life in the remote provinces means, very often, living in a primitive log cabin, drawing water from a rope-and-bucket well, walking to work a couple of miles in icy winter and dusty summer. It means few stores and not much variety on their shelves, little entertainment and not much contact with the world beyond the horizon other than a static-filled radio program which consists mostly of propaganda statements.

Soviet youngsters at 18 must start a three-year hitch in the service. However, the Soviet draft law differs considerably from the American. Youngsters in school are deferred, just as Americans usually are. But Soviet youngsters in higher education—that is, in university and university-level education—are normally exempt entirely from military duty. One result of this is that the Soviet army is largely made up of peasant boys. The officers, however, are mostly from the cities.

No matter how critical they may be of life in Russia—and Soviet youngsters speak their minds very freely these days—they are usually filled with patriotism and pride for Russia's achievements. "The Russian bear is patient," a 16-year-old told me during a discussion of the cold war, "but beware when he is aroused."

Soviet boys are excited by Soviet space achievements. They want to study physics, higher mathematics, space science. Their favorite heroes are cosmonauts. They talk about landing on the moon and the possibility of life on other planets. The bookstores are filled

A 12-year-old learns to operate machine tool.

with popular books and magazines on science topics. Science fiction is a favorite. The Russians don't go in for comic books, as we do, but they have their own literary equivalent for Superman and all the heroes of the modern world of Jules Verne.

But the most enduring and universal interest of Soviet youngsters is the automobile. Cars are still not common in Russia. Russia makes several kinds of automobiles—the ZIL, the Volga, the Pobeda, the Moskvich, the Zaporozhets. They are roughly equivalent to the Buick, the Chevrolet, the compact, and our smallest foreign imports like the Renault or the Fiat. However, only about 150,000 units a year are produced, compared with our 5,000,-000 or 6,000,000.

In these circumstances owning a car, or even driving one, is as much of a dream to a Soviet youngster as going to the moon.

A French film about the United States was shown in Russia recently. It was exhibited because of its emphasis on the seamier side of American life, but the reaction of Soviet youngsters was not exactly what the Communist propagandists had expected.

I was bombarded with questions from Russian youngsters who had seen the picture. "Is it true that in America you deliberately wreck cars—just for fun?" one youngster demanded. (One scene in the picture showed a county fair sequence in which daredevil drivers hurl their cars into a concrete wall.) "Are there really automobile graveyards in the United States?" asked another after seeing shots of car junkyards. Others asked incredulously if it were true that cars cost only $50 or $100 in the United States, whether young people could really own their own cars and drive back and forth to school, whether there were super highways where persons were *compelled* to drive at a minimum of 70 miles an hour.

Only a few foreign sports cars have been seen in all of Russia. A friend of mine who drove a white MG in Moscow often found the car surrounded by such throngs of boys and young men that it was almost impossible to get the car away from the curb. Policemen were constantly stopping the car—ostensibly because of some minor traffic violation, but really just to get a closer look at the strange little car. In the last two years a group of young Moscow auto enthusiasts has formed a sports-car club. They build their own sports cars, using Pobeda frames and constructing the bodies on the models of pictures in foreign sports-car magazines. They have even held a couple of rallies on a cornfield track and dirt roads outside the city.

Russian youngsters are fond of sports and outdoor life. They like to hike and camp in the summer. Thousands of them go to the mountains of the Caucasus for three-week climbing and camping trips. Thousands more go to the endless forest and lake country of Siberia—much like northern Maine or Minnesota, a beautiful primitive camping area in summertime.

Younger children go in large numbers to camps nearer the big cities or camps on the shores of the Black Sea or in the Crimea. There are other big resorts on the sandy coasts of the Baltic Sea. But until recent years swimming was not a major Soviet interest.

Skiing is the big winter sport. Even seven-year-olds are taken for their recreation periods to Moscow parks and learn to glide down gentle slopes. Because so much of Russia is flat, cross-country skiing is more common than mountain or downhill skiing. Skating has only begun to be popular on a mass basis in recent years. Now each winter the paths of the big-city parks are flooded, loudspeaker music is installed, and the parks are filled with skaters all day and all evening.

Sports clubs and the Pioneer and Komsomol organizations are the centers for organized athletics rather than schools and universities. Encouraged by lavish expenditures and propaganda, the Russians have won a major place for themselves in international athletic competition, as evidenced by their remarkable Olympic performances. Much more can be expected as their training broadens and intensifies. The Russians are great competitors.

The top spectator sport is soccer. This is the game every Russian youngster plays on his hometown sandlot. He also plays *lapta*, which is a bat-and-ball game with a vague similarity to baseball. Once, in a fervor of chauvinistic propaganda, the Russian press claimed that the United States had "stolen" the Russian game of *lapta* and turned it into baseball. Another favorite game is *gorodki*, in which players try to knock blocks of wood out of a circle by hurling sticks about half the length of a ball bat.

Television has become a big thing in Russia. There are TV stations now in most Soviet cities. Moscow has two channels and will soon have more. The programming, however, is much different from that in our country. No

Gunsmoke. No late shows. No horror films. No singing commercials.

There is little or no daytime programming except on weekends. Programs start about 6:00 P.M. Not many of them are specially devised for TV. They are live pickups of concerts, stage plays, ballet, opera or poetry recitations (very popular). Sports events—especially soccer—are broadcast. So are big parades, ceremonies, speeches by Premier Khrushchev, and so on. There are quite a few educational broadcasts, and there are going to be many more. There are also special children's plays, travelogues and showings of popular films, newsreels and the like. Commercials are limited to simple announcements: The GUM Department Store has a sale of carpet sweepers. Travel by Soviet Airlines. Buy Soviet State Insurance. Subscribe to State Savings Bonds.

Religion plays little part in the lives of most Russian youngsters, largely because of the fierce propaganda against it. However, a high percentage of Russian boys and girls do go to church in their preschool years, and many of them are baptized and christened in church. In their school years they usually drop out. Under the instigation of the Komsomol organization, some engage in antireligious activities. Recently the teen-agers of some small towns have been organized by the Communist Youth into demonstrators who have shouted taunts and thrown stones at churches and churchgoers.

On the other hand, the persecution of religious faith has stirred some young people to the defense of their church. With the revival of anti-Semitism in Russia, many Jewish youngsters have become militant defenders of their beliefs.

And, in spite of all the pressure and propaganda, many young people like to be married in church because of tradition and the beauty of the Russian Orthodox service. The Communist Party has begun to set up "Wedding Palaces" in the big cities where couples can be married with some ceremony. Before this the Communist procedure was simply for the man and woman to go to a registry office and record their marriage.

One thing which has infuriated the Communist Party has been the interest which young people show in the Baptist Church. There have been several instances in which whole units of the Komsomol organization have joined the Baptists—despite the Party's insistence upon atheism. The Baptist faith apparently has attracted the interest of Russian young people because of its uniqueness. Russia traditionally has been a land in which the Orthodox Church has held almost universal sway. The Baptists, with their closer feeling for the contemporary world, seem to have a special appeal to Russian young people.

A great source of hope that changes in Russia may be to our liking is the lively, persistent interest of Soviet youth in the West. It is rare to meet a Russian boy who is rude and hostile because of anti-American propaganda. Instead, he smothers his American visitor with questions about American schools, Hollywood, New York skyscrapers, American cars and every other detail of American life. They imagine that the wild West still exists and that Indians roam the prairies scalping white men,

hunting buffalo and living in their old ways.

At college age the effects of their exposure to Western literature and their attraction toward Western ideas takes a more striking form. Here, in classes and in informal get-togethers, you hear them challenging the basic premises of totalitarianism, demanding the answers to fundamental questions such as what is truth and what is the reality of the world. They angrily reject the Party doctrines which are fed to them by the propaganda and agitation department of the Communist Party.

Young Russian poets declaim passionate poems, denouncing policies of their government, not only in private meetings but in public squares. Often they are dispersed or chased away by the Soviet police. Sometimes they are arrested. But this does not seem to discourage them. Young artists paint in Western abstract style. Musicians try to compose in Western atonal forms.

Of course, there are many Soviet youngsters who go along with the system, who never challenge authority, who obediently carry out the dictates of the Communist Party.

But dissent has reached the level at which old-line Party workers shake their heads sadly and say: "I don't know what has happened to our young people. We can't seem to hold them. They are going another way. This is our greatest defeat."

It is too early to know whether these old Party workers are overly pessimistic. But it is in these symptoms of dissent among Russia's young Ivans that the best hopes for ultimate change in the totalitarian nature of the Soviet system would seem to lie.   THE END

Below, a Russian teacher has written a sentence on the blackboard for an English lesson. Above the words is a portrait of Lenin.

PHOTO BY ELLIOTT ERWITT, MAGNUM

A Boy Talks Across the Continent

Melville Bell Grosvenor, Age 13, Telephones from New York to San Francisco.

(1) FAMOUS MEN WHO FIRST TALKED FROM NEW YORK TO SAN FRANCISCO.

(2) "TRAIN" OF THE MEN WHO FINISHED THE LINE.

(3) HAULING POLES IN THE SAGE-BRUSH COUNTRY.

(4) BORING POSTHOLES IN LAKE BED.

(5) MAP SHOWING ROUTE OF THE ATLANTIC-TO-PACIFIC TELEPHONE LINE.

(6) SETTING A POLE IN A SALT SINK.

THE first boy to telephone across the continent is Melville Bell Grosvenor, a thirteen-year-old lad of Washington, D. C. Melville is a grandson of Alexander Graham Bell, the inventor of telephony, and he was one of the guests of honor at the formal opening of the transcontinental telephone line on January 25.

Along with Mayor Mitchel of New York, "Grandfather" Bell and other distinguished guests at this opening ceremony, Melville conversed with distinguished men at the other end of the line in San Francisco, 3,400 miles away.

Of course every boy in the country has heard of this wonderful new telephone line connecting San Francisco with New York, Philadelphia, Boston and other eastern cities, and has felt a thrill of pride knowing that this remarkable achievement has been made possible through the genius and persistence of American inventors and electrical engineers. But there are some very interesting things connected with this

The Pictures

(1) *Beginning at the left end, those in the historic group at the top are: Mr. T. T. McCarty, Chief Engineer, American Telephone and Telegraph Company; Mr. George McAneny, President, Board of Aldermen, New York City; Mr. U. N. Bethell, Senior Vice-President, American Telephone and Telegraph Company; Dr. Bell, the inventor; Mayor Mitchel, of New York City; Mr. O. E. Yost, of Nebraska, and Mr. W. A. Prendergast, Comptroller, City of New York.*

(2) *In Nevada the construction crews, far from railroads, moved by these trains in finishing their great work.*

(3) *Carting poles in the roadless deserts was no easy job, as this picture shows.*

(4) *In Humboldt Lake, Nev., two miles of poles (80 in number) were set in water from 18 inches to 3 feet deep; the picture shows the machine used to bore the holes.*

(5) *Note the enormous distances between the largest cities on this transcontinental telephone line.*

(6) *This shows some of the difficulties of polesetting in the "wild" parts of the West.*

new telephone achievement of the American Telephone and Telegraph Company which most boys probably have not heard about.

How THE VOICE FLIES

Suppose a boy in New York were able to speak loud enough for his voice to carry to San Francisco. How long do you think it would take the sound to travel across the continent? Sound travels at the rate of 1,160 feet per second. The distance from New York to San Francisco is 3,400 miles. So it would take a boy's voice about four hours to travel from New York to the Golden Gate.

How, then, is it possible for your voice to be transmitted almost instantaneously over the telephone? As a matter of fact, transmission of sound by telephone is not instantaneous, although for short distances the length of time consumed is too brief to be measured. When Melville Grosvenor

A Boy Talks Across the Continent

spoke into the telephone in New York on January 25, it was only one-fifteenth of a second before his voice was heard at the other end of the wire, 3,400 miles away.

The explanation of this wonderful feat of sending the sound of a voice across the continent in one-fifteenth of a second is found in the fact that it is not sound, or air, waves which are transmitted, but electrical waves.   Electrical waves have a speed of 56,000 miles per second.   When you speak into a telephone transmitter the sound waves of your voice are converted into electrical waves.   These waves travel over the wire to the telephone receiver at the rate of 56,000 miles per second, and the receiver picks up these electrical waves and transforms them into air waves so that the sound of the voice is accurately reproduced although the actual sound of the voice of the speaker goes no farther than the transmitter into which he speaks.

"WAVES" MUSTN'T GET TANGLED UP

This seems simple, but it is really a most complex problem.   These waves, having been faithfully converted from air waves into electrical waves and sent out on their journey over the line, must not interfere with each other; they must not tumble over each other, so to speak, or get in each other's way; they must be sent out, nearly 50,000 of them, every minute.   Some of them have one shape and some another. They are just as different from each other as the waves of the sea.   These differences in shape, the distance between them, the time between them, must be faithfully preserved and conserved, so that at no point in their journey will they be changed sufficiently to be noticed.   It is not the problem of sending one simple current, but as many as 120,000 a minute.   All of these minute currents, millions of them—millions and millions in a conversation—must be carried electrically over the line to San Francisco and then converted back again into sound waves which agitate the air of the room and affect the ear as air waves.

130,000 POLES

It may be interesting to the readers of BOYS' LIFE to know something about the material required in building this transcontinental telephone line.   From New York to San Francisco there are 3,400 miles of hard drawn copper wire of No. 8 B. W. G. gauge.   There are four such wires from which are derived two physical circuits, and one phantom circuit.   The diameter of each wire is .165 inch. The weight is 870 pounds per circuit mile; that is 435 pounds per mile of each wire, two wires being required for a circuit.   The total weight of one circuit of two such wires is 2,960,000 pounds, or 1,480 tons. In the line itself there are 130,000 poles. In addition to this there is the wire used in the Pupin coils.   This wire used in these coils is of .004 of an inch in diameter.   For each physical circuit of the line, in addition to the 6,800 miles of copper wire, 13,600 miles of this hair-like wire is used.

If you will look at the map reproduced in this issue you will see the enormous distance between the largest cities on this new across-the-continent telephone line, which will give you a clearer idea of the wonderful thing that happened on January 25, 1915.

THE COMING DECADES IN SPACE

By ISAAC ASIMOV

Illustrated by ROBERT McCALL

In 1957, mankind launched its first satellite into space. That satellite, unmanned and small, circled Earth, barely skimming the main body of the atmosphere. In 1969, a large, three-man vessel traveled safely to the moon, 237,000 miles from Earth. There, it deposited the first human beings on the soil of an alien world, then brought them safely back.

So much for what can be done in a dozen years. What will we do in the next two and a half dozen?

Reaching the moon by three-man vessels in one long bound from Earth is like casting a thin thread across space. The main effort, in the coming decades, will be to strengthen this thread; to make it a cord, a cable, and, finally, a broad highway.

Can we stand the expense of doing this?

The manned space program has cost the United States $24 billion, but it was $24 billion spent right here in the United States (not on the moon). Part of it went into the development of many materials, devices, and techniques that will have—and already do have—applications here on Earth. Part of it went into laying the groundwork for future advances that will be less expensive and that promise greater returns.

To make the moon landing more than a sort of glorious feat and to bring it into the realm of the commonplace, we are going to need some sort of base between Earth and moon. We will need a large manned satellite, orbiting Earth permanently at a distance from us far less than the moon. The Soviet Union has been gearing its space program toward the establishment of such a "space station," and the United States plans to have its first space station in orbit in 1973. The American space station will be powered, in part, by solar batteries. It has been planned to include a large reflecting telescope.

The telescope indicates the most immediate use of the space station. It will be an observation post. Though the station may be just a few hundred miles up from Earth's surface, in a certain way it will be millions of miles closer to the rest of the universe than we are down here.

Why? Because it will be outside the atmosphere.

Our atmosphere is a crowded mass of molecules that lets hardly anything through. Most of the visible light gets through and most of a band of short-wave radio radiation called microwaves. Everything else is absorbed. What's more, the water vapor in the atmosphere forms mist, fog, and clouds that frequently cut off the visible light, too.

There are some areas in deserts and on plateaus where the air is clearer. But even there, temperature differences from one part of the atmosphere to another bend light beams, make stars apparently shift position, blur planet-surfaces. And even in the most isolated spots, the dust in the air is increasing, and distant light from man-made cities grows brighter. It becomes harder to see.

Every year the atmosphere becomes harder to look through, and a space station will take us beyond all that. Since the vacuum of space is absolutely clear, a telescope with no air between itself and the stars is an astronomer's dream come true.

One thing we would see most clearly from a space sta-

tion (and something we cannot see at all from Earth's surface) is a large swath of Earth taken as a whole.

Earth can be mapped from space with an instant accuracy available by no other means, and the map always could be kept up to date. It would be an extraordinary map—one that would show details no other map could. It would show the character of the ground, and from small changes we could deduce the location of mineral and oil deposits. We could study geologic faults more precisely and perhaps learn to predict landslides and earthquakes. We could follow the changing patterns of vegetation, study the progress of plant diseases, make farming more efficient.

It may be only by studies from space stations that we will learn enough about the earth as a whole to make real progress in studying ecology; in studying the worldwide relationship of life-forms to each other and to the environment.

Nor is it only Earth that can tell us about Earth. From a space station, we can study the sun as it has never been studied. We can study *all* its radiation in detail and in full, and not just the radiation that gets through our thick and dusty atmosphere.

We will understand better the amount and kind of energy that Earth receives, and the amount and kind it radiates from different portions of its surface. We will understand its weather systems better and learn, perhaps, how to introduce controls that will make the environment better for man and for life generally.

We will understand better the cosmic-ray particles and the neutrinos that fill all of space, and learn what they can tell us of the inner workings of stars and the evolution of galaxies. We may discover new particles that will reveal mysteries now undreamed of. But—will new facts about these particles be useful?

Certainly! Knowledge is *always* useful; if not at once, then some day. Knowledge is all one piece. No matter where we increase the knowledge; no matter what we learn about the universe; no matter how far-off and unimportant it all seems, it could have ways of helping us right here on Earth.

For instance, what could seem more unimportant to the average human being than the fact that quadrillions of miles away from us there are dust clouds in space?

Well, by studying the kind of light emitted from the dust clouds and the kind of light they absorb, astronomers have been able to deduce what kind of atoms exist there. Mostly, they are hydrogen and helium atoms, but with some oxygen, carbon, and nitrogen atoms thrown in. These atoms are spread out so thinly that it didn't seem likely that very many would just happen to collide and stick together.

But then, in the 1960's, microwaves were studied instead of just light waves. That made more delicate decisions possible about any atom-combinations that could exist there. In 1963, oxygen-hydrogen combinations were detected. Then, beginning in late 1968, more and more atom-combinations were found; two, three, four, even six atoms in combination have been located in those clouds. To detect them requires the most delicate work with radio-telescopes.

In space, though, away from interference by Earth's man-made radio waves, ➡

Man continues the greatest adventure of all—exploring the universe.

U.S. aim: a manned space station in 1973.

and with the ability to observe waves of all sizes and lengths, it would be possible to study the substances in the dust clouds much more carefully.

And if we can do that . . . well, remember that the sun and Earth were formed out of such dust clouds. We might end up with a better idea of the chemistry of Earth as it was first formed, and of what chemical changes must have taken place thereafter to form still more complicated molecules.

If we have a better idea of the starting chemistry of Earth, we may be able to conduct experiments that will allow us to deduce the pathway to life. We may be able to construct the very simple systems that would begin to hint of life. From them we may be able to learn some of the basic behavior of cells, behavior that now is masked by all the complicated additional molecules and systems that have been added by three billion years of evolution.

In other words, a clear line of research may extend from the constitution of the dust

This transportation center of the future shows how space exploration will affect man's life on Earth.

clouds (as determined from a space station) to a better understanding of the fundamentals of life.

Naturally, a space station will have to be kept supplied. It may need repairs. Scientists and engineers who have served their hitch will have to be taken off and replaced with others. There will have to be a continual line of ships shuttling between Earth's surface and the space station.

A space shuttle is now being planned: a double vessel, with the smaller (the orbiter) being carried piggyback by the larger (the booster). Both the booster and the orbiter will be equipped with rocket engines carrying fuel and oxygen for use in deep space, but each also will be equipped with jet engines that make use of atmospheric oxygen. And each will have wing and tail elements to help them navigate in the atmosphere.

This represents an important revolution in space flight. Until now, nothing sent into space has ever been used again. Objects in orbit stay in orbit forever, or drop into the atmosphere and ➡

are destroyed. Even manned vessels that have returned to Earth are not used again. All this means that valuable structures representing many millions of dollars are constantly being destroyed or retired from use.

Not so the space shuttle. The booster will lift itself and the orbiter into the thin upper atmosphere. At a height of nearly 40 miles, the orbiter will fire its engines and break away from the booster. The orbiter, having a head start in the booster's own motion, and with very little atmosphere to offer resistance, will be able to go into an orbit that will take it to the space station by the use of very little fuel.

The booster will cruise back to Earth, making use of its jet engine and its aerodynamic properties to take full advantage of the atmosphere. On landing, it will be gone over, refurbished, and made ready for refueling and repeating its task. It is reasonable to anticipate that, with proper main-

tenance, a booster might be used many times over. This represents an important saving. If a single booster is used 10 times, it represents a much smaller expense than 10 boosters each used one time.

The orbiter will be carrying men or supplies to the space station; objects needed for repairs; new instruments. It will carry back other men or objects, coasting down the gravity hill to Earth's surface. It, too, can be used over and over again.

The space shuttle also can be used to service and repair ordinary satellites: the weather satellites that automatically check Earth's cloud cover, the navigational satellites that can be used as guides by ocean-going ships on Earth, the communications satellites that will make it possible for all parts of Earth to be continually in touch with each other.

These satellites will, as a result, be longer lasting, more efficient, and can be made much more complex and useful.

They will free scientists on the space station from having to do the more mechanical work of observation that automatic devices can do.

The communications satellites, if properly serviced, may be most important of all. Since they probably will be using laser beams eventually, there will be much more room for different wavelength channels for television, radio, and telephone. "Intelsat IV" already is in orbit, with an average capacity for 5,000 voice circuits and 12 TV channels.

By 1980 much more elaborate communications satellites will be in orbit, and our whole planet may be closely linked. Perhaps this will make it more possible to develop friendships between peoples, talk out quarrels instead of fighting them out, reach compromises instead of impasses.

The space shuttle should make it possible to expand the space stations. By the 1980's, there will be in orbit stations that are larger, more complex,

more efficient and much more livable. The advanced space station will be not only a base for observing Earth, the sun and the universe; it will become a laboratory for experimentation. It will make use of the vacuum of space, of the hard radiation from the sun, of gravity-free conditions—all of which are difficult or impossible to duplicate on Earth's surface.

The space station may even be a factory that will produce devices impossible to make on Earth. Metals and other substances can be prepared without contamination by gas molecules. Welds can be made more perfectly in the absence of air of any kind. Very thin films could be applied more evenly. Anything that requires a vacuum would have a better one in space, without effort, than can be produced on Earth except with a great deal of effort.

The absence of a gravitational effect on the space station would make it possible to grow crystals ➤

Mars . . . Venus . . . Mercury . . . and beyond, as man expands his horizons.

closer to perfection, make mixes more efficiently, produce better casts, blow thinner bubbles. For delicacy and precision, the mark "Made on Space Station" may represent the ultimate.

Most important, the space station will be the testing ground for life away from Earth. Mankind will learn how to become independent of the planet of his birth. The space station will help us learn that gently. Earth will still be there close by; always ready to reach out and help; always ready to take her astronauts back. Then, through practice, through trial, through error sometimes, mankind will learn to manipulate the environment of space more efficiently.

As he does this, he will be ready to probe out to the moon more strongly, more surely. By the 1980's, we will have "space tugs" more powerful than any space vessel in existence now. They will be nuclear-powered, so that they will have more thrust per weight of fuel.

These "workhorses of space" will be able to carry the men and supplies needed to build space stations much farther out in space; stations that circle the moon rather than Earth. From such a lunar station, the moon can be surveyed as Earth can from our own stations. More than that, the lunar station will serve as a base for us to reach and explore the moon's surface.

Specially designed space shuttles will maneuver between the lunar station and the lunar surface, making a lunar colony possible and, very likely, practical. Life on the moon actually would be less difficult in some ways than life on a station. There would be the substance of the moon's crust to serve as raw materials.

Since the moon is airless, observations from its surface would be as efficient as those on the station, and there would be considerable room for work and equipment. Observatories on the far side, away from Earth, would be free of the interference of earthlight during the long lunar night and from the radio noise emanating from our planet.

The moon itself could be explored and its geological history worked out. Its geology may tell us more of the evolution of the solar system than our own would, for whatever took place on the moon in the way of meteoric bombardment, volcanic action, and solar radiation has not been obscured by the action of wind, water, and life, as it has been on Earth.

From the moon, or from the space stations, we will be launching manned spaceships on the long voyage to Mars by the 1990's. Those spaceships will be far more elaborate than the simple vessels that first carried men to the moon. They probably will be launched in pairs, each with a minimum crew of three. If anything happens to one vessel, the other will be available for repair or rescue.

With the experience gained on the surface of the moon, it will be that much simpler for man to operate on the surface of Mars. It is difficult to predict what we will find on the Martian surface. But if even the simplest life forms exist there, the information that would give us would be of extreme importance.

And, of course, unmanned vessels can be launched in far greater numbers than manned vessels can, and for far greater distances. By the time we are ready to send men to Mars, instrument packages will be sailing through space toward every one of the planets of the solar system; to the asteroids, to the giant planets far beyond, each with its complex satellite system. There will be probes sent into comets, also; and, in the other direction, to Venus and Mercury, and into an orbit that will skim the sun as closely as can be managed.

Earth's transportation will be affected by all this. Knowledge always laps over its boundaries and it is impossible to advance in one area without affecting all others. Thus, the computer systems used to control and direct spaceflight may well be used to control our own increasingly complex traffic on air and ground.

Aircraft may become hybridized; passing through the atmosphere into space, and then back into the atmosphere, in carrying men and cargo from one point on Earth to another.

The vehicles developed for use on the moon's surface may find applications on Earth's surface as well. In fact, a transportation center on Earth in 1995 may turn out to be a combination spaceflight-airflight nerve center from which some vessels leave for a space station, some for the moon, and some for other parts of the Earth.

If we can only tackle space exploration with a sure and firm hand, with courage and imagination, and tackle our earthbound problems in the same way—preserving our environment through increasing our knowledge and wisdom—our children will see a world far different from our own. And far better.

PRESIDENT WILSON DELIVERING HIS INAUGURAL ADDRESS

What the Boy Scouts Did at the Inauguration

NOTE.—In the last Presidential campaign Theodore Roosevelt made a hit when he said his hat was in the ring. People under-
stood the simile and liked it. They knew it meant he was going to make a fight for his principles. And that is the kind
of man everybody likes to see climb into the ring, whether they approve of his principles or not.

Prior to March 3 last, the Boy Scouts of America, and by that is meant the boy scouts themselves, never found occasion to throw
their hats into the ring in a large way. But on that day they did. It was a mighty disagreeable ring, too. Yet in went fifteen hun-
dred scout hats, each with a determined scout under it. And they soon showed the country what a boy scout is made of. What
they did in justice to the scout oath and law is best known by the people who saw it. And it has had full measure of appreciation,
both in hearty thanks and words of praise from high and low and in laudatory comment in the public press. What follows here is
a simple chronicle of facts unadorned, to let the rest of the boy scouts, and other boys interested, know what these fifteen hun-
dred scouts were up against.—Editor.

THE National Capital at Inauguration time is far from the
peaceful, dignified city that usually greets the visitor.
Great crowds throng in, in such numbers that even the
whole of New York City's great and wonderfully efficient police

MR. WILSON WAITING AT PRINCETON FOR THE TRAIN THAT TOOK
HIM TO WASHINGTON FOR HIS INAUGURATION

force would be hard put to it to handle them. For the most part
the people are, of course, anxious to see the Inaugural ceremonies, but a great many roughs and toughs are also present,
for no good purpose. In addition, there is the element who, while
not of the criminal class, have a way of making a holiday, especially a big one like the inauguration of a President, an excuse
for resorting to rowdyism. So with it all, the task of protecting
the respectable visitors is so great that every Washington official,
from the Chairman of the Inaugural Committee down to the
humblest policeman on his beat, looks forward to it with dread.

About 1,500 boy scouts, from the District of Columbia, Maryland, Georgia, New Jersey, Kentucky, Pennsylvania, and Virginia, manfully tackled the inaugural problem this year, volun-
teering to help the Inaugural Committee. Of course, they also
wanted to see the parade and the ceremonies. They were confronted by a task which staggered the police and certainly ap-
palled many an onlooker. But with the cheerfulness born of
grit and determination they threw their strength on the side of
law, order and good citizenship—and won out!

"Law and order" in reality became noticeable by their absence
for a time on March 3, during the Suffrage parade. And Washington and its respectable visitors will not soon forget the spec-
tacle of boys in the uniform that stands for *learning* the principles of good citizenship actually restraining grown men from
acting the part of brutes. For it is a fact that the boy scouts
did their part, and more, to keep the city from approaching a
state of riot.

Up to the time of the Suffrage parade the scouts had been on
duty in the Union Station and around the city, rendering what
assistance they could to the incoming crowds. On Monday they

received detailed instructions concerning their part in keeping order during the parade. Under the American Red Cross plan, emergency stations were designated and scouts detailed to their posts. All others received this order: "All scouts not otherwise detailed to duty are to report in full uniform, with staves, to the north side of Pennsylvania avenue, between First and Seventh streets, at 2 p.m. They will be detailed to special duty by the police in charge."

This simple order contained the germs of some remarkable opportunities for the scouts.

The Superintendent of Police sent instructions to Scout Commissioner Edgar S. Martin that the boy scouts must remain behind the police cables and must not carry their staves. The burden of keeping back drunken ruffians, hostile and insulting gangs and holding the enormous crowd in check was too much for the police, and they were soon begging the scouts to help them and borrowing their staves. Scout Commissioner Martin ordered the scouts outside the police cables. They found the task of keeping the way open for the parade was, in itself, tremendous, but in addition they had to render first aid in hundreds of instances, and their wits were exerted to the utmost in dealing with one difficult incident after another.

On Tuesday the line of march of the Inaugural parade was

THE WEST POINTERS ADMIRED THE SCOUTS

WAITING FOR THE SUFFRAGE PARADE. THE SCOUTS' WORK WAS NOT VERY DIFFICULT AT THIS STAGE

THE PRINCETON SCOUTS WITH THE WILSON BAGGAGE

covered by the scouts—they were there for service, not for the glory of marching in the parade—and their first aid work was a feature of the day. The boys had canteens and water bottles, and there is record that one boy handled sixteen cases of fainting. The police on many occasions requested assistance from the boys, and once a mounted policeman descended upon the Baltimore troop and asked for twelve to assist in the control of the crowds at the Court of Honor and near the President's box.

Two patrols of Princeton, N. J., scouts, whose troops assisted at the farewell to President Wilson in Princeton, turned up at Washington to welcome him. They were given charge of the baggage of the Presidential party, from the time it came on the train till it was delivered by two of the scouts at the hotel. On Tuesday they reported for duty at the White House reviewing stand, where they sold programs on the stand. Afterward, during the parade, the police sergeant in charge called upon them to guard the rear of the stand from accidents, whether from malice or ignorance, especially as there was danger of fire from carelessly thrown matches or cigarette butts. And here comes in a touch of the scout spirit that is not to be passed by. Acting Scout Commissioner John H. Traeger, who had charge of the Princeton troop, afterward said:

"In this patrol service of the White House reviewing stand, several other scouts who happened along shared with the Prince-

CONCLUSIVE EVIDENCE THAT THE BOY SCOUTS MADE THEMSELVES USEFUL

ton troop. Unfortunately, I did not make memorandum of their names. There was one scout, about thirteen or fourteen years old, the only scout from some New Jersey town, who was placed with our troop in the forenoon. There was an eagle scout from Georgia. There was also a young Washington scout who gave our troop a great deal of valuable service. I regret very much that I have not his name. He deserves high commendation for his untiring energy, courtesy, willingness, and a most cheerful disposition. He wore a Red Cross arm-band."

An interesting commentary on the question of the usefulness of the staves came from witnesses of the parades. Mr. Arthur C. Moses, President of the Washington Local Council, says that without the staves the boys would have been powerless to hold back the thousands of people who were closing in on the marchers on every side. "The staff of the boy scout proved to be more effectual than the baton of the policeman," he says. Over and over the use of the staves in forming stretchers was demonstrated. The boys also used them in forming a barricade around persons who were overcome in the crowd.

Among the scouts who patrolled Pennsylvania avenue on Inaugural Day was Lord Eustace Perry, Secretary of the British Embassy, and a scout master. He was on duty in uniform from eight o'clock in the morning till eleven at night, directing the scouts under him in first aid work.

After the Inauguration, Major Charles Lynch, of the United States Army Medical Corps, wrote to Scout Commissioner Martin and said: "You will hear many golden opinions of the splendid work which the boy scouts did, but perhaps no one was better situated to form a correct judgment of their work than I was, as I had charge of the Red Cross arrangements on the third and fourth of March. On both days I was materially assisted by the boy scouts, who always showed themselves to be manly, self-reliant, and helpful." The Inaugural Committee appreciated the help, and Mr. Isaac Gans, the chairman, wrote: "The boys did yeoman work. They showed the training they have received, and

I believe that every citizen is proud of these lads and the showing they made." From Rear-Admiral Richard Wainwright came commendation just as hearty: "The courage and discipline displayed by the boy scouts in their endeavor to protect the parading women excited the admiration and respect of all who were in a position to witness it." Major General Leonard Wood, Chief of Staff of the War Department and Grand Marshal of the Inaugural parade, wrote to Mr. Martin, praising the scouts. He said: "Not only did they serve as policemen . . . but as very efficient administrators of first aid. From both suffrage and anti-suffrage parties came many grateful messages; for days afterward Scout Commissioner Martin was swamped by them with letters, telegrams, and personal visits.

In the booklet of instruction given to the boys by the Boy Scout Inaugural Committee, after the detailed instructions for the different days, comes a general statement of the duties. A short sentence gives the gist of the attitude of the entire representation of scouts throughout the Inaugural ceremonies: "To be active, attentive, and alert at all times while on duty." This, however, expresses very modestly the great service which the boy scouts rendered to the visitors and residents of the city. Indeed, the suffragists, who are already preparing to march in 1917, have declared they will ask the boy scouts to come to Washington to protect them. And as evidence of their sincerity they have appointed a committee to prepare a design for a medal which is to be presented to every boy scout who took part in the protection of women who marched on March 3. Designs have been submitted to National Headquarters of the Boy Scouts of America for approval.

Naturally, everybody concerned, scout officials and scouts, is glad of all this appreciation. But most of all there is felt a deep-seated satisfaction in having shown so unmistakably the kind of stuff a scout is made of. The situation at Washington could not have been staged had it been tried. Things just naturally developed.

HOLDING THEM   KEEP BACK!

WALTER P. McGUIRE, Editor
DAN BEARD, Associate Editor
FREDERIC L. COLVER,
Business Manager

Copyright, 1917, by the Boy Scouts
of America. Entered as second-
class matter in the Post Office at
New York City.

BOYS' LIFE
THE BOY SCOUTS' MAGAZINE

Published by the Boy Scouts
of America
at National Headquarters
200 Fifth Ave., New York

VOL. VII, No. 1

MAY, 1917

Our Country Is At War

CONGRESS DECLARED, on April 5th, that war exists between the United States and the Imperial German Government.

This declaration was made in response to an address of President Wilson, made to Congress on April 2nd.

Every boy in the United States should read that message and should remember that, among other things, the President said:

"On the 3rd of February last I officially laid before you the extraordinary announcement of the Imperial German Government that on and after the 1st day of February, it was its purpose to put aside all restraints of law or of humanity and use its submarines to sink every vessel that sought to approach either the ports of Great Britain and Ireland or the western coasts of Europe or any of the ports controlled by the enemies of Germany within the Mediterranean.

"I was for a little while unable to believe that such things would in fact be done by any government that had hitherto subscribed to the humane practices of civilized nations.

"The present German warfare against commerce is a warfare against mankind. It is a war against all nations. American ships have been sunk, American lives taken, in ways which it has stirred us very deeply to learn of, but the ships and people of other neutral and friendly nations have been sunk and overwhelmed in the waters in the same way. There has been no discrimination.

"The challenge is to all mankind. Each nation must decide for itself how it will meet it.

"When I addressed the Congress on the 26th of February last, I thought that it would suffice to assert our neutral rights with arms, our rights to use the seas against unlawful interference, our rights to keep our people safe against unlawful violence. But armed neutrality, it now appears, is impracticable.

"With a profound sense of the solemn and even tragical character of the step I am taking, and of the grave responsibilities which it involves, but in unhesitating obedience to what I deem my constitutional duty, I advise that the Congress declare the recent course of the Imperial German Government to be in fact nothing less than war against the Government and people of the United States; that it formally accept the status of belligerent which has thus been thrust upon it, and that it take immediate steps not only to put the country in a more thorough state of defense but also to exert all its power and employ all its resources to bring the Government of the German Empire to terms and end the war."

Your Flag and My Flag

Your flag and my flag,
  And how it flies today
In your land and my land
  And half a world away!
Rose-red and blood-red
  The stripes forever gleam;
Snow-white and soul-white—
  The good forefathers' dream;
Sky-blue and true blue, with stars to gleam
  aright—
The gloried guidon of the day; a shelter through
  the night.

Your flag and my flag!
  To every star and stripe
The drums beat as hearts beat
  And fifers shrilly pipe!
Your flag and my flag—
  A blessing in the sky;
Your hope and my hope—
  It never hid a lie!
Home land and far land and half the world
  around,
Old Glory hears our glad salute and ripples to
  the sound!

Your flag and my flag!
  And, oh, how much it holds—
Your land and my land—
  Secure within its folds!
Your heart and my heart
  Beat quicker at the sight;
Sun-kissed and wind-tossed—
  Red and blue and white.
The one flag—the great flag—the flag for me
  and you—
Glorified all else beside—the red and white and
  blue!

Wilbur D. Nesbit.

Copyright, 1916
P. F. Volland & Co.

Every possible effort was made to avoid war, you see, but because, as the President said, "right is more precious than peace," our Country was forced into war—into the greatest war the world has ever known. Every boy, especially every Boy Scout, now has his big opportunity to prove his patriotism.

DID you ever think that the chance would come to *you* some day to really help your country do something great for mankind? You know what it has done in the past. There was the Revolutionary War, after which a Republic was established here which since has come to be an ideal for oppressed men the world over. There was the Civil War, and millions who had been slaves were made free. We sent our men to Cuba, to fight and to die that a people cruelly treated by a foreign master might be independent. We took upon us the danger and the responsibility of driving an oppressor from the Philippines, in the far Pacific, and remain there only to help the little brown men learn (what their old rulers would not let them learn) to govern themselves as free men.

Our armed forces, with those of other nations, punished offenders in China and exacted from them a penalty of millions of dollars for their crimes, and then our Government returned all that money to China to be used to pay for the education of Chinese boys in American schools and colleges.

That is why "your flag and my flag" is a symbol loved throughout the world.

THIS is our glorious history as a nation—the history your school books tell—you know it well. The men who helped to make that history are heroes of the past.

We are writing a *new* page of history, and in it *you* will have a part. We shall have new heroes. You can be one.

BOYS' LIFE
STORIES

Boys' Life was a fledgling, year-old magazine when the Boy Scouts of America (BSA) purchased it in 1912. The reason for the purchase? The BSA had launched a literacy initiative. Scouts were encouraged to be readers so that they could grow up to be informed citizens. That goal continues to this day. The current edition of **The Boy Scout Handbook** states: "Reading is a window to the past and the future. It is a doorway to discovery. Read, read and read some more...."

The early issues of the magazine were filled with stories designed to fascinate boys. Over the decades the magazine has continued to publish award-winning fiction by notable writers, accompanied by award-winning illustrations. Genres have included adventure, science fiction, sports, thrillers, westerns, mystery, even humor.

The works of distinguished authors such as Jack London, Ray Bradbury, Arthur C. Clarke, and Isaac Asimov have graced the pages of the magazine. London was an early contributor, with his story of a boy's courage against claim jumpers in the days of the Klondike gold rush, first published in 1911. A wartime story from 1944 is a fictionalized account of a British commando raid on German supply bases in North Africa. Bradbury's contribution is a fantasy about a restless space captain searching the galaxy for something he will never find. Two of Clarke's stories are included here: a 1964 tale of a race to the moon using the solar wind yachts, and a 1967 account of an ascent of Mt. Everest using anti-gravity "levitators." Today, the fiction published features a boy protagonist between 8 and 17 years old.

Tales of true-life adventure and history are also popular. A 1962 story recounts the mystery surrounding ships that have disappeared at sea, never to be found, and of ships discovered with the entire crew missing, who were also never found. A 1978 story recounts the U.S. Navy's astounding victory over a Japanese fleet at the Battle of Midway during the Second World War.

To engage beginning readers (and to give them a chuckle) and for quick snippets of information, **Boys' Life** publishes comics and brief illustrated stories. "The Tracy Twins," featuring two Cub Scouts and their grandfather, ran for many years. Dik Browne, who earned fame with the comic strip "Hagar the Horrible," was the original artist for the comic. And to support the 12th point of the Scout Law—a Scout is reverent—the magazine includes "Bible Stories," incidents taken from the Old Testament.

Boys' Life, with a readership between the ages of 6 and 17 years old, now publishes demographic editions. The low edition, edited for boys aged 6–11, contains more comics, word games, puzzles, and Cub Scout–specific program material. The high edition, edited for boys ages 11–17, contains more challenging reading and Boy Scout–specific program material. At times, the fiction selections are demographically split, with a story at a more elementary reading level included in the low edition, and a different story at a more advanced reading level in the high edition. The goal is to keep the boy engaged—and of course, reading.

The Man

DRIVEN BY A FORCE HE DID NOT UNDERSTAND

A RESTLESS CAPTAIN SAILED HIS SHIP FROM STAR TO

STAR BUT COULD NOT SEE THE THING HE SOUGHT

By RAY BRADBURY

CAPTAIN HART stood in the door of the rocket. "Why don't they come?" he asked.

"Who knows?" said Martin, his lieutenant.

"Do I know, Captain?"

"What kind of a place is this, anyway?" The captain lighted a cigar. He tossed the match out into the glittering meadow. The grass started to burn.

Martin moved to stamp it out with his boot.

"No," ordered Captain Hart, "let it burn. Maybe they'll come see what's happening then, the ignorant fools."

Martin shrugged and withdrew his foot from the spreading fire.

Captain Hart examined his watch. "An hour ago we landed here, and does the welcoming committee rush out with a brass band to shake our hands? No indeed! Here we ride millions of miles through space and the fine citizens of some silly town on some unknown planet ignore us!" He snorted, tapping his watch. "Well, I'll just give them five more minutes, and then—"

"And then what?" asked Martin, ever so politely, watching the captain's jowls shake. "We'll fly over their city again and give

"You can't talk to me this way," shouted the captain, violently.

THE SERPENT IN THE GARDEN

THE SERPENT WAS THE SLIEST BEAST IN THE GARDEN OF EDEN.

ONE DAY, HE ENTICED THE WOMAN TO EAT THE FRUIT OF THE TREE OF KNOWLEDGE OF GOOD AND EVIL WHICH GOD HAD WARNED WAS FORBIDDEN.

AND WHEN SHE HAD EATEN, SHE GAVE SOME TO ADAM...AND SUDDENLY THEY BOTH BECAME ASHAMED OF THEIR NAKEDNESS AND HID THEMSELVES FROM GOD'S SIGHT.

THEN GOD, KNOWING ALL, CURSED THE SERPENT AND TOLD ADAM AND THE WOMAN THAT THEY WOULD SUFFER, FOR THEIR DISOBEDIENCE SAYING, "BY THE SWEAT OF YOUR BROW SHALL YOU EARN YOUR FOOD TIL YOU RETURN UNTO THE GROUND; FOR OUT OF IT WERE YOU TAKEN; FOR DUST YOU ART, AND UNTO DUST SHALL YOU RETURN."

AND ADAM CALLED HIS WIFE'S NAME EVE; BECAUSE SHE WAS THE MOTHER OF ALL LIVING.

THEN GOD BANISHED ADAM AND EVE FROM THE GARDEN OF EDEN AND PLACED CHERUBS TO THE EAST OF THE GARDEN AND A FLAMING SWORD WHICH TURNED EVERY WAY TO GUARD THE PATH TO THE TREE OF LIFE.

GENESIS: 3

THE BATTLE OF MIDWAY

BY CHARLES MERCER
ILLUSTRATED BY JIM SHARPE

"The enemy planned a lethal blow . . ."

IN MAY, 1942, the American situation in the Pacific was desperate. Following the Japanese sneak attack on Pearl Harbor of December 7, 1941, our fighting forces were outmatched in ships, planes, guns, and men. By May, the enemy was clenching its fist to deal the Americans a knockout blow. Where and when would it come? How could vastly outnumbered American forces hope to withstand it? Swift aircraft carriers had succeeded the slow battleships as the new ▶

Conclusion

THE CRUEL SKY

By ARTHUR C. CLARKE

Begin story here: Dr. Jules Elwin and George Harper have scaled the peak of Everest with the aid of anti-gravity Levitators. The "Levvies" are marvelous power-packs stored with enough energy to lift a 250-pound weight through a vertical distance of ten miles. Elwin had invented the Levvies and now, in spite of his severely crippled legs, he had fulfilled a lifelong wish to conquer the world's highest mountain. But the old scientist and his young partner did not reckon on Nature's fury. As they started back down the mountain, a sudden windstorm caught them in its blast and tossed the two climbers out into space.

Illustrated by ROBERT J. LEE

The Man

DRIVEN BY A FORCE HE DID NOT UNDERSTAND

A RESTLESS CAPTAIN SAILED HIS SHIP FROM STAR TO

STAR BUT COULD NOT SEE THE THING HE SOUGHT

By RAY BRADBURY

CAPTAIN HART stood in the door of the rocket. "Why don't they come?" he asked.

"Who knows?" said Martin, his lieutenant. "Do I know, Captain?"

"What kind of a place is this, anyway?" The captain lighted a cigar. He tossed the match out into the glittering meadow. The grass started to burn.

Martin moved to stamp it out with his boot.

"No," ordered Captain Hart, "let it burn. Maybe they'll come see what's happening then, the ignorant fools."

Martin shrugged and withdrew his foot from the spreading fire.

Captain Hart examined his watch. "An hour ago we landed here, and does the welcoming committee rush out with a brass band to shake our hands? No indeed! Here we ride millions of miles through space and the fine citizens of some silly town on some unknown planet ignore us!" He snorted, tapping his watch. "Well, I'll just give them five more minutes, and then—"

"And then what?" asked Martin, ever so politely, watching the captain's jowls shake.

"We'll fly over their city again and give

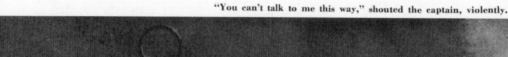

"There's no way," the mayor said gently, "to tell you anything."

'em a good scare." His voice grew quieter. "Do you think, Martin, maybe they didn't see us land?"

"They saw us. They looked up as we flew over."

"Then why aren't they running across the field? Are they hiding? Are they yellow?"

Martin shook his head. "No. Take these binoculars, sir. See for yourself. Everybody's walking around. They're not frightened. They—well, they just don't seem to care."

Captain Hart placed the binoculars to his tired eyes. Martin looked up and had time to observe the lines and the grooves of irritation, tiredness, nervousness there. Hart looked a million years old; he never slept, he ate little, and drove himself on, on. Now his mouth moved under the held binoculars, his voice came sharply.

"Really, Martin, I don't know why we bother. We build rockets, we go to all the trouble of crossing space, searching for them, and this is what we get. Neglect. Look at those idiots wander about in there. Don't they realize how big this is? The first space flight to touch their provincial land. How many times does that happen? Are they that blasé?"

Martin didn't know.

Captain Hart gave him back the binoculars wearily. "Why do we do it, Martin? This space travel, I mean. Always on the go. Always searching. Our insides always tight, never any rest."

"Maybe we're looking for peace and quiet. Certainly there's none on Earth," said Martin.

"No, there's not, is there?" Captain Hart was thoughtful, the fire damped down. "You think maybe that's why we're going out to the stars, eh, Martin? Looking for our lost souls, is that it? Trying to get away from our evil planet to a good one?"

"Perhaps, sir. Certainly we're looking for something."

Captain Hart cleared his throat and tightened back into sharpness. "Well, right now

we're looking for the mayor of that city there. Run in, tell them who we are, the first rocket expedition to Planet Forty-three in Star System Three. Captain Hart sends his salutations and desires to meet the mayor. On the double!"

"Yes, sir." Martin walked slowly across the meadow.

"Hurry!" snapped the captain.

"Yes, sir!" Martin trotted away. Then he walked again, smiling to himself.

The captain had smoked two cigars before Martin returned. Martin stopped and looked up into the door of the rocket, swaying, seemingly unable to focus his eyes or think.

"Well?" snapped Hart. "What happened? Are they coming to welcome us?"

"No." Martin had to lean dizzily against the ship.

"Why not?"

"It's not important," said Martin. He was looking at the golden city and blinking.

"Say something!" cried the captain. "Aren't they interested in our rocket?"

Martin said, "What? Oh. The rocket?" "No, they're not interested. Seems we came at an inopportune time."

"Inopportune time!"

Martin was patient. "Captain, listen. Something big happened yesterday in that city. It's so big, so important that we're second-rate—second fiddle. I've got to sit down." He lost his balance and sat heavily, gasping for air.

The captain chewed his cigar angrily. "What happened?"

Martin lifted his head slowly. "Sir, yesterday, in that city, a remarkable man appeared—good, intelligent, compassionate, and infinitely wise!"

The captain glared at his lieutenant. "What's that to do with us?"

"It's hard to explain. But he was a man for whom they'd waited a long time—a million years maybe. And yesterday he walked into

ILLUSTRATED BY BOB FINK

their city. That's why today, sir, our rocket landing means nothing."

The captain sat down violently. "Who was it? Not Ashley? He didn't arrive in his rocket before us and steal my glory, did he?" He seized Martin's arm. His face was pale and dismayed.

"Not Ashley, sir."

"Then it was Burton! I knew it. Burton stole in ahead of us and ruined my landing! You can't trust anyone any more."

"Not Burton, either, sir," said Martin quietly.

The captain was incredulous. "There were only three rockets. We were in the lead. This man who got here ahead of us? What was his name!"

"He didn't have a name. He doesn't need one. It would be different on every planet, sir."

The captain stared at his lieutenant with hard, cynical eyes.

"Well, what did he do that was so wonderful that nobody even looks at our ship?"

"For one thing," said Martin steadily, "he healed the sick and comforted the poor. He fought hypocrisy and dirty politics and sat among the people, talking, through the day."

"Is that so wonderful?"

"Yes, Captain."

"I don't get this." The captain confronted Martin, peered into his face and eyes. "You been drinking, eh?" He was suspicious. He backed away. "I don't understand."

Martin looked at the city. "Captain, if you don't understand, there's no way of telling you."

The captain followed his gaze. The city was quiet and beautiful and a great peace lay over it. The captain stepped forward, taking his cigar from his lips. He squinted first at Martin, then at the golden spires of the buildings.

"You don't mean—you can't mean—That man you're talking about couldn't be—"

Martin nodded. "That's what I mean, sir."

The captain stood silently, not moving. He drew himself up.

"I don't believe it," he said at last.

At high noon Captain Hart walked briskly into the city, accompanied by Lieutenant Martin and an assistant who was carrying some electrical equipment. Every once in a while the captain laughed loudly, put his hands on his hips and shook his head.

The mayor of the town confronted him. Martin set up a tripod, screwed a box onto it, and switched on the batteries.

"Are you the mayor?" The captain jabbed a finger out.

"I am," said the mayor.

The delicate apparatus stood between them, controlled and adjusted by Martin and the assistant. Instantaneous translations from any language were made by the box. The words sounded crisply on the mild air of the city.

"About this occurrence yesterday," said the captain. "It occurred?"

"It did."

"You have witnesses?"

"We have."

"May we talk to them?"

"Talk to any of us," said the mayor. "We are all witnesses."

In an aside to Martin the captain said, "Mass hallucination." To the mayor, "What did this man look like?"

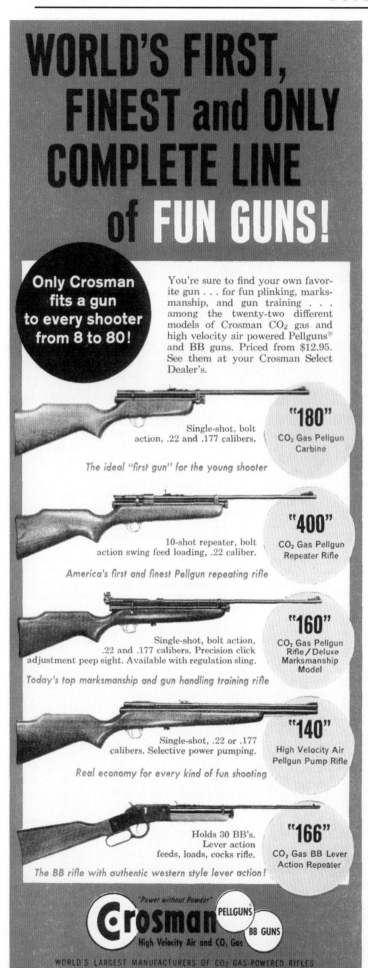
The Man

"That would be hard to say," said the mayor, smiling a little.

"Why would it?"

"Opinions might differ slightly."

"I'd like your opinion, sir, anyway," said the captain. "Record this," he snapped to Martin over his shoulder. The lieutenant pressed the button of a hand recorder.

"Well," said the mayor of the city, "he was a very gentle and kind man. He was of a great and knowing intelligence."

"Yes—yes, I know, I know." The captain waved his fingers. "Generalizations. I want something specific. What did he look like?"

"I don't believe that is important," replied the mayor.

The captain snapped his fingers. "There was something or other—a healing?"

"Many healings," said the mayor.

"May I see one?"

"You may," said the mayor. "My son." He nodded at a small boy who stepped forward. "He was afflicted with a withered arm. Now, look upon it."

AT THIS THE CAPTAIN laughed tolerantly. "Yes, yes. This isn't even circumstantial evidence, you know. I didn't see the boy's withered arm. I see only his arm whole and well. That's no proof. What proof have you that the boy's arm was withered yesterday and today is well?"

"My word is my proof," said the mayor simply.

"My dear man!" cried the captain. "You don't expect me to go on hearsay, do you? Oh no!"

"I'm sorry," said the mayor, looking upon the captain with what appeared to be curiosity and pity.

"Do you have any pictures of the boy before today?" asked the captain.

After a moment a large oil portrait was carried forth, showing the son with a withered arm.

"My dear fellow!" The captain waved it away. "Anybody can paint a picture. Paintings lie. I want a photograph of the boy."

There was no photograph. Photography was not a known art in their society.

"Well," sighed the captain, face twitching, "let me talk to a few other citizens. We're getting nowhere." He pointed at a woman. "You." She hesitated. "Yes, you; come here," ordered the captain. "Tell me about this man you saw."

The woman looked steadily at the captain. "He walked among us and was very fine and good."

"What color were his eyes?"

"The color of the sun, the color of the sea, the color of a flower, the color of the mountains, the color of the night."

"That'll do." The captain threw up his hands. "See, Martin? Absolutely nothing. Some charlatan wanders through whispering sweet nothings in their ears and—"

"Please, stop it," said Martin.

The captain stepped back. "What?"

"You heard what I said," said Martin. "I like these people. I believe what they say. You're entitled to your opinion, but keep it to yourself, sir."

"You can't talk to me this way," shouted the captain.

"I've had enough of your high-handedness," replied Martin. "Leave these people alone. They've got something good and decent, and you come and foul up the nest and sneer at it. Well, I've talked to them too. I've gone through the city and seen their faces, and they've got something you'll never have—a little simple faith, and they'll move mountains with it. You, you're boiled because someone stole your act, got here ahead and made you unimportant!"

"I'll give you five seconds to finish," remarked the captain. "I understand. You've been under a strain, Martin. Months of traveling in space, nostalgia, loneliness. And now, with this thing happening, I sympathize, Martin. I overlook your petty insubordination."

"I don't overlook your petty tyranny," replied Martin. "I'm stepping out. I'm staying here."

"You can't do that!"

"Can't I? Try and stop me. This is what I came looking for. I didn't know it, but this is it. This is for me. Take your filth somewhere else and foul up other nests with your doubt and your—scientific method!" He looked swiftly about. "These people have had an experience, and you can't seem to get it through your head that it's really happened and we were lucky enough to almost be in on it.

"People on Earth have talked about this man for centuries after he walked through the old world. We've all wanted to see him and hear him and never had the chance. And now, today, we just missed seeing him by a few hours."

Captain Hart looked at Martin's cheeks. "You're crying like a baby. Stop it."

"I don't care."

"Well, I do. In front of these natives we're to keep up a front. You're overwrought. As I said, I forgive you."

"I don't want your forgiveness."

"You idiot. Can't you see this is one of Burton's tricks, to fool these people, to bilk them, to establish his oil and mineral concerns under a religious guise! You fool, Martin. You absolute fool! You should know Earthmen by now. They'll do anything—lie, cheat, steal, kill, to get their ends. Anything is fine if it works; the true pragmatist, that's Burton. You know him!"

THE CAPTAIN SCOFFED heavily. "Come off it, Martin, admit it; this is the sort of scaly thing Burton might carry off, polish up these citizens and pluck them when they're ripe."

"No," said Martin, thinking of it.

The captain put his hand up. "That's Burton. That's him. That's his dirt, that's his criminal way. I have to admire the old dragon. Flaming in here in a blaze and a halo and a soft word and a loving touch, with a medicated salve here and a healing ray there. That's Burton all right!"

"No." Martin's voice was dazed. He covered his eyes. "No, I won't believe it."

"You don't want to believe." Captain Hart kept at it. "Admit it now. Admit it! It's just the thing Burton would do. Stop daydreaming, Martin. Wake up! It's morning. This is a real world and we're real, dirty people—Burton the dirtiest of us all!"

Martin turned away.

"There, there, Martin," said Hart, mechanically patting the man's back. "I understand. Quite a shock for you. I know. A rotten shame, and all that. That Burton is a rascal. You go take it easy. Let me handle this."

Martin walked off slowly toward the rocket.

Captain Hart watched him go. Then, taking a deep breath, he turned to the woman he had been questioning. "Well. Tell me some more about this man. As you were saying, madam?"

LATER THE OFFICERS of the rocket ship ate supper on card tables outside. The captain correlated his data to a silent Martin who sat red-eyed, brooding over his meal.

"Interviewed three dozen people, all of them full of the same milk and hogwash," said the captain. "It's Burton's work all right, I'm positive. He'll be spilling back in here tomorrow or next week to consolidate his miracles and beat us out in our contracts. I think I'll stick on and spoil it for him."

Martin glanced up sullenly. "I'll kill him," he said.

"Now, now, Martin! There, there, boy."

"I'll kill him—so help me, I will."

"We'll put an anchor on his wagon. You have to admit he's clever. Unethical but clever."

"He's dirty."

"You must promise not to do anything violent." Captain Hart checked his figures. "According to this, there were thirty miracles of healing performed, a blind man restored to vision, a leper cured. Oh, Burton's efficient, give him that."

A gong sounded. A moment later a man ran up. "Captain, sir. A report! Burton's ship is coming down. Also the Ashley ship, sir!"

"See!" Captain Hart beat the table. "Here come the jackals to the harvest! They can't wait to feed. Wait till I confront them. I'll make them cut me in on this feat—I will!"

Martin looked sick. He stared at the captain.

"Business, my dear boy, business," said the captain.

Everybody looked up. Two rockets swung down out of the sky. When the rockets landed they almost crashed.

"What's wrong with those fools?" cried the captain, jumping up. The men ran across the meadowlands to the steaming ships. The captain arrived. The airlock door popped open on Burton's ship. A man fell out into their arms.

"What's wrong?" cried Captain Hart.

The man lay on the ground. They bent over him and he was burned, badly burned. His body was covered with wounds and scars and tissue that was inflamed and smoking. He looked up out of puffed eyes and his thick tongue moved in his split lips.

"What happened?" demanded the

captain, kneeling down, shaking the man's arm.

"Sir, sir," whispered the dying man. "Forty-eight hours ago, back in Space Sector Seventy-nine DFS, off Planet One in this system, our ship, and Ashley's ship, ran into a cosmic storm, sir." Liquid ran gray from the man's nostrils. Blood trickled from his mouth. "Wiped out. All crew. Burton dead. Ashley died an hour ago. Only three survivors."

"Listen to me!" shouted Hart, bending over the bleeding man. "You didn't come to this planet before this very hour?"

Silence.

"Answer me!" cried Hart.

The dying man said, "No. Storm. Burton dead two days ago. This first landing on any world in six months."

"Are you sure?" shouted Hart, shaking violently, gripping the man in his hands. "Are you sure?"

"Sure, sure," mouthed the dying man.

"Burton died two days ago? You're positive?"

"Yes, yes," whispered the man. His head fell forward. The man was dead.

The captain knelt beside the silent body. The captain's face twitched, the muscles jerking involuntarily. The other members of the crew stood back of him looking down. Martin waited. The captain asked to be helped to his feet, finally, and this was done. They stood looking at the city. "That means—"

"That means?" said Martin.

"We're the only ones who've been here," whispered Captain Hart. "And that man—"

"What about that man, Captain?" asked Martin.

The captain's face twitched senselessly. He looked very old indeed, and gray. His eyes were glazed. He moved forward.

"Come along, Martin. Come along. Hold me up; for my sake, hold me. I'm afraid I'll fall. And hurry. We can't waste time—"

They moved, stumbling, toward the city, in the long dry grass, in the blowing wind.

SEVERAL HOURS later they were sitting in the mayor's auditorium. A thousand people had come and talked and gone. The captain had remained seated, his face haggard, listening, listening. There was so much light in the faces of those who came and testified and talked he could not bear to see them. And all the while his hands traveled, on his knees, together; on his belt, jerking and quivering.

When it was over, Captain Hart turned to the mayor and with strange eyes said: "But you must know where he went?"

"He didn't say where he was going," replied the mayor.

"To one of the other nearby worlds?" demanded the captain.

"I don't know."

"You must know."

"Do you see him?" asked the mayor, indicating the crowd.

The captain looked. "No."

"Then he is probably gone," said the mayor.

"Probably, probably!" cried the captain weakly. "I've made a horrible mistake, and I want to see him now. Why, it just came to me,

this is a most unusual thing in history. To be in on something like this. Why, the chances are one in billions we'd arrived at one certain planet among millions of planets the day after he came! You must know where he's gone!"

"Each finds him in his own way," replied the mayor gently.

"You're hiding him." The captain's face grew slowly ugly. Some of the old hardness returned in stages. He began to stand up.

"No," said the mayor.

"You know where he is then?" The captain's fingers twitched at the leather holster on his right side.

"I couldn't tell you where he is, exactly," said the mayor.

"I advise you to start talking."

"There's no way," said the mayor, "to tell you anything."

"Liar!" The captain took out a small steel gun. An expression of pity came into the mayor's face as he looked at Hart.

"You're very tired," he said. "You've traveled a long way and you belong to a tired people who've been without faith a long time, and you want to believe so much now that you're interfering with yourself. You'll only make it harder if you kill. You'll never find him that way."

"Where'd he go? He told you; you know. Come on, tell me!" The captain waved the gun.

The mayor shook his head.

"Tell me! Tell me!"

The gun cracked once, twice. The mayor fell, his arm wounded.

Martin leaped forward. "Captain!"

The gun flashed at Martin. "Don't interfere."

ON THE FLOOR, HOLDING his wounded arm, the mayor looked up. "Put down your gun. You're hurting yourself. You've never believed, and now that you think you believe, you hurt people because of it."

"I don't need you," said Hart, standing over him. "If I missed him by one day here, I'll go on to another world. And another and another. I'll miss him by half a day on the next planet, maybe, and a quarter of a day on the third planet, and two hours on the next, and an hour on the next, and half an hour on the next, and a minute on the next. But after that, one day I'll catch up with him! Do you hear that?" He was shouting now, leaning wearily over the man on the floor. He staggered with exhaustion. "Come along, Martin." He let the gun hang in his hand.

"No," said Martin. "I'm staying here."

"You're a fool. Stay if you like. But I'm going on, with the others, as far as I can go."

The mayor looked up at Martin. "I'll be all right. Leave me. Others will tend my wounds."

"I'll be back," said Martin. "I'll walk as far as the rocket."

They walked with vicious speed through the city. One could see with what effort the captain struggled to show all the old iron, to keep himself going. When he reached the rocket he slapped the side of it with a trembling hand. He holstered his gun. He looked at Martin.

"Well, Martin?"

Martin looked at him. "Well, Captain?"

The captain's eyes were on the sky. "Sure you won't—come with—with me, eh?"

"No, sir."

"It'll be a great adventure. I know I'll find him."

"You are set on it now, aren't you, sir?" asked Martin.

The captain's face quivered and his eyes closed. "Yes."

"There's one thing I'd like to know."

"What?"

"Sir, when you find him—if you find him," asked Martin, "what will you ask of him?"

"Why—" The captain faltered, opening his eyes. His hands clenched and unclenched. He puzzled a moment and then broke into a strange smile. "Why, I'll ask him for a little peace and quiet." He touched the rocket. "It's been a long time, a long, long time since— since I relaxed."

"Did you ever just try, Captain?"

"I don't understand," said Hart.

"Never mind. So long, Captain."

"Goodby, Mr. Martin."

The crew stood by the port. Out of their number only three were going on with Hart. Seven others were remaining behind, they said, with Martin.

Captain Hart surveyed them and uttered his verdict: "Fools!"

He, last of all, climbed into the airlock, gave a brisk salute, laughed sharply. The door slammed.

The rocket lifted into the sky on a pillar of fire. Martin watched it go far away and vanish. At the meadow's edge the mayor, supported by several men, beckoned.

"He's gone," said Martin.

"Yes, poor man, he's gone," said the mayor. "And he'll go on, planet after planet, seeking and seeking, and always and always he will be an hour late, or a half hour late, or ten minutes late, or a minute late. And finally he will miss out by only a few seconds. And when he has visited three hundred worlds and is seventy or eighty years old he will miss out by only a fraction of a second, and then a smaller fraction of a second. And he will go on and on, thinking to find that very thing which he left behind here, on this planet, in this city—"

Martin looked steadily at the mayor.

The mayor put out his hand. "Was there ever any doubt of it?" He beckoned to the others and turned. "Come along now. We mustn't keep him waiting."

They walked into the city.

THE END

ABOUT THE AUTHOR: *Ray Bradbury, best known as the author of many distinguished science fiction tales, has also written general interest stories for the "Saturday Evening Post" and other magazines; the screenplay for such movies as "Moby Dick;" and several books, including one for children, "Switch on the Night." He has always been interested in the Boy Scouts of America, and although his family consists of four daughters, is a subscriber to BOYS' LIFE. He was born in Waukegan, Illinois, and now lives in California.*

© Copyright 1958 by Standard Magazines Inc. Originally published in Thrilling Wonder Stories, Feb., 1949. Reprinted by permission of Harold Matson Co.

Quarles simply allowed the first truck to pass, then he pulled the pin of a grenade and lobbed it toward the second truck

Desert Raiders

By JOHN B. STANLEY

ILLUSTRATED BY BOB FINK

Behind Rommel's lines ten men operated with the craftiness of wolves and left fire and devastation along their trail

THERE were ten of them.

In the moonlight of the early evening as he looked at them, Keith thought of how fit they all looked. These were *real* soldiers, he told himself, and if anyone could do the job that lay ahead, these men could. A sense of pride surged through him, and he was thankful for the fate that had made him their commander. His gaze shifted from face to face. Then suddenly a twinge of anxiety shook him. He wasn't sure whether it was caused by the sight of young Quarles or simply by his concern for the entire group; but he was disturbed, and there flashed through his mind in kaleidoscopic series the misfortunes that might befall his little band on this raid behind Rommel's line.

A moment later he spoke, his disquiet banished:

"Well, chaps, let's review the plan one last time. Lieutenant Higgins will lead his party to the airdrome so as to attack at 21:30. All aircraft on the ground will be destroyed and petrol storage tanks fired. Shoot up airdrome personnel—and any other jerries that get in your way—and destroy or damage whatever facilities you can. Join me here at Wadi Selim not later than 22:45."

He paused before continuing with the remainder of his orders. In the uniform of a colonel of the German general staff, erect, tall and broad shouldered, he looked Prussian rather than British. But in the hardness of his weather worn face there were no cruel lines; and the blue-steel eyes, widely separated over a rather sharp nose, were warmed by a mouth more natural when stretched in smile than when drawn in the tight lines it could assume.

"Quarles and I," he continued, "with Rumsey driving the jeep will leave for Bardo immediately. We'll first reconnoiter the harbor and waterfront. Then we'll probably tackle the bosche headquarters before leaving for Wadi Selim. At 22:45 we'll all leave here for our desert landing field. The transport plane that's to pick us up should be there between 23:30 and 23:45.

"Whether or not all of us are at the landing field, the plane will take off at 24:00. If we're pursued too closely we may have to signal the plane not to land; or maybe it can land and take off immediately. In any event, if some of us don't make the plane, they'll have to try and make their own way back to our lines as best they can. Are there any questions?"

The silence that settled over the group was unbroken. Then Keith spoke again.

"Set your watches. It is now eighteen thirty-nine—thirty-nine thirty—thirty-nine forty-five—fifty—eighteen forty."

Once more there was a pause, and uneasily the men shifted about in place. Abruptly Keith turned to Higgins and stuck out his hand.

"Good luck, Ned. See you later on."

"Luck, sir," Higgins' reply was low. "Take care of yourself."

WITH the six of Higgins' group he also shook hands; and with each clasp he gave a bit of jocular advice, like a coach patting a player on the back before sending him into a big game. There was a natural reserve between them, even at this parting; but through the wall of constraint, as they exchanged comments, penetrated a sense of reciprocal respect and admiration, almost love. It was a feeling shared only by those who had been through hardships and dangers together; it was what made men fight and die together. This was a moment that would live forever in the memories of all these men; but it was only a moment and it passed quickly.

A few seconds later Keith climbed into the little *volkswagen* that they had taken from the Germans on their last raid and had renamed a jeep because of its resemblance to the similar American vehicle. Then, as Lieutenant Quarles settled himself beside him, he tapped Rumsey on the shoulder and said simply, "Let's go."

Fifteen minutes of driving over the rough Libyan desert road brought them to the coastal highway. Effortlessly the little car turned onto the smooth macadam and they rolled toward Bardo. Only the rhythmic humming of the tires disturbed the night stillness and, like gentle music, it lulled the three men to silence.

Through Keith's mind ran thoughts of the past ten days, days that had brought them through the last British mine field south of El Alamein to the wadi they had just left. It was like one long day rather than ten, he felt, for all of those daylight hours under the everlasting blue of the Libyan sky and the fiery desert sun really had merged into one. Ten bivouacs, remembered only as begun in the chilly half light of dawn when camouflage nets were raised to shield from prying Axis planes men and vehicles alike, because indistinct and inseparate. Unnumbered meals, some cold, others warmed in concealed fires, but all shared with clouds of voracious flies that seemed as numerous as they did careless of whether they feasted on man or food, were remembered only as one.

He thought, too, of those long nights of silent travel to this, the djebel country. Like the days, they fused into a single period of time, a space in which the occasional pauses, the rare engine trouble, and the daylight halts, were the only highlights. He wondered how many times he had doubted the verity of his navigational calculations and how often he had verified his course. How many hours, he asked himself, had they spent checking their maps?

His mind leapt to the plans they had made for this night. Did everyone understand his job? Had he neglected any details? Had he forgotten anything? All these things he asked himself and had to be content with the simple answer that only the next few hours would tell.

Fondly, he considered the men he had just left. He knew them, he felt, as a father knows his children; like a father he knew he would have no rest until he should see them all again. He had no doubt that they would give a good account of themselves, for he had been on raids with all of them. But veterans or no, they were *his* men and tonight each one of them would be in danger. Until the danger had passed he would know no peace.

Their faces flashed before his mind: Higgins, quiet, capable, red-headed Higgins, who had proved himself a dozen times over; McKenna the Scot, fierce in his hatred of everything German since that day when he had heard of his wife's death in a winter bombing; the ebullient, leathery faced O'Meara, who laughed so as he sprayed lead with his Tommy gun; Porter, who looked like a clod but whose quick-thinking had saved his mates more than once; Jamison, the slim London boy who seemed so out of place in the desert yet who got along so well with the Arabs; Newberry, swearing every raid would be his last but the first to ask new assignments. It was indeed a good crew, he told himself; and he wished he were with them instead of alone with Rumsey and Quarles.

RUMSEY seemed to sense that his commander was thinking of him, for he took his eyes off the road long enough to turn his head and twist his face into that slow smile of his. He was an eager, quiet chap, sometimes too quiet thought Keith. But at any rate, he was experienced and had proved his coolness if not his audacity in the last two forays.

He wished that he had the same confidence in Quarles that he had in Rumsey. His brow wrinkled in worry as he reflected that the youth by his side when matched with the other men in the band was like a piece of unpainted furniture in a smart drawing room. Inexperienced and untrained in the operations of the Long Range Desert Groups, this was Quarles' first raid and Keith felt that he was certain to be much more of a liability than an asset. For the hundredth time since they had begun their trek he belabored himself for having been persuaded by the Colonel to permit Quarles to come along. And again, as always, he told himself that he had given in only because the lad spoke German so fluently—almost, in fact, as well as Keith did himself.

Out of the corner of his eye he glanced at Jeffrey Quarles, some day to be the eleventh Lord Crestwicke. He had to admit that the boy was rugged and physically well equipped for this type of work, for the hundred and sixty pounds or so that he carried were trimly distributed over his tall frame. The squared shoulders and tapering waist set off well the uniform of a captain of the Afrika Korps. If, even in the moonlight that illumined it now, the face beneath that jauntily placed canvas cap had some signs of maturity, Keith admitted to himself he would have felt better. But the slightly turned up nose, the clear blueness of the eyes, and the unconcerned mouth gave no evidence of the toughness that comes to the veteran only through trial by fire.

"Jerries up the road, sir."

Rumsey's words, barely loud enough to be heard above the singing tires, startled Keith. Precipitately his mind switched to the import of the warning. Every nerve and sense alert, he peered ahead. By degrees his eyes focused and he distinguished what appeared to be a roadside hut with a small group of men clustered about it. As the car gradually slowed, he made out the figures to be German soldiers. Instinctively he loosened his holster, a tense, tight feeling sweeping over him. The first test was upon them.

Even before the little vehicle had rolled to a halt, a beam of light from the sentry's flashlight struck them. There was but a semblance of hesitation as the man recognized the general staff insignia. Then, without question, he saluted smartly, and waved that they could continue their way.

THEY were in Bardo.

Slower now, the car threaded its way through the narrow streets. Surely and without error Rumsey steered his way down one quiet thoroughfare and up another; hours of patient pouring over maps had given him expert knowledge of the town. Occasionally they passed German soldiers, the guttural conversations and clash of hobnailed boots against pavement echoing into the night as groups of twos and threes wandered aimlessly about. Only rarely did they spot the silent, robed Arab townsfolk; but the clinging, fetid odors that seemed to rise out of the ground like steam never for a moment let them forget that this was Africa.

In spite of their leisurely pace it was not long before they had traversed the width of Bardo and arrived at the breakwater which stretched out from the southern shore of the bay that had made the town a port. Silently, the low grinding of brakes lost in the crashing roar of the Mediterranean surf, the car came to a halt. Then Keith, followed by Quarles, clambered out and wordlessly waved Rumsey off to carry out the pre-arranged plan of awaiting the two officers in an alley near the German headquarters.

They stood motionless for a minute taking in the view before them. Across the mouth of the half-moon bay they saw the breakwater that extended almost to the tiny cape jutting out from the northern shore. In front of them loomed a pier warehouse and beyond, reaching like fingers into the glistening harbor waters, they could see the tips of five other wharves. The cobbled waterfront road bent with the semi-circular shore, all but a small portion hidden from their view by the sharp bend it took near the second dock.

Slowly they began to walk.

As they drew closer to the first wharf a large number 6 became visible. Two small sailing ships, masts pointing skyward above the pier warehouse, lay moored to the wharf stanchions. Then in the shadows of the entrance they discerned a lone sentry standing immobile as the pier house itself. A dozen steps further on they were challenged, saluted, and passed on as they identified themselves as "Colonel von Kalb" and "Captain Schmidt."

Like number six, Pier Five showed ➡

But even before they had come within a few yards of the group Quarles squeezed the trigger

Desert Raiders

few signs of activity as they approached. There a small coastwise freighter, fires banked and apparently unloaded, sat quietly next to the warehouse, slapping wavelets emphasizing the shipboard silence. Again a single guard challenged, saluted, and permitted them to pass.

The warehouse on Pier Five, like the others, overlapped from the quay onto land. As they rounded one corner of this building there came into view the remainder of the waterfront road. Almost as they made the turn, the moon ducked behind a cloud. Almost, but not quite, the blanketing gloom shut out the sight of row upon row of vehicles. Crowding the dockside thoroughfare in the blackness, the ranks merged into shapeless lumps. Even so, a curious excitement swept over Keith at the scene and he nudged Quarles to move to the landward side of the street.

THEY crossed diagonally, but had not quite reached the first line of trucks when the moonlight again poured down.

"Petrol carriers!" whispered Quarles, galvanized by the revelation of the long line of gasoline tank trucks that stretched from in front of Pier Four as far as they could see. "What can they be doing here? Do you suppose—"

"Sh! Quiet, boy! That's what we have to find out," interrupted Keith warningly. His muffled remarks were out before he realized, but even in that crowded moment he regretted his words as out of a corner of his eyes he saw Quarles' lips tighten at the rebuke.

"Let's move along, Quarles; there's something strange about all of this," he growled more kindly.

Still walking slowly, the British officers approached the first line of trucks. Standing silent, five in a row, and without a sign of drivers, all the trucks apparently were empty. Long hose lines, stretched out between the ranks, indicated readiness for some sort of a fueling operation.

They had moved past a dozen or so ranks before Keith spoke again: "Looks as if they're getting ready to fill up, but I don't see a sign of any tankers in the harbor or at the docks. Do you make anything of it?"

"No, sir, but we've only had a look at three piers. There may be tankers tied up at the others," said Quarles quietly.

"That's hardly possible," replied Keith. "Our air and naval reconnaissance keeps a good check on that sort of thing, and we probably would see some evidence of recent bombing here if anything had moved in within the past two weeks. We'd better move across the road again, though, and check each dock to be sure."

Quarles nodded and the two moved through the rows of trucks to the seaward side of the street. They were about to emerge from between the vehicles when Quarles pulled on Keith's coat sleeve and pointed out into the harbor.

"Look there, Sir," he said.

As quickly as he spoke, Keith turned his head.

"So," he breathed softly, "subs."

Two submarines, barely discernible, were passing through the narrow entrance between the breakwater and the north shore cape. Even as they looked, others followed and they counted a total of twelve in the harbor. Then, as the procession of submersibles seemed to end, they moved out from behind the truck that had shielded them and proceeded towards the other piers.

Hardly had they taken a step when the sound of a voice, stridently piercing the silence, stopped them in their tracks. Instinctively they ducked back behind the trucks. Then, cautiously, both worked forward in the shadows of the huge vehicles towards Dock Number Two. There, they were just able to see, was a large group of soldiers, apparently being addressed by an officer.

Bits of phrases floated to them.

"—docks—pumps—U-boats—panzers —first trucks fueled are to—"

They edged closer and the words of the speaker registered more clearly.

"—U-boats will be moored at—pumps should be ready to operate by—o'clock. All trucks must be fueled by five a.m. They will proceed individually to the assembly points 'A' and 'B', fifteen miles and five miles, respectively, south of Bardo on the Bardo-Tobruk road. They will remain there all day in the camouflaged areas prepared. Orders for the movement forward tomorrow night will be issued at the assembly points.

"The Field Marshal himself has sent instructions from his forward headquarters that this operation must be carried out successfully if our valiant panzer divisions are to have fuel to attack. All of us must therefore leave nothing undone that will speed the operation. All must work doubly hard to see that it is carried out in the efficient manner that has already brought glory to our irresistible army."

KEITH looked significantly at Quarles and nodded his head in the direction of the center of town. Like two wraiths they dodged into the shadows of the trucks. Soon they were plodding up one of the narrow side streets towards headquarters.

Tersely and somewhat as if he were thinking aloud, Keith spoke to his companion: "Here's how I figure it. The U-boats are submarine tankers. The jerries are using them to bring in petrol to the panzers. This is the big

leak that our navy and air force have not been able to plug up. The petrol carriers will fill up tonight and by dawn will be moved to two assembly points. They'll stay in those two camouflaged areas tomorrow and then tomorrow night will take the fuel to the panzer divisions. Rommel and his staff are not in Bardo. That means that we can change the plans we've made to bomb and shoot up the bosche GHQ. We must get back word to our intelligence tonight so they can send bombers here by dawn and then scout around for those two camouflaged assembly points in daylight tomorrow and bomb them. We can't risk taking chances of not getting back, so we'll go straight to the alley and get Rumsey."

He finished speaking and as he did so became conscious of footsteps behind them. Discreetly he glanced backward as they strode along. Two figures, though seemingly attempting to take advantage of the shadowy street, appeared more than once in bold outline. It was obvious that they were dogging the two Britishers, though they were making every effort not to attract the attention of their prey.

"Quarles," Keith spoke quietly, "we're being followed. We'll keep on our way as if we didn't know about it till I figure this thing out. Don't look back, and for heaven's sake, don't get excited."

To his relief Keith saw that the youngster did not so much as wince at the news. Only that same tightening of the lips marked his receipt of the information. And that expression, the older man was sure, was only a sign of the other's resentment of the tenor of the warning. Again he regretted his words. They continued on their way.

A short while later he spoke again: "There's only one thing to do. Too many soldiers in the streets and we're too near headquarters. We can't take a chance on luring them into an alley and slugging them. I've got to throw them off the scent some other way. I'm going to try a stunt at headquarters. You just carry out what I tell you to do when we get there. Haven't time to tell you more now."

They emerged from the side street a

few feet from the headquarters building. Boldly, though they knew their two pursuers could not be far behind, they sauntered up to the entrance.

"Major Rintel is the commandant?" casually asked Keith of the sentry after he had returned the salute.

"No, Herr Colonel, Major Mueller is our commandant. I have never heard of Major Rintel," replied the guard.

"Ah, yes. Mueller, of course," said the British officer as if wondering how he could possibly have failed to remember such a simple name as Mueller. "Have the sergeant of the guard call Major Mueller. I wish to speak to him."

"Would not the Herr Colonel care to enter? The Major is in his office," politely rejoined the soldier.

"Have the Major come out," said Keith sternly. "I am in a hurry and must travel tonight. Schmidt," turning to Quarles, "have Hans bring round the car."

Immediately the guard spoke to another soldier inside the doorway, giving the message that "a colonel of the General Staff wished to see the Commandant outside right away." Simultaneously, Quarles quit the side of the pseudo-colonel to search out Rumsey and the car.

Keith looked at his watch and out of a corner of his eye towards the corner of the headquarters building near which he was sure his two trailers were lurking. He couldn't see them; but they were there, he was sure. At any rate, he felt, Quarles would know when he came back, for he had to pass that spot on his way to the entrance.

A SHORT, roly-poly major bustled through the door, obviously very distressed as he tried to fasten his blouse at the same moment that he smoothed his hair. He looked almost ready to burst into tears as he pulled himself up short in front of "the colonel." Clearly he was a very poor example of the race of supermen and he seemed well aware of his shortcomings.

"Good evening, Herr Colonel. Good evening, Sir. I didn't know you were in this accursed town, Sir. Won't you come in, Sir? I assure you, Herr Colonel, my poor office is at your disposal. Won't you—" All in one breath the skittish officer spouted his words which seemed to trip over each other like little school children pouring from a classroom.

"Major Mueller!" The clipped words of the impostor were searing in tone and damned the verbal flood of the distressed major.

"Yes, Herr Colonel?" weakly answered the other.

"I wish to speak to you. Let us move away from this door. I will speak to you in private and I cannot waste time going into this pig-pen."

"Yes, Herr Colonel. Of course, Sir. As you wish, Sir."

The major was now in worse case than before. His face, which in the light streaming through the doorway had had some semblance of color, was now a pasty yellow. He twitched feverishly and scampered after Keith like a puppy as the latter began walking to the corner.

They stopped out of earshot of the headquarters sentry, but, Keith was sure, still within hearing distance of the two men who had been following him and Quarles. The moment they halted, Quarles drove up with Rumsey and jumped out of the car. He said only that the Herr Colonel's car was ready and was motioned to silence by an imperious wave of the hand. Not unnoticed, however, was his meaningful eye movement that signalled the presence of the two pursuers in the nearby shadows.

"And now, Major Mueller," said

Keith coldly, looking at the German. "You know me, of course."

"But certainly," quavered the major, uneasy but sure now that he must not confess to anything that might make him appear worse in the eyes of the visitor. "Had I known the Herr Colonel was in Bardo, I would have—"

"I did not wish my presence known," interrupted Keith with all the Prussian austerity that he could muster.

"Naturally, naturally," agreed the major, "I under—"

"But," interrupted Keith again, "I have serious charges to lodge against you, for you have failed to take proper measures to maintain the security of this port."

"Oh, Herr Colonel, that can't be, Sir," expostulated the now frightened officer in a voice that shook as it mounted in shrillness. "I have taken every possible measure—all precautions, Herr Colonel. I have guards for every warehouse on the waterfront. A motor patrol constantly goes through the town. There are foot patrols in the streets. I have done everything, Herr Colonel, I assure you—there must be some mistake, Herr Colonel—I—I—"

"There is no mistake, Major Mueller." Keith's words were harsh and brought the man's outflow to a halt.

"Yes, of course, Herr Colonel. What is it that the Herr Colonel finds incorrect?" The little major was not abject in his anxiety.

"The Captain," motioning to Quarles, "and I have inspected the waterfront. We walked its length and were challenged by your sentries. But not once, Major, not once did your sentries make us identify ourselves. We walked through the vehicles parked on the waterfront and were not stopped. We heard an officer giving instructions to his men. We walked back to headquarters and, can you believe me, were followed by two clumsy fools who even now are probably trying to overhear what I am saying to you."

THE scorn in the British officer's voice was searing; and as he finished he noticed what seemed to be a flurry of shadows from the direction of the corner. Apparently the two men who had trailed them had considered it better not to be found in the vicinity of the distraught Major and his two important visitors. As for the Major, he was completely downcast. Only a mumbled half-croak, half-squeal came from his throat.

"Ordinarily I would only reprimand you, Major," said Keith in the same cold tone but now much relieved, "but in view of yesterday's intelligence warning of the expected British paratroop raid, I fear that I must relieve you of your command."

A gleam of hope darted into the Major's stricken face as the import of the last few words came to him.

"Intelligence warning? But I have not received any such warning. I swear to you, Herr Colonel, that no such message was received. I—"

"What!" grated Keith in well-simulated consternation, "are you sure?"

"I swear it, Herr Colonel. I myself check every incoming message and none has been received. I will show you our files—" Breaking off in the middle of his explanations the German darted to the headquarters entrance like a scared rabbit.

More slowly the two British officers walked to the doorway as Quarles whispered, "One minute to go before the airport attack."

In a moment the Major was back with a bulky message file in his hands. But now there was a note of confidence as he spoke.

"You can see for yourself, Herr Colo-

nel. Right here, sir. You see—" He began thumbing through the file and the words poured out as fast as he could voice them.

"Of course I shall revoke my decision," said Keith reassuringly, "if I find you have not received the message. Here, Captain," he said, taking the file from the shaking hands of the German officer and handing it over to Quarles, "look through these messages and see if yesterday's intelligence warning was received. The Major and I must talk over some—"

The staccato sound of distant small arms fire and the dull booms of explosions shattered the hush of the night. A sheet of flame reared skyward, then more thudding rumbles resounded. With a start the major yelped, "The British. Airport! Got to get troops there! Sergeant! Lieutenant Schultz!"

"Quiet, you fool. Do nothing of the sort," barked Keith as he grabbed the almost hysterical Major. "That's probably only a diversion at the airport. The real attack will come on the town and waterfront. British planes are now probably near by. Order your men down to the waterfront to protect the docks and transportation. Have all anti-aircraft guns open fire and maintain it for thirty minutes. I myself will go to the airport. You stay here."

With a nod of understanding, but still screaming for the sergeant and Lieutenant Schultz, the Major bounded off again. Keith and Quarles climbed into the jeep and sped off, the message file with them.

As anti-aircraft guns barked, searchlights weaved in and out of clouds, and sirens wailed; as booming thumps and the faint crackling of rifles and machine guns floated in from the direction of the airfield, the three invaders drew near the outpost at which they had been halted on their way into Bardo. Now, though, a tremendous sheet of flame from the airdrome illumined the scene and in the light they could see at least a half dozen soldiers in the roadway.

"'Fraid we may get into trouble if we stop this time," shouted Keith over the wind and noise. "Better take a chance on rushing 'em. Step on it as soon as they think we're about to stop," he yelled to Rumsey as he picked up a sub-machine gun from the floor of the car.

GRADUALLY they slowed down. Then they saw the Nazi soldiers relax, sliding their cradled weapons to less ready positions. But even before they had come within a few yards of the group Quarles squeezed the trigger of the Tommy gun he held. One or two of the soldiers staggered, clutched their bodies, and slumped to the ground. The others hit the earth, ducking behind whatever cover was at hand.

In the brief interval before Keith opened fire and the jeep accelerated to full speed, Quarles caught the bitter look on his superior's face and knew he had done wrong. Then, as the bullets began chipping the ground about the flying car, he realized his blunder. In the screaming wind he heard one snatches of his commander's recriminations, "—should've waited—too soon, dash it—fire before—"

The words faded into a groan. Then Keith lunged and toppled to the floor of the speeding car.

Numbly, the youth gathered the unconscious body into his arms. Without thinking he ripped open the blood-soaked tunic and applied a first aid compress to the torn flesh. In the darkness he could not tell how seriously Keith was hurt; he was not even sure that he was not dead.

Of only one thing was he sure: he was responsible for this catastrophe.

By his fault the Germans had been given time to fire a few well-aimed shots at the retreating car. The few seconds had made all the difference; and now Keith, who had gone through a dozen raids unscratched, was stretched out bleeding, maybe dying, maybe dead.

He hardly knew they had turned off the highway on to the rougher desert road. And when they stopped, short of the wadi, it was only mechanically that he perceived Rumsey signalling with his flashlight. A few seconds later, when they had progressed the length of the ravine, the car turned off the road and halted. Then with tenderness, the two lifted the body of their chief to the ground.

In the light of a flashlight held by Rumsey, Quarles removed the compress he had applied and examined the wound. Tears of relief came to his eyes as he saw that the German bullet had been too high to be fatal. Quickly, with sure fingers, he bandaged the injury; then they made the unconscious officer as comfortable as they could. Through it all, not a word was spoken.

The sound of a motor brought them to their feet just as they were finishing with Keith. Warily they waited as the noise came closer. Then the shape of the approaching vehicle formed itself in the moonlight and three spaced dashes of light came from it. They relaxed, and Rumsey flashed back the answering signal.

In a moment the truck had pulled up near them. It was Davis who first dismounted and reached Quarles.

"Where's the Captain?" he asked, as if unwilling that anyone but Keith should hear his report.

"He's wounded," replied Quarles. "Not badly," he added as he saw the other's face fall, "but he's still unconscious."

"We all got away," said Davis, anticipating the officer's question, "but Lt. Higgins, O'Meara, and Jamison were shot up. I don't know how badly any of them are wounded. We were followed, too. I don't know how far behind us the jerries are nor how many of them there are. I think we'd better move right away and try to get to the airfield."

FOR a few seconds Quarles was silent as he sensed the situation. Now, he knew, he was in command. This time, he swore, he would not fail Keith and the others. It did not take him long to give his orders.

"Have everyone stay in the lorry, Davis," he said. "You help Rumsey and me lift the Captain into it. Then drive as fast as you can to the landing field. Take off as soon as you can."

"Yes, sir," said Davis. "Will you follow in the jeep or are you coming with us?"

"No," said Quarles calmly, "No. I'm staying here. This wadi is a natural ambush and if you've been followed too closely I'll be able to delay them for a while."

Davis stood silent for a minute. Then he stuck out his hand and said, "Very well, Sir. And good luck. I'll tell the Captain."

"Thanks, Davis," said Quarles, "now let's get the Captain in the lorry."

Carefully they lifted the now conscious but groggy Keith into the truck. Then Quarles walked over to the jeep that had been parked a short distance away. He was reaching into one of the compartments for some grenades when he heard the truck roar off to the airfield.

Hardly had it gone when he heard the crunch of a step behind him. He whirled about quickly, his pistol in hand.

It was Rumsey.

"What are you doing here, Rumsey?" he asked angrily. "I told Davis I wanted every man to get in the lorry and get to that plane."

"Well, Sir," said Rumsey, almost self-consciously, "there's two reasons. One is that the Captain sort of told me to look out for you and help you to keep out of trouble."

"I don't need your help or anyone else's," said Quarles hotly. "And I don't appreciate the fact that you have disobeyed orders that I gave. If I could, I'd send you on to the others, but I suppose it's too late for that," Rumsey's statement had done nothing to make him feel better, for now he realized that Keith had always had a low opinion of him; and his actions on the raid had certainly borne out the Captain's fears.

"You haven't asked me the other reason, Lieutenant," said Rumsey smilingly as he broke in on Quarles' lugubrious line of thought.

Quarles did not answer, so Rumsey spoke again.

"The other reason is, Sir, that I thought this would be the best show of the trip and I—well, I thought I'd like to be with you to see it through."

In spite of himself, his anger, and his dejection, Quarles was touched. Somehow, he felt, it couldn't be so bad if Rumsey had faith in him. And as for Keith, well, perhaps after tonight Keith would think a little better of him.

"Thanks, Rumsey," he said, without a trace of his former anger, "I'm really glad you're with me, you know. But," after a slight pause, "we've some work to do yet, so let's get started."

The plan that Quarles outlined to him was simple enough and after the two of them had loaded themselves down with grenades, tommy guns, and plenty of ammunition, they walked back along the wadi road. Midway they parted, as Quarles clambered up the side of the little ravine and Rumsey continued to the entrance to place himself above that portion of the wadi road.

They didn't have long to wait.

It was only five minutes or so after Quarles had ensconced himself that he heard the sound of motors. He strained to see the number, and gradually, as they drew closer, he made out three vehicles. They were troop carrier trucks and as they drew near the wadi they moved slowly over the rough surface.

It was all over in a short time.

QUARLES simply allowed the first truck to pass, then he pulled the pin of a grenade and lobbed it toward the second truck as it drew abreast. A second and a third he hurled, then he scrambled along the side of the little gorge and heaved more grenades after the leading vehicle. Flung to the ground by the force of the first few blasts, he climbed to one knee and pressed the trigger of his sub-machine gun. He used it as a gardener would a hose, pointing it first in the direction of the leading truck and then spraying it over the second. To his rear he felt the concussions of the grenades that Rumsey had thrown and as he fired he heard the staccato sound of his companion's gun.

Determinedly he got to his feet and walked towards the first truck. Clip after clip he loaded, unconscious of the shrieks and groans, unmindful of the scattered fire that came from what remained of the leading troop carrier. He drew closer, had almost reached the bulk of the truck when he felt a searing, burning stab in his shoulder. He spun around, clutched for the air, then knew no more.

It was quiet when he regained consciousness and he was being lifted into the jeep. Dimly he saw Rumsey, felt him adjust a compress, sensed he was being placed into the seat. He realized he was wounded, somewhere near the chest or shoulder.

"Rumsey," he said weakly.

"Yes, Lieutenant," said the other,

"how're you feeling?"

"A little weak," he replied. "What happened?"

"We got 'em all, Sir. Your first grenade landed right in the middle of the second lorry. It was a beautiful lob, Sir. As good as any I've ever seen. Mine were a little short but they stopped the last one all right. I had a little trouble with some of those jerries, but finally got 'em all."

"How about the first lorry? It was blasted wasn't it?"

"Yes, Sir," said Rumsey. "Your first volley and the grenades got most of them. But one of them pinked you before I could get up to help. I finished them all off, though, Lieutenant."

Quarles felt Rumsey jab him with something. He guessed it was one of those little ampules of morphine. The jeep began rolling and the world seemed to whirl about. He fought to keep conscious and tried to speak.

"Where—you—going now—Rumsey?" he asked feebly.

"To the desert landing field, Sir. We're going to join the others," replied Rumsey.

"No—can't do that—I—told them—not to—wait for me." He felt giddy as the sound of his own words reached his ears.

"Yes, Sir. I know you did. But you didn't say anything about not waiting for me and I told Davis we'd be there by 24:00. And we're going to make it and have time to spare, Sir."

"Shouldn't—have done—that—Rumsey—" The words trailed away into nothingness and he relapsed into darkness.

The pulsing roar of airplane motors came to his ears as he woke again. He looked up and his eyes focused on the face of the man who was adjusting a blanket about him. He closed his eyes again, then reopened them. He had made no mistake, it was Keith and he was smiling.

"How are you feeling, Jeff?" he asked.

New energy surged through him as he realized that Keith had called him by his first name, had shown no signs of displeasure.

"Fine, Sir. How are you feeling?" he asked. "And how are the others? Did you get word back about Bardo? Are there—"

"Sh! Quiet, Jeff. One thing at a time. Everything is all right. I just have a slight wound in my shoulder. Guess it was the creasing in the head that I got that knocked me out. The others are o.k. except Higgins who's going to be laid up for some time. We sent back the message by our plane wireless and unless I miss my guess our bombers are on their way to Bardo now. What they don't get at dawn, they'll finish off in daylight tomorrow."

Quarles breathed a deep sigh.

"I'm glad, Sir. But I'm sorry about Higgins. He's a fine officer and you'll miss him. I'm sorry about tonight, too. I—"

"Don't worry about tonight, Jeff. That's all right. As for Higgins, I hate to lose him, but we've found a good replacement," said Keith gently.

"You have, Sir. Who is he?" asked the youth drowsily.

"It's you, Jeff. Now go to sleep. We'll be landing in a little while."

Quarles dropped off to sleep again. This time there was a smile on his face.

THE son of Norman Thomas, Evan Thomas, tells in AMBULANCE IN AFRICA (Appleton-Century, $2.00) his experiences as an ambulance driver with the British 8th Army during its retreat before Rommel and during the turn of the tide at Alamein in October of 1942. The book is written in a fresh, somewhat naive, collegiate style.

It looks bad—get yourself another tree

What happened to the *Cyclops*? Why was the *Mary Celeste* abandoned?
Where is the *Waratah*? In history's log these ships are listed as

UNSOLVED MYSTERIES OF THE SEA

BY LYMAN M. NASH

ILLUSTRATED BY J. J. FLOHERTY, JR.

BUNDLED AGAINST the damp, biting cold of that early November morning in 1872, Captain Benjamin Briggs barked orders to the helmsman as *Mary Celeste* moved slowly down channel toward the open sea. When the last buoy marking the narrows between Staten Island and Brooklyn had been passed, he joined his wife and small daughter at the rail, to watch the New Jersey coast disappear astern.

Then he set course for Gibraltar.

His ship, the *Mary Celeste,* was a brigantine of 282 tons, carrying square sails on her foremast and fore and aft sails on her mainmast. Built of sturdy Nova Scotian timber at Parrsborough, Canada, in 1861, she was 98 feet from stem to stern, with a beam of 25 feet and a draft of 11 feet 2 inches. For eleven years she had plied the trade routes of the North Atlantic, bringing profit to her owners and satisfaction to the men who sailed her.

In October, 1872, with Briggs, of Marion, Massachusetts, in command, *Mary Celeste* had sailed into New York to take on 1,700 barrels of alcohol for Genoa, Italy. By odd coincidence, she was docked next to the brig *Dei Gratia*, and on the evening of November 6, Captain Briggs invited her master, Captain Morehouse, to dine with him, his wife and their small daughter.

Early the next morning, with an icy mist hanging over the Hudson, *Mary Celeste* cleared New York harbor.

A month later, on the afternoon of December 5, the Gibraltar-bound *Dei Gratia* was sailing easily before a northerly wind, some 380 miles off the coast of Portugal. Shortly after two o'clock the lookout shouted, "Sail ho!"

As *Dei Gratia* drew nearer, Captain Morehouse turned to his mate. "Looks like the *Mary Celeste*," he said. "Wonder what Briggs is doing in these waters. He should have been in the Mediterranean by now."

"If you ask me," said first mate Oliver Deveau, "that whole crew is drunk. Look how crazy the ship is acting."

The other ship was, indeed, acting strange. Although running on a port tack, several of her sails were set for a starboard tack, and whenever the wind shifted she came about to run before it.

When the two ships were less than half a mile apart, Morehouse hailed her. He received no answer. Repeated hailings failed to raise an answering voice.

"Something is wrong over there," he said to Deveau. "Maybe the crew is sick. You'd better lower a boat and investigate."

With two seamen, Deveau rowed to the silent vessel. Approaching her, he saw the name *Mary Celeste* painted in an arc on her stern, and beneath it the words *New York*. Her davits were swung out, her lifeboat gone. He grabbed a line and swung aboard.

Deveau found no hand at the helm, the deck deserted. "Hello," he shouted. "Anyone below?" The forlorn slap of a sail was his only reply. A quick glance in the cabins assured him that *Mary Celeste* was derelict.

But why? She seemed perfectly sound; her rigging was in good shape. Thoroughly puzzled, Deveau signaled Captain Morehouse to join him.

Together the two men walked forward, then aft. Their footfalls and the gentle creaking of the blocks were all that disturbed the awesome silence. Cautiously, not knowing what to expect, they went below. Everything was shipshape. They began a complete search.

In the captain's cabin the bunks were made, though one of the pillows bore the imprint of a child's head. A few pieces of Mrs. Briggs' jewelry were on a wardrobe. The *Mary Celeste's* log lay open on Captain Briggs' desk.

The last entry was dated November 24, placing the ship a little over 100 miles west of the Azores. Other ship's pa- ➡

Unsolved Mysteries of the Sea

pers were missing, and the ship's chronometer could not be found.

The main cabin gave further evidence of hasty abandonment, but yielded no clues as to why. At one end of a large table was a sewing machine with part of a child's dress in it, several spools of thread, and a thimble. At the other end was an unfinished letter beginning, "My dear wife," later proven to be in the mate's handwriting.

Unable to discover any reason for abandonment, and mindful of his salvage rights, Captain Morehouse decided to take *Mary Celeste* to Gibraltar.

Arriving at the Rock, Captain Morehouse hustled to the Admiralty office to claim salvage. He told his story to Solly Flood, who bore the impressive nomenclature, "Her Majesty's Advocate-General and Proctor for the Queen in Her Office of Admiralty, and Attorney-General for Gibraltar."

Mr. Flood, realizing he had a first-class puzzler on his hands, ordered the *Mary Celeste* fully surveyed. The results merely deepened the already dark mystery.

ON BOTH SIDES of her bow, three feet above waterline, was a gash of recent origin about seven feet long and nearly a half inch deep. Several naval officers, plus an engineer, inspected this gash. They said it had been made intentionally, that there was no possible way for it to be accidental, but that it in no way affected the boat's seaworthiness.

Except for that curious gash, the ship was in excellent shape. There were plenty of provisions aboard and an adequate supply of fresh water. There was no indication of fire or explosion, no sign of trouble from any cause. Smears on the cutlass proved to be rust, as did those "bloodstains" on deck.

As the survey report stated, *Mary Celeste* "was thoroughly sound, staunch, strong, and in every way seaworthy and well found."

Furthermore, weather reports showed the ship had encountered no storms or heavy weather. So when the court of inquiry convened, it was greatly perplexed. It had a mass of questions, but no available answers. For some reason, in mid-ocean, the crew of *Mary Celeste* upped and departed or had been spirited away. Why?

Unable to answer the big question, the board awarded the captain and crew of *Dei Gratia* $8,500 for salvage services, one-fifth the total value of ship and cargo. Then it adjourned. Mr. Flood promptly forwarded to London a report, stating that no logical explanation of the strange affair could be arrived at, although it was his personal opinion that the crew mutinied, murdered Captain Briggs, his wife Sarah, their daughter, and the mate, then sailed off in the small boat probably to be lost at sea.

This theory was semi-officially endorsed by the United States Government when the Treasury Department alerted its customs officers to watch for the mutineers,

Conservation Pledge

I GIVE MY PLEDGE AS AN AMERICAN TO SAVE AND FAITHFULLY TO DEFEND FROM WASTE THE NATURAL RESOURCES OF MY COUNTRY - ITS SOIL AND MINERALS, ITS FORESTS, WATERS, AND WILDLIFE

should they try to re-enter the country.

On that note, official interest in the enigma of the *Mary Celeste* ended. The case was tucked away in Admiralty files and left there to gather dust.

At Gibraltar a new crew was signed aboard the ship and she finished her voyage to Genoa, delivering her cargo of alcohol with no further ado. But from that day on, *Mary Celeste* was a jinxed ship. During the following years she was sold several times, each sale bringing financial ruin to the new owner. In 1884 she sailed on her last voyage, being wrecked on Roshell's Reef, off the coast of Haiti. The crew was saved, but seemed to be cursed by the *Mary Celeste*, for every one of them died or came to grief soon afterward.

MEANWHILE, THE mystery of why her crew had abandoned and what happened to them was not allowed to die. Periodically, nautical experts came forth to offer their theories, and right on their tails came other experts to prove them wrong.

One of the first with a solution was no less a personage than Sir Arthur Conan Doyle, creator of Sherlock Holmes. He believed that two of the seamen mutinied, dispatched the remainder of the crew by dumping them overboard, and were taken off the ship by accomplices. Unfortunately, Sir Arthur further obscured the riddle by calling her the *Marie Celeste*, and saying her lifeboat was aboard. Both errors have persisted to the present.

Among the more feather-brained theories was one that linked Captain Briggs and Captain Morehouse in a gargantuan conspiracy to defraud the owners. Another claimed the owners arranged the whole thing for their own dark purposes. A third named Morehouse and Deveau as the real culprits. A fourth, wishing to settle the case for all time, stated that the *Mary Celeste* never even existed, that the entire story was a myth.

From the known facts we can assume that whatever happened aboard the ship occurred on the morning of November 25, 1872. Had she been abandoned at night, the beds in the captain's cabin would not have been made.

But why was she abandoned at all? You don't desert a sound ship in favor of the perils of an open boat, unless there is something seriously wrong.

Was it mutiny, as expressed in many theories? More than likely not. It is difficult enough to overpower a ship at night, let alone in broad daylight, and there wasn't the slightest evidence of violence. Nor would mutineers be likely to leave the ship without first scuttling her. Nothing could more upset their plans than to have *Mary Celeste* remain afloat.

Piracy is also ruled out. No pirate worth his salt would capture a ship, murder its crew, and then leave behind valuable jewelry, much less a British banknote.

Some years ago the theory of a sea monster was propounded. Attacked by this denizen of the deep, the crew fought back, accounting for the gash in *Mary Celeste's* bow. When they saw it was a losing battle, they took to the lifeboat in panic and were shortly gobbled up. This is as highly improbable as another recent theory—that the ten persons aboard *Mary Celeste* were carried off to a distant planet by a flying saucer.

Coming closer to believable fact, was Captain Morehouse's theory. *Mary Celeste* was becalmed a few miles north of Santa Maria island, with a current driving her hard toward that perilous coast. For safety's sake the crew took to the boat, planning to reboard the ship if a breeze sprang up. But they forgot to attach a line to the ship, and when the desired breeze did come they were unable to regain her. Later, they themselves were driven onto that rugged shore and drowned, their boat dashed to pieces.

But Captain Briggs was a man born to the sea, not a mere amateur. No matter how desperate the situation, it is unlikely he would forget the very important precaution of trailing out a line.

Many people, Captain Briggs' relatives included, believed that the solution to the mystery lay in *Mary Celeste's* cargo. Under normal conditions, if properly stowed, alcohol is not dangerous. However, in certain circumstances the alcohol might generate gas, and given sufficiently high temperature, the gas might explode.

Perhaps, as the *Mary Celeste* sailed under a cloudless sky that warm morning long ago, an odor of gas was detected. A hatch cover was removed to let the gas escape, and until the danger was past, the crew took to the boat. Then, while they waited, the breeze freshened, *Mary Celeste* picked up speed and left them far behind. They may have perished of hunger, or died in the surf of a lonesome beach.

This explanation accounts for most of the facts. It explains the hatch cover lying on deck, and the haste of abandonment. The rusted cutlass may only have been a seaman's souvenir. The gash in the bow might not have had any connection with the mystery.

While the riddle of the *Mary Celeste* is a classic, lesser known is the poser, "What happened to the *Cyclops*?" A U. S. Navy collier, she was one of the largest fuel ships afloat, carrying the latest safety devices, and designed to weather the worst storms.

IN MID-FEBRUARY, 1918, she left Brazil with 7,000 tons of manganese and fifty-seven passengers, among them Alfred Gottschalk, American Consul-General in Rio de Janiero. Early in March *Cyclops* put in at Barbados for supplies. Two days later she steamed on her way, bound for Hampton Roads, Virginia.

On April 15, six weeks after the *Cyclops* left Barbados, the Navy announced she had been overdue for a month.

In the greatest search up to that time, ships of the United States, Britain, France, and Italy quartered every rod of ocean along her route. They visited every island dotting the Caribbean, investigated every isolated bay, examined every stretch of beach. But no trace of *Cyclops* was ever found.

142 BOYS' LIFE

Naval authorities could not account for the complete lack of wreckage. In even the most sudden sinkings, they said, life jackets, furniture, rafts, and bodies are found floating weeks and months afterward. In the case of the *Cyclops* there was nothing.

But the oddest event in the *Cyclops* mystery was yet to come. Months later it was learned that a Rio newspaper had printed an advertisement announcing memorial services for Alfred Gottschalk, "lost with the *Cyclops* at sea."

The advertisement appeared five weeks before the disappearance of Cyclops *was made public.*

Nine years earlier, and half a world away, another great ship sailed to oblivion. On July 26, 1909, the steamer *Waratah* slipped her moorings in the port of Durban, South Africa, and headed for the Cape of Good Hope. A combination passenger-freighter, she was returning to England by way of Capetown.

Shortly after dawn on July 27, she passed the *Clan MacIntyre*. The two ships exchanged greetings. Then *Waratah*'s twin screws picked up speed. An hour later she disappeared over the horizon. As the last wisp of smoke faded, she vanished forever from the sight of man, carrying 211 people to an unknown doom.

MARINE EXPERTS pointed out it was impossible for a ship of *Waratah*'s size to go down without a trace. But she disappeared nonetheless, within sight of land on a busy sea route, as completely as if she never existed.

When it comes to ghostly tales, none can surpass the true story of *Seabird*, a gallant square-rigger that wrote its name on the pages of history a hundred years ago.

One morning in 1850 she sailed proudly into Easton's Beach, Rhode Island, her white sails glistening in the sun. But instead of turning toward the wharf, *Seabird* drove madly for the shore. At the very last moment she slowed miraculously, coming to rest gently on the beach.

Startled townsmen clambered aboard. They found everything as it should be. Breakfast was laid on the table. Coffee boiled merrily on the stove. The smell of tobacco smoke still lingered in the cabins. No boats were missing. But the only living thing on board was a mongrel dog.

A thorough investigation failed to shed any light on what became of the missing crew. As weeks passed, *Seabird* ground deeper into the sandy shore. Finally her cargo of coffee and lumber was unloaded. *Seabird* refused to budge.

A few nights later the wind rose to gale force and mountainous waves rolled in from the broad Atlantic. Next morning she was gone. Like her captain and crew, *Seabird* vanished, never to be seen again.

Will these mysteries of the sea ever be solved? Probably not, for the sea grudgingly keeps her secrets. Yet the fate of *Cyclops* and *Waratah* and what happened to the crew of the *Mary Celeste* are questions that continue to tantalize us. Chances are they will tantalize men until the end of time. THE END

CASTLE HEIGHTS Military Academy

Accredited. Preparation for College and Gov't Academies. Junior School in separate plant. Boys taught to *study* and inspired to excel. High standards. Guidance program. R. O. T. C. 17 buildings. Every boy in athletics. Outdoor sports year round. Nonprofit. Swimming pool, golf, aviation. Summer school and camp. Apply early for 1962-63. For "22 Points" and catalog, address: Col. H. E. Armstrong, President, Lebanon, Tenn. (Near Nashville)

GMA

GEORGIA MILITARY ACADEMY

For Quality Education

Successful preparation for best colleges and Service Academies. Fully accredited. Grades 6-12. Small classes. Sports; two gyms, pool. ROTC highest rating. 25 acres in suburb of Atlanta. Moderate inclusive fee. Est. 1900. Summer school. Catalog.

Comdr. W. R. Brewster, Jr., President, Box 119-B, College Park, Georgia

CULVER

FOUNDATION FOR MANHOOD

Prepares boys, grades 8-12, for leading colleges and adult life. Promotes character, courtesy, leadership. Outstanding faculty and facilities. Fully accredited. All sports. ROTC. Artillery, Cavalry, Infantry, Band. 1400-acre campus on Lake Maxinkuckee. Scholarships available. Catalog. 220 Pershing Parkway, Culver, Ind.

KENTUCKY MILITARY INSTITUTE

A School with a winter home in Florida

Preparation for college under ideal climatic conditions all year. Winter months at Venice, Fla. Oldest private Military School in America. Fully accredited. ROTC. Land and water sports. *Early application advisable.* For catalog and "Why Florida", address: Col. C. B. Richmond, Box L, Lyndon, Ky.

HARGRAVE MILITARY ACADEMY

"The School Where Character Counts"

NDCC Honor School. Fully accredited. College preparatory, general courses. Grades 6-12. How-to-study training; remedial and developmental reading; individual guidance. Christian influence. Separate Junior School. All sports. Summer School. Est. 1909. Catalog. Col. Joseph H. Cosby, President, Box F, Chatham, Virginia.

COLUMBIA MILITARY ACADEMY

Fully accredited. Prepares for Colleges and Gov't. Academies. 14 buildings, 9 built by U. S. Gov't. 2 gyms, pool, ROTC. Supervised study. Weekly reports. Junior School. All Sports. Band. Orchestra, Glee Club. Summer School. Write for Catalog and "47 Features." Dept. L. Columbia, Tenn.

MIAMI MILITARY ACADEMY

NATIONALLY ACCREDITED HONOR NDCC SCHOOL

37th yr. College Prep. Separate junior school. Grades 5-12. Boys learn to study in small classes under certified men instructors. Sports, sailing, rifle team. New Gym, pool, golf, tennis, band. 30 acres on Biscayne Bay. Fireproof masonry buildings. Moderate all inclusive fee. *Summer School and Camp.* Illustrated Catalog. 10608 Biscayne Blvd., Miami 38-B, Fla.

★ Carson Long ★

Military School. Educates the whole boy—physically, mentally, spiritually. How to learn, how to labor, how to live. Prepare for college and life. Grades 6-12. 126th yr. of character building. Rates $1450.00. Box 42, New Bloomfield, Pa.

CHARLOTTE HALL MILITARY ACADEMY

188th year. 33 miles from Washington, 65 miles from Baltimore. Nonsectarian. Supervised study. Emphasis on fundamentals; how to study. Grades 7-12. All sports. Band, orchestra. 320-acre campus. Limited enrollment. Accredited. Catalog: Registrar, Box 401, Charlotte Hall, Md.

Patterson School for Boys

Fully accredited college preparation. Grades 7-12. Small classes. Emphasis on Christian character. On 1300-acre estate. Gymnasium, sports, lake. Summer camp with tutoring for boys 7 to 15 years. For "Happy Valley" catalog, write George F. Wiese, Box L, Legerwood Sta., Lenoir, N. C.

Fishburne MILITARY SCHOOL

A distinguished military school for the young man seriously concerned with making adequate preparation for college entrance. Accredited since 1897. Grades 9-12. Highest ROTC rating. Summer School. Catalog. Colonel E. P. Childs, Jr., Superintendent, Box L, Waynesboro, Virginia.

ANY OF THESE SCHOOLS WILL BE GLAD TO SEND CATALOGS ON REQUEST

SCHOOLS

FORK UNION MILITARY ACADEMY

Our ONE SUBJECT PLAN of study in Upper School (grades 9-12) has increased honor roll 50%. Develops capacity to concentrate. Fully accredited. ROTC highest rating. 560 acres. 17 modern buildings, 2 indoor pools, 2 beautiful spacious gyms. Separate infirmary, three nurses. Splendid environment, excellent health record. Junior School (grades 5-8) has own separate buildings, gym, pool. Housemothers. All athletics. Band, Glee Club. Activities. 64th year. For ONE SUBJECT PLAN booklet and catalog write

Dr. J. C. WICKER, President

Box 502, Fork Union, Virginia

RIVERSIDE MILITARY ACADEMY

6 MONTHS IN THE BLUE RIDGE MTS. ★ 3 WINTER MONTHS IN SUNNY FLORIDA

Distinguished military preparatory school—Health and interest assured by Spring and Fall in foothills of Blue Ridge Mts. (one hour from Atlanta), Winter on Southeast Florida seashore at Hollywood (16 miles Miami)—Two complete school plants with all facilities—Outdoor sports year round—Expert coaching. Fully accredited preparation all colleges—Grades 8 - 12, and P.G.

Constant association with selected teachers who live and eat with cadets—Weekly reports—ROTC directed by U.S. Army Officers. Develops self-discipline and good study habits—All-inclusive School Bill $1694—Boys 37 states. Nonsectarian. Catalog, write Gen. Sandy Beaver, Pres., Box 602, Gainesville 6, Ga.

STAUNTON MILITARY ACADEMY Founded 1860

In Beautiful Shenandoah Valley. Thorough college preparation; fully accredited. Individual guidance. Band. All sports. 2 gyms. Pool. Fine health record. Fireproof buildings. Separate Junior School. Illus. Catalog write Supt. S.M.A. Box F2, Staunton, Va.

BASIC COURSE R.O.T.C. BY U. S. ARMY INSTRUCTORS

Georgia Military College

Accredited 4-year High School and Junior College. 83rd year. Modern equipment. Personal guidance. Varsity and intramural sports. Quarterly registration—September, January, March. ROTC—Highest Gov't rating. Moderate cost. Write for catalog. Col. R. A. Thorne, Box B, Milledgeville, Georgia.

Junior Military Academy Boys 4-14

Semi-military. Kindergarten-8th grade. Family life and affectionate care. Food from our own farm. 12 months' enrollment includes 8 weeks at Camp Whooppee. Enter any time. Moderate rate. 43rd year. Write for catalog. Maj. Roy DeBerry, Box B, Bloomington Springs, Tenn.

SUMMER SCHOOLS AND CAMPS

VALLEY FORGE MILITARY ACADEMY SUMMER CAMPS

A summer of fun and recreation in heart of America's National Shrine. Ranger Camp (12-14). Pioneer Camp (8-12). Full program on 300 wooded acres for active boys. Permanent staff assures excellent instruction and individualized attention in camp lore—swimming, athletics, Indian lore, archery, rifle marksmanship, wood and leathercraft, scouting and nature study. Training in leadership and courtesy. Optional tutoring and developmental reading. Aquacade! Overnight hikes! Campfires! Separate Band Camp (13-18) under renowned musical director. Individual instrument instruction. Catalog Box 43, Wayne, Pa.

ALL AMERICA CAMP

ALL SPORTS *supervised by* FAMOUS COACHES

on the Campus of NEW YORK MILITARY ACADEMY

Boys 9 through 16 will enjoy the most wonderful summer of their lives on the 480 acres of this famous School of Distinction. 8 weeks beginning July 1. Indoor and Outdoor Pools. The nation's sports leaders direct participation in all major sports: Baseball, Basketball, Football Skills, Golf, Swimming, Tennis, Track & Field. Also: Bowling, Boxing, Camping, Trips and Wrestling. Non-Military. No extras. REMEDIAL READING, MATHEMATICS & Instrumental Music available. Write ALL AMERICA CAMP, NYMA, 30 Campus Drive, Cornwall-on-Hudson, N. Y.

WENTWORTH SUMMER CAMP AND SCHOOL

Camp for Boys 8½ and over. Finest fun program and training under regular Academy personnel. Indian Tribe. Ozark Mountain Camp. Riding, canoeing, swimming, fishing, crafts, rifle firing, military. Optional tutoring. Summer School includes high school and junior college. Write: Wentworth Military Academy, 522-C Main Street, Lexington, Missouri

Fair Haven $25 per week (all incl.). Harrisonburg, Va. In the beautiful Blue Ridge Mountains. Boys and girls, 7-15 years. June 23-August 25. Campers accepted for one to nine weeks. Riding, swimming, sports, trips to caverns, nature study. Good food, accommodations; understanding counselors. Folder. P.O. Box 629-B, Harrisonburg, Virginia

CAMP NORTHWESTERN

Boys 8-15. Sail, swim, boat, fish, water-ski on magnificent Lake Geneva. A. R. C. awards. Golf, tennis, soccer, riflery, baseball, riding, archery, crafts. Mature counselors. 19th season. Tutoring. Program for advanced study available. Catalog. 62 So. L. Shore Dr., Lake Geneva, Wisconsin.

NOTTINGHAM CAMPS

A summer of fun and friendship for boys & girls, 8-16. Separate camps; 360 acres. All sports; riding, riflery, fishing, sailing, golf. Pool. Dramatics. Summer School. Between Philadelphia and Baltimore. Near Chesapeake Bay. Catalog. C. C. Burley, Director, Box 160, Colora, Maryland.

Namequoit—Cape Cod 100 boys, 7-16; 3 age groups.

On salt-water bay and fresh-water lake. Orleans, Mass. Swimming, sailing, canoeing, fishing. Tennis, riflery, baseball, gymnastics. Educational trips; crafts. Modern facilities, mature staff. Tutoring available. Write for catalog. A. B. Farnham, One Glover Road, Wayland, Mass.

FARRAGUT NAVAL CAMPS

Summer of adventure on Toms River. Boys 9-16 inclusive in 2 age groups. Trips on 63-ft. flagship. 42 land and water activities. Modern buildings. 2 gyms, 2 athletic fields. Approved summer school program. Write for literature. Farragut Naval Camps, Box BC, Toms River, New Jersey

WOODCRAFT CAMP

8 WEEKS OF FUN FOR BOYS 9½ to 14

Exciting, educational camping on beautiful Lake Maxinkuckee. Indian and Nature lore, handicraft, campcraft. Swimming, canoeing, river trips. Tennis, baseball; other sports. 1400 wooded acres. Excellent food. Founded in 1912. Regular Culver Military Academy staff. Just enough military to teach neatness, promptness, courtesy. Optional tutoring. Nationwide enrollment. Catalog. CULVER 230 Lake Shore Parkway, Culver, Ind.

Camp Easton for Boys 7-16. ELY, MINN. Established 1927 in Superior National Forest. Excellent counseling. All sports; crafts, nature, riflery, Indian Lore, water sports & swimming. 5-day canoe trips in famous Minn. & Can. canoe country. Supervised travel. Resident nurse. Catalog. Douglas B. Bobo, 420 W. Chicago, Buchanan, Michigan.

SHATTUCK SUMMER SCHOOL-CAMP

Six weeks' recreation and study for boys 9-18. Two age groups. Regular Shattuck faculty and facilities. Basic military training. Sailing, swimming, tennis, golf, other sports. Dietitian. In southern Minnesota. *Write for Catalog.* Director of Admissions, A-627 Shumway Hall, Faribault, Minn.

CAMP TOSEBO 60 boys 7-15 Manistee, Michigan

Portage Lake. Sand beach. 51st year. Swimming, sailing, water skiing, riding, athletics, crafts, dramatics, Indian Lore, canoe trips. Nurse. Tutoring. Individual attention. Homelike atmosphere. 8 weeks, 4 weeks. Catalog. Mr. & Mrs. Ross L. Taylor, Box 1023, Warrenville, Illinois.

Adirondack Woodcraft Camps

37th yr. Fun & Adventure in the Woods. Boys 7-18. Five separate age groups. 2 private lakes near Old Forge. Adirondack. Canadian canoe trips. Riding. Forestry, riflery. Tutoring. Mature councilors. 3 nurses. Bklt. William H. Abbott, Director, Box 2378, Fayetteville, N.Y.

Howe Military Camp

A summer of constructive fun for Juniors (8-14) on lake. July 1 to Aug. 11. Completely modern equipment and facilities. Staff from Winter School faculty. All sports; boating, swimming. Review studies if desired. Low rate. Catalog. Burrett B. Bouton, M.A., 17 Academy Place, Howe, Indiana

CARRIER FORCE
ADM. NAGUMO

ADM. YAMAMOTO
MAIN FORCE

Yamamoto

Nagumo

Jim Sharpe

THE BATTLE OF MIDWAY

BY CHARLES MERCER
ILLUSTRATED BY JIM SHARPE

"The enemy planned a lethal blow . . ."

IN MAY, 1942, the American situation in the Pacific was desperate. Following the Japanese sneak attack on Pearl Harbor of December 7, 1941, our fighting forces were out-matched in ships, planes, guns, and men. By May, the enemy was clenching its fist to deal the Americans a knockout blow. Where and when would it come? How could vastly outnumbered American forces hope to withstand it? Swift aircraft carriers had succeeded the slow battleships as the new ▶

4 JUNE 42

MIDWAY

Spruance

TASK FORCE 17
ADM. FLETCHER

ADM. SPRUANCE
TASK FORCE 16

Fletcher

Pearl Harbor

HAWAII

Lcdr. John Waldron

Torpedo 8

weapon of naval warfare—and in carriers alone, the Japanese had 10 while the U.S. had but two ready for action.

This was the staggering problem that tough-minded Admiral Chester W. Nimitz faced in that month as Commander in Chief of the Pacific Fleet. When Nimitz tried to count his blessings, he could not add up much more than two. There was the unbreakable will of the Americans to win the war despite all odds. And there was one vital secret weapon: the United States had broken some of the codes in which the Japanese sent their war messages. They had an idea of enemy intentions. Many messages that the Americans intercepted they could decipher only in part, yet often through inklings, they read the minds of enemy leaders.

At their Pearl Harbor headquarters, the Commander in Chief and his staff knew something momentous and mysterious was developing. Nimitz had great faith in the Navy's codebreakers—especially in Lieutenant Commander Joseph J. Rochefort and the men who toiled with him at the headquarters codebreaking unit called Hypo. Now Rochefort warned that the Japanese Combined Fleet was preparing for a massive action against American naval strength focused on some place code-named AF.

But where was AF? Rochefort, with his fine intuition, was certain it was Midway—1,135 miles west northwest of Pearl Harbor. He settled the question with a clever trick. Midway was a station on a trans-Pacific cable line. Over this closed-circuit cable, Rochefort ordered the naval station there to send out a plain-language radio message announcing that the fresh-water evaporators had broken down. Before long the codebreakers intercepted an enemy message to Admiral Isoruku Yamamoto, Commander in Chief of the Combined Fleet, stating that AF was short of water.

Midway, like all land that poked above the surface of the Central Pacific, was an atoll. It was a desolate place, but one of its small islands had a good airstrip: in enemy hands it would be invaluable for bombing raids against Hawaii.

Locating Midway as the target was just the start of Nimitz's problems. Next he had to find the strength to meet the attack. A month before, the Americans had possessed four battle-ready carriers, but then the codebreakers had warned of an enemy invasion in the Coral Sea. To thwart the attack, Nimitz had sent a task force commanded by Rear Admiral Frank Jack Fletcher and built around the carriers *Lexington* and *Yorktown*. *Lexington* was sunk and Fletcher reported *Yorktown* so severely damaged in the Battle of the Coral Sea that it would take 90 days to make her fit for action again. That left only carriers *Enterprise* and *Hornet* under Rear Admiral William F. Halsey, Jr.

Nimitz counted on Halsey to serve as tactical commander in the forthcoming battle. But when *Enterprise* and *Hornet* steamed into Pearl, Nimitz found that Halsey was too ill with a skin ailment to put to sea again. Fletcher, not as aggressive as Halsey, would have to be in command. But who could serve as Fletcher's backup? Nimitz's choice of Rear Admiral Raymond A. Spruance seemed surprising, but it would have historic consequences. Spruance, then 55, had no experience in operating carriers. For months he had commanded the cruisers that screened the flattops of his friend Bill Halsey, who recommended him for the job. Spruance was ice compared to Halsey's fire: reserved in manner while Halsey was gregarious.

Meanwhile, Nimitz was beefing up the defenses of Midway until the atoll bristled with guns, determined Marines, and bomber and fighter planes from the Army, Navy, and Marine Corps. Yet the commanders realized that the fate of Midway would be determined by air action at sea.

Soon *Yorktown* limped into Pearl. Nimitz, a former engineering official, descended into her depths with an inspection party. Ninety days to make her seaworthy? Nimitz turned his icy blue eyes on the inspectors and said, "We must have this ship in three days!" And they did: 1,400 men labored around the clock for three days to make *Yorktown* fit and ready for action once again.

The Americans' most potent weapon remained the codebreakers' signal intelligence. This showed that Yamamoto planned to divide his Combined Fleet into three forces: (1) A northern group would attack the Aleutians. (2) The First Carrier Striking Force would come down on Midway from the northwest and launch the main attack with an air raid on the atoll. (3) The Midway Invasion Force, bringing troops to storm the atoll, would approach from the southwest. American officers were pleased to find a flaw in Yamamoto's planning: he was dividing his superior forces.

Spruance, with *Enterprise* as his flagship, would command Task Force 16, which also comprised *Hornet* under Captain Marc A. Mitscher, six cruisers, and 12 destroyers. Fletcher would command Task Force 17, comprising *Yorktown*, two cruisers, and six destroyers. The two forces would operate independently of each other, but Fletcher, with more carrier experience than Spruance, would have overall tactical command. Nimitz ordered them first to go after the carrier striking force coming from the northwest. Signal intelligence indicated that these attackers would include four big enemy carriers—*Akagi, Kaga, Hiryu,* and *Soryu* with a screen of two battleships, three cruisers, and 11 destroyers.

On June 2, the American task forces gathered northeast of Midway. The American commanders realized that Yamamoto's design was not just to seize Midway but to draw the American main fleet into a decisive action and destroy it. Then nothing could stop the Japanese from seizing Hawaii and turning the Western and Central Pacific into Emperor Hirohito's private lake. Understanding this, Nimitz told his commanders that, if necessary, it was better to lose Midway and preserve their carriers.

Midway search planes spotted the enemy land invasion force slowly approaching the atoll from the southwest, but where was the First Carrier Striking Force? Restlessly Spruance prowled the flag deck where he had set up his headquarters high above the *Enterprise* flight deck. He planned to hit the enemy carriers before they struck him—hit them quickly and hard. *But where was the enemy?*

At 4 A.M. on June 3, the Japanese striking force was 250 miles northwest of Midway, precisely where Hypo had forecast it would be at that hour. Its commander was Vice Admiral Chuichi Nagumo, victor in the December 7 attack on Pearl Harbor. He flew his flag aboard *Akagi*, pride of the Japanese carrier fleet. From the decks of the four big flattops, which Hypo had said would be the heart of the enemy force, 108 bombers and fighters took off through the

T
he enemy carrier crews, busy rearming their planes, were taken by surprise."

dawn to strike Midway.

Spruance was pacing his flag bridge listening to the loudspeaker which blared incoherent fragments on the Midway radio frequencies. Suddenly at 5:34 A.M., the voice of a Midway search pilot hawked out of the static: "Enemy carriers!"

But where? More than 40 minutes passed before the enemy's position was reported, authenticated, and plotted. After Spruance estimated that the enemy was about 175 miles from Task Force 16 and within range of his torpedo planes, he said, "Launch the attack!" It was 6:15 A.M.

In making his fateful command decision to send off all his air strength at once, there were several things Spruance did not know. One thing—something not even the codebreakers knew—was that Yamamoto himself was present to direct the Japanese in the battle. He was with another big force that the codebreakers had not detected, a force composed of ▶

seven battleships, a carrier, three cruisers, and 21 destroyers lurking behind the enemy striking and landing forces. Yamamoto was aboard an extraordinary battleship named *Yamato*, the largest warship ever built. Impervious to any air or naval weapon of the time, *Yamato* mounted nine 18-inch guns—more firepower than any ship in history.

Spruance planned a coordinated attack with *Enterprise* and *Hornet* air groups flying together and then each attacking one of the enemy carriers. Dive bombers would hurtle from on high while torpedo planes skimmed the waves, all protected by fighter escorts. Browning set a launch hour of 7 A.M. From the flight deck rose the roar of engines as pilots gunned their craft and loudspeakers blared orders. Above the noise and flurry Spruance stood quietly, tensely. Things were going badly. The launchings were very slow. An enemy plane spotted them. At 7:45 A.M., the torpedo planes still had not been launched. Spruance abandoned his plan of a coordinated attack and signaled the planes aloft to go after the enemy. Ten miles to the north, Fletcher was being more cautious about sending his *Yorktown* planes into action.

Meanwhile Nagumo's 108 carrier planes homed in on Midway with an umbrella of fighters overhead. Marine Corps fighters rose gallantly from their strip to intercept, but their old Buffaloes and Wildcats were completely outclassed. Of 26 Marine interceptors, 17 were destroyed and seven badly damaged. At the same time, American bombers sought out the enemy carriers, but in their inexperience, they did no damage and suffered heavy losses.

Nagumo, after launching his attack against Midway, reserved 108 planes with armor-piercing bombs and torpedoes to use against any American ships he might find. About 8:30 A.M., when his planes were coming back from Midway and wanting to land, he had to make a crucial decision upon receiving a report of an American carrier. He could (1) launch the bombers on deck and send them against the Americans without fighter escort, or (2) recover his Midway attackers and rearm them. But he could not do both at the same time. He decided to recover his planes. The four Japanese carriers were in a boxlike formation. Nagumo, after recovering his raiders at 9:17 A.M., ordered his force to make a 90-degree turn and search for the American carriers.

This turn by Nagumo caused the *Hornet* attack commander to miss the enemy altogether. He made a wrong

"Yamamoto himself was present to direct the Japanese in the battle."

guess and led his planes in the opposite direction from the enemy. All the fighters ran out of fuel and had to ditch at sea, while 13 dive bombers landed at Midway for gas. All missed the battle—all but the 15 planes of the *Hornet* torpedo squadron, led by Lieutenant Commander John C. Waldron, which became separated from the others and suddenly found the enemy. As the slow, heavy Devastators bore in just above the waves, enemy fighters screamed down and anti-aircraft fire joined in chopping them to pieces.

Ensign George H. Gay saw his radio man killed and the Devastators ahead of his bursting into flames, then he dropped his torpedo and pulled out sharply above an enemy carrier's deck. A pursuing fighter shot away Gay's left rudder control, and his Devastator plowed into the sea. Miraculously, the young ensign found himself afloat in his inflated life jacket with a ringside view of the greatest naval air battle ever. All 15 planes of his squadron had been destroyed, and of their 30 crewmen, only he was still alive.

While Gay watched, Lieutenant Commander Eugene E.

Lindsey led in the *Enterprise* torpedo planes as bravely as Waldron had led those from *Hornet*. Within minutes, 10 of 14 Devastators were shot down. Then fighters destroyed nearly all of the *Yorktown* torpedo squadron that came lumbering behind. It appeared to be a complete Japanese victory. They had shot down all but six of 47 American torpedo planes, while their ships had not been touched by a single torpedo. (It turned out to be faulty torpedoes.)

Neither Spruance nor Fletcher knew that this was happening. American pilots had not yet even reported the new location and direction of the enemy fleet, probably because they were too excited about attacking it. Spruance especially wanted to know the whereabouts of Lieutenant Commander Clarence W. McCluskey, the air group commander of *Enterprise* who was leading the dive bombers.

Since 7:52 A.M., McCluskey had been hunting the enemy with his bombers. At 9:55, while flying at 19,000 feet, he spotted a Japanese destroyer high-tailing to the northwest. McClusky pointed his bombers in the same direction, and in minutes the pilots saw the First Carrier Striking Force.

McCluskey informed the tensely waiting officers on *Enterprise* of the enemy location, then issued crisp orders to the commanders of his two squadrons. With a cry of "Tally ho!" the pilots tipped over their Dauntless dive bombers and came shrieking down at a 70-degree angle.

Luck, which had eluded the Americans all morning, at last was with them. The enemy carrier crews, busy rearming their planes, were taken by total surprise as the bombs smashed into them like sledge hammers. American luck still had not run out. Sheer coincidence rather than planning caused Commander M. F. Leslie of *Yorktown* to find the enemy fleet with 17 dive bombers at almost the precise moment McCluskey and his men attacked. The *Yorktown* planes also roared down.

Fires raged on *Kaga*, *Akagi*, and *Soryu*, while *Hiryu* fled full speed to the north. Nagumo refused to leave the bridge and had to be escorted away. Miraculously, within minutes, disorganized American air squadrons had destroyed three of Japan's most powerful carriers.

Meantime, the fleeing *Hiryu* launched bombers which found *Yorktown* that afternoon and mauled her so badly she had to be abandoned. Fletcher passed command of the battle to Spruance. Then, late in the afternoon, Spruance sent off bombers which struck *Hiryu* and started fires that eventually consumed her. Now the score was four big enemy carriers destroyed against *Yorktown* abandoned, but still afloat. Her officers put a salvage party aboard.

Next day, June 5, Spruance concluded the enemy was withdrawing west in two groups. He kept planes searching for the Japanese and followed slowly with his surface ships. On June 6, the planes sank an enemy heavy cruiser and severely damaged another. But another event at almost the same hour tempered American jubilation. By that day, the salvage workers were positive they could save *Yorktown*. The destroyer *Hammann* was alongside the damaged carrier supplying electric power to the salvage party while other destroyers circled the vessels protectively. Nevertheless, the enemy submarine *I-168* slipped through the protective screen and sank both *Yorktown* and *Hammann*.

Some armchair strategists criticized Spruance for not pursuing the enemy. But that was what Yamamoto wanted him to do. If Spruance had chased the retreating Japanese, his vessels would have been destroyed by the big guns of *Yamato*, the battleship that the Americans did not even know existed.

The Japanese had suffered their first naval defeat in three centuries. Despite their overwhelming strength, they had lost four big carriers and a heavy cruiser, 322 planes, and 2,500 men. The Americans who still held Midway, lost one carrier and one destroyer, 147 planes, and 307 men. Never again did the Japanese mount a serious attack to the east against the Americans. It was the first turning point of World War II in the Pacific. ♣

PART I of a 2-part story

THE CRUEL SKY

By ARTHUR C. CLARKE

Everest's ghostly summit lured the scientist and his young companion to sky-high perils.

By midnight, the summit of Everest was only a hundred yards away, a pyramid of snow, pale and ghostly in the light of the rising moon. The sky was cloudless, and the wind that had been blowing for days had dropped almost to zero. It must be rare indeed for the highest point on Earth to be so calm and peaceful; they had chosen their time well.

Perhaps *too* well, thought George Harper; it had been almost disappointingly easy. Their only real problem had been getting out of the hotel without being observed. The management objected to unauthorized midnight excursions up the mountain; there could be accidents, which were bad for business.

But Dr. Elwin was determined to do it this way, and he had the best of reasons, though he never discussed them. The presence of one of the world's most famous scientists — and certainly the world's most famous cripple — at Hotel Everest during the height of the tourist season had already aroused a good deal of polite surprise. Harper had allayed some of the curiosity by hinting that they were engaged on gravity measurements, which was at least part of the truth. But a part of the truth which, by this time, was vanishingly small.

Anyone looking at Jules Elwin now, as he forged steadily towards the 29,000-foot level with 50 pounds of equipment on his shoulders, would never have guessed that his legs were almost useless. He had been born a victim of the 1961 thalidomide disaster, which had left more than 10,000 partially deformed children scattered over the face of the world. Elwin was one of the lucky ones. His arms were quite normal, and had been strengthened by exercise until they were considerably more powerful than most men's. His legs, however, were mere wisps of flesh and bone; with the aid of braces, he could stand and even totter a few uncertain steps, but he could never really walk.

Yet now he was 200 feet from the top of Everest . . .

A travel poster had started it all, more than three years ago. As a junior computer programmer in the Applied Physics Division,

George Harper knew Dr. Elwin only by sight and by reputation. Even to those working directly under him, Astrotech's brilliant director of research was a slightly remote personality, cut off from the ordinary run of men both by his body and by his mind. He was neither liked nor disliked, and though he was admired and pitied, he was certainly not envied.

Harper, only a few months out of college, doubted if the doctor even knew of his existence, except as a name on an organization chart. There were ten other programmers in the division, all senior to him, and most of them had never exchanged more than a dozen words with their research director. When Harper was co-opted as messenger boy to carry one of the classified files into Dr. Elwin's office, he expected to be in and out with nothing more than a few polite formalities.

That was almost what happened, but just as he was leaving he was stopped dead by the magnificent panorama of Himalayan peaks covering half of one wall. It had been placed where Dr. Elwin could see it whenever he looked up from his desk, and it showed a scene that Harper knew very well indeed. For he had photographed it himself, as an awed and slightly breathless tourist standing on the trampled snow at the crown of Everest.

There was the white ridge of Kanchenjunga, rearing through the clouds almost a hundred miles away. Nearly in line with it, but much nearer, were the twin peaks of Makalu; and closer still, dominating the foreground, was the immense bulk of Lhotse—Everest's neighbor and rival. Further round to the west, flowing down valleys so huge that the eye could not appreciate their scale, were the jumbled ice rivers of the Khumbu and Rongbuk glaciers. From this height, their frozen wrinkles looked no larger than the furrows in a ploughed field; but those ruts and scars of iron-hard ice were hundreds of feet deep.

Harper was still taking in that spectacular view, reliving old memories, when he heard Dr. Elwin's voice behind him.

"You seem interested. Have you ever been there?"

"Yes, Doctor—my folks took me, after I graduated from high school. We stayed at the hotel for a week, and thought we'd have to go home before the weather cleared. But on the last day the wind stopped blowing, and about 20 of us made it to the summit. We were there for an hour, taking photos of each other."

Dr. Elwin seemed to digest this information for rather a long time; then he said, in a voice which had lost its previous remoteness and now held a definite undercurrent of excitement: "Sit down, Mr.—ah—Harper. I'd like to hear more."

As he walked back to the chair facing the director's big, uncluttered desk, George Harper found himself somewhat puzzled. What he had done was not in the least unusual; every year, thousands of people went to the Everest Hotel, and a good many of them reached the summit. Only last year, in fact, there had been a much-publicized presentation to the 10,000th tourist to stand on top of the world. Some cynics had commented on the extraordinary coincidence that Number 10,000 had just happened to be a rather well-known video starlet.

There was nothing that Harper could tell Dr. Elwin that he couldn't discover just as easily from a dozen other sources—the tourist brochures, for example. However, no young and ambitious scientist would miss this opportunity of impressing a man who could do so much to help his career. Harper was neither coldly calculating nor inclined to dabble in office politics, but he knew a good chance when he saw one.

"Well, Doctor," he began, speaking slowly at first as he tried to put his thoughts and memories into order, "the jets land you at a little town called Namche, about 20 miles from the mountain. Then the bus takes you along a spectacular road up to the hotel, which overlooks the Khumbu Glacier. It's at an altitude of 18,000 feet, and there are pressurized rooms for anyone who finds it hard to breathe. Of course, there's a medical staff in attendance, and the management won't accept guests who aren't physically fit. You have to stay at the hotel for at least two days, on a special diet, ▨▨▨→

before you're allowed to go higher.

"From the hotel you can't actually see the summit, as you're too close to the mountain, and it seems to loom right above you. But the view is fantastic; you can see Lhotse and half a dozen other peaks. And it can be scary, too—especially at night. For the wind is usually howling somewhere high overhead, and there are weird noises from the moving ice. It's easy to imagine that there are monsters prowling round up in the mountains . . .

"There's not much to do at the hotel, except to relax and watch the scenery, and to wait until the doctors give you the go-ahead. In the old days it used to take weeks to acclimatize to the thin air; now they can make your blood count shoot up to the right level in 48 hours. Even so, about half the visitors—mostly the older ones—decide that this is quite high enough for them.

"What happens next depends on how experienced you are, and how much you're willing to pay. A few expert climbers hire guides and make their own way to the top, using standard mountaineering equipment. That isn't too difficult nowadays, as there are shelters at various strategic spots. Most of these groups make it, but the weather is always a gamble and every year a few people get killed.

"The average tourist does it the easier way. No aircraft are allowed to land on Everest itself, except in emergencies, but there's a lodge near the crest of Nuptse and a helicopter service to it from the hotel. From the lodge it's only three miles to the summit, via the South Col—an easy climb for anyone in good condition, with a little mountaineering experience. Some people do it without oxygen, though that's not recommended. I kept my mask on until I reached the top; then I took it off and found I could breathe without much difficulty."

"Did you use filters, or gas cylinders?" the doctor interrupted.

"Oh, filters—they're quite reliable now, and increase the oxygen concentration over 100 percent. They've simplified high-altitude climbing enormously; no one carries compressed gas anymore."

"How long did the climb take?"

"The full day; we left just before dawn and were back at nightfall. *That* would have surprised the old-timers—but of course we were starting fresh and traveling light. There are no real problems on the route from the lodge, and steps have been cut at all the tricky places. As I said, it's easy for anyone in good condition."

The instant he repeated those words, Harper wished that he had bitten off his tongue. It seemed incredible that he could have forgotten to whom he was talking, but the wonder and excitement of that climb to the top of the world had come back so vividly that for a moment he was once more on that lonely, windswept peak. The one spot on Earth where Dr. Elwin could never stand . . .

But the scientist did not appear to have noticed—or else he was so used to such unthinking tactlessness that it no longer bothered him. Why, wondered Harper, was he so interested in Everest? Probably because of that very inaccessibility; it stood for all that had been denied to him by the accident of birth.

Yet now, only three years later, George Harper paused a bare hundred feet from the summit, and drew in the nylon rope as the doctor caught up with him. Though nothing had ever been said about it, he knew that the scientist wished to be the first to the top. He deserved the honor, and the younger man would do nothing to rob him of it.

"Everything OK?" he asked, as Dr. Elwin drew abreast of him. The question was quite unnecessary, but Harper felt an urgent need to challenge the great loneliness that now surrounded them. They might have been the only men in all the world; nowhere amid this white wilderness of peaks was there any sign that the human race existed.

Elwin did not answer, but gave an absent-minded nod as he went past, his shining eyes fixed upon the summit. He was walking with a curiously stiff-legged gait, and his feet made remarkably little impression in the snow. And as he walked, there came a faint but unmistakable whine from the bulky backpack he was carrying on his shoulders.

That pack, indeed, was carrying him—or three-quarters of him. As he forged steadily along the last few feet to his once-impossible goal, Dr. Elwin and all his equipment weighed only 50 pounds. And if *that* was still too much, he had only to turn a dial and he would weigh nothing.

The Cruel Sky

Amid the moon-washed Himalayas was the greatest secret of the 21st century. In all the world, there were only five of these experimental Elwin Levitators, and two of them were here.

Even though he had known about them for two years, and understood something of their basic theory, the "Levvies"—as they had soon been christened at the lab—still seemed like magic to Harper. Their powerpacks stored enough electrical energy to lift a 250-pound weight through a vertical distance of ten miles.

The lift—and—descent cycle could be repeated almost indefinitely as the units reacted against the Earth's gravitational field; on the way up, the battery discharged—on the way down, it was charged again. Since no mechanical process is completely efficient, there was a slight loss of energy on each cycle, but it would be repeated at least a hundred times before the units were finally exhausted.

Climbing the mountain, with most of their weight neutralized, had been an exhilarating experience. The vertical tug of the harness made it feel that they were hanging from invisible balloons, whose buoyancy could be adjusted at will. They needed a certain amount of weight in order to get traction on the ground, and after experimenting had settled on 20 percent. With this, it was easy to ascend a one-in-one slope as to walk normally on the level.

Several times they had cut their weight almost to zero, to rise hand-over-hand up vertical rock faces. This had been the strangest experience of all, demanding complete faith in their equipment. To hang suspended in midair, apparently supported by nothing but a box of gently humming electronics—that required a considerable effort of will. But after a few minutes, the sense of power and freedom overcame all fear; for here indeed was the realization of one of man's dreams.

A few weeks ago one of the library staff had found a line from an early 20th-century poem which described their achievement perfectly: "To ride secure the cruel sky." Not even birds had ever possessed such freedom of the third dimension; this was the *real* conquest of space. The Levitator would open up the mountains, and the high places of the world, as a lifetime ago the Aqualung had opened up the sea. Once these units had passed their tests and were mass-produced cheaply, every aspect of human civilization would be changed. Transport would be revolutionized; space travel would be no more expensive than ordinary flying; all mankind would take to the air.

But Dr. Elwin, Harper felt sure, was not thinking of this, in his lonely moment of triumph. Later, he would receive the world's applause (and perhaps its curses); none of them would mean as much to him as standing here on Earth's highest point. This was truly a victory of mind over matter—of sheer intelligence over a frail and crippled body. All the rest would be anticlimax.

When Harper joined the scientist on the flattened, snow-covered pyramid, they shook hands with rather formal stiffness, because that seemed the right thing to do. But they said nothing; the wonder of their achievement, and the panorama of peaks that stretched as far as the eye could see in every direction, had robbed them of words.

Harper relaxed in the buoyant support of his harness, and slowly scanned the circle of the sky. As he recognized them, he mentally called off the names of the surrounding giants—Makalu, Lhotse, Baruntse, Cho Oyu, Kanchenjunga. . . . Even now scores of these peaks had never been climbed. Well, the Levvies would soon change that.

There were many, of course, who would disapprove. But back in the 20th century there had also been mountaineers who thought it was "cheating" to use oxygen. It was hard to believe that, even after weeks of acclimatization, men had attempted to reach these heights without artificial aids. Harper remembered Mallory and Irvine, whose bodies still lay undiscovered within perhaps a mile of this very spot . . .

Dr. Elwin cleared his throat.

"Let's go, George," he said quietly, his voice muffled through the oxygen filter. "We must get back before they start looking for us."

With a silent farewell to all those who had stood here before them, they turned away from the summit and started down the gentle slope. The night, which had been brilliantly clear until now, was becoming darker; some high clouds were slipping across the face of the moon, so rapidly that its light switched on and off in a manner that sometimes made it hard to see the route. Harper did not like the look of the weather, and began to mentally rearrange their plans. Perhaps it would be better to aim for the shelter on the South Col, rather than the lodge. But he said nothing to Dr. Elwin, not wishing to raise any false alarms.

Now they were moving along a knife-edge of rock, with utter darkness on one side and a faintly glimmering snowscape on the other. This would be a terrible place, Harper could not help thinking, to be in a storm——

He had barely shaped the thought when the gale was upon them. From out of nowhere, it seemed, came a shrieking blast of air, as if the mountain had been husbanding its strength for this moment. There was no time to do anything; even had they possessed normal weight, they would have been swept off their feet. In seconds, the wind had tossed them out over the shadowed, empty blackness.

It was impossible to judge the depths beneath them; when Harper forced himself to glance down, he could see nothing. Though the wind seemed to be carrying him almost horizontally, he knew that he must be falling; his residual weight would be taking him downwards at a quarter of the normal speed. But that would be ample; if they fell 4,000 feet, it would be poor consolation to know that it would seem only 1,000 . . .

He had not yet had time for fear—*that* would come later, if he survived—and his main worry, absurdly enough, was that the expensive Levitator might be damaged. He had completely forgotten his partner. The sudden jerk on the nylon rope filled him with puzzled alarm; then he saw Dr. Elwin slowly revolving round him at the end of the line, like a planet circling a sun.

The sight snapped him back to reality, and to a consciousness of what must be done. His paralysis had probably lasted only a fraction of a second; then he shouted across the wind: "Doctor, use emergency lift."

As he spoke, he fumbled for the seal on his control unit, tore it open, and pressed the button.

At once, the pack began to hum like a hive of angry bees. He felt the harness tugging at his body, as it tried to drag him up into the sky, away from the invisible death below. The simple arithmetic of the Earth's gravitational field blazed in his mind, as if written in letters of fire. One kilowatt could lift a hundred kilograms through a meter every second, and the packs could convert energy at a maximum rate of ten kilowatts—though they could not keep this up for more than a minute. So allowing for his initial weight-reduction, he should be lifting at well over 100 feet a second.

There was a violent jerk on the rope, as it took up the slack between them. Dr. Elwin had been slow to punch the emergency button, but at last he too was ascending. It would be a race between the lifting power of their units, and the wind that was sweeping them towards the icy face of Lhotse, now scarely a thousand feet away.

That wall of snow-streaked rock loomed above them in the moonlight, a frozen wave of stone. It was impossible to judge their speed accurately, but they could hardly be moving at less then 50 miles an hour. Even if they survived the impact, they could not expect to escape serious injury; and injury here would be as good as death.

Then, just when it seemed that a collision was unavoidable, the current of air suddenly shot skywards, dragging them with it. They cleared the ridge of rock with a comfortable 50 feet to spare; it seemed like a miracle, but after a dizzying moment of relief, Harper realized that what had saved them was only simple aerodynamics. The wind *had* to rise in order to clear the mountain; on the other side, it would descend again. But that no longer mattered, for the sky ahead was empty.

Now they were moving quietly beneath the broken clouds. Though their speed had not slackened, the roar of the wind had suddenly died away, for they were traveling with it through emptiness. They could even converse comfortably, across the 30 feet of space that still separated them.

"Dr. Elwin!" Harper called, "are you OK?"

"Yes, George," said the scientist, perfectly calmly. "Now what do we do?"

"We must stop lifting. If we go any higher, we won't be able to breathe—even with the filters."

"You're right. Let's get back into balance."

The angry humming of the packs died to a barely audible electric whine as they cut out the emergency circuits. For a few minutes they yo-yoed up and down on their nylon rope—first one uppermost, then the other—until they managed to get into trim. When they had finally stabilized, they were drifting at a little below 30,000 feet. Unless the Levvies failed—which, after their overload, was quite possible—they were out of immediate danger.

Their troubles would start when they tried to return to earth.

(To be concluded)

Conclusion

THE CRUEL SKY

By ARTHUR C. CLARKE

Begin story here: Dr. Jules Elwin and George Harper have scaled the peak of Everest with the aid of anti-gravity Levitators. The "Levvies" are marvelous power-packs stored with enough energy to lift a 250-pound weight through a vertical distance of ten miles. Elwin had invented the Levvies and now, in spite of his severely crippled legs, he had fulfilled a lifelong wish to conquer the world's highest mountain. But the old scientist and his young partner did not reckon on Nature's fury. As they started back down the mountain, a sudden windstorm caught them in its blast and tossed the two climbers out into space.

Illustrated by ROBERT J. LEE

Trapped in the Himalyas, they grappled with death and their own sense of terror.

No men in all history had ever greeted a stranger dawn. Though they were tired and stiff and cold, and the dryness of the thin air made every breath rasp in their throats, they forgot all these discomforts as the first dim glow spread along the jagged eastern horizon. The stars faded one by one; last to go, only minutes before the moment of daybreak, was the most brilliant of all the space stations—Pacific Number Three, hovering 22,000 miles above Hawaii. Then the sun lifted above a sea of nameless peaks, and the Himalayan day had dawned.

It was like watching sunrise on the moon. At first, only the highest mountains caught the slanting rays, while the surrounding valleys remained flooded with inky shadows. But slowly the line of light marched down the rocky slopes, and more and more of this harsh, forbidding land climbed into the new day.

Now, if one looked hard enough, it was possible to see signs of human life. There were a few narrow roads, thin columns of smoke from lonely villages, glints of reflected sunlight from monastery roofs. The world below was waking, wholly unaware of the two spectators poised so magically 15,000 feet above.

During the night, the wind must have changed direction several times, and Harper had no idea where they were. He could not recognize a single landmark; they could have been anywhere over a 500-mile-long strip of Nepal and Tibet.

The immediate problem was to choose a landing place—and that soon, for they were drifting rapidly toward a forbidding jumble of peaks and glaciers where they could hardly expect to find help. The wind was carrying them in a northeasterly direction, toward China. If they floated over the mountains and landed there, it might be weeks before they could contact one of the UN Famine Relief Centers and find their way home. They might even be in some personal danger, if they descended out of the sky in an area where there was only an illiterate and superstitious peasant population.

"We'd better get down quickly," said Harper. "I don't like the look of those mountains." His words seemed utterly lost in the void around them; although Dr. Elwin was only ten feet away, it was easy to imagine that his companion could not hear anything he said. But at last the doctor nodded his head, in almost reluctant agreement.

"I'm afraid you're right—but I'm not sure we can make it, with this wind. Remember—we can't go down as quickly as we can rise."

That was true enough; the power-packs could be charged at only a tenth of their discharge rate. If they lost altitude and pumped gravitational energy back into them too fast, the cells would overheat and probably explode. The startled Tibetans (or was it Nepalese?) would think that a large meteorite had detonated in their sky—and no one would ever know exactly what had happened to Dr. Jules Elwin and his promising young assistant . . .

Five thousand feet above the ground, Harper began to expect the explosion at any moment. They were falling swiftly, but not swiftly enough; very soon they would have to decelerate, lest they hit at too high a speed. To make matters worse, they had completely miscalculated the air speed at ground level. That infernal, unpredictable wind was blowing a near-gale once more; they could see streamers of snow, torn from exposed ridges, waving like ghostly banners beneath them. While they had been moving with the wind, they were unaware of its power; now they must once again make the dangerous transition between stubborn rock and softly yielding sky.

The air current was funneling them into the mouth of a canyon. There was no chance of lifting above it. They would have to choose the best landing place that they could find.

The canyon was narrowing at a fearsome rate; now it was little more than a vertical cleft, and the rocky walls were sliding past at 30 or 40 miles an hour. From time to time random eddies would swing them to the right, then the left; often they missed collisions by only a few feet. Once, when they were sweeping scant yards above a ledge thickly covered with snow, Harper was tempted to pull the quick release that would jettison the Levitator. But that would be jumping from the frying pan into the fire: They might get safely back on to firm ground—only to find themselves trapped unknown miles from all possibility of help.

Yet even now, at this moment of renewed peril, he felt very little fear. It was all like an exciting dream—a dream from which he would presently wake up to find himself safely in his own bed. This fantastic adventure could not really be happening to him——

"George!" shouted the doctor. "Now's our chance—if we can manage to snag that boulder!"

They had only seconds in which to act. At once, they both began to play out the nylon rope, until it hung in a great loop beneath them, its lowest portion only a yard above the racing ground. A large rock, some 20 feet high, lay exactly in their line of flight; beyond it, a wide patch of snow gave promise of a reasonably soft landing.

The rope skittered over the lower curves of the boulder, seemed about to slip clear, then caught beneath an overhang. Harper felt the sudden jerk; then he was swung around like a stone on the end of a sling.

I never thought that snow could be so hard, he told himself. After that there was a brief and brilliant explosion of light; then nothing.

HE WAS BACK at the university, in the lecture room. One of the professors was talking, in a voice that was very familiar, yet somehow did not seem to belong here. He ran—in a sleepy, half-hearted fashion—through the names of his college instructors. No, it was certainly none of them, yet he knew the voice so well, and it was undoubtedly lecturing to *someone*——

". . . still quite young when I realized that there was something wrong with Einstein's Theory of Gravitation. In particular, there seemed to be a fallacy underlying the Principle of Equivalence. According to this, there is no way of distinguishing between the effects produced by gravitation, and those of acceleration.

"But this is clearly false. One can create a uniform acceleration—but a uniform gravitational field is impossible, since it obeys an inverse square law, and therefore must vary even over quite short distances. So tests can easily be devised to distinguish between the two cases, and this made me wonder if . . . "

The softly spoken words left no more impression on Harper's mind than if they were in a foreign language. He realized dimly that he *should* understand all this, but it was too much trouble to look for the meaning. Anyway, the first problem was to decide where he was.

Unless there was something wrong with his eyes, he was in complete darkness. He blinked—and the effort to do so brought on such a splitting headache that he gave a cry of pain.

"George! Are you all right?"

Of course! That had been Dr. Elwin's voice, talking softly there in the darkness. But talking to *whom*?

"I've got a terrible headache. And there's a pain in my side when I try to move. What's happened? Why is it dark?"

"You've had a concussion—and I think you've cracked a rib. Don't do any unnecessary talking. You've been unconscious all day—it's night again, and we're inside the tent. I'm saving our batteries."

The sudden glare from

They had to pick a landing place—and soon! For they were drifting rapidly toward a forbidding jumble of jagged peaks and glaciers—far beyond the reach of help.

the flashlight was almost blinding when Dr. Elwin switched it on, and Harper saw the walls of the tiny tent around them. How lucky that they had brought full mountaineering equipment, just in case they got trapped on Everest! But perhaps it would only prolong the agony . . .

He was surprised that the crippled scientist had managed, without any assistance, to unpack all their gear, erect the tent, and drag him inside. Everything was laid out neatly: the first-aid kit, the concentrated-food cans, the water containers, the tiny red gas cylinders for the portable stove. Only the bulky Levitator units were missing; presumably they had been left outside to give more room.

"You were talking to someone when I woke up," Harper said. "Or was I dreaming?" Though the indirect light reflected from the walls of the tent made it hard to read the other's expression, he could see that Elwin was embarrassed. Instantly, he knew why, and wished that he had never asked the question.

The scientist did not believe that they would survive. He had been recording his notes, in case their bodies were ever discovered. Harper wondered bleakly if he had already recorded his last will and testament.

Before Elwin could answer, he quickly changed the subject.

"Have you called Lifeguard?"

"I've been trying every half-hour, but I'm afraid we're shielded by the mountains. I can hear them, but they don't receive us."

Dr. Elwin picked up the little recorder-transceiver, which he had unstrapped from its normal place on his wrist, and switched it on.

"This is Lifeguard Four," said a faint mechanical voice. "Listening out now."

During the five-second pause, Elwin pressed the SOS button, then waited.

"This is Lifeguard Four. Listening out now."

They waited for a full minute, but there was no acknowledgment of their call. *Well,* Harper told himself grimly, *it's too late to start blaming each other now.* Several times, while they had been drifting above the mountains, they had debated whether to call the global rescue service, but had decided against it, partly because there seemed no point in doing so while they were still airborne, partly because of the unavoidable publicity that would follow. It was easy to be wise after the event: Who would have dreamed that they would land in one of the few places beyond Lifeguard's reach?

Dr. Elwin switched off the transceiver, and the only sound in the little tent was the faint moaning of the wind along the mountain walls within which they were doubly trapped—beyond escape, beyond communication.

"Don't worry," he said at last. "By morning, we'll think of a way out. There's nothing we can do until dawn —except make ourselves comfortable. So drink some of this hot soup . . . "

NOW, SEVERAL HOURS LATER, the

headache no longer bothered Harper. Though he suspected that a rib was indeed cracked, he had found a position that was comfortable as long as he did not move, and he felt almost at peace with the world.

He had passed through successive phases of despair, anger at Dr. Elwin, and self-recrimination at having become involved in such a crazy enterprise. Now he was calm again, though his mind, searching for ways of escape, was too active to allow sleep.

Outside the tent, the wind had almost died away, and the night was very still. It was no longer completely dark, for the moon had risen. Though its direct rays would never reach them here, there must be some reflected light from the snows above. Harper could just make out a dim glow at the very threshold of vision, seeping through the translucent heat-retaining walls of the tent.

First of all, he told himself, they were in no immediate danger. The food would last for at least a week; there was plenty of snow that could be melted to provide water. In a day or two, if his rib behaved itself, they might be able to take off again—this time, he hoped, with happier results.

From not far away there came a curious, soft thud, which puzzled Harper until he realized that a mass of snow must have fallen somewhere. The night was now so extraordinarily quiet that he almost imagined he could hear his own heartbeat; every breath of his sleeping companion nearby seemed unnaturally loud.

He turned his thoughts back to the problem of survival. (Curious, how the mind was distracted by trivialities!) Even if he were not fit enough to move, the doctor could attempt the flight by himself. This was a case where one man would have just as good a chance of success as two.

There was another of those soft thuds—slightly louder this time. It was a little odd, Harper thought fleetingly, for snow to move in the cold stillness of the night. He hoped that there was no risk of a slide; having had no time for a clear view of their landing place, he could not assess the danger. He wondered if he should awaken the doctor— who must have had a good look around before he erected the tent. Then, fatalistically, he decided against it: If there *was* an impending avalanche, they probably could not do much to escape.

Back to problem number one. Here was an interesting solution well worth considering: They could attach the transceiver to one of the Levvies, and send the whole thing aloft. The signal would be picked up as soon as the unit left the canyon, and Lifeguard would find them within a few hours—or, at the very most, a few days.

Of course, it would mean sacrificing one of the Levvies, and if nothing came of it they would be in an even worse plight. But all the same——

What was that? This was no soft thudding of loose snow. It was a faint but unmistakable 'click,' as of one pebble knocking against another. And pebbles did not move themselves. . .

You're imagining things, Harper told himself. The idea of anyone, or anything, moving around one of the high Himalayan passes in the middle of the night was completely ridiculous. But his throat became suddenly dry, and he felt the flesh crawl at the back of his neck. He had heard *something,* and it was impossible to argue it away.

Hang the doctor's breathing; it had suddenly become noisy, so that it was hard to focus on any sounds from outside. Did this mean that Dr. Elwin, fast asleep though he was, had also been alerted by his ever-watchful subconscious? He was being fanciful again. . .
Click!

Perhaps it was a little closer; it certainly came from a different direction. It was almost as if something—moving with uncanny but not complete silence —were slowly circling the tent.

This was the moment when George Harper devoutly wished he had never heard of the Abominable Snowman. It was true that he knew little enough about it, but even that little was certainly far too much.

He remembered that the Yeti—as the Nepalese called it—had been a persistent Himalayan myth for more than a hundred years. A dangerous monster larger than a man, it had never been captured, photographed or even described by reputable witnesses. Most Westerners were quite certain that it was pure fantasy, and were totally unconvinced by the scanty evidence of tracks in the snow, or patches of skin preserved in obscure monasteries. The mountain tribesmen knew better; and now Harper was afraid that they were right.

Then, as nothing more happened for long seconds, his fears began slowly to dissolve. Perhaps his overwrought imagination had been playing tricks; in the circumstances, that would hardly be surprising. With a deliberate and determined effort of will, he turned his thoughts once more toward the problem of rescue. He was making fair progress when—something hit the tent.

Only the fact that his throat muscles were paralyzed with sheer fright prevented him from yelling. He was utterly unable to move; then, in the darkness beside him, he heard Dr. Elwin begin to stir sleepily.

"What is it?" muttered the scientist. "Are you all right?"

Harper felt his companion turn over, and knew that he was groping for the flashlight. He wanted to whisper: "For God's sake, keep quiet!" but no words could escape his parched lips. Then there was a click, and the beam of the flashlight formed a brilliant circle on the wall of the tent.

That wall was now bowed in toward them as if a heavy weight were resting upon it. And in the center of the bulge was a completely unmistakable pattern —the imprint of a distorted hand or claw. It was only about two feet from the ground; whatever was outside seemed to be kneeling as it fumbled at the fabric of the tent. . .

The light must have disturbed it, for

➤➤➤

MAKE LIKE A FISH

By DICK PRYCE

Wouldn't it be great if you could dive under the water, open your eyes and see like a fish? Swimmers wearing face masks can, because a mask prevents distortion caused by water pressing directly against opened eyes. It's not really difficult to increase underwater vision without a face mask —if you know how.

Next time you're in a pool, submerge and open your eyes. What do you see? Nothing that is really in focus. Cup both hands and form a canopy above the eyes. Exhale. If you have pressed tightly enough with the sides of your fingers to form an airtight seal, you can trap air bubbles in the canopy and directly

If you want to swim like a fish—as well as see like one—dive for rocks in a lake or river. Toss a 20-pound smooth boulder—no jagged edges— into the water. It's no cinch to get a rock this big to the surface. But learning to retrieve from the bottom may help you save a life sometime.

Here's a good water game for beginners and nonswimmers: riding the rapids on a plastic air mattress. Well, would you believe a riffle? If your creek has a riffle a foot deep (make sure the water below the riffle is not over your head) you can float down this rapid, racing your buddies all the way.

Never regard an air mattress as a

in front of your eyes. Vision improves immediately. The reason is that an air bubble is a face mask of sorts. All a mask really does is provide a permanent air bubble through which you look. Using this method you can see for ten feet in clear water.

When you and your friends have mastered this technique, then you're ready to plan an interesting game. Have someone write words in various parts of the pool—on the bottom. The first person able to report all the words to a leader wins. If you are prohibited from writing on the pool bottom, use crayon to write a word on aluminum dishes from a cook kit.

Swimming is really more fun if you can find games that provide action and exercises that increase your swimming skills. In the excitement of playing water games, don't get beyond your depth—literally. Nonswimmers should stay in water no deeper than 3½ feet. Beginners can swim in water over their heads, but shouldn't venture beyond depths of six feet. Good swimmers, of course, can swim in any depth—but even then they must swim with a buddy. And forget about horseplay! Crying wolf in the water is dangerous business. The trouble: Who can really tell when you're acting or when you're drowning? No one but you, if you're a clown who's always acting.

safety device. In water use air mattresses only to have fun. They are harder to stay on than you might imagine. Don't inflate to full capacity or you'll keep rolling off—much as you roll off an overinflated mattress while sleeping.

Once you have learned how to ride the riffles on the mattress, try floating down without it. Go feetfirst and on your back, using your arms to keep your body afloat. The speed of the water propels you. This is not idle practice. If you're ever in a boat that overturns in rapids, this feet-first method is the safest way to descend: It allows you to see where you are going and push off rocks blocking your way.

It isn't necessary to have expensive equipment to have fun in the water. A wet cotton pillowcase can be filled with air and used as a flotation device. Simply slam the mouth of the case down hard against the water to trap air. Start a fad on your beach by using a pillowcase to help you body surf. If a pillowcase is too small to hold you on top of a wave, make a big sack of unbleached muslin.

Water games primarily teach you to take care of yourself in the water, while allowing you to develop skills that enable you to aid swimmers in trouble. But it isn't a crime to have fun at the same time. ∎

The Cruel Sky

the imprint abruptly vanished, and the tent wall sprang flat once more. There was a low, snarling growl; then, for a long time, silence.

Harper found that he was breathing again. At any moment he had expected the tent to tear open, and some unimaginable horror to come rushing in upon them. Instead—almost anticlimactically—there was only a faint and far-off wailing from a transient gust of wind in the mountains high above. He felt himself shivering uncontrollably; it was nothing to do with the temperature, for it was comfortably warm in their little insulated world.

Then there came a very familiar— indeed, almost friendly—sound. It was the metallic ring of an empty can striking on stone, and it somehow relaxed the tension a little. For the first time, Harper found himself able to speak, or at least to whisper.

"It's found our food containers. Perhaps it'll go away now."

Almost as if in reply, there was a low snarl that seemed to convey anger and disappointment—then the sound of a blow, and the clatter of cans rolling away into the darkness. Harper suddenly remembered that all the food was here in the tent; only the discarded empties were outside. That was not a cheerful thought; he wished that, like superstitious tribesmen, they had left an offering for whatever gods or demons the mountains could conjure forth.

What happened next was so sudden, so utterly unexpected, that it was all over before he had time to react. There was a scuffling sound, as of something being banged against rock; then a familiar electric whine; then a startled grunt——

——and then, a heart-stopping scream of rage and frustration that turned swiftly to sheer terror, and began to dwindle away at ever-increasing speed, up, up into the empty sky——

The fading sound triggered the one appropriate memory in Harper's mind. Once he had seen an early 20th-century movie on the history of flight, and it had contained a ghastly sequence showing a dirigible launching. Some of the ground crew had hung onto the mooring lines just a few seconds too long, and the airship had dragged them up into the sky, dangling helplessly beneath it. Then, one by one, they had lost their hold and dropped back to the Earth . . .

Harper waited for a distant thud, but it never came. Then he realized that the doctor was saying, over and over again: "I left the two units tied together—I left the two units tied together——"

He was still too much in a state of shock for even that information to worry him. Instead, all he felt was a detached and admirably scientific sense of disappointment.

Now he would never know what it was that had been prowling around their tent, in the lonely hours before the Himalayan dawn.

ONE OF THE MOUNTAIN-RESCUE helicopters, flown by a skeptical Sikh who still wondered if the whole thing was an elaborate joke, came nosing down the canyon in the late afternoon. By the time the machine had landed in a flurry of snow, Dr. Elwin was already waving frantically with one arm and supporting himself on the tent framework with the other.

As he recognized the crippled scientist, the helicopter pilot felt a sensation of almost superstitious awe. So the report *must* be true; there was no other way in which Elwin could possibly have reached this place. And that meant that everything flying in and above the skies of Earth was, from this moment, as obsolete as an oxcart. . .

"Thank God you found us," said the doctor, with heartfelt gratitude. "How did you get here so quickly?"

"You can thank the radar tracking networks, and the telescopes in the orbital met stations. We'd have been here earlier, but at first we thought it was all a hoax."

"I don't understand."

"What would *you* have said, Doctor, if someone reported a very dead Himalayan Snow Leopard, mixed up in a tangle of straps and boxes—and holding constant altitude at 90,000 feet?"

Inside the tent, George Harper started to laugh, despite the pain it caused round his rib. The doctor put his head through the flap and asked anxiously: "What's the matter?"

"Nothing—*ouch!* But I was wondering how we are going to get the poor beast down, before it's a menace to navigation."

"Oh, someone will have to go up with another Levvy and press the buttons. Maybe we should have a radio control on all units. . ."

Dr. Elwin's voice faded out in midsentence. Already he was far away, lost in dreams that would change the face of many worlds.

In a little while he would come down from the mountains, bearing the laws of a new civilization. For he would give back to all mankind the freedom lost so long ago, when the first amphibians left their weightless home beneath the waves.

The billion-year battle against the force of gravity was over. ∎

CLOSE COVER BEFORE STRIKING

Vol. I, No. 2   MARCH 15, 1911   5c a Copy

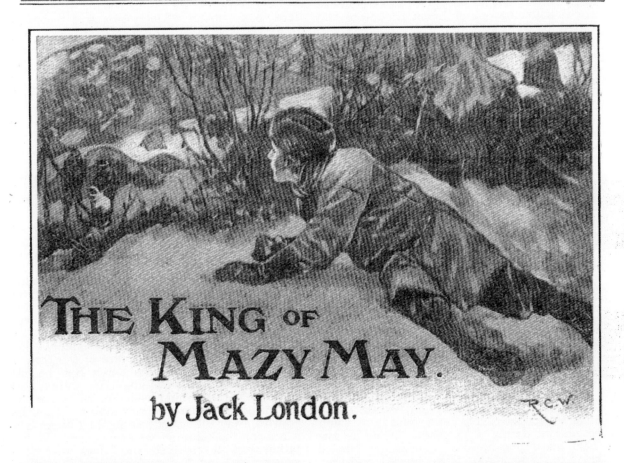

THE KING OF MAZY MAY.
by Jack London.

WALT MASTERS is not a very large boy, but there is manliness in his make-up, and he himself, although he does not know a great deal that most boys know, knows much that other boys do not know. He has never seen a train of cars nor an elevator in his life, and for that matter he has never once looked upon a corn-field, a plough, a cow, or even a chicken. He has never had a pair of shoes on his feet, nor gone to a picnic or a party, nor talked to a girl. But he has seen the sun at midnight, watched the ice-jams on one of the mightiest of rivers, and played beneath the northern lights, the one white child in thousands of square miles of frozen wilderness.

Walt has walked all the fourteen years of his life in sun-tanned, moose-hide moccasins, and he can go to the Indian camps and "talk big" with the men, and trade calico and beads with them for their precious furs. He can make bread without baking-powder, yeast, or hops, shoot a moose at three hundred yards, and drive the wild wolf-dogs fifty miles a day on the packed trail.

Last of all, he has a good heart, and is not afraid of the darkness and loneliness, of man or beast or thing. His father is a good man, strong and brave, and Walt is growing up like him.

Walt was born a thousand miles or so down the Yukon, in a trading-post below the Ramparts. After his mother died, his father and he came on up the river, step by step, from camp to camp, till now they are settled down on the Mazy May Creek in the Klondike country. Last year they and several others had spent much toil and time on the Mazy May, and endured great hardships; the creek, in turn, was just beginning to show up its richness and to reward them for their heavy labor. But with the news of their discoveries, strange men began to come and go through the short days and long nights, and many unjust things they did to the men who had worked so long upon the creek.

Si Hartman had gone away on a moose-hunt, to return and find new stakes driven and his claim jumped. George Lukens and his brother had lost their claims in a like manner, having delayed too long on the way to Dawson to record them. In short, it was the old story, and quite a number of the earnest, industrious prospectors had suffered similar losses.

But Walt Masters' father had recorded his claim at the start, so Walt had nothing to fear now that his father had gone on a short trip up the White River prospecting for quartz. Walt was well able to stay by himself in the cabin, cook his three meals a day, and look after things. Not only did he look after his father's claim, but he had agreed to keep an eye on the adjoining one of Loren Hall, who had started for Dawson to record it.

Loren Hall was an old man, and he had no dogs, so he had to travel very slowly. After he had been gone some time, word came up the river that he had broken through the ice at Rosebud Creek and frozen his feet so badly that he would not be able to travel for a couple of weeks. Then Walt Masters received the news that old Loren was nearly all right again, and about to move on afoot for Dawson as fast as a weakened man could.

Walt was worried, however; the claim was liable to be jumped at any moment because of this delay, and a fresh stampede had started in on the Mazy May. He did not like the looks of the newcomers, and one day, when five of them came by with crack dog-teams and the lightest of camping outfits, he could see that they were prepared to make speed, and resolved to keep an eye on them. So he locked up the cabin and followed them, being at the same time careful to remain hidden.

He had not watched them long before he was sure that they were professional stampeders, bent on jumping all the claims in sight. Walt crept along the snow at the rim of the creek and saw them change many stakes, destroy old ones, and set up new ones.

In the afternoon, with Walt always trailing on their heels, they came back down the creek, unharnessed their dogs, and went into camp within two claims of his cabin. When he saw them make preparations to cook, he hurried home to get something to eat himself, and then hurried back. He crept so close that he could hear them talking quite plainly, and by pushing the underbrush aside he could catch occasional glimpses of them. They had finished eating and were smoking round the fire.

"The creek is all right, boys," a large, black-bearded man, evidently the leader, said, "and I think the best thing we can do is to pull out tonight. The dogs can follow the trail; besides, it's going to be moonlight. What say you?"

"But it's going to be beastly cold," objected one of the party. "It's forty below zero now."

"An' sure, can't ye keep warm by jumpin' off the sleds an' runnin' afther the dogs?" cried an Irishman. "An' who wouldn't? The creek's as rich as a United States mint! Faith, it's an ilegant chanst to be gettin' a run fer yer money! An' if ye don't run, it's mebbe you'll not get the money at all, at all."

"That's it," said the leader. "If we can get to Dawson and record, we're rich men; and there's no telling who's been sneaking along in our tracks, watching us, and perhaps now

off to give the alarm. The thing for us to do is to rest the dogs a bit, and then hit the trail as hard as we can. What do you say?"

Evidently the men had agreed with their leader, for Walt Masters could hear nothing but the rattle of the tin dishes which were being washed. Peering out cautiously, he could see the leader studying a piece of paper. Walt knew what it was at a glance—a list of all the unrecorded claims on Mazy May. Any man could get these lists by applying to the gold commissioner at Dawson.

"Thirty-two," the leader said, lifting his face to the men. "Thirty-two isn't recorded, and this is thirty-three. Come on; let's take a look at it. I saw somebody had been working on it when we came up this morning."

Three of the men went with him, leaving one to remain in camp. Walt crept carefully after them till they came to Loren Hall's shaft. One of the men went down and built a fire on the bottom to thaw out the frozen gravel, while the others built another fire on the dump and melted water in a couple of gold-pans. This they poured into a piece of canvas stretched between two logs, used by Loren Hall in which to wash his gold.

In a short time a couple of buckets of dirt were sent up by the man in the shaft, and Walt could see the others grouped anxiously about their leader as he proceeded to wash it. When this was finished, they stared at the broad streak of black sand and yellow gold grains on the bottom of the pan, and one of them called excitedly for the man who had remained in camp to come. Loren Hall had struck it rich and his claim was not yet recorded. It was plain that they were going to jump it.

Walt lay in the snow, thinking rapidly. He was only a boy, but in the face of the threatened injustice to old lame Loren Hall he felt that he must do something. He waited and watched, with his mind made up, till he saw the men begin to square up new stakes. Then he crawled away till out of hearing, and broke into a run for the camp of the stampeders. Walt's father had taken their own dogs with him prospecting, and the boy knew how impossible it was for him to undertake the seventy miles to Dawson without the aid of dogs.

Gaining the camp, he picked out, with an experienced eye, the easiest running sled and started to harness up the stampeders' dogs. There were three teams of six each, and from these he chose ten of the best. Realizing how necessary it was to have a good head-dog, he strove to discover a leader amongst them; but he had little time in which to do it, for he could hear the voices of the returning men. By the time the team was in shape and everything ready, the claim-jumpers came into sight in an open place not more than a hundred yards from the trail, which ran down the bed of the creek. They cried out to Walt, but instead of giving heed to them he grabbed up one of their fur sleeping-robes, which lay loosely in the snow, and leaped upon the sled.

"Mush! Hi! Mush on!" he cried to the animals, snapping the keen-lashed whip among them.

The dogs sprang against the yoke-straps, and the sled jerked under way so suddenly as to almost throw him off. Then it curved into the creek, poising perilously on one runner. He was almost breathless with suspense, when it finally righted with a bound and sprang ahead again. The creek bank was high and he could not see the men, although he could hear their cries and knew they were running to cut him off. He did not dare to think what would happen if they caught him; he just clung to the sled, his heart beating wildly, and watched the snow-rim of the bank above him.

Suddenly, over this snow-rim came the flying body of the Irishman, who had leaped straight for the sled in a desperate attempt to capture it; but he was an instant too late. Striking on the very rear of it, he was thrown from his feet, backward, into the snow. Yet, with the quickness of a cat, he had clutched the end of the sled with one hand, turned over, and was dragging behind on his breast, swearing at the boy and threatening all kinds of terrible things if he did not stop the dogs; but Walt cracked him sharply across the knuckles with the butt of the dog-whip till he let go.

It was eight miles from Walt's claim to the Yukon—eight very crooked miles, for the creek wound back and forth like a snake, "tying knots in itself," as George Lukens said. And because it was so crooked the dogs could not get up their best speed, while the sled ground heavily on its side against the curves, now to the right, now to the left.

Travellers who had come up and down the Mazy May on foot, with packs on their backs, had declined to go round all the bends, and instead had made short cuts across the narrow necks of creek bottom. Two of his pursuers had gone back to harness the remaining dogs, but the others took advantage of these short cuts, running on foot, and before he knew it they had almost overtaken him.

"Halt!" they cried after him. "Stop, or we'll shoot!"

But Walt only yelled the harder at the dogs, and dashed round the bend with a couple of revolver bullets singing after him. At the next bend they had drawn up closer still, and the bullets struck uncomfortably near to him; but at this point the Mazy May straightened out and ran for half a mile as the crow flies. Here the dogs stretched out in their long wolf swing, and the stampeders, quickly winded, slowed down and waited for their own sled to come up.

Looking over his shoulder, Walt reasoned that they had not given up the chase for good, and that they would soon be after him again. So he wrapped the fur robe about him to shut out the stinging air, and lay flat on the empty sled, encouraging the dogs, as he well knew how.

At last, twisting abruptly between two river islands, he came upon the mighty Yukon sweeping grandly to the north. He could not see from bank to bank, and in the quick-falling twilight it loomed a great white sea of frozen stillness. There was not a sound, save the breathing of the dogs, and the churn of the steel-shod sled.

No snow had fallen for several weeks, and the traffic had packed the main-river trail till it was hard and glassy as glare ice. Over this the sled flew along, and the dogs kept the trail fairly well, although Walt quickly discovered that he had made a mistake in choosing the leader. As they were driven in single file, without reins, he had to guide them by his voice, and it was evident the head-dog had never learned the meaning of "gee" and "haw." He hugged the inside of the curves too closely, often forcing his comrades behind him into the soft snow, while several times he thus capsized the sled.

There was no wind, but the speed at which he travelled created a bitter blast, and with the thermometer down to forty below, this bit through fur and flesh to the very bones. Aware that if he remained constantly upon the sled he would freeze to death, and knowing the practice of Arctic travellers, Walt shortened up one of the lashing-thongs, and whenever he felt chilled, seized hold of it, jumped off, and ran behind till warmth was restored. Then he would climb on and rest till the process had to be repeated.

Looking back he could see the sled of his pursuers, drawn by eight dogs, rising and falling over the ice hummocks like a boat in a seaway. The Irishman and the black-bearded leader were with it, taking turns in running and riding.

Night fell, and in the blackness of the first hour or so Walt toiled desperately with his dogs. On account of the poor lead-dog, they were continually floundering off the beaten track into the soft snow, and the sled was as often riding on its side or top as it was in the proper way. This work and strain tried his strength sorely. Had he not been in such haste he could have avoided much of it, but he feared the stampeders would creep up in the darkness and overtake him. However, he could occasionally hear them yelling to their dogs, and knew from the sounds that they were coming up very slowly.

When the moon rose he was off Sixty Mile, and Dawson was only fifty miles away. He was almost exhausted, and breathed a sigh of relief as he climbed on the sled again. Looking back, he saw his enemies had crawled up within four hundred yards. At this space they remained, a black speck of motion on the white river-breast. Strive as they would, they could not shorten this distance, and strive as he would he could not increase it.

Walt had now discovered the proper lead-dog, and he knew he could easily run away from them if he could only change the bad leader for the good one. But this was impossible, for a moment's delay, at the speed they were running, would bring the men behind upon him.

When he was off the mouth of Rosebud Creek, just as he was topping a rise, the report of a gun and the ping of a bullet on the ice beside him, told him that they were this time shooting at him with a rifle. And from then on, as he cleared the summit of each ice-jam, he stretched flat on the leaping sled till the rifle-shot from the rear warned him that he was safe till the next ice-jam was reached.

Now it is very hard to lie on a moving sled, jumping and plunging and yawing like a boat before the wind, and to shoot through the deceiving moonlight at an object four hundred yards away on another moving sled performing equally wild antics. So it is not to be wondered at that the black-bearded leader did not hit him.

After several hours of this, during which, perhaps, a score of bullets had struck about him, their ammunition began to give out and their fire slackened. They took greater care, and only whipped a shot at him at the most favorable opportunities. He was also beginning to leave them behind, the distance slowly increasing to six hundred yards.

Lifting clear on the crest of a great jam off Indian River, Walt Masters met with his first accident. A bullet sang past his ears, and struck the bad lead-dog.

The poor brute plunged in a heap, with the rest of the team on top of him.

Like a flash Walt was by the leader. Cutting the traces with his hunting-knife, he dragged the dying animal to one side and straightened out the team.

He glanced back. The other sled was coming up like an express train. With half the dogs still over their traces, he cried "Mush on!" and leaped upon the sled just as the pursuing team dashed abreast of him.

The Irishman was just preparing to spring for him—they were so sure they had him that they did not shoot—when Walt turned fiercely upon them with his whip.

He struck at their faces, and men must save their faces with their hands. So there was no shooting just then. Before they could recover from the hot rain of blows, Walt reached out from his sled, catching their wheel-dog by the fore-legs in midspring, and throwing him heavily. This brought the whole team into a snarl, capsizing the sled and tangling his enemies up beautifully.

Away Walt flew, the runners of his sled fairly screaming as they bounded over the frozen surface. And what had seemed an accident proved to be a blessing in disguise. The proper lead-dog was now to the fore, and he stretched low to the trail and whined with joy as he jerked his comrades along.

By the time he reached Ainslie's Creek, seventeen miles from Dawson, Walt had left his pursuers, a tiny speck, far behind. At Monte Cristo Island he could no longer see them. And at Swede Creek, just as daylight was silvering the pines, he ran plump into the camp of old Loren Hall.

Almost as quick as it takes to tell it, Loren had his sleeping-furs rolled up, and had joined Walt on the sled. They permitted the dogs to travel more slowly, as there was no sign of the chase in the rear, and just as they pulled up at the gold commissioner's office in Dawson, Walt, who had kept his eyes open to the last, fell asleep.

And because of what Walt Masters did on this night, the men of the Yukon have become very proud of him, and always speak of him now as the King of Mazy May.

These stories are the best that can be purchased in the world, and in order to be able to give them to you we need more subscribers. Are you with us? $1.20 pays your dues for a whole year—24 issues.

We aim to give the boys the very best stories, and if you are pleased with our efforts let us know. We want to give you only that which you like.

KNOTS WORTH KNOWING
How To Tie Some Useful Knots

Here you can learn the best knots. We shall tell you each issue how to tie a fresh one. Last issue described the making of the overhand knot. —Editor.

THE FIGURE OF EIGHT KNOT

The Flemish or figure of eight is a better and more reliable knot than the overhand knot, and it is more ornamental. The way to make it is to pass the end back, over, and round the standing part and down through the loop. See that you commence by forming a loop, as though you were about to make a simple overhand knot, but then, instead of bringing the end up through the loop, turn it over the standing part and *down* through the loop.

It is well as to use a rather firm material such as blind-cord, for practicing small common knots; or, better still, line used for sea-fishing. Either can be tied up over and over again,

which is not the case with common string, and it is easier to see which way the parts of a knot lie.

The figure of eight is a very useful and interesting knot. It will not jam like the overhand knot, as the turns are longer, and it is not so likely to slip. There is never any necessity to take a knife to cut it, as it can be untied in an instant, no matter how tight it has been pulled.

Sometimes this knot is used to join two ropes. The ends are laid together alongside one another, the double parts are taken in each hand, and when the knot is formed it is made taut by hauling on both parts at once.

Next issue: The Sailor's Square Knot.

In the explanations which are given the *standing part* of a rope means the main part, or long portion; the loop (most knots begin with a loop) is termed the *bight*, and the short part of the rope, which is used in forming the knots, is called the *end*.

Employer: "Yes, I advertised for a strong boy. Do you think you will suit?"

Applicant: "Well, I've just finished throwing nineteen other applicants out of the building."

"Yes, madam, I remember very well your buying a stamp," said a post-office assistant.

"Well, I put it on a very important letter and posted it. It has not been received. I want you to understand that I shall buy my stamps elsewhere if this occurs again."

THE SUNJAMMER

BY ARTHUR C. CLARKE, *who as a boy made his own telescopes and mapped the moon. As a teen-ager he began to write science-fiction and facts. In 1945 he was the first to propose the use of satellites for communication transmittal. Mr. Clarke is an expert skin-diver as well as an astronomer, and he has written 25 books and hundreds of stories and articles on both space and oceanography. A native of Great Britain, he lives at present in Ceylon, where he is doing underwater exploration. In 1962 he received the international Kalinga Prize, most important award in the science-writing field.*

T HE ENORMOUS disk of sail strained at its rigging, already filled with the wind that blew between the worlds. In three minutes the race would begin, yet now John Merton felt more relaxed, more at peace, than at any time for the past year. Whatever happened when the commodore gave the starting signal, whether *Diana* carried him to victory or defeat, he had achieved his ambition. After a lifetime spent in designing ships for others, now he would sail his own.

"T minus two minutes," said the cabin radio. "Please confirm your readiness."

One by one, the other skippers answered. Merton recognized all the voices—some tense, some calm—for they were the voices of his friends and rivals. On the four inhabited worlds, there were scarcely twenty men who could sail a sun-yacht; and they were all here, on the starting line or aboard the escort vessels, orbiting twenty-two thousand miles above the equator.

"Number One—*Gossamer*—ready to go."

"Number Two—*Santa Maria*—all O.K."

"Number Three—*Sunbeam*—O.K."

"Number Four — *Woomera* — all systems GO."

Merton smiled at that last echo from the early, primitive days of astronautics. But it had become part of the tradition of space; and there were times when a man needed to evoke the shades of those who had gone before him to the stars.

"Number Five—*Lebedev*—we're ready."

"Number Six—*Arachne*—O.K."

Now it was his turn, at the end of the line; strange to think that the words he was speaking in this tiny cabin were being heard by at least five billion people.

"Number Seven—*Diana*—ready to start."

"One through Seven acknowledged," answered that impersonal voice from the judge's launch. "Now T minus one minute."

Merton scarcely heard it; for the last time, he was checking the tension in the rigging. The needles of all the dynamometers were steady; the immense sail was taut, its mirror surface sparkling and glittering gloriously in the sun.

To Merton, floating weightless at the periscope, it seemed to fill the sky. As well it might —for out there were fifty million square feet of sail, linked to his capsule by almost a hundred miles of rigging. All the canvas of all the tea-clippers that had once raced like clouds across the China seas, sewn into one gigantic sheet, could not match the single sail that *Diana* had spread beneath the sun. Yet it was little more substantial than a soap bubble; that two square miles of aluminized plastic was only a few millionths of an inch thick.

"T minus ten seconds. All recording cameras ON."

Something so huge, yet so frail, was hard for the mind to grasp. And it was harder still to realize that this fragile mirror could tow him free of Earth, merely by the power of the sunlight it would trap.

". . . Five, Four, Three, Two, One, CUT."

Seven knife blades sliced through the seven thin lines tethering the yachts to the mother-ships that had assembled and serviced them. Until this moment, all had been circling Earth

together in a rigidly held formation, but now the yachts would begin to disperse, like dandelion seeds drifting before the breeze. And the winner would be the one that first drifted past the Moon.

Aboard *Diana*, nothing seemed to be happening. But Merton knew better; though his body could feel no thrust, the instrument board told him that he was now accelerating at almost one thousandth of a gravity. For a rocket, that figure would have been ludicrous—but this was the first time any solar yacht had ever attained it. *Diana's* design was sound; the vast sail was living up to his calculations. At this rate, two circuits of the Earth would build up his speed to escape velocity—and then he could head out for the Moon, with the full force of the Sun behind him.

The full force of the Sun. He smiled wryly, remembering all his attempts to explain solar sailing to those lecture audiences back on Earth. That had been the only way he could raise money, in those early days; he might be chief designer of the Cosmodyne Corporation, with a whole string of successful spaceships to his credit, but his firm had not been exactly enthusiastic about his hobby.

"Hold your hands out to the Sun," he'd said. "What do you feel? Heat, of course. But there's pressure as well—though you've never noticed it, because it's so tiny. Over the area of your hands, it only comes to about a millionth of an ounce.

"But out in space, even a pressure as small as that can be important—for it's acting all the time, hour after hour, day after day. Unlike rocket fuel, it's free and unlimited. If we want to, we can use it; we can build sails to catch the radiation blowing from the Sun."

At that point, he would pull out a few square yards of sail material and toss it toward the audience. The silvery film would coil and twist like smoke, then drift slowly to the ceiling in the hot-air currents.

"You can see how light it is," he'd continue. "A square mile weighs only a ton, and can collect five pounds of radiation pressure. So it will start moving—and we can let it tow us if we attach to it.

"Of course, its acceleration will be tiny—about a thousandth of a 'g.' That doesn't seem much, but let's see what it means.

"It means that in the first second, we'll move about a fifth of an inch. I suppose a healthy snail could do better than that. But after a minute, we've covered sixty feet, and will be doing just over a mile an hour. That's not bad, for something driven by pure sunlight! After an hour, we're forty miles from our starting point, and will be moving at eighty miles an hour. Please remember that in space there's no friction, so once you start anything moving, it will keep going forever. You'll be surprised when I tell you what our thousandth-of-a-'g' sailboat will be doing at the end of a day's run. *Almost two thousand miles an hour*. If it starts from orbit—as it has to, of course—it can reach escape velocity in a couple of days. All without burning a single drop of fuel!"

Well, he'd convinced them, and in the end he'd even convinced Cosmodyne. Over the last twenty years, a new sport had come into being.

It had been called the sport of billionaires, and that was true—but it was beginning to pay for itself in terms of publicity and TV coverage. The prestige of four continents and two worlds was riding on this race, and it had the biggest audience in history.

Diana had made a good start; time to take a look at the opposition. Moving very gently though there were shock absorbers between the control capsule and the delicate rigging, he was determined to run no risks—Merton stationed himself at the periscope.

There they were, looking like strange silver flowers planted in the dark fields of space. The nearest, South America's *Santa Maria*, was only fifty miles away; it bore a close resemblance to a boy's kite—but a kite more than a mile on a side. Further away, the University of Astrograd's *Lebedev* looked like a Maltese cross; the sails that formed the four arms could apparently be tilted for steering purposes. In contrast, the Federation of Australasis' *Woomera* was a simple parachute, four miles in circumference. General Spacecraft's *Arachne*, as its name suggested, looked like a spiderweb —and had been built on the same principles, by robot shuttles spiraling out from a central point. Eurospace Corporation's *Gossamer* was an identical design, on a slightly smaller scale. And the Republic of Mars's *Sunbeam* was a flat ring, with a half-mile-wide hole in the center, spinning slowly so that centrifugal force gave it stiffness. That was an old idea, but no one had ever made it work; and Merton was fairly sure that the colonials would be in trouble when they started to turn.

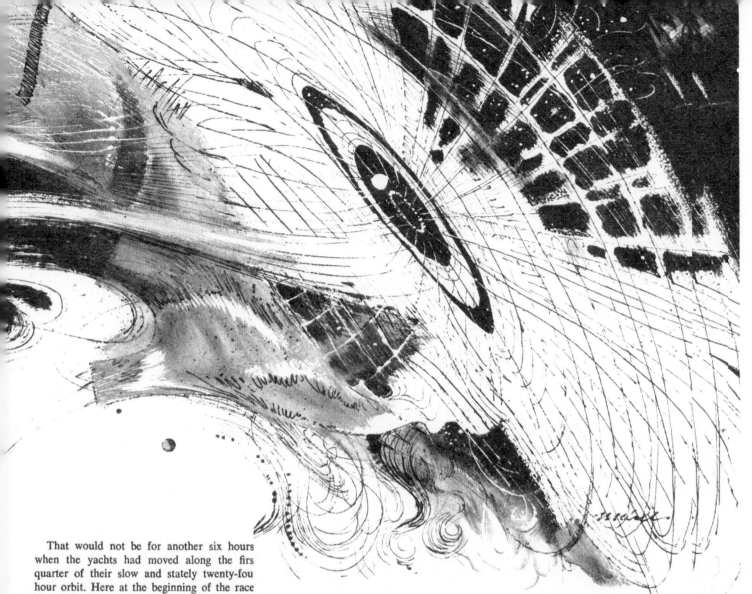

ILLUSTRATED BY ROBERT McCALL

That would not be for another six hours when the yachts had moved along the firs quarter of their slow and stately twenty-fou hour orbit. Here at the beginning of the race they were all heading directly away from the Sun —running as it were, before the solar wind. One had to make the most of his lap, before the boats swung round to the other side of Earth and then started to head back into the Sun.

Time for the first check, Merton told himself, while he had no navigational worries. With the periscope, he made a careful examination of the sail, concentrating on the points where the rigging was attached to it. The shroud lines —narrow bands of unsilvered plastic film— would have been completely invisible had they not been coated with fluorescent paint. Now they were taut lines of colored light, dwindling away for hundreds of yards toward that gigantic sail; each had its own electric windlass, not much bigger than a game fisherman's reel. The little windlasses were continually turning, playing lines in or out, as the auto-pilot kept the sail trimmed at the correct angle to the Sun.

The play of sunlight on the great flexible mirror was beautiful to watch. It was undulating in slow, stately oscillations, sending multiple images of the Sun marching across the heavens, until they faded away at the edges of the sail. Such leisurely vibrations were to be expected in this vast and flimsy structure; they were usually quite harmless, but Merton watched them carefully. Sometimes they could build up to the catastrophic undulations known as the "wriggles," which could tear a sail to pieces.

When he was satisfied that everything was shipshape, he swept the periscope around the sky, rechecking the positions of his rivals. It was as he had hoped; the weeding-out process had begun, as the less efficient boats fell astern. But the real test would come when they passed into the shadow of Earth; then maneuverability would count as much as speed.

It seemed a strange thing to do, now that the race had just started, but it might be a good idea to get some sleep. The two-man crews on the other boats could take it in turns, but Merton had no one to relieve him. He must rely on his physical resources—like that other solitary seaman Joshua Slocum, in his tiny *Spray,* sailing *Spray* single-handed round the world.

Merton snapped the elastic bands of the cabin seat around his waist and legs, then placed the electrodes of the sleep-inducer on his forehead. He set the timer for three hours and relaxed.

Very gently, hypnotically, the electronic pulses throbbed in the frontal lobes of his brain. Colored spirals of light expanded beneath his closed eyelids, widening outward to sleep.

"Number Six—*Arachne*—O.K."

The brazen clamor of the alarm dragged him back from his dreamless sleep. He was instantly awake, his eyes scanning the instrument panel. Only two hours had passed but above the accelerometer, a red light was flashing. Thrust was failing; *Diana* was losing power.

Merton's first thought was that something had happened to the sail; perhaps the antispin devices had failed, and the rigging had become twisted. Swiftly, he checked the meters that showed the tension in the shroud lines. Strange; on one side of the sail they were reading normally—but on the other, the pull was dropping slowly even as he watched.

In sudden understanding, Merton grabbed the periscope. Yes—there was the trouble.

A huge, sharp-edged shadow had begun to slide across the gleaming silver of the sail. Darkness was falling upon *Diana,* as if a cloud had passed between her and the Sun. And in the dark, robbed of the rays that drove her, she would lose all thrust and drift helplessly through space.

But, of course, there were no clouds here, more than twenty thousand miles above the Earth. If there was a shadow, it must be made by man.

Merton grinned as he swung the periscope

toward the Sun, switching in the filters that would allow him to look full into its blazing face without being blinded.

"Maneuver 4a," he muttered to himself. "We'll see who can play best at *that* game."

It looked as if a giant planet was crossing the face of the Sun; a great black disk had bitten deep into its edge. Twenty miles astern, *Gossamer* was trying to arrange an artificial eclipse—specially for *Diana's* benefit.

The maneuver was a perfectly legitimate one. Back in the days of ocean racing, skippers had often tried to rob each other of the wind.

Merton had no intentions of being caught so easily. There was time to take evasive action.

Diana's tiny computer—the size of a matchbox, but the equivalent of a thousand human mathematicians—considered the problem for a full second and then flashed the answer. He'd have to open control panels three and four, until the sail had developed an extra twenty degrees of tilt; then the radiation pressure would blow him out of *Gossamer's* dangerous shadow, back into the full blast of the Sun. It was a pity to interfere with the autopilot, which had been carefully programed to give the fastest possible run—but that, after all, was why he was here. This was what made solar yachting a sport, rather than a battle between computers.

Out went control lines 1 to 6, slowly undulating like sleepy snakes as they momentarily lost their tension. Two miles away, the triangular panels began to open lazily, spilling sunlight through the sail. Yet, for a long time, nothing seemed to happen. It was hard to grow accustomed to this slow-motion world, where it took minutes for the effects of any action to become visible to the eye. Then Merton saw that the sail was indeed tipping toward the Sun—and that *Gossamer's* shadow was sliding harmlessly away, its cone of darkness lost in the deeper night of space.

Long before the shadow had vanished, and the disk of the Sun had cleared again, he reversed the tilt and brought *Diana* back on course. Her new momentum would carry her clear of the danger; no need to overdo it and upset his calculations by side-stepping too far. That was another rule that was hard to learn; the very moment you had started something happening in space, it was already time to think about stopping it.

He reset the alarm, ready for the next natural or man-made emergency; perhaps *Gossamer* or one of the other contestants would try the same trick again. Meanwhile, it was time to eat, though he did not feel particularly hungry. One used little physical energy in space, and it was easy to forget about food. Easy—and dangerous; for when an emergency arose, you might not have the reserves needed to deal with it.

He broke open the first of the meal packets and inspected it without enthusiasm. The name on the label—SPACETASTIES—was enough to put him off. And he had doubts about the promise printed underneath: "Guaranteed Crumbless." It had been said that crumbs were a greater danger to space vehicles than meteorites. They could drift into the most unlikely places, causing short circuits, blocking vital jets and getting into all of the instruments that

were supposed to be hermetically sealed.

Still, the liverwurst went down pleasantly enough; so did the chocolate and the pineapple puree. The plastic coffee-bulb was warming on the electric heater when the outside world broke in upon his solitude, as the radio operator on the commodore's launch called him.

"Dr. Merton? If you can spare the time, Jeremy Blair would like a few words with you." Blair was one of the more responsible news commentators, and Merton had been on his program many times. "I'll take it," he answered.

"Hello, Dr. Merton," said the commentator immediately. "Glad you can spare a few minutes. And congratulations—you seem to be ahead of the field."

"Too early in the game to be sure of *that*," Merton answered cautiously.

"Tell me, doctor—why did you decide to sail *Diana* yourself? Just because it's never been done before?"

"Well isn't that a very good reason? But it wasn't the only one, of course?" He paused, choosing his words carefully. "You know how critically the performance of a sun-yacht depends on its mass. A second man, with all his supplies, would mean another five hundred pounds. That could easily be the difference between winning and losing."

"And you're quite certain that you can handle *Diana* alone?"

"Reasonably sure, thanks to the automatic controls I've designed. My main job is to supervise and make decisions."

"But—two square miles of sail! It just doesn't seem possible for one man to cope with all that!"

Merton laughed.

"Why not? Those two squares miles produce a maximum pull of just ten pounds. I can exert

He placed the electrodes of the sleep-inducer on his head and set the timer for three hours.

that much force with my little finger," he said.

"Well, thank you, doctor. And good luck. I'll be calling you again."

As the commentator signed off, Merton felt a little ashamed of himself. For his answer had been only part of the truth; and he was sure that Blair was shrewd enough to know it.

There was just one reason why he was here, alone in space. For almost forty years he had worked with teams of hundreds or even thousands of men, helping to design the most complex vehicles that the world had ever seen. For the last twenty years he had led one of those teams and watched his creations go soaring to the stars. (Sometimes; but there were failures that he could never forget, even though the fault had not been his.) He was famous, with a successful career behind him. Yet he had never done anything by himself; always he had been one of an army.

This was his very last chance of individual achievement, and he would share it with no one. There would be no more solar yachting for at least five years, as the period of the quiet Sun ended and the cycle of bad weather began, with radiation storms bursting through the solar system. When it was safe again for these frail, unshielded craft to venture aloft, he would be too old.

He dropped the empty food containers into the waste disposal and turned once more to the periscope. At first, he could find only five of the other yachts; there was no sign of *Woomera*. It took him several minutes to locate her—a dim, star-eclipsing phantom, neatly caught in the shadows of *Lebedev*. He could imagine the frantic efforts the Australasians were making to extricate themselves, and wondered how they had fallen into the trap. It suggested that *Lebedev* was unusually maneuverable; she would bear watching, though she was too far away to menace *Diana* at the moment.

Now the Earth had almost vanished; it had waned to a narrow, brilliant bow of light that was moving steadily toward the Sun. Dimly outlined within that burning bow was the nightside of the planet, with the phosphorescent gleams of great cities showing here and there through gaps in the clouds. The disk of darkness had already blanked out a huge section of the Milky Way; in a few minutes it would start to encroach upon the Sun.

The light was fading; a purple, twilight hue—the glow of many sunsets, thousands of miles below—was falling across the sail, as *Diana* slipped silently into the shadow of Earth. The Sun plummeted below that invisible horizon; within minutes, it was night.

Merton looked back along the orbit he had traced, now a quarter of the way around the world. One by one he saw the brilliant stars of the other yachts wink out, as they joined him in the brief night. It would be an hour before the Sun emerged from that enormous black shield, and through all that time they would be completely helpless, coasting without power.

He switched on the external spotlight and started to search the now darkened sail with its beam. Already, the thousands of acres of film were beginning to wrinkle and become flaccid; the shroud lines were slackening, and must be wound in lest they become entangled. But all

THE SUNJAMMER

this was expected; everything was going as planned. Fifty miles astern, *Arachne* and *Santa Maria* were not so lucky. Merton learned of their troubles when the radio burst into life on the emergency circuit.

"Number Two—Number Six—this is Control. You are on a collision course—your orbits will intersect in sixty-five minutes! Do you require assistance?"

There was a long pause while the two skippers digested this bad news. Merton wondered who was to blame; perhaps one yacht had been trying to shadow the other, and had not completed the maneuver before they were both caught in darkness. Now there was nothing that either could do.

Yet—sixty-five minutes! That would just bring them out into sunlight again, as they emerged from the shadow of the Earth. They still had a slim chance, if their sails could snatch enough power to avoid a crash. There must be some frantic calculations going on, aboard *Arachne* and *Santa Maria*.

Arachne answered first; her reply was just what Merton had expected.

"Number Six—calling Control. We don't need assistance, thank you. We'll work this out for ourselves."

I wonder, thought Merton; but at least it will be interesting to watch. The first real drama of the race was approaching—exactly above the line of midnight on the sleeping Earth.

For the next hour, Merton's own sail kept him too busy to worry about *Arachne* and *Santa Maria*. It was hard to keep a good watch on that fifty million square feet of dim plastic out there in the darkness, illuminated only by his narrow spotlight and the rays of the still distant Moon. From now on, for almost half his orbit around the Earth, he must keep the whole of this immense area edge-on to the Sun. During the next twelve or fourteen hours, the sail would be a useless encumbrance; for he would be heading *into* the Sun, and its rays could only drive him backward along his orbit. It was a pity that he could not furl the sail completely, until he was ready to use it again; but no one had yet found a practical way of doing this.

Far below, there was the first hint of dawn along the edge of the Earth. In ten minutes, the Sun would emerge from its eclipse; the coasting yachts would come to life again as the blast of radiation struck their sails. That would be the moment of crisis for *Arachne* and *Santa Maria* and, indeed, for all of them.

Merton swung the periscope until he found the two dark shadows drifting against the stars. They were very close together—perhaps less than three miles apart. They might, he decided, just be able to make it.

Dawn flashed like an explosion along the rim of Earth, as the Sun rose out of the Pacific. The sail and shroud lines glowed a brief crimson, then gold, then blazed with the pure white light of day. The needles of the dynamometers began to lift from their zeros—but only just. *Diana* was still almost completely weightless, for with the sail pointing toward the Sun, her acceleration was now only a few millionths of a gravity.

But *Arachne* and *Santa Maria* were crowding on all the sail that they could manage, in their desperate attempt to keep apart. Now, while there was less than two miles between them, their glittering plastic clouds were unfurling and expanding with agonizing slowness, as they felt the first delicate push of the Sun's rays. Almost every TV screen on Earth would be mirroring this protracted drama.

The two skippers were stubborn men. Either could have cut his sail and fallen back to give the other a chance; but neither would do so. Too much prestige, too many millions, too many reputations, were at stake. And so, silently and softly as snowflakes falling on a winter night, *Arachne* and *Santa Maria* collided.

The square kite crawled almost imperceptibly into the circular spider web; the long ribbons of the shroud lines twisted and tangled together with dreamlike slowness. Even aboard *Diana*, busy with his own rigging, Merton could scarcely tear his eyes away from this silent, long-drawn-out disaster.

For more than ten minutes the billowing, shining clouds continued to merge into one inextricable mass. Then the crew capsules tore loose and went their separate ways, missing each other by hundreds of yards. With a flare of rockets, the safety launches hurried to pick them up.

That leaves five of us, thought Merton. He felt sorry for the skippers who had so thoroughly eliminated each other, only a few hours after the start of the race; but they were young men, and would have another chance.

Within minutes, the five had dropped to four. From the very beginning, Merton had had doubts about the slowly rotating *Sunbeam*; now he saw them justified.

The Martian ship had failed to tack properly; her spin had given her too much stability. Her great ring of a sail was turning to face the Sun, instead of being edge-on to it; she was being blown back along her course at almost her maximum acceleration.

That was about the most maddening thing that could happen to a skipper—worse even than a collision, for he could blame only himself. But no one would feel much sympathy for the frustrated colonials, as they dwindled slowly astern. They had made too many brash boasts before the race, and what had happened to them was poetic justice.

Yet it would not do to write off *Sunbeam* completely; with almost half a million miles yet to go, she might still pull ahead.

However, the next twelve hours were uneventful, as the Earth waxed in the sky from new to full. There was little to do while the fleet drifted round the unpowered half of its orbit, but Merton did not find the time hanging heavily on his hands. He caught a few hours sleep, ate two meals, wrote up his log, and became involved in several more radio interviews. Sometimes, though rarely, he talked to the other skippers, exchanging greetings and friendly taunts. But most of the time he was content to float in weightless relaxation, beyond all the cares of Earth, happier than he had been for many years. He was—as far as any man could be in space—master of his own fate, sailing the ship upon which he had lavished so much skill, so much love, that it had become part of his very being.

The next casualty came when they were passing the line between Earth and Sun, and were just beginning the powered half of the orbit. Aboard *Diana*, Merton saw the great sail stiffen as it tilted to catch the rays that drove it. The acceleration began to climb up from the microgravities, though it would be hours yet before it would reach its maximum value.

It would never reach it for *Gossamer*. The moment when power came on again was always critical, and she failed to survive it.

Blair's radio commentary, which Merton had left running at low volume, alerted him with the news; "Hello, *Gossamer* has the wriggles!" He hurried to the periscope, but at first could see nothing wrong with the great circular disk of *Gossamer's* sail. It was difficult to study it, as it was almost edge-on to him and so appeared as a thin ellipse; but presently he saw that it was twisting back and forth in slow, irresistible oscillations. Unless the crew could damp out these waves, by properly timed but gentle tugs on the shroud lines, the sail would tear itself to pieces.

They did their best, and after twenty minutes it seemed that they had succeeded. Then, somewhere near the center of the sail, the plastic film began to rip. It was slowly driven outward by the radiation pressure, like smoke coiling upward from a fire. Within a quarter of an hour, nothing was left but the delicate tracery

of the radial spars that had supported the great web. Once again there was a flare of rockets, as a launch moved in to retrieve the *Gossamer's* capsule and her dejected crew.

"Getting rather lonely up there, isn't it?" said a conversational voice.

"Not for you, Dimitri," retorted Merton. "You've still got company back there at the end of the field. *I'm* the one who's lonely, up here in front." It was not an idle boast; by this time *Diana* was three hundred miles ahead of the next competitor, and his lead should increase still more rapidly in the hours to come.

Aboard *Lebedev*, Dimitri Markoff gave a good-natured chuckle. He did not sound, Merton thought, at all like a man who had resigned himself to defeat.

"Remember the legend of the tortoise and the hare," answered the Russian. "A lot can happen in the next quarter million miles."

It happened much sooner than that, when they had completed their first orbit of Earth and were passing the starting line again—though thousands of miles higher, thanks to the extra energy the Sun's rays had given them. Merton had taken careful sights on the other yachts, and had fed the figures into the computer. The answer it gave for *Woomera* was so absurd that he immediately did a recheck.

There was no doubt of it—the Australasians were catching up at a completely fantastic rate.

A swift look through the periscope gave the answer. *Woomera's* rigging, pared back to the very minimum of mass, had given away. It was her sail alone, still maintaining its shape, that was racing up behind him like a handkerchief blown before the wind. Two hours later it fluttered past, less than twenty miles away; but long before that, the Australasians had joined the crowd aboard the commodore's launch.

So now it was a straight fight between *Diana* and *Lebedev*—for though the Martians had not given up, they were a thousand miles astern and no longer counted as a serious threat. For that matter, it was hard to see what *Lebedev* could do to overtake *Diana's* lead; but all the way round the second lap—through eclipse again, and the long, slow drift against the Sun, Merton felt a growing unease.

He knew the Russian pilots and designers. They had been trying to win this race for twenty years—and, after all, it was only fair that they should, for had not Pyotr Nikolayevich Lebedev been the first man to detect the pressure of sunlight, back at the very beginning of the twentieth century? But they had nev-

er succeeded.

And they would never stop trying. Dimitri was up to something—and it would be spectacular.

Aboard the official launch, a thousand miles behind the racing yachts, Commodore van Stratten looked at the radiogram with angry dismay. It had traveled more than a hundred million miles, from the chain of solar observatories swinging high above the sun's blazing surface. It brought the worst possible news.

The commodore—his title, of course, was purely honorary; back on Earth he was professor of astrophysics at Harvard—had been half expecting it. Never before had the race been arranged so late in the season; there had been many delays, they had gambled and now, it seemed, they might all lose.

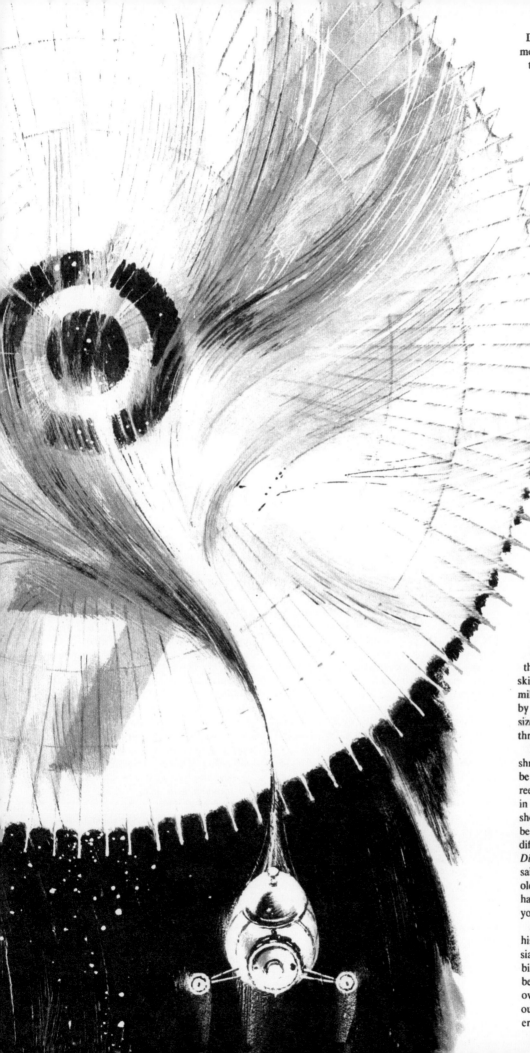

Deep beneath the surface of the Sun, enormous forces were gathering. At any moment, the energies of a million hydrogen bombs might burst forth in the awesome explosion known as a solar flare. Climbing at millions of miles an hour, an invisible fireball many times the size of Earth would leap from the Sun, and head out across space.

The cloud of electrified gas would probably miss the Earth completely. But if it did not, it would arrive in just over a day. Spaceships could protect themselves with their powerful magnetic screens; but the lightly built solar yachts, with their paper-thin walls, were defenseless against such a menace. The crews would have to be taken off.

John Merton still knew nothing of this as he brought *Diana* round the Earth for the second time. If all went well, this would would be the last circuit, both for him and for the Russians. They had spiraled upwards by thousands of miles, gaining energy from the Sun's rays. On this lap, they should escape from Earth completely —and head outward on the long run to the Moon. It was a straight race now; *Sunbeam's* crew had finally withdrawn exhausted, after battling valiantly with their spinning sail for more than a hundred thousand miles.

Merton did not feel tired; he had eaten and slept well, and *Diana* was behaving herself admirably. The autopilot, tensioning the rigging like a busy little spider, kept the great sail trimmed to the Sun more accurately than any human skipper. Though by this time the two square miles of plastic sheet must have been riddled by hundreds of micrometeorites, the pinhead-size punctures had produced no falling-off of thrust.

He had only two worries. The first was shroud line Number 8, which could no longer be adjusted properly. Without any warning, the reel had jammed; bearings sometimes seized up in vacuum. He could neither lengthen nor shorten the line, and would have to navigate as best he could with the others. Luckily, the most difficult maneuvers were over; from now on, *Diana* would have the Sun behind her as she sailed straight down the solar wind. And as the old-time sailors had often said, it was easy to handle a boat when the wind was blowing over your shoulder.

His other worry was *Lebedev,* still dogging his heels three hundred miles astern. The Russian yacht had shown remarkable maneuverability, thanks to the four great panels that could be tilted around the central sail. All her flip-overs as she rounded Earth had been carried out with superb precision; but to gain maneuverability she must have sacrificed speed. You could not have it both ways; in the long, straight haul ahead, Merton should be able to hold his own. Yet he could not be certain of victory until, three or four days from now, *Diana* went flashing past the far side of the Moon.

And then, in the fiftieth hour of the race, near the end of the second orbit round Earth, Markoff sprang his little surprise.

"Hello, John," he said casually over the ship-to-ship circuit. "I'd like to watch this. It should be interesting."

Merton drew himself across to the periscope, turned up the magnification to the limit. There in the field of view, a most improbable sight against the background of the stars, was the glittering Maltese cross of *Lebedev*, very small but very clear. And then, as he watched, the four arms of the cross slowly detached themselves from the central square, and went drifting away, into space.

Markoff had jettisoned all unnecessary mass, now that he was coming up to escape velocity and need no longer plod patiently around the Earth, gaining momentum on each circuit. From now on, *Lebedev* would be almost unsteerable—but that did not matter; all the tricky navigation lay behind her. It was as if an old-time yachtsman had deliberately thrown away his rudder and heavy keel—knowing that the rest of the race would be straight downwind over a calm sea.

"Congratulations, Dimitri," Merton radioed. "It's a neat trick. But it's not good enough—you can't catch up with me now."

"I've not finished yet," the Russian answered. "There's an old winter's tale in my country, about a sleigh being chased by wolves. To save himself, the driver has to throw off the passengers one by one. Do you see the analogy?"

MERTON did, all too well. On this final straight lap, Dimitri no longer needed his co-pilot *Lebedev* could really be stripped down for action.

"Alexis won't be very happy about this," Merton replied. "Besides, it's against the rules."

"Alexis isn't happy, but I'm the captain; he'll just have to wait around for ten minutes until the commodore picks him up. And the regulations say nothing about the size of the crew—*you* should know that."

Merton did not answer; he was too busy doing some hurried calculations, based on what he knew of *Lebedev's* design. By the time he had finished, he knew the race was still in doubt. *Lebedev* would be catching up with him about the time he hoped to pass the Moon.

But the outcome of the race was already being decided, ninety-two million miles away.

On Solar Observatory Three, far inside the orbit of Mercury, the automatic instruments recorded the whole history of the flare. A hundred million square miles of the Sun's surface suddenly exploded in such blue-white fury that, by comparison, the rest of the disk paled to a dull glow. Out of that seething inferno, twisting and turning like a living creature in the magnetic fields of its own creation, soared the electrified plasma of the great flare. Ahead of it,

moving at the speed of light, went the warning flash of ultraviolet and Xrays. That would reach Earth in eight minutes, and was relatively harmless. Not so the charged atoms that were following behind at their leisurely four million miles an hour—and which, in just over a day, would engulf *Diana*, *Lebedev*, and their accompanying little fleet in a cloud of lethal radiation.

The commodore left his decision to the last possible minute. Even when the jet of plasma had been tracked past the orbit of Venus, there was a chance that it might miss the Earth. But when it was less than four hours away, and had already been picked up by the Moon-based radar network, he knew that there was no hope. All solar sailing was over, for the next five or six years—until the Sun was quiet again.

A great sigh of disappointment swept across the solar system. *Diana* and *Lebedev* were halfway between Earth and Moon, running neck and neck—and now no one would ever know which was the better boat. The enthusiasts would argue the result for years; history would merely record; "Race canceled owing to solar storm."

WHEN John Merton received the order, he felt a bitterness he had not known since childhood. Across the years, sharp and clear, came the memory of his tenth birthday. He had been promised an exact scale of the famous spaceship *Morning Star*, and for weeks had been planning how he would assemble it, where he would hang it up in his bedroom. And then, at the last moment, his father had broken the news. "I'm sorry, John—it costs too much money. Maybe next year. . . ."

Half a century and a successful lifetime later, he was a heartbroken boy again.

For a moment, he thought of disobeying the commodore. Suppose he sailed on, ignoring the warning? Even if the race were abandoned, he could make a crossing to the Moon that would stand in the record books for generations.

But that would be worst than stupidity; it would be suicide—and a very unpleasant form of suicide. He had seen men die of radiation poisoning, when the magnetic shielding of their ships had failed in deep space. No—nothing was worth *that*. . . .

He felt as sorry for Dimitri Markoff as for himself; they had both deserved to win, and now victory would go to neither. No man could argue with the Sun in one of its rages, even though he might ride upon its beams to the edge of space.

Only fifty miles astern now, the commodore's launch was drawing alongside *Lebedev*, preparing to take off her skipper. There went the silver sail, as Dimitri—with feelings that he would share—cut the rigging. The tiny capsule would be taken back to Earth, perhaps to be used again; but a sail was spread for one voyage only.

He could press the jettison button now and save his rescuers a few minutes of time. But he could not do so; he wanted to stay aboard to the very end, on the little boat that had been for so long a part of his dreams and his life. The great sail was spread now at right angles

to the Sun, exerting its utmost thrust. Long ago it had torn him clear of Earth—and *Diana* was still gaining speed.

Then, out of nowhere, beyond all doubt or hesitation, he knew what must be done. For the last time, he sat down before the computer that had navigated him halfway to the Moon.

When he had finished, he packed the log and his few personal belongings. Clumsily—for he was out of practice, and it was not an easy job to do by oneself—he climbed into the emergency survival suit. He was just sealing the helmet when the commodore's voice called over the radio.

"We'll be alongside in five minutes, Captain." And then he added, "Please cut your sail so we won't foul it."

John Merton, first and last skipper of the sun-yacht *Diana*, hesitated for a moment. He looked for the last time round the tiny cabin, with its shining instruments and its neatly arranged controls, now all locked in their final positions. Then he said to the microphone: "I'm abandoning ship. Take your time to pick me up. *Diana* can look after herself."

There was no reply from the commodore, and for that he was grateful. Professor van Stratten would have guessed what was happening—and would know that, in these final moments, he wished to be left alone.

HE DID not bother to exhaust the airlock, and the rush of escaping gas blew him gently out into space; the thrust he gave her then was his last gift to *Diana*. She dwindled away from him, sail glittering splendidly in the sunlight that would be hers for centuries to come. Two days from now she would flash past the Moon; but the Moon, like the Earth, could never catch her. Without his mass to slow her down, she would gain two thousand miles an hour in every day of sailing. In a month, she would be traveling faster than any ship that man had ever built.

As the Sun's rays weakened with distance, so her acceleration would fall. But even at the orbit of Mars, she would be gaining a thousand miles an hour in every day. Long before then, she would be moving too swiftly for the Sun itself to hold her. Faster than a comet had ever streaked in from the stars, she would be heading out into the abyss, beyond the knowledge and imagination of man.

The glare of rockets, only a few miles away, caught Merton's eye. The launch was approaching to pick him up—at thousands of times the acceleration that *Diana* could ever attain. But its engines could burn for a few minutes only, before they exhausted their fuel—while *Diana* would still be gaining speed, driven outward by the Sun's eternal fires, for ages yet to come.

"Good-by little ship," said John Merton. "I wonder what eyes will see you next, how many thousand years from now?"

At last he felt at peace, as the blunt torpedo of the launch nosed up beside him. He would never win the race to the Moon; but his would be the first of all man's ships to set sail in the long journey to the stars. THE END

THE TRACY TWINS
by DIK BROWNE

THE SERPENT IN THE GARDEN

THE SERPENT WAS THE SLIEST BEAST IN THE GARDEN OF EDEN.

ONE DAY, HE ENTICED THE WOMAN TO EAT THE FRUIT OF THE TREE OF KNOWLEDGE OF GOOD AND EVIL WHICH GOD HAD WARNED WAS FORBIDDEN.

AND WHEN SHE HAD EATEN, SHE GAVE SOME TO ADAM...AND SUDDENLY THEY BOTH BECAME ASHAMED OF THEIR NAKEDNESS AND HID THEMSELVES FROM GOD'S SIGHT.

THEN GOD, KNOWING ALL, CURSED THE SERPENT AND TOLD ADAM AND THE WOMAN THAT THEY WOULD SUFFER FOR THEIR DISOBEDIENCE SAYING, "BY THE SWEAT OF YOUR BROW SHALL YOU EARN YOUR FOOD TIL YOU RETURN UNTO THE GROUND; FOR OUT OF IT WERE YOU TAKEN; FOR DUST YOU ART, AND UNTO DUST SHALL YOU RETURN."

AND ADAM CALLED HIS WIFE'S NAME EVE; BECAUSE SHE WAS THE MOTHER OF ALL LIVING.

THEN GOD BANISHED ADAM AND EVE FROM THE GARDEN OF EDEN AND PLACED CHERUBS TO THE EAST OF THE GARDEN AND A FLAMING SWORD WHICH TURNED EVERY WAY TO GUARD THE PATH TO THE TREE OF LIFE.

GENESIS:3

BOYS' LIFE
FEATURES

Everything of interest to a boy will find its way into the pages of *Boys' Life*, and consequently the magazine's features range from the somber to the scientific to the silly.

The assassination of President John F. Kennedy in 1963 rocked the nation. The magazine published a memorial to the fallen president in 1964, offering a message of hope and resolve to Scouts. Kennedy was the first Boy Scout to become president of the United States, having achieved the rank of Star Scout as a youth.

The exploration of Mars never fails to captivate readers, and an astronomer explained in 1950 what was known about the Red Planet. A month before man landed on the moon in 1969, Isaac Asimov's June article laid out the rationale for spending billions of dollars to accomplish this feat, and explained the scientific advances that could be achieved by visiting (and eventually colonizing) our nearest planetary neighbor.

Astronaut John Glenn addressed Scouts directly in 1965, challenging them to develop new ways of thinking and to determine their roles for the future in line with the explosion of technology. More than half of the astronauts in the U.S. space program had some previous involvement with Scouting.

Named an honorary Scout in 1927 by the Boy Scouts of America, Orville Wright explained to *Boys' Life* readers in 1914 how he and his brother Wilbur had learned to fly and succeeded in the first engine-powered airplane flight.

Legendary film directory Alfred Hitchcock found his way into the magazine in 1973, wryly discussing the techniques he used in making movies; he explained how his interest lay in creating suspense (giving information) rather than mystery (withholding information) to create an emotional impact—useful information for film buffs. Movies are always popular with boys, and the magazine previews suitable releases. In 1964, five upcoming movies were promoted (including one starring Elvis Presley). In 1967, the movies previewed included "Chitty, Chitty, Bang, Bang," based on the Ian Fleming novel. There is a discussion of the future of radio in the same column, and the 14-year-old winner of a teen movie contest is announced. Popular culture is also grist for the magazine's mill.

Pedro the Mailburro appears in a 1962 feature as Swami Pedro, giving his prognosis of what the world will look like in the year 2000. The floppy-eared hayburner is wrong, as usual, on all counts.

Boys' Life has entertained and educated America's youth for nearly a century with a proven mix of nature, sports, history, fiction, science, comics and Scouting. Lively writing and colorful graphics and photos help readers develop a taste for good reading, and the magazine brings the program of Scouting into homes every month. The overall message of the magazine is that it is great to be a boy in America—such a wonderful place to experience life and all it has to offer.

How I Learned to Fly

By ORVILLE WRIGHT

As told by him to Leslie W. Quirk, for the readers of BOYS' LIFE

THE FIRST FLIGHT WITH AN ENGINE, DECEMBER 17, 1903, ORVILLE WRIGHT AT THE HELM; WILBUR WRIGHT ALONGSIDE OF MACHINE.*

I SUPPOSE my brother and I always wanted to fly. Every youngster wants to, doesn't he? But it was not till we were out of school that the ambition took definite form.

We had read a good deal on the subject, and we had studied Lilienthal's tables of figures with awe. Then one day, as it were, we said to each other: "Why not? Here are scientific calculations, based upon actual tests, to show us the sustaining powers of planes. We can spare a few weeks each year. Suppose, instead of going off somewhere to loaf, we put in our vacations building and flying gliders." I don't believe we dared think beyond gliders at that time—not aloud, at least.

That year—it was 1900—we went down to North Carolina, near Kitty Hawk. There were hills there in plenty, and not too many people about to scoff. Building that first glider was the best fun we'd ever had, too, despite the fact that we put it together as accurately as a watchmaker assembles and adjusts his finest timepiece. You see, we knew how to work because Lilienthal had made his tables years before, and men like Chanute, for example, had verified them.

To our great disappointment, however, the glider was not the success we had expected. It didn't behave as the figures on which it was constructed vouched that it should. Something was wrong. We looked at each other silently, and at the machine, and at the mass of figures compiled by Lilienthal. Then we proved up on them to see if we had slipped somewhere. If we had, we couldn't find the error; so we packed up and went home. We were agreed that we hadn't built our glider according to the scientific specifications. But there was another year coming and we weren't discouraged. We had just begun.

We wrote to Chanute, who was an engineer in Chicago at the time. We told him about our glider; we drew sketches of it for him; we set down long rows of figures. And then we wound up our letter by begging him to explain why the tables of Lilienthal, which he had verified by experiments of his own, could not be proved by our machine.

Chanute didn't know. He wrote back it might be due to a different curve or pitch of surfaces on the planes, or something like that. But he was interested just the same, and when we went down to Kitty Hawk in 1901 we invited him to visit our camp.

Chanute came. Just before he left Chicago, I recall his telling us, he had read and O. K.'d the proofs of an article on aeronautics which he had prepared for the Encyclopedia Britannica, and in which he again told us of verifying Lilienthal's tables.

Well, he came to Kitty Hawk, and after he had looked our glider over carefully he said frankly that the trouble was not with any errors of construction in our machine. And right then all of us, I suspect, began to lose faith in Lilienthal and his gospel figures.

We had made a few flights the first year, and we made about 700 in 1901. Then we went back to Dayton to begin all over. It was like groping in the dark. Lilienthal's figures were not to be relied upon. Nobody else had done any scientific experimenting along these lines. Worst of all, we did not have money enough to build our glider with various types and sizes of planes or wings, simply to determine, in actual practice, which was the best. There was only the alternative of working out tables of our own. So we set to work along this line.

We took little bits of metal and we fashioned planes from them. I've still a deskful in my office in Dayton. There are flat ones, concave ones, convex ones, square ones, oblong ones and scores and scores of other shapes and sizes. Each model contains six square inches. When we built our third glider the following year, ignoring Lilienthal altogether and constructing it from our own figures, we made the planes just 7,200 times the size of those little metal models back at Dayton.

It was hard work, of course, to get our figures right; to achieve the plane giving the greatest efficiency—and to know before we built that plane the exact proportion of efficiency we could expect. Of course, there were some books on the subject that were helpful. We went to the Dayton libraries and read what we could find there; afterwards, when we had reached the same ends by months and months of study and experiment, we heard of other books that would have smoothed the way.

But those metal models told us how to build. By this time, too, Chanute was convinced that Lilienthal's tables were obsolete or inaccurate, and was wishing his utmost that he was not on record in an encyclopedia as verifying them.

During 1902 we made upward of 1,400 flights, sometimes going up a hundred times or more in a single day. Our runway was short, and it required a wind with a velocity of at least twelve miles an hour to lift the machine. I recall sitting in it, ready to cast off, one still day when the breeze seemed approaching. It came pres-

* This and other illustrations used with this article are published by Boys' Life through the courtesy of Mr. Henry Woodhouse, Managing Editor of "Flying" Magazine.

EXCITEMENT ON THE MOON

America takes the first giant step to the moon —and into the universe.

By ISAAC ASIMOV

Americans have circled the moon closely and returned to Earth. Russians have linked two ships in space and transferred men from one to the other. The Space Age is progressing at a fantastic rate.

But why bother?

Don't laugh: Many people ask that. We are sinking billions into reaching the moon; but when we get there, what have we got? Isn't it just a desolate desert without air or water and no good for anything? Ought we to spend billions just for prestige when so many problems face us on Earth?

Or can we expect something important and useful to come out of exploring the moon? The answer to that is a definite, Yes! We can!

The Space Age has already brought us communications satellites, weather satellites, and a better understanding of the exact shape and structure of Earth, its oceans and its atmosphere. And we will get more, much more, the very instant that astronauts reach the moon. When they set foot upon the lunar soil, they can begin to study it at once. They will dig in selected places, make tests and analyses, and bring back perhaps 50 pounds of moon-stuff for thorough analysis on Earth.

This cannot be done by instruments alone. Even our soft-landing Surveyors can only study the spots on which they land, can only tell us something about the very outermost skin of the moon. That is not enough. We want to get below, well below.

For one thing, getting below the surface may show us the past history of the moon and where it came from. The moon, you see, is quite a mystery. It is a giant satellite, and the only other worlds to have giant satellites are the huge outer planets, such as Jupiter and Saturn. The small planets have either tiny satellites or none at all. Our Earth is an exception. It has a satellite more than one-quarter its own diameter.

Astronomers don't know why and three theories have been advanced to account for the moon being where it is.

making the scene:

MOVIES

A MAN FOR ALL SEASONS (Columbia) Young, dynamic, but already willful and despotic—this was King Henry VIII in the year 1528. Sir Thomas More was a friend, well loved and respected in Britain. But the times were rife with political connivance. On this background, here is a powerful story of conflict between men of evil, men of mixed good and bad, and one man of stubborn integrity. It opens dramatically when a messenger from the chancellor of England rushes to the dark dockside of London's River Thames, hails a boat taxi and is rowed through the mists to the home of Thomas More. The letter he carries is the beginning of intolerable years of pressure on More to support Henry in his break with the church of Rome, which More's conscience will not let him do. The main drama, however, is not the struggle between state and church, but the clash of forces trying to break down More, the unbreakable man. More's honesty has earned the enmity of ruthless Richard Rich, who gives false evidence in court, thus convicting More as a traitor, and causing him to be executed by the ax that took so many heads in Henry's reign. This graphic motion picture portrays the sights, sounds and colors of 16th-century life. Photography is magnificent, suspense strong, acting excellent, especially that of Paul Scofield as More. Of interest to any teen-ager who likes historical drama.

TOBRUK (Universal) A tense war film. The fictionalized story of a small group of British soldiers who made a hazardous secret journey across the African desert to attack the German fortifications at the port of Tobruk in World War II.

. . . THE MIKADO (Warner Bros.) A movie version of Gilbert and Sullivan's great comedy-drama in music will be released this month on a two-shows-a-day basis in a number of cities.

. . . In CHITTY, CHITTY, BANG, BANG, Dick Van Dyke will portray an inventor-explorer—Comdr. Caracatacus Pott, whose magical car carries his family through a whirlwind fantasy tour. Roald Dahl, a writer of fine imagination, is doing the screenplay from an Ian Fleming novel. The music will be composed by Richard and Robert Sherman, who did the score for MARY POPPINS.

SPORTS & SCHOOL

How does he do it? Is his flying talent inherited? The fellow in midair is 11-year-old James Lovell, son of Gemini 12 Command Pilot James Lovell, Sr. Power source for the son's flight is a trampoline, but he too knows how to leave the Earth.

. . . March is big for ski competitions. The U.S. Ski Association schedule shows an even dozen national race events to be held on various dates in Maine, New Hampshire, Vermont, Minnesota, Wyoming, Colorado and Alaska. For information contact headquarters of your regional division of USSA.

. . . The Sports Car Club of America, which makes the rules for sports-car racing, stipulated this year that every racing driver must use seat belt and shoulder harness. The new 1967 rules, however, have made it easier for novice drivers to win, because the rules now prohibit most of the secret gear ratios and other modifications that some professional drivers have previously made on production-model cars.

TELEVISION & RADIO

Radio? it is necessary in this day of fat TV and colossal movies? Well, some guys still can't do their homework without it—can't drive without the beat. It clues you in on what disks for the discothèque. In clock form it can put you to sleep at night and wake you without shock next morning. You can carry it in a pocket to follow the ball games and the blast-offs. You can telephone to it and sound off about anything. It brings news while it's happening. But radio never gets big publicity. Is it just an unglamorous old workhorse of communications?

I asked Bob Wogan, vice-president, programs, NBC Radio Network, where radio is going. Will it ever fade away like an old soldier? Not likely, he says.

"There are more radio sets sold now than ever before. It's estimated that there is an average of four working radios in every home. Radio is going where the world goes. Radio is flexible. It's for people on the go. So programs are a variety of shorts."

How does it get to you? Some of it of course originates in your town and carries the payload for local ads. Some of it comes from the national networks on disks and tapes, and live over telephone wire. NBC's weekend *Monitor*, for example, goes to 205 network stations. Bob Wogan explained that facts of news and entertainment are compressed into small capsules—literally put into tape cartridges—and people with only a few minutes to listen get a whole bit instead of a fragment. Personalities become important. Men like cartoonist-philosopher Al Capp just being himself, sports specialists like Joe Garagiola and Mel Allen, and newsmen like Chet Huntley and Merrill Muller are like friends to listeners as well as being always ahead of what's new.

Hot news, like a natural disaster—earthquake, flood—or a big personal story, uses a hot line. It's taped as phoned in by reporters on the scene and transmitted in a full form to local stations, which can use as much or little as needed. A staff of more than 800 persons are involved in the news programs in radio central and all over the world as reporters, stringers and interviewers.

Radio is go-go all the way, not only from the local deejay.

. . . Several good TV specials will be aired in March. "Trilogy; the American Boy" will show in three freestyle short films the pain

SWAMI PEDRO'S
Forecast for 2000 A.D.
OUR SELF-APPOINTED SWAMI, PEDRO, HAS POLISHED UP HIS CRYSTAL BALL AND IS CONCENTRATING ALL HIS EXTRA-SENSORY BRAIN-POWER (THAT'S HIS STATEMENT) TO GAZE INTO THE FUTURE AND LET A WAITING WORLD (HIS WORDS) KNOW WHAT TO EXPECT WHEN THE NEXT CENTURY ROLLS AROUND.
MOON COLONIES WILL BE ESTABLISHED WITH A REGULAR SHUTTLE SERVICE BETWEEN THEM AND EARTH. AN ABUNDANCE OF VALUABLE METAL-BEARING ORES WILL BE DISCOVERED WHICH WILL BE PROCESSED AT LUNAR REFINING PLANTS TO SAVE SHIPPING WEIGHT.
CANCER, HEART, MENTAL AND OTHER DISEASES WILL BE CONQUERED. OUR LIFE SPAN WILL BE INCREASED TO AN AVERAGE EXPECTANCY OF OVER 250 YEARS! ELECTRONIC "KNIVES" WILL DO AWAY WITH THE NEED FOR CUTTING WITH SCALPELS IN OPERATIONS.
SPACE BEACONS WILL BE PLACED IN PRE-DETERMINED ORBITS AS NAVIGATION AIDS FOR SPACESHIPS. SOLAR BATTERIES WILL KEEP THESE "SKY LIGHTHOUSES" OPERATING INDEFINITELY!
SPACE PROBERS WILL LAND TELEVISION-EQUIPPED ROBOTS THAT WILL TRANSMIT ON-THE-SPOT PICTURES BACK TO EARTH FROM ALL PLANETS IN OUR SOLAR SYSTEM.
WHEELS WILL BE DISCARDED ON CARS. THEY'LL RUN ON CUSHIONS OF AIR...BOATS, TOO. SOLAR HEATING UNITS WILL KEEP OUR HOUSES COMFORTABLE ALL WINTER. EVERY SCHOOL CLASSROOM WILL BE EQUIPPED WITH "TELEVISION TEACHERS." THE PROBLEM OF FEEDING A WORLD POPULATION OF 20 BILLION PEOPLE WILL BE SOLVED...THERE'LL BE NO MORE HUNGER AND WANT ANYWHERE ON EARTH!
SO SAYS OUR PROGNOSTICATING PAL, PEDRO.
THAT'S ALL FOR TODAY—IT'S TOO EXHAUSTING! MY POOR BRAIN!
POP

"Ask not what your country can do for you— ask what you can do for your country."

President John F. Kennedy, The Inaugural Address, Jan. 20, 1961

By BOB HOOD

IT WAS A BLACK FRIDAY in American history, that November day in Dallas. The bullets that struck John F. Kennedy sent shock waves around the world. Now the first shock is spent, but the memory of the tragedy will stay with us always.

United in grief, America wept. It was as though, on the same day, every home in the nation had a death in the family. And the family of man around the globe—big people and little people—shared our sorrow:

President Betancourt of Venezuela cried when he heard the news. Foreign Minister Paul-Henri Spaak of Belgium sobbed, "I cannot speak tonight." In Nigeria the eight-year-old daughter of the Minister of State recited President Kennedy's entire inaugural address by—and from— heart. Her father, Dr. K. O. Mbadiwe, was moved to tears. In Japan a farmer and his family walked 18 miles and then stood quietly in the darkness outside the American embassy in Tokyo. When word reached Warsaw, Poland, a bus driver stopped his vehicle and burst into tears. Students in Berlin carried memorial torches.

Famous statesmen came to the funeral: the majestic Charles de Gaulle of France; Emperor Haile Selassie of Ethiopia; distinguished prime ministers and presidents; kings and queens and princes. Thousands and thousands of Americans poured into Washington, D. C., to pay their respects to John Fitzgerald Kennedy. As he lay in the rotunda of the Capitol, American leaders eulogized him. Speaker of the House John McCormack praised his "bravery" and "sense of personal duty"; his "warmth and sense of humanity"; and his "tenacity and the determination to carry each stage of his great work through to its successful conclusion."

Senate Majority Leader Mike Mansfield said: "He gave us of a good heart from which the laughter came. He gave us of a profound wit . . . of a kindness and a strength fused into a human courage to seek peace without fear." Chief Justice Earl Warren called him "a believer in the dignity and equality of all human beings, a fighter for justice and apostle of peace."

Former Vice-President Richard M. Nixon appeared on television. "President Kennedy," he said, "yesterday wrote the last and greatest chapter of his 'Profiles in Courage'. . . . The greatest tribute we can pay to his memory is in our everyday lives to do everything we can to reduce the forces of hatred which drive men to do such terrible deeds."

On November 27, 1963, President Lyndon B. Johnson told Congress: "Today John Fitzgerald Kennedy lives on in the immortal words and works that he left behind. He lives on in the minds and memories of mankind. He lives on in the hearts of his countrymen."

America's youngest President, John F. Kennedy's story is part of our nation's heritage of success.

His father, Joseph P. Kennedy, was wealthy, but his Irish forefathers were poor. His great-grandfather, Patrick Kennedy, left a peasant's cottage in County Kilkenny around 1845 during the terrible potato famine. He emigrated to the Boston area and there the American clan Kennedy began to sprout. Industrious, enterprising, ambitious—American characteristics, these—the Kennedys were to prosper. Patrick J. Kennedy, grandfather of John F., started as a longshoreman and eventually wound up a prominent businessman and the owner of a bank. Like many Irish-Americans he plunged into politics, winning election after election. So victory became a part of the Kennedy tradition.

At the same time that Patrick J. was prospering, John Kennedy's maternal grandfather, John F. Fitzgerald, was making his way. Called "Honey Fitz," "The Little General," and "Little Nap," he was a merry little man with sparkling eyes. He bounced out of the Boston slums and into the political ring. He was elected councilman, alderman, state legislator; he twice won seats in the U. S. House of Representatives; he became mayor of Boston.

ILLUSTRATED BY ROBERT LEVERING

In 1914, the daughter of "Honey Fitz," Rose Fitzgerald, and the son of Patrick J. Kennedy, Joseph P., were married. Two successful, vigorous families were united, and on May 29, 1917, John Fitzgerald Kennedy was born.

Joseph Kennedy encouraged his children to be independent and self-reliant. For years the shining star of the family was Joseph, Junior (later killed in World War II). Two years older than Jack, he was bright, quick-tempered and aggressive. He was bigger and tougher, too, and the boys fought, as brothers do, to see who would rule the roost. This rivalry probably helped develop the determination and competitive spirit which marked the President's character.

A photograph of John F. Kennedy at age ten shows a smiling face sprinkled with freckles—and the thick head of hair which would become a kind of Presidential mantle. In 1927 the Kennedys moved to Bronxville, New York, and, in 1929, Jack became a Boy Scout in Troop 2. At that time he showed some of the power of persuasion that turned up later in his adult political career. He wrote a "plea for a raise" to his father:

"My recent allowance is 40¢. This I used for aeroplanes and other playthings of childhood but now I am a scout and I put away my childish things. Before I would spend 20¢ of my 40¢ allowance and in five minutes I would have empty pockets and nothing to gain and 20¢ to lose. When I am a scout I have to buy canteens, haversacks, blankets, searchlights, poncho—things that will last for years and I can always use it while I can't use chocolate marshmallow ice cream sundaes and so I put in my plea for a raise of thirty cents for me to buy scout things and pay my own way around . . ."

YOUNG JACK loved sports and he was a fierce, fearless competitor. During his school days he played football, baseball, and other sports, but his will-to-win outstripped his skill. Swimming was his favorite and he did excel at it. At age 13 he could swim 50 yards in 30 seconds. As a boy he showed signs of a phenomenal, almost photographic memory for facts, conversations, correspondence and the like. But he was absent-minded and often could not recall where he had placed his clothing, books and other possessions.

He was well liked by students and teachers, but he gave little sign of brilliance throughout his private school education. His marks were not outstanding; Latin always gave him a lot of trouble. "If it were not for Latin," he once wrote to his mother, "I would probably lead the lower school but I am flunking that by ten points." He didn't show his potential until his senior year at Harvard University. He worked very hard that year and graduated *cum laude* in political science. His thesis, "Appeasement at Munich," won a *magna cum laude*. He later developed this into his first book, "Why England Slept."

Like many Americans, John F. Kennedy served his country honorably and heroically in World War II. As skipper of PT boat 109 his brave actions won him the Purple Heart and the Navy and Marine Corps Medal with a citation from Admiral William F. Halsey, in tribute to his "courage, endurance and excellent leadership in keeping with the highest traditions of the United States Naval Service."

After the war he began his career as a public servant. Three times he was elected to the House of Representatives, twice to the United States Senate, and, in 1960, to the Presidency.

The Presidency is the toughest job in the world, as he would learn. It demands sacrifice and service, courage and conviction, a sense of duty and dedication—and vision. Like Presidents Truman and Eisenhower, President Kennedy was committed to the welfare of all the people in the nation and to the cause of freedom around the world. In his inaugural address he declared:

"Let the word go forth from this time and place, to friend and foe alike, that the torch has been passed to a new generation of Americans —born in this century, tempered by war, disciplined by a hard and bitter peace, proud of our ancient heritage—and unwilling to witness or permit the slow undoing of those human rights to which this nation has always been committed, and to which we are committed today at home and around the world."

The American Presidency symbolizes all our ideals. Electing a man to this office is the highest honor we can bestow upon him. Our Presidents strive to repay this honor with their words and deeds. In the process some of them give their lives, and the cruelest death is death by assassination. Slain: Lincoln, Garfield, McKinley, Kennedy—such a sorry way to repay our debt to their dedication!

For we do owe our President a debt. We owe a debt to all our public servants who work honestly for us. Of course, it is our right and obligation as free Americans to discuss and debate issues, to agree or disagree with an elected official, to oppose him or to support him. But it also is our duty to respect a mailman or policeman, teacher or judge, mayor or President.

Our elected officials, especially the President, must understand us, what we want and what we need. To do this the President of the United States must walk among us, to shake our hands, to listen to our voices, to accept words of praise or blame. He should not be called a coward or a traitor, for no man reaches this high office who is not of outstanding character. When we say hateful things about our President we undermine our own freedom. For hate breeds violence and violence can only lead to an evil government where the strong rule by force alone.

President John F. Kennedy was murdered while serving us. He was a decent man, brilliant and dashing, with a flashing smile. Like Theodore Roosevelt, he believed in the active life, in feeling fit and having fun. And like Teddy, he enjoyed his job, the most challenging one in the world. His mind was a literal warehouse of facts, his wit quick and sharp. He believed in the pursuit of excellence. The rewards he found in his job, he once said, were those of the Greek definition of happiness: "the full use of your powers along lines of excellence."

He had great appeal to young people, because of his youth, vitality and idealism. In June, 1962, he spoke to a group of students at the White House:

"Recently I heard a story of a young Peace Corpsman, Tom Scanlon, who is working in Chile. He worked in a village about 40 miles from an Indian village which prides itself on being Communist. Scanlon paid many visits to the village trying to see the chief, who delighted in sending him away. Finally, he got to speak to the chief, who declared:

" 'You are not going to talk us out of being Communist.'

" 'I am not trying to do that,' Scanlon said. 'I only want to talk to you about how I can help.'

"The chief looked at him and replied:

" 'In a few weeks the snow will come. Then you will have to park your jeep 20 miles from here and come through five feet of snow on foot. The Communists are willing to do that. Are you?'

"A friend saw Scanlon a few days after his visit with the chief, and asked what he was doing. The young Peace Corpsman replied:

" 'I am waiting for the snow.' "

The President finished his little talk by saying he hoped the same spirit motivated the students.

JOHN FITZGERALD KENNEDY was Honorary President of the Boy Scouts of America. He was also the first Boy Scout to become President of the United States. He lived up to the highest ideals of Scouting. He, too, once said, just as you say now: "On my honor I will do my best to do my duty to God and my country and to obey the Scout Law; to help other people at all times; to keep myself physically strong, mentally awake, and morally straight."

In the gloom of that grim weekend last November, there were things to be proud of. Through its grief and through the presence of its great leaders at the funeral, the world paid respect not only to a fine man but to the Presidency itself, an office which has great meaning to all people. And although an assassin cut down the President, the Presidency lived on, as always. We should all take pride in our government, in how it pulled together in crisis, reassuring its citizens and people of the free world that the Union stood firm. We should take pride that our nation did not falter, that it continues in the spirit of President Kennedy's inaugural address:

"Finally, whether you are citizens of America or citizens of the world, ask of us here the same high standards of strength and sacrifice which we ask of you. With a good conscience our only sure reward, with history the final judge of our deeds, let us go forth to lead the land we love, asking His blessing and His help, but knowing that here on earth God's work must truly be our own."   THE END

PHOTO BY HENRY GROSSMAN

"This is our challenge: Not to hesitate, not to pause, not to turn about and linger over this evil moment, but to continue on our course so that we may fulfill the destiny that history has set for us."

—President Lyndon B. Johnson. Address to Congress. November 27, 1963

EXCITEMENT ON THE MOON

America takes the first giant step to the moon —and into the universe.

By ISAAC ASIMOV

Americans have circled the moon closely and returned to Earth. Russians have linked two ships in space and transferred men from one to the other. The Space Age is progressing at a fantastic rate.

But why bother?

Don't laugh: Many people ask that. We are sinking billions into reaching the moon; but when we get there, what have we got? Isn't it just a desolate desert without air or water and no good for anything? Ought we to spend billions just for prestige when so many problems face us on Earth?

Or can we expect something important and useful to come out of exploring the moon? The answer to that is a definite, Yes! We can!

The Space Age has already brought us communications satellites, weather satellites, and a better understanding of the exact shape and structure of Earth, its oceans and its atmosphere. And we will get more, much more, the very instant that astronauts reach the moon. When they set foot upon the lunar soil, they can begin to study it at once. They will dig in selected places, make tests and analyses, and bring back perhaps 50 pounds of moon-stuff for thorough analysis on Earth.

This cannot be done by instruments alone. Even our soft-landing Surveyors can only study the spots on which they land, can only tell us something about the very outermost skin of the moon. That is not enough. We want to get below, well below.

For one thing, getting below the surface may show us the past history of the moon and where it came from. The moon, you see, is quite a mystery. It is a giant satellite, and the only other worlds to have giant satellites are the huge outer planets, such as Jupiter and Saturn. The small planets have either tiny satellites or none at all. Our Earth is an exception. It has a satellite more than one-quarter its own diameter.

Astronomers don't know why and three theories have been advanced to account for the moon being where it is.

Excitement on the Moon

One theory is that it was born in some other part of the solar system. For some reason it managed to get close enough to the Earth under conditions that were just right for it to be captured. The most likely place for it to have been formed is in what is now the asteroid belt. Some astronomers think that a planet exploded

there, that the asteroids are the fragments of that explosion. There aren't enough fragments to make a planet of respectable size, though, and perhaps that's because the largest fragment was somehow blown toward Earth and was captured.

If that is so, we ought to find that the composition of the moon's crust is like that of certain meteorites which also probably come from the asteroid belt. A huge "meteorite" like the moon may tell us a great deal about conditions farther from the sun and about how the solar

system came to be formed.

Before its explosion and capture, the moon may have had an atmosphere and surface water. Pictures taken by lunar orbiters that have circled the moon show crooked depressions that look as though they are dried-up riverbeds.

Perhaps life began to form on the moon in its original location.

Chemists feel quite certain that before the first living things formed on earth, there was a period of hundreds of millions of years in which simple chemicals changed into more complex ones. Finally,

the chemicals became complex enough to represent a very simple form of life. They have no way of telling for sure the details of how this went on. They can only guess from small laboratory experiments.

On the moon, they may find a whole array of complicated chemicals under the surface, and they will then be able to deduce the route to life much more accurately than from laboratory experiments.

Indeed, there may well be water under the moon's surface, trapped as ice, or in loose combination with minerals. There may be scraps of free water and air in small underground cavities. Perhaps there may even be tiny living cells that have formed over the billions of years and which still hang on to life under the harsh conditions of the moon.

This would be a wonderful discovery. If the cells are chemically like cells on Earth, it would be strong evidence that there may be only one chemistry possible for our kind of life. If the cells are of different chemistry, it means we would double our knowledge of living systems at once.

What the moon can tell us about primitive life and about pre-life chemistry may help us understand a great deal about life on Earth. We have trouble in biology, because Earth life is so complicated. Very simple moon life can make many things clear to us.

Someone once said to me, "Why do we spend so much money on reaching the moon, instead of spending it on cancer research?"

"All science is one," I answered. "You can't learn something anywhere without its possibly being useful everywhere else. If we study the moon's crust, we may find its chemistry helps us understand what goes wrong in the cancer cell. It may even turn out that by reaching the moon, we may soon cure cancer as well."

A second theory of the moon's origin is that it was always near Earth. Perhaps when Earth formed out of the original cloud of gas, dust and particles, a double body formed—a large one, Earth, which kept its atmosphere and ocean; and a small one, the moon, which lost them.

If that were the case, the moon's crust might be very like Earth's, but it would remain very much as it was at the beginning.

On Earth, the original nature of the crust was changed by waves and wind, and also by the action of life. Because of those changes, it is very difficult for us to work out what things were like even a few hundred million years ago.

The moon's crust, on the other hand, has been in a kind of deepfreeze for perhaps three or four billion years. What it tells us may be true of our Earth three or four billion years ago. The complex chemicals it may contain would be even more likely to be those that originally formed on Earth.

A few weeks' work on the samples brought back from the moon may revolutionize the entire science of geology, and it may turn out that we will have had to spend billions of dollars to go to the moon in order to understand properly the secrets of our own planet.

Still a third theory of Earth's origin arises from the fact that, because of the effect of the tides, the moon is steadily drifting farther from Earth. In the long-ago past it was considerably closer to the Earth. One or two billion years ago, it was very close. Could it have originally

been part of Earth which somehow broke away?

If this happened, it may have happened after life developed on Earth. In that case, the moon's crust may contain fossil traces of very early Earth-life: fossils that have long since been wiped out on Earth. Who knows, if living cells still exist on the moon, they may have developed from very early forms of Earth-life.

Even if there are no traces of life on the moon, or even of complicated chemicals, we still haven't lost. We would have to figure out why the chemicals developed on Earth but not on the moon. From that we might work out exactly what is needed for life to form and therefore get a better idea of the route it took.

Whatever we find on the moon will tell us a great deal about Earth, about life, about ourselves.

But there's more to moon exploration than landing on it and bringing back supplies of soil. After the first trip there will be others. Men will establish laboratories and observatories on the moon, scientific centers that can do things that cannot be done on Earth.

Over the moon's surface is a high-grade vacuum, better than any we can make on Earth, and there are millions of square miles of it. There are all sorts of technical processes and research programs that require a vacuum and these could be carried through much more easily on the moon. New chemicals could be formed; old chemicals could be prepared in greater purity; metals could be studied under unusual conditions; weldings and coatings could be made in new ways.

The moon's sunlit side can get very hot and it is exposed to hard radiation from the sun. Radiation-exposure of materials can be carried on over large areas and for long times in ways which cannot possibly be done on Earth. Again, additional knowledge and new processes may result.

The moon's night side can get very cold and stays dark for two weeks at a time. In the shadow of certain craters, it is always dark. It would be much easier, in certain places on the moon, to get down to extremely low temperatures. There are many devices on Earth which make use of extremely low temperatures at which a phenomenon called "superconductivity" takes place. At such low temperatures, electric currents are conducted with super-ease against no resistance whatever. Tiny electric currents can remain flowing in wires forever. Very strong magnets and very tiny switches are produced through making use of such easy-flowing currents which can be turned on and off at will. Such devices could be produced and used much more easily on the moon than on Earth.

A hundred years from now, the moon may be a great industrial complex, manufacturing high-quality chemicals and devices essential to Earth's technology. These could not be made on Earth except much more expensively, if at all.

Because the moon has no atmosphere, much more can be seen there in the heavens. On Earth, clouds blanket the sky; mist, fog and dust obscure it; temperature differences in the atmosphere make everything shimmer; light scattered by the air makes everything dimmer. Astronomers are beginning to have trouble finding places high enough in the mountains or far enough in the deserts to give them a clean look at the universe.

The moon gives us a clean look everywhere. An observatory on the moon would be an astronomer's idea of heaven. A small telescope could see Mars more clearly and in greater detail from the moon than any instrument on Earth could make out. Phenomena which, on Earth, are just on the dim edge of being sensed, would be sharp and clear on the moon.

This is true of radio astronomy, too. In the last quarter-century most of our new knowledge of the universe has grown out of radio waves which we detect coming from various spots in the sky. But the "radio noise" produced by Earth's civilization is beginning to interfere dangerously with the heavenly radio broadcasts. On the far side of the moon, 2,000 miles of lunar rock will blank out any radio noise the Earth cares to make. The universe can be studied in absolute silence.

Who knows what fabulous mysteries of the infancy of the universe and of its makeup can be solved from the moon? Perhaps we will begin to understand the mysterious flickering light of the distant quasars or the steady radio signals of the equally mysterious pulsars. We may learn of utterly new energy sources, new laws of nature; knowledge will put unimaginable new tools in our hands.

We can go farther still. We won't just establish factories and observatories on the moon and have them serviced by people who come from Earth, stay a few weeks or months, and then return.

Eventually there will be a moon colony, independent of Earth. The colonists can use solar batteries or, even-

Excitement on the Moon

tually, nuclear fusion plants, for energy. They might get a water supply from beneath the moon's surface and break up some of it to get oxygen. With air and water in underground caverns, they can grow plants for food and eventually raise small animals, too.

Generations may be born, live and die on the moon, and the colonists may not even particularly want to return to Earth. They would be living under gravity only one-sixth that of ours and they may not want to expose themselves to a tremendous weight they are not used to. They may not like the open, dirty air; the wind; the rain and snow; the vast sky. They may prefer their own comfortable, underground life.

And if so, such a colony would be useful, too. In fact, a working colony of human beings could be our most useful accomplishment on the moon. For one thing, mankind as a species would be safer. Right now we believe there are men on only one world in all the universe. If we do something horrible to our planet, man may be through forever. Once a moon colony is established, men may survive, even if Earth does not.

Then, too, the moon colony may be a wonderful laboratory experiment for Earthmen, an experiment in sociology. For a million years or more, man and his ape-like ancestors have lived in a huge world, where he could kill as he pleased, ravage as he pleased, pollute as he pleased. The world was so large and man so small, that he could do no real damage.

Now, however, there are so many Earthmen and they work with so huge a technology, that the world is being destroyed. The air is full of smog, the water is full of industrial waste, the soil is being eroded, many species of life are being wiped out; in short, our world is becoming less livable every day.

A colony on the moon, with only a small supply of food, water and air, cooped up inside limited caverns, would have to live very carefully. They would have to develop protection against pollution; they would have to learn to use their resources very efficiently; they would have to learn to maintain civilization, peace and decency under crowded conditions. Perhaps Earthmen would be able to observe all this, and learn from it before it was too late.

Then, too, a moon colony may lead the way to further manned exploration of the solar system.

Our own difficulties with rocket ships are two-fold. Earth's gravity is so oppressive that rocket ships must build up a speed of seven miles per second to move permanently away from the Earth. The moon's gravity is much less than Earth's, and a speed of 1.5 miles a second would be sufficient to move a ship away from the moon.

Secondly, on Earth a rocket ship must build up speed most carefully, for it has to pass through a thick atmosphere, and air resistance can dangerously heat up the skin of the ship. On the moon, there is no atmosphere to create a heat danger.

It would take much less fuel to launch spaceships toward Mars or Venus starting from the moon, than from the Earth.

Furthermore, moon colonists might be more suitable than Earthmen to man these spaceships.

To reach the moon and return requires only a couple of weeks, even allowing for several days' stay on the surface of the moon. To get to Mars and back would take well over a year. To explore the giant planets of the outer solar system would take many years.

There would undoubtedly be serious psychological problems for Earthmen restricted to small spaceship cabins, gravity-free, for months or years at a time—considering that they had spent all their lives in a wide and open world.

It might be different for moon colonists. They would be accustomed to be living in small caverns, under artificial conditions. They would be accustomed, too, to low gravity. Their normal condition of life would be very much like that inside a spaceship.

It might not be very hard for them to transfer from such a spaceship to another one with a thinner wall—to transfer from a spaceship that goes round and round the Earth to another one that is heading out to Mars or Jupiter.

Indeed, we may not really be able to explore the solar system in a useful fashion, unless we let the colonists do the exploring.

But why go on to explore the solar system? Because it is bound to gain mankind far more knowledge and far more understanding. It may gain him enough knowledge and understanding to make it possible for him to head out, at last, to the stars . . . where we may find new worlds like the Earth itself. And in this way mankind will reach farther and farther into the universe, continuing his quest to grow wiser and better. ∎

Slide of the Month   By WHITTLIN' JIM

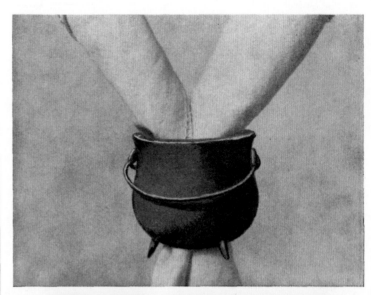

IRON KETTLE

Both Johnny Bruce of Ringgold, Ga., and Bob Gary of Bordentown, N.J., originated the idea of a slide modeled after a cooking pot. On his slide, Johnny wrote, "Cook or starve." Naturally, you can't really cook in this pot—but it makes a dandy and unusual slide.

If you own a lathe, you're in luck when you make this slide. Otherwise, bore a ¾-inch hole down the center of a 1½-inch square piece of white pine about four inches long (lower right). Then you'll have something to hold onto until your slide is almost finished. Use a narrow sharp blade for whittling. The handle and lugs (shown in drawing) are of iron wire. The kettle feet are the ends of toothpicks. Paint the pot dull black. Drawings are exact size. ∎

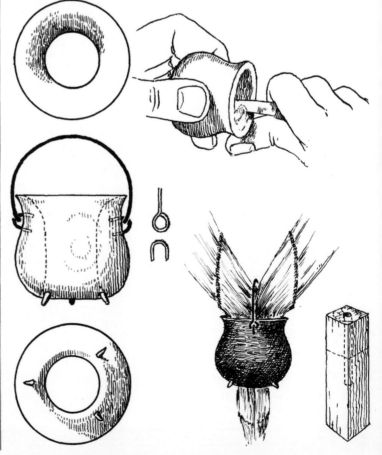

Movies

Alfred Hitchcock talks about suspense.

"What is film all about? A series of images coming along the screen."

Alfred Hitchcock heaves his rotund body out of an impressively large chair and illustrates. "Maybe you start with a long shot of a man running down the street. The next image is of his head and shoulders; his hair is flying, and he's out of breath. The next shot might be of his feet, of running feet only. Those are all images, and assembling those images creates an idea. The idea is that a man is running. Now we ask, why is the man running? Because in his hand—the next image—is a bundle of dollar bills, maybe a packet of 200 of them. What is the inference? That the man has stolen the money. Because a man running with money in his hand can have only two reasons, and it would be highly undramatic to show him trying to get to the bank before it closes.

"So why is he running so desperately? Because down the street is a policeman. The image of the policeman supports our theory that the man has stolen the money. So you see how films are dealing with images all the time. And you see how we break the images up. We show the man. We show his desperate face. We show his speed through his feet. And then we show the money in his hand. We are telling a story by the ORDER in which we assemble those images."

To Alfred Hitchcock, certainly the most famous of living American directors and one of the best (*Frenzy, North by Northwest, Rebecca, To Catch a Thief*), the most important aspect of directing is to plan each image ahead of time. When Hitchcock looks through the camera for the first time, he already has sketched on paper every image that will be in every scene of his picture.

He believes that all directors should sketch out each scene of a movie before they start shooting. "The sketches can be very rough. They don't have to be drawings or anything like that."

Hitchcock recommends that filmmakers look at art books and sketch books to sharpen their visual sense and gain an understanding of composition.

By RICHARD and ALJEAN HARMETZ

"Take a painter like Paul Klee. His is the kind of painting where the uninitiated would look and say, 'My little boy could do as well as that.' Yet a Klee painting is a matter of complete design."

Because everything in a Hitchcock film is worked out in advance, the shooting itself is an anticlimax. "The camera is just an instrument," he says, "like a painter's brush. It is the rectangular white screen that is important. You must fill it with images, just as a painter fills his canvas. Write it all down first. *Long shot:* Man running. *Close-up:* Desperate face of man, hair flying. *Close-up:* Feet pattering along. *Close-up:* Hand hiding money. *Long shot:* Policeman running in the distance. Then we can see how to improve it. For example, in our close-up of the money—which we take from a fast-moving dolly or camera car—we can pan from the money. The money goes out of the picture. What are we panning to? The long shot of the policeman. That way we are saying that the money is stolen because in the distance a policeman is on his way.

"Then we can use the images even more creatively. We can use them to put thoughts into a man's mind. In *Rear Window*, Jimmy Stewart must stay in one position. His leg is in a cast. He can't move, but he can look out the window. *Close-up:* Mr. Stewart. What does he see? We cut to a man and wife in an apartment in the distance. They are quarreling. *Close-up:* Mr. Stewart smiling. What does the smile mean? It can mean, *I'm glad I'm not married.* Later in the picture Mr. Stewart looks at the same window. There is no wife there, but the man has roped up a trunk. *Close-up:* Mr. Stewart. He is frowning, with a touch of concern. In a book, that would be written, *That's funny. The wife is no longer there.* We have done the same thing with images. Mr. Stewart's expression of concern starts the audience thinking. We've taken separate images, put them together, shown the effect on the face of Mr. Stewart. And he, in turn, has transferred an idea and implanted it in the audience's mind."

Particularly in building suspense, it is important that a director never put in a shot that has no meaning—no matter how pretty or exciting the shot might be.

"Every piece of film a director puts together must have a meaning or an implication. In the opening of *Frenzy*, there's the body of a girl in the river. She has been strangled with a necktie. A cabinet minister or government official looks and says, 'She's wearing my club

tie!' That is a joke, but the next cut after he says that is another close-up of the girl with a tie around her neck. And the very next cut is of a young man standing in front of a mirror putting a tie on. The implication is that he might be a murderer. I'm not saying he really is, because actually he isn't, but I'm letting the audience infer that he is. You can call it a trick if you like, but there is pure use of film—the juxtaposition of the close-up of the girl and the necktie and then the young man putting the tie around his neck."

The audience usually knows who the master spy or murderer is long before an Alfred Hitchcock movie is over. Hitchcock is not the slightest bit interested in mysteries. "Mystery is withholding information from an audience. Suspense is giving information to the audience. Terror is not a consequence of mystery. It is a consequence of suspense.

"Let's say two men are sitting at a table and talking about baseball for five minutes and, at the end of that five minutes, a bomb goes off and blows the room to smithereens. The audience will get 10 seconds of shock, of the surprise that comes at the end of a whodunit. To create suspense, a director must do exactly the opposite. Show the audience the bomb and tell them it is going to go off in five minutes. Have the man who plants the bomb set the thing. Then two men come in and talk about baseball, and the talk gets the audience on edge. The audience says, 'Don't talk about baseball. There's a bomb under the table. It's going to go off in five minutes. Get out of the room.' Look at the emotion you put the audience through. Because they've got information."

Hitchcock has no sympathy for the "instant director." He says—slowly and emphatically, with long pauses between the words—"I am a true believer in art. It takes a long time to become an artist. First you must master the technique of your craft. Only when you have learned your craft can you express yourself artistically. In filmmaking, a lot of people start the other way around."

making the scene:

MOVIES

A MAN FOR ALL SEASONS (Columbia) Young, dynamic, but already willful and despotic—this was King Henry VIII in the year 1528. Sir Thomas More was a friend, well loved and respected in Britain. But the times were rife with political connivance. On this background, here is a powerful story of conflict between men of evil, men of mixed good and bad, and one man of stubborn integrity. It opens dramatically when a messenger from the chancellor of England rushes to the dark dockside of London's River Thames, hails a boat taxi and is rowed through the mists to the home of Thomas More. The letter he carries is the beginning of intolerable years of pressure on More to support Henry in his break with the church of Rome, which More's conscience will not let him do. The main drama, however, is not the struggle between state and church, but the clash of forces trying to break down More, the unbreakable man. More's honesty has earned the enmity of ruthless Richard Rich, who gives false evidence in court, thus convicting More as a traitor, and causing him to be executed by the ax that took so many heads in Henry's reign. This graphic motion picture portrays the sights, sounds and colors of 16th-century life. Photography is magnificent, suspense strong, acting excellent, especially that of Paul Scofield as More. Of interest to any teen-ager who likes historical drama.

TOBRUK (Universal) A tense war film. The fictionalized story of a small group of British soldiers who made a hazardous secret journey across the African desert to attack the German fortifications at the port of Tobruk in World War II.

. . . **THE MIKADO** (Warner Bros.) A movie version of Gilbert and Sullivan's great comedy-drama in music will be released this month on a two-shows-a-day basis in a number of cities.

. . . In **CHITTY, CHITTY, BANG, BANG,** Dick Van Dyke will portray an inventor-explorer—Comdr. Caracatacus Pott, whose magical car carries his family through a whirlwind fantasy tour. Roald Dahl, a writer of fine imagination, is doing the screenplay from an Ian Fleming novel. The music will be composed by Richard and Robert Sherman, who did the score for MARY POPPINS.

SPORTS & SCHOOL

How does he do it? Is his flying talent inherited? The fellow in midair is 11-year-old James Lovell, son of Gemini 12 Command Pilot James Lovell, Sr. Power source for the son's flight is a trampoline, but he too knows how to leave the Earth.

. . . March is big for ski competitions. The U.S. Ski Association schedule shows an even dozen national race events to be held on various dates in Maine, New Hampshire, Vermont, Minnesota, Wyoming, Colorado and Alaska. For information contact headquarters of your regional division of USSA.

. . . The Sports Car Club of America, which makes the rules for sports-car racing, stipulated this year that every racing driver must use seat belt and shoulder harness. The new 1967 rules, however, have made it easier for novice drivers to win, because the rules now prohibit most of the secret gear ratios and other modifications that some professional drivers have previously made on production-model cars.

TELEVISION & RADIO

Radio? it is necessary in this day of fat TV and colossal movies? Well, some guys still can't do their homework without it—can't drive without the beat. It clues you in on what disks for the discothèque. In clock form it can put you to sleep at night and wake you without shock next morning. You can carry it in a pocket to follow the ball games and the blast-offs. You can telephone to it and sound off about anything. It brings news while it's happening. But radio never gets big publicity. Is it just an unglamorous old workhorse of communications?

I asked Bob Wogan, vice-president, programs, NBC Radio Network, where radio is going. Will it ever fade away like an old soldier? Not likely, he says.

"There are more radio sets sold now than ever before. It's estimated that there is an average of four working radios in every home. Radio is going where the world goes. Radio is flexible. It's for people on the go. So programs are a variety of shorts."

How does it get to you? Some of it of course originates in your town and carries the payload for local ads. Some of it comes from the national networks on disks and tapes, and live over telephone wire. NBC's weekend *Monitor,* for example, goes to 205 network stations. Bob Wogan explained that facts of news and entertainment are compressed into small capsules—literally put into tape cartridges—and people with only a few minutes to listen get a whole bit instead of a fragment. Personalities become important. Men like cartoonist-philosopher Al Capp just being himself, sports specialists like Joe Garagiola and Mel Allen, and newsmen like Chet Huntley and Merrill Muller are like friends to listeners as well as being always ahead of what's new.

Hot news, like a natural disaster—earthquake, flood—or a big personal story, uses a hot line. It's taped as phoned in by reporters on the scene and transmitted in a full form to local stations, which can use as much or little as needed. A staff of more than 800 persons are involved in the news programs in radio central and all over the world as reporters, stringers and interviewers.

Radio is go-go all the way, not only from the local deejay.

. . . Several good TV specials will be aired in March. "Trilogy; the American Boy" will show in three freestyle short films the pain

news and reviews of the month by FRAN SMITH

and joy of growing up. ABC-TV *Stage 67*, March 9. One film is set in Southern California, another in Louisiana bayou country, and the third in New York City.

...**"100 Years of Laughter,"** also on *Stage 67*, will trace Negro humor from the days of slavery to the present. Sidney Poitier is host with top Negro comedians performing. March 16.

...**"End of the Trail"** is another fine special from NBC-TV *Project 20*, portraying the long conflict between white men and the Plains Indians. You will see both Indian and whites as they really were, shown by the technique of still-in-motion. Photographs and drawings made at the time of the events make up the visual story. The audio part is an eloquent script narrated by veteran Western actor Walter Brennan. Background focuses on the Northern plains in the region of Greasy Grass River (Little Big Horn). The end of the trail was Custer's battle there, for although the Indians won, it was their last victory.

...CBS-TV has announced that its cameramen and reporters will start for the North Pole this month. They will accompany the first over-the-ice polar expedition in 58 years, a private project designed to test men and equipment and do certain medical experiments. Lightweight snowmobiles will have flotation devices to cross open water between ice floes. CBS plans to film a color documentary for broadcast later and to provide progress reports en route.

trends

Some teen-agers are not afraid to tackle serious subjects in an art form—especially if it moves! John Dentino, 14, of Stockton, Calif., won a top prize in the 1966 Kodak Teen-age Movie Contest. His 15-minute film, titled "The Trip," depicts what happened to a boy who took a piece of LSD just to see what would happen. John showed on film all the hallucinations, at first beautiful, later full of torment and torture. An unusual technique was his use of color in the imaginary scenes, and black-and-white in the documentary parts. A taped narration accompanied the film. The judges called it "the best film on all counts." More than 200 teen-agers participated in the 1966 Teenage Movie Awards. For information about the 1967 Kodak competition, write Eastman Kodak Co., Rochester, N.Y. 14650

... The Lexington (Mass.) Center of Modern Art reported that pupils under 15 do all the work of making films, from script to projection. At the center, Stephen Detore

made a film about an invasion from outer space. Other students, many of them working in animated technique, also tried various thrillers, although interest in documentaries is growing.

... Something new in music: "Gee, I thought you picked a piccolo!" ... "Can a fourth-grader learn to play a tuba?" ... "The air was full of music and so exciting I wanted to play myself." These were typical remarks at a Young Audience concert in Las Vegas, Nev. The kids heard a percussion quartet, a university string quartet, and the Nevada Brass Quintet in a series. Music-minded fellows who want to hear live music (not just rock) occasionally might ask their parents or teachers to write Young Audiences, Inc., 115 E. 92nd St., New York, N.Y. 10028. This group forms chapters to sponsor informal concerts at which kids can talk with the musicians and try out various orchestral instruments for themselves.

... Mathew Spence, 16, of Cranbury, N.J., went to Europe with the crew of the Brooks School, North Andover, Mass. But Matt did more than row for his school, apparently. He became a goodwill ambassador for the American teen-ager just by being himself. While abroad he was a guest in the home of British author James Morris, who had lived in Cranbury for a time when Matt was much younger. Shortly after Matt's visit, Morris wrote an article about Americans which was published in *The Saturday Evening Post*. He said that some Europeans might profitably cultivate "the charm of the American teenager." About Matt, he wrote, "He was like a shot in the arm for us: so eager, so original, so dedicated to miscellaneous causes and so exceedingly funny that we are chuckling gratefully still."

SCOUTING

Berlin, Germany, may be a divided city, but Scouting goes on apace on the Western side, and last fall celebrated the 50th anniversary of the movement in Berlin. Cub Scouts of four nations met in what was the first international meeting in the memory of Scout officials in Berlin. The boys represented the United States, Great Britain, France and Germany. They enjoyed a day of games and wound up the celebration with a bonfire and songfest.

... Scouts of Troop 269 Richwood, W.Va., spent a total of 196 man-hours in a conservation project on Cranberry River. The project was lacking in glamour, but full of value. It was picking up litter along the shores. Seventy-five large bags of trash and debris were the result. This comprised almost a ton and a half of paper, oil cans, beer cans, discarded furniture and assorted junk. The Scouts received a letter of appreciation from the U.S. Forest Service for this conservation Good Turn.

... Moon Craft I is a replica of the moon module is to be landed on the moon by American astronauts within a few years. It was designed and built by the Scouts of the First Methodist Church and the Explorers from the Idaho Department of Fish and Game, Post 60 at Boise, Idaho. Manned by a Scout and an Explorer, it was "landed" (hauled?) to a point in Idaho's Craters of the Moon National Monument. It was all part of a program whereby 300 Scouts and Explorers earned the Space Exploration and the Atomic Energy merit badges.

How I Learned to Fly

By ORVILLE WRIGHT

As told by him to Leslie W. Quirk, for the readers of BOYS' LIFE

THE FIRST FLIGHT WITH AN ENGINE, DECEMBER 17, 1903, ORVILLE WRIGHT AT THE HELM; WILBUR WRIGHT ALONGSIDE OF MACHINE.*

I SUPPOSE my brother and I always wanted to fly. Every youngster wants to, doesn't he? But it was not till we were out of school that the ambition took definite form.

We had read a good deal on the subject, and we had studied Lilienthal's tables of figures with awe. Then one day, as it were, we said to each other: "Why not? Here are scientific calculations, based upon actual tests, to show us the sustaining powers of planes. We can spare a few weeks each year. Suppose, instead of going off somewhere to loaf, we put in our vacations building and flying gliders." I don't believe we dared think beyond gliders at that time—not aloud, at least.

That year—it was 1900—we went down to North Carolina, near Kitty Hawk. There were hills there in plenty, and not too many people about to scoff. Building that first glider was the best fun we'd ever had, too, despite the fact that we put it together as accurately as a watchmaker assembles and adjusts his finest timepiece. You see, we knew how to work because Lilienthal had made his tables years before, and men like Chanute, for example, had verified them.

To our great disappointment, however, the glider was not the success we had expected. It didn't behave as the figures on which it was constructed vouched that it should. Something was wrong. We looked at each other silently, and at the machine, and at the mass of figures compiled by Lilienthal. Then we proved up on them to see if we had slipped somewhere. If we had, we couldn't find the error; so we packed up and went home. We were agreed that we hadn't built our glider according to the scientific specifications. But there was another year coming and we weren't discouraged. We had just begun.

We wrote to Chanute, who was an engineer in Chicago at the time. We told him about our glider; we drew sketches of it for him; we set down long rows of figures. And then we wound up our letter by begging him to explain why the tables of Lilienthal, which he had verified by experiments of his own, could not be proved by our machine.

Chanute didn't know. He wrote back it might be due to a different curve or pitch of surfaces on the planes, or something like that. But he was interested just the same, and when we went down to Kitty Hawk in 1901 we invited him to visit our camp.

Chanute came. Just before he left Chicago, I recall his telling us, he had read and O. K.'d the proofs of an article on aeronautics which he had prepared for the Encyclopedia Britannica, and in which he again told us of verifying Lilienthal's tables.

Well, he came to Kitty Hawk, and after he had looked our glider over carefully he said frankly that the trouble was not with any errors of construction in our machine. And right then all of us, I suspect, began to lose faith in Lilienthal and his gospel figures.

We had made a few flights the first year, and we made about 700 in 1901. Then we went back to Dayton to begin all over. It was like groping in the dark. Lilienthal's figures were not to be relied upon. Nobody else had done any scientific experimenting along these lines. Worst of all, we did not have money enough to build our glider with various types and sizes of planes or wings, simply to determine, in actual practice, which was the best. There was only the alternative of working out tables of our own. So we set to work along this line.

We took little bits of metal and we fashioned planes from them. I've still a deskful in my office in Dayton. There are flat ones, concave ones, convex ones, square ones, oblong ones and scores and scores of other shapes and sizes. Each model contains six square inches. When we built our third glider the following year, ignoring Lilienthal altogether and constructing it from our own figures, we made the planes just 7,200 times the size of those little metal models back at Dayton.

It was hard work, of course, to get our figures right; to achieve the plane giving the greatest efficiency—and to know before we built that plane the exact proportion of efficiency we could expect. Of course, there were some books on the subject that were helpful. We went to the Dayton libraries and read what we could find there; afterwards, when we had reached the same ends by months and months of study and experiment, we heard of other books that would have smoothed the way. But those metal models told us how to build. By this time, too, Chanute was convinced that Lilienthal's tables were obsolete or inaccurate, and was wishing his utmost that he was not on record in an encyclopedia as verifying them.

During 1902 we made upward of 1,400 flights, sometimes going up a hundred times or more in a single day. Our runway was short, and it required a wind with a velocity of at least twelve miles an hour to lift the machine. I recall sitting in it, ready to cast off, one still day when the breeze seemed approaching. It came pres-

* This and other illustrations used with this article are published by Boys' Life through the courtesy of Mr. Henry Woodhouse, Managing Editor of "Flying" Magazine.

ently, rippling the daisies in the field, and just as it reached me I started the glider on the runway. But the innocent-appearing breeze was a whirlwind. It jerked the front of the machine sharply upward. I tilted my rudder to descend. Then the breeze spun downward, driving the glider to the ground with a tremendous shock and spinning me out headfirst. That's just a sample of what we had to learn about air currents; nobody had ever heard of "holes" in the air at that time. We had to go ahead and discover everything for ourselves.

But we glided successfully that summer, and we began to dream of greater things. Moreover, we aided Chanute to discover the errors in Lilienthal's tables, which were due to experimental flights down a hill with a descent so acute that the wind swept up its side and out from its surface with false buoying power. On the proper incline, which would be one parallel with the flight of the machine, the tables would not work out. Chanute wrote the article on aeronautics for the last edition of that encyclopedia again, but he corrected his figures this time.

The next step, of course, was the natural one of installing an engine. Others were experiments, and it now became a question of which would be the first to fly with an engine. But we felt reasonably secure, because we had worked out all our own figures, and the others were still guessing or depending upon Lilienthal's or somebody's else that were inaccurate. Chanute knew we expected to try sustained flights later on, and while abroad that year mentioned the fact, so we had competition across the water, too.

We wrote to a number of automobile manufacturers about an engine. We demanded an eight-horse one of not over 200 pounds in weight. This was allowing twenty-five pounds to each horsepower, and did not seem to us prohibitive.

Several answers came. Some of the manufacturers politely declined to consider the building of such an engine; the gasoline motor was comparatively new then, and they were having trouble enough with standard sizes. Some said it couldn't be built according to our specifications, which was amusing, because lighter engines of greater power had already been used. Some seemed to think we were demented—"Building a flying machine, eh?" But one concern, of which we had never heard, said it could turn out a motor such as we wanted, and forwarded us figures. We were suspicious of figures by this time, and we doubted this concern's ability to get the horsepower claimed, considering the bore of the cylinders, etc. Later, I may add, we discovered that such an engine was capable of giving much greater horsepower. But we didn't know that at the time; we had to learn our A, B, C's as we went along.

Finally, though, we had a motor built. We had discovered that we could allow much more weight than we had planned at first, and in the end the getting of the engine became comparatively simple. The next step was to figure out what we wanted in the way of a screw propeller.

We turned to our books again. All the figures available dealt with the marine propeller—the thrust of the screw against the water. We had only turned from the solution of one problem to the intricacies of another. And

ORVILLE WRIGHT IN HIS "GLIDER" AT KITTY HAWK.

the more we experimented with our models the more complicated it became.

There was the size to be considered. There was the material to be decided. There was the matter of the number of blades. There was the delicate question of the pitch of the blades. And then, after we had made headway with these problems, we began to scent new difficulties. One pitch and one force applied to the thrust against still air; what about the suction, and the air in motion, and the vacuum, and the thousand and one changing conditions? They were trying out the turbine engines on the big ocean liners at that time, with an idea of determining the efficiency of this type. The results were amazing in the exact percentage of efficiency developed by fuel and engine and propeller combined. A little above 40 per cent. efficiency was considered wonderful. And the best we could do, after months and months of experimenting and studying, was to conceive and build a propeller that had to deliver 66 per cent. of efficiency, or fail us altogether.

THE COLLIER TROPHY.

Granted to Orville Wright in 1913, by the Aero Club of America for the development and demonstration of his automatic stabilizer.

But we went down to Kitty Hawk pretty confident, just the same.

There were the usual vexatious delays. But finally, in December, 1903, we were ready to make the first flight. My brother and I flipped a coin for the privilege of being the first to attempt a sustained flight in the air. Up to now, of course, we had merely taken turns. But this was a much bigger thing. He won.

The initial attempt was not a success. The machine fluttered for about 100 feet down the side of the hill, pretty much as gliders had done. Then it settled with a thud, snapping off the propeller shaft, and thus effectually ending any further experiments for the time being.

It was getting late in the fall. Already the gales off Hatteras were beginning to howl. So I went back to Dayton personally to get a new shaft, and to hurry along the work as rapidly as I could.

It was finished at last. As I went to the train that morning, I heard for the first time of the machine constructed by Langley, which had dropped into a river the day before. You see, others were working just as desperately as we were to perfect a flying machine.

We adjusted the new shaft as soon as I reached Kitty Hawk. By the time we had finished it was late in the afternoon, with a stiff wind blowing. Our facilities for handling the machine were of the crudest. In the past, with our gliders, we had depended largely upon the help of some men from a life saving station, a mile or two away. As none of them happened to be at our camp that afternoon, we decided to postpone the next trial till morning.

It was cold that night. A man named Brinkley—W. C. Brinkley—dropped in to warm himself. He was buying salvage on one or more of the ships that had sunk during a recent storm that raged outside Kitty Hawk Point. I remember his looking curiously at the great frame-work, with its engine and canvas wings, and asking, "What's that?" We told him it was a flying machine which we were going to try out the next morning, and asked him if he thought it would be a success. He looked out toward the ocean, which was getting rough and which was battering the sunken ships in which he was interested. Then he said, "Well you never can tell what will happen—if conditions are favorable." Nevertheless, he asked permission to stay over-night and watch the attempted flight.

Morning brought with it a twenty-seven mile gale. Our instruments, which were more delicate and more accurate than the Government's, made it a little over twenty-four; but the official reading by the United States was twenty-seven miles an hour. As soon as it was light we ran up our signal flag for help from the life saving station. Three men were off duty that day, and came pounding over to camp. They were John T. Daniels, A. D. Etheridge and W. S. Daugh. Before we were ready to make the flight a small boy of about thirteen or fourteen came walking past.

Daniels, who was a good deal of a joker, greeted him. The boy said his name was Johnny Moore, and was just strolling by. But he couldn't get his eyes off the machine that we had anchored in a sheltered place. He wanted to know what it was.

"Why, that's a duck-snarer," explained Daniels soberly. North Carolina, of course, is noted for its duck shooting. "You see, this man is going up in the air over a bay where there are hundreds of ducks on the water. When he is just over them, he will drop a big net and snare every last one. If you'll stick around a bit, Johnny, you can have a few ducks to take home."

So Johnny Moore was also a witness of our flights that day. I do not know whether the lack of any ducks to take away with him was a disappointment or not, but I suspect he did not feel compensated by what he saw.

The usual visitors did not come to watch us that day. Nobody imagined we would attempt a flight in such weather, for it was not only blowing hard, but it was also very cold. But just that fact, coupled with the knowledge that winter and its gales would be on top of us almost any time now, made us decide not to postpone the attempt any longer.

My brother climbed into the machine. The motor was started. With a short dash down the runway, the machine lifted into the air and was flying. It was only a flight of twelve seconds, and it was an uncertain, wavy, creeping sort of a flight at best; but it was a real flight at last and not a glide.

Then it was my turn. I had learned a little from watching my brother, but I found the machine pointing upward and downward in jerky undulations. This erratic course was due in part to my utter lack of experience in controlling a flying machine and in part to a new system of controls we had adopted, whereby a slight touch accomplished what a hard jerk or tug made necessary in the past. Naturally, I overdid everything. But I flew for about the same time my brother had.

He tried it again, the minute the men had carried it back to the runway, and added perhaps three or four seconds to the records we had just made. Then, after a few secondary adjustments, I took my seat for the second time. By now I had learned something about the controls, and about how a machine acted during a sustained flight, and I managed to keep in the air for fifty-seven seconds. I couldn't turn, of course—the hills wouldn't permit that—but I had no very great difficulty in handling it. When I came down I was eager to have another turn.

But it was getting late now, and we decided to postpone further trials until the next day. The wind had quieted, but it was very cold. In fact, it had been necessary for us to warm ourselves between each flight. Now we carried the machine back to a point near the camp, and stepped back to discuss what had happened.

My brother and I were not excited nor particularly exultant. We had been the first to fly successfully with a machine driven by an engine, but we had expected to be the first. We had known, down in our hearts, that the machine would fly just as it did. The proof was not astonishing to us. We were simply glad, that's all.

But the men from the life saving station were very excited. Brinkley appeared dazed. Johnny Moore took our flights as a matter of course, and was presumably disappointed because we had snared no ducks.

And then, quite without warning, a puff of wind caught the forward part of the machine and began to tip it. We all rushed forward, but only Daniels was at the front. He caught the plane and clung desperately to it, as though thoroughly aware as were we of the danger of an upset of the frail thing of rods and wings. Upward and upward it lifted, with Daniels clinging to the plane to ballast it. Then, with a convulsive shudder, it tipped backward, dashing the man in against the engine, in a great tangle of cloth and wood and metal. As it turned over, I caught a last glimpse of his legs kicking frantically over the plane's edge. I'll confess I never expected to see him alive again.

But he did not even break a bone, although he was bruised from head to foot. When the machine had been pinned down at last, it was almost a complete wreck, necessitating many new parts and days and days of rebuilding. Winter was fairly on top of us, with Christmas only a few days off. We could do no more experimenting that year.

After all, though, it did not matter much. We could build better and stronger and more confidently another year. And we could go back home to Dayton and dream of time and distance and altitude records, and of machines for two or more passengers, and of the practical value of the heavier-than-air machine. For we had accomplished the ambition that stirred us as boys. We had learned to fly.

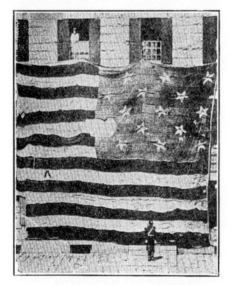

THE FLAG THAT WAS STILL THERE

O NE hundred years ago Baltimore was attacked by a powerful British expeditionary force. The flower of the British army and navy struggled to take the town, but untrained soldiery under gallant leaders held in check the invaders, who were seasoned veterans to the man. At the very gates of the city the British came upon a line of trenches they dared not assail.

Fort McHenry was bombarded by the naval forces for twenty-five hours. When the smoke of battle cleared "our flag was still there," and the British weighed anchor and withdrew. It was during this fight that Francis Scott Key, a young patriot, detained aboard the flag-of-truce ship "Minden," inspired by the thrilling sight,

National Anthem's Birthday

It Will Be Celebrated This Month

wrote the words of our national anthem, "The Star Spangled Banner."

The final gun of the attack on Baltimore marked the close of the last important engagement of the War of 1812. Jackson and his brave followers defeated the British at New Orleans several months later, ignorant of the fact that peace had been proclaimed several days before, and American independence, so proudly heralded in 1776, became an actuality.

Plans have been completed to celebrate the Centennial anniversary of the important event from September 6 to 13. For fifteen months the National Star Spangled Banner Centennial Commission, of which Mayor James H. Preston, of Baltimore, is president, has been at work completing plans for this patriotic anniversary.

At a recent meeting of this body, Scout Commissioner H. L. Eddy, was appointed chairman of a committee to take charge of the Boy Scouts during the celebration. First aid work, assisting the police force and acting as guides to visitors is the big task that has been placed on the Boy Scouts. The efficient work of the Scouts at Washington when President Wilson was inaugurated, at Gettsburg during the recent reunion and at other places, was foremost in the minds of the Managing Directors when they solicited the aid of Mr. Eddy and his co-workers.

This Centennial celebration promises to be one of the most important events of the kind ever held in this section of the country. The first day, Sunday, will be "Parti-

THE FRANCIS SCOTT KEY MEMORIAL SHIELD

ots' Day." There will be music by a chorus of 5,000 people. On Monday, "Industrial Day" there will be an immense pageant with 500 floats in line. Tuesday will be "Francis Scott Key Day," on which there will be another parade of 60,000 men in line and 50 bands of music. Thursday will be "Baltimore Day" and Friday "Army and Navy Day," on which there will be a great military parade of regular troops, militia, naval reserves, etc. Saturday will be "Star Spangled Banner Day," and the principal feature will be an address by President Woodrow Wilson. These are merely the more spectacular parts of the program. A great many other features have been arranged. There will be official delegates from all the States of the Union, and it is expected that an immense crowd will be present to help celebrate the birth of the national anthem.

D O you think the challenges of today are open to only a select few?

Well, I don't. This is a new age of exploration—not only in space, but in many, many fields, and there is opportunity for each of us to serve.

Did you know that about half of the young people graduating from college this year will go into jobs and positions that didn't exist when they were born? Many of these jobs have been created within the last few years by space exploration, but our

THE NEW AGE OF EXPLORATION

BY JOHN GLENN JR.

advances go far beyond the space program.

I heard a man from General Electric state that half of the products they are making didn't even exist 10 years ago! And think of the advances in medicine.

Recently I was privileged to be in the operating room with Doctor De Bakey, the famous heart surgeon in Houston. I looked over his shoulder as he did five heart operations in one day. He used such things as plastic heart valves and nylon arteries. It was one of the most fascinating days I have ever spent anywhere.

You have heard of the Stone Age, the Bronze Age and the Iron Age, those great eras marking the advancement of man to a higher civilization. These mileposts, however, had been separated by *thousands* of years. But in the last 20 years of our history we have had two outstanding technological developments meriting the titles of ages, the Atomic Age and the Space Age. Go back a little more than 60 years, and we can even include the Air Age.

The time scales have been compressed, until today we can speak of a technological explosion, with the space program at the forefront.

Our knowledge is expanding so rapidly that no one can fully understand or forecast its extent. We cannot even begin to predict the benefits that may come, for the main purpose of the space program is to explore, to seek out the new, the unknown, the unimaginable. We have learned from the past that time, effort and money spent on research and exploration have a way of paying off in the future far beyond our wildest expectations.

And this is just the beginning of the grandest exploration of all time.

Space accomplishments are but *one* fruit of a greater advancement. There have been matching advances in technical fields that will continue to influence our lives—from our homes, to roads, to medicine, to education.

If our nation is to be as complete and strong as we know it can be, we need not only great thinking and talent in space, but in all fields. How do we get it? Well, each of us is blessed with certain talents and capabilities. And while some of us might not show much talent now, it is there just the same. Each of us has to discover what he can do best and determine how and where to use his talents.

M AKE the best of what you have. Maintain an intense curiosity in everything you do. Get a good education. Be prepared to contribute to whatever field that best suits your talents and interests.

In this connection, I heard a man at a graduation address some time ago say that he didn't think a college should really grant degrees at graduation. He thought the students should come back 15 years later to see what they'd *done* with their education, how they *used* it, what they *made* of themselves. Then they could get the diploma if they'd really used their abilities.

Many scientific advances have been necessary for space flight, advances that we call "R & D"— Research and Development. Through *research* we investigate what capabilities and talents we have and then *develop* them by performing new tasks— in this case, manned space flight.

S COUTING, which started many years before we thought of building spacecraft, is an R & D program. It provides an opportunity for varied experiences—*research* into what talents, capabilities and interests each possesses.

There is a place in Scouting for every interest, capability and type boy, no matter how he looks, thinks, or feels. But it goes beyond just *research;* it also provides opportunity to *develop* all these talents—physically, mentally and morally. And just as in Space R & D, we know from past experience that effort expended in this direction on boys will pay off in the future beyond our greatest hopes.

At this point it might be interesting for you to know that out of the 28 astronauts now on duty with NASA, 26 had been members of Scout troops when they were younger!

I think that one of the best lessons Scouting can teach is to do the best you can, without just setting standards by what someone else does. Remember what the Scout Oath says? "On *my* honor *I* will do *my* best to do *my* duty to God and *my* country."

You notice that the words don't say "us," and "our" and "we," so that we can put off responsibility to someone else. "I will do my best . . ." is all very personal.

Astronaut Scott Carpenter lives next door to me. His son Jay was chinning himself and trying like crazy, really trying, to get that last one in. He finished and had broken his old record.

Scott asked him who he was trying to beat. Jay said, "Just me."

Scott remarked that he thought Jay had learned one of the most important lessons in life.

"What do you mean?" I said.

"Jay learned how to compete with himself," Scott told me.

I think that Jay learned how to demand the best of himself without expecting someone else to set his standards.

Scouting, like space, is exploration—exploring ourselves and our talents and trying to determine what role we are going to play in the future through our interests of this moment.

This is a time for new thinking. There are new environments to get into and old ones to be further developed.

The cliché, "The sky is the limit," is no longer appropriate. THE END

Think of it—feeling the solid ground underfoot and saying to yourself, "This is not the good old Earth but the planet Mars!"

Exploring Mars

By DR. R. S. RICHARDSON
of the Mount Wilson and Palomar Observatories

ILLUSTRATED BY ROBERT MOORE

You would be a real superman on the Red Planet, but don't forget your gas mask and oxygen tank

ELEVEN years have passed since the nation was aroused out of its Sunday afternoon calm by one of the most startling reports ever heard over the radio. Men from Mars were invading the Earth! Armed with poison gas and a deadly heat ray they were sweeping men and objects before them. Details of the invasion were described so vividly that thousands of people were terrified, convinced that the end of the world was at hand. The actors who put on the now famous broadcast were amazed when told of the panic their play had produced.

In February, 1949, another "invasion" from Mars occurred, the target for which was this time in Ecuador, South America. When the people there discovered that they had been hoaxed, an infuriated mob invaded the radio station and burned down the building.

People usually fear an unknown danger more than one they can see. A few reassuring words might have stopped the trouble before it began.

This spring Mars is scheduled to swing near the Earth for a few weeks and become the brightest star in the evening sky. There is sure to be the customary wild speculation about life on Mars. Let us take a look in advance so that we may see for ourselves what astronomers know about conditions on the Red Planet.

Don't Forget Your Oxygen Mask

O.K. here you go. You have travelled to Mars by rocket and have just brought your spaceship to rest upon the level surface. Naturally you are anxious to get outside and explore this strange world. Think of it—feeling the solid ground underfoot and saying to yourself, "This is not the good old Earth but the planet Mars."

Before you dared venture outside, however, you would have to put on a gas mask and oxygen tank similar to the kind that firemen wear in a smoke-filled building. Mars has a thin atmosphere of some kind, but there is certainly not enough oxygen in it for beings like ourselves. Though it's probably not poisonous, a man would be dead in a few seconds from suffocation if he had nothing else to breathe. Therefore, the length of your visit would depend entirely upon your supply of oxygen.

You Can't Build a Fire

Air without oxygen would make life difficult in several ways besides forcing you to wear breathing apparatus continuously. For example, on Mars you couldn't light a match, or build an open fire, or run an ordinary automobile engine. (One piece of equipment you would *not* need on Mars is a fire extinguisher). On the other hand, machinery left exposed out of doors would never rust, since rust is simply the "ash" that forms by iron slowly burning in the oxygen.

All cooking would have to be done by electricity but here you would be faced by still another difficulty. Although electrical heat would soon set a pot of water to boiling vigorously it would take hours to cook anything in it. The reason is that on Mars water boils when it is not much hotter than lukewarm, as you could easily discover by testing it with your fingers. The temperature at which water boils depends on the pressure of the air, the boiling ➡

Exploring Mars

point going down as you go higher
and the air becomes thinner. Thus
on the top of Mount Everest, the
highest mountain on Earth with an
altitude of 29,000 feet, water would
boil at 160° F. instead of 212° F. as it
does at sea level. But on Mars the air
pressure everywhere is so low that
water must boil at about 145° F. It
would be like living on a mountain
37,000 feet high.

You would not be on Mars an hour
before noticing a strange new feeling
of strength and power. Your body
would seem wonderfully light while
your muscles had become as strong as
steel bands. In fact, you would have
suddenly developed into a miniature
superman, able to make huge leaps
through the air and lift heavy objects
with ease. You would notice also that
bodies fell in a peculiar manner, floating gently downward as if they were
in a slow motion picture.

A Track Meet for the Record

These effects are due to the low
surface gravity on Mars. Gravity is
the force that gives bodies weight and
makes them fall. On Mars the force
of gravity is thirty-eight per cent as
much as upon the Earth. Thus everything would feel only about one third
as heavy as it does on the Earth, but
your muscles would remain as strong
as ever. A one hundred pound sack of
cement (Earth-weight) would feel so
light that you could throw it over one
shoulder with ease, for on Mars it
would weigh only thirty-eight pounds.

The low force of gravity would help
produce some remarkable records if a
track meet were to be held on Mars.
An athlete who can toss the sixteen-
pound shot fifty feet on the Earth
should be able to get off a heave of
about 150 feet on Mars, and do about
500 feet in the discus throw. In the
broad jump a leap of fifty-five feet
would probably not be enough to
qualify a man for the finals. A high
jumper who is consistent at six feet
should be able to clear the bar at
better than fourteen feet. But whether
a man could run faster on Mars than
on the Earth is a question. He should
be able to drive harder with his legs,
but if he happened to get both feet
off the ground it would take longer
for him to hit the track again.

A track meet or a baseball game
should be possible on Mars, although
the baseball diamonds would all have
to be made much larger than on Earth
because of the vast distances that the
players could knock the ball. Football,
however, would seem to be definitely
ruled out. Remember that the athletes
would all have to wear gas masks,
and it is hard to see how a man could
buck the line wearing a gas mask.

The Desert Is Cold

If you went to Mars expecting to
see some marvellous scenery the
chances are that you would be badly
disappointed. Practically the entire
surface of the planet is a barren desert,
and there is no reason to think that
a desert on Mars would look so very
different from a desert upon the Earth.
The chief difference is that on Mars
the deserts are cold instead of being
hot. Have you ever been on a hike or
camping trip when you felt about as
cold as you thought a person could
possibly feel? Well, you wouldn't know

anything about cold weather until you
had spent a night on Mars.

During the day you would feel comfortable enough wearing ordinary
heavy winter clothing, for the temperature at noon near the equator is as
high as 45° F. But as the afternoon
wore on and a thin mist began to
obscure the sun, you would begin to
feel a penetrating, numbing cold that
would send you looking for warmer
surroundings in a hurry. By sunset
the thermometer would be down to
zero with the mercury still falling fast.
And by midnight it must fall to about
-70° F., which is about the record low
temperature in the United States.

Water is so scarce on Mars that the
sight of a small lake would be as
strange to a Martian as boiling hot
springs are to us. For there are no
seas or oceans on this world, only endless miles and miles of dry red colored
desert. You would have to land your
spaceship near the edge of one of the
polar ice caps to be sure of a plentiful
water supply.

Is There Life on Mars?

Perhaps you are asking. "On a world
where there is little or no oxygen in
the air and an extremely limited
amount of water, how can there be
any life?"

To be strictly truthful about it,
astronomers don't know whether or
not there is any life whatever on Mars.
Yet it is conceivable that if our supply
of oxygen and water were to diminish
very gradually, say over a period of
millions and millions of years, some
forms of life might be able to adapt
themselves and survive. A small highly
selected breed of men could probably
live indefinitely within huge glass en-
closures filled with air containing

oxygen supplied artificially from
chemicals. But it is doubtful if men
would be aware of such a slow death
creeping upon them until it was too
late to struggle against it.

There is evidence, however, that
vegetable life still exists on Mars. Not
all the surface is red desert. There
are certain dark regions that change
color with the seasons, from gray or
brown in the autumn and winter to
blue-green in the spring, as if plants
were starting to sprout. They must be
hardy plants that can stand a daily
range in temperature of more than a
hundred degrees.

Yet even upon the Earth there is
one family of plants that might be
able to grow on Mars—the lichens.
Next time you are in the woods pay
particular attention to the little plants
growing on rotten logs or on the bare
surface of a rock. They don't look
very impressive but among all the
plants in the vegetable kingdom these
are the toughest fighters in the struggle for existence. Lichens can grow
in the burning heat of the desert and
on the frigid plains of Siberia. You
will find them at sea level and on the
highest mountains. A lichen can be so
dry that it crumbles to powder, but
give it a little water and it starts
growing again. You must not take
this to mean that there are lichens
growing on Mars. We have no idea
what kind of plants may be growing
there, but it would be astonishing if
they bore the least resemblance to
plants upon the Earth.

Two Little Moons

No matter how long you remained
on Mars you would never see a big
yellow moon in the sky. Instead of
one large moon the planet Mars has
two tiny ones revolving around it.
They were discovered in 1877 by Professor Asaph Hall at the United States
Naval Observatory in Washington,

"Come on out, honey—there's a full earth tonight"

"The boys'll never believe I took this picture"

D. C. Afterward Professor Hall said that he undertook the search because he had grown tired of reading in the school books that "Mars has no moons." These two bodies, which are no bigger than flying mountains, were named Phobos and Deimos (Fear and Terror), after the two horses that drew the chariot of the War God, Mars, in the old Greek myths. Phobos revolves only 3700 miles above the planet's surface, not much farther than the distance across the United States. Phobos moves so fast that to a Martian it would appear to rise in the west and set in the east twice during the course of a single day. Deimos at a distance of 14,600 miles rises in the east and sets in the west as a well-behaved moon should.

The strangest and most mysterious thing about Mars is what has been called "canals," the fine lines that some astronomers have seen covering the surface of the planet like a network. The whole conception of super-intelligent beings rests upon the nature of these lines. Are they real or are they merely illusions in the eye of the observer himself? This is a question that has been argued back and forth for seventy years and nobody knows the answer yet.

Nobody had ever heard of canals on Mars until 1877, when they were first seen by an Italian astronomer with the imposing name of Giovanni Virginio Schiaparelli. He made this famous discovery with a telescope not much larger than that of the street-corner astronomer who lets you look at the moon for ten cents. People think that all the great discoveries are made at big observatories, but important work has been done by amateurs observing in their backyards with little homemade telescopes. If you are handy with tools, you can easily learn to make a telescope and become a backyard astronomer yourself.

What Are the Canals?

Schiaparelli made many drawings of Mars which he combined into a map of the planet. This map created a sensation when it was published, for astronomers had never seen anything like it before. They recognized the old familiar markings but what were these dozens of fine lines criss-crossing the surface? He referred to them as "canali," apparently a shorthand name which he had adopted while hastily sketching at the telescope when time was precious. But the word was translated into English as "canals," a word signifying an artificially constructed waterway and something quite differ-

ent from a mere channel. Of course the news created intense excitment, for if there are canals on Mars there must also be people to build them.

It was nine years before anybody but Schiaparelli could see canals on Mars. Eventually, however, they were sighted at observatories all over the world. Yet some astronomers noted for their keen eyesight were never able to see a single canal regardless of how long and hard they looked. You can hardly blame these men for believing that the canals originated not on Mars but in the eyes of those who claimed to see them.

A theory to explain the canals was proposed fifty years ago by an American astronomer named Percival Lowell. It is a fascinating theory whether you want to believe it or not.

A Controversial Theory

We have seen that water is an exceedingly scarce article on Mars, the sole remaining source of supply being the thin layer of ice and snow at the poles. Lowell became convinced that the lines which he saw were indeed real canals which the Martians had constructed to bring water from the melted polar snows down over the arid desert surface. We do not see the canals themselves (which are much too narrow for visibility) but rather the strips of vegetation growing along their sides. Building canals a thousand miles long would not be such a big engineering job on Mars as on the Earth, due to the lower surface gravity and the absence of mountains.

Most astronomers consider Lowell's theory to be too fantastic for serious consideration. (Maybe you can think of some objections to it yourself). It is hoped that the question of the canals can be settled once for all when Mars makes a close approach to the Earth in September, 1956. Present plans call for photographing the planet with a motion picture camera of special design attached to the new 200-inch telescope on Palomar Mountain, or some other large glass. If photographs can be obtained that show the canals clear and sharp then we will have proof at last that they cannot be optical illusions.

But until such photographs are obtained we have not the slightest evidence of intelligent beings on Mars, or animal or plant life of any kind, for that matter. It is possible that the canals will turn out to be real. But of one thing you can be absolutely sure. *Any invaders from Mars exist entirely in our own imagination.*

THE END

ON THE SCREENS By FRAN SMITH

THE GUNS OF AUGUST (Universal). This unusual film uses film clips and still photographs made 50 years ago. These are woven into the story of the tragic opening days of World War I. WW I has been a sort of forgotten war, overshadowed by WW II and the uneasy peace called the cold war. But the great conflict that started in the tense hot days of August, 1914, was a nasty one, fascinating to us now because it has

Winston Churchill, as he appeared in World War I, is third man from left.

receded far enough into history so that we can look at it as a kind of puzzle to be solved. This movie, from the best-selling book by Barbara Tuchman, deals mostly with the dramatic personalities that were the key figures in the puzzle: Kaiser Wilhelm of Germany, Czar Nicholas of Russia, Winston Churchill as a young British officer, Woodrow Wilson, America's wartime president, and many others.

FATE IS THE HUNTER (20th Century-Fox). Glenn Ford plays an airline executive who goes out on a long, long limb. He's trying to prove that the cause of a plane crash was not pilot error. The pilot who died in the crash was his wartime buddy. The challenge for Ford is not only to absolve his friend, but to make sure the crash investigations are ab-

Glenn Ford prepares to bail out in a flashback scene of World War II.

solutely thorough. The result provides a mystery story, with a melodramatic "Hollywood" ending, when an attempt is made to duplicate exactly the fatal flight in order to find the missing scrap of evidence. Flashback scenes of aviation combat add tension to this screen play.

THE LIVELY SET (Universal). Here's one for the racing-car buffs. James Darren is the college student whose plans for an engineering career are almost smashed on the track. Sharing honors with the human stars is

Doug McClure and James Darren, car buffs, are rivals, then partners.

the Chrysler Corporation's experimental gas-turbine car. This was driven in the final scene—an endurance road race, filmed on the spectacular roads of Death Valley National Park. The big idea in this movie is that young automotive geniuses ought to stay in college and develop their talents for design. This is James Darren's final decision, as you may guess, but not before he has built and driven several cars to victory or to smashup. There's romance in it, too, mainly provided by Pamela Tiffin.

ROUSTABOUT (Paramount) brings together the surprising combination of Elvis Presley and Barbara Stanwyck in a slambang tale of carnival life. Elvis careens around on a motor-

Elvis Presley is a rambling troubadour who joins up with a carnival.

cycle, but he also sings (11 songs). Elvis fans will find the same likable toughie with a heart of gold.

MY FAIR LADY (Warner). The unforgettable characters of George Bernard Shaw's humorous and warmly human play *Pygmalion* comes to the screen in fine form. Rex Harrison is Henry Higgins, the professor who makes a society lady out of Eliza Doolittle, the beautiful, uncouth flower girl from the London slums—and she is Audrey Hepburn. The show will open first in big cities only.

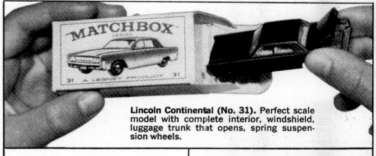

SWAMI PEDRO'S

Forecast for 2000 A.D.

Our self-appointed Swami, Pedro, has polished up his crystal ball and is concentrating all his extra-sensory brain-power (that's his statement) to gaze into the future and let a waiting world (his words) know what to expect when the next century rolls around.

Moon colonies will be established with a regular shuttle service between them and Earth. An abundance of valuable metal-bearing ores will be discovered which will be processed at lunar refining plants to save shipping weight.

Cancer, heart, mental and other diseases will be conquered. Our life span will be increased to an average expectancy of over 250 years! Electronic "knives" will do away with the need for cutting with scalpels in operations.

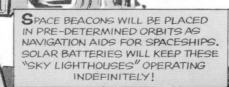

Space beacons will be placed in pre-determined orbits as navigation aids for spaceships. Solar batteries will keep these "sky lighthouses" operating indefinitely!

Space probers will land television-equipped robots that will transmit on-the-spot pictures back to Earth from all planets in our solar system.

Wheels will be discarded on cars. They'll run on cushions of air...boats, too. Solar heating units will keep our houses comfortable all winter. Every school classroom will be equipped with "television teachers." The problem of feeding a world population of 20 billion people will be solved...there'll be no more hunger and want anywhere on Earth!

So says our prognosticating pal, Pedro.

That's all for today—it's too exhausting! My poor brain!

POP

1209